(*Left*) The seriousness of slum problems the world over is illustrated by this view of Indian children in their single tiny room, in which family members cook, eat, and sleep. There are no electricity, no plumbing, no ventilation, and water is carried from long distances.

(*Above*) The bulging living quarters of this Delhi slum drive many residents into teeming, smelly lanes, whose surfaces and drains are clogged because of poor sanitation. Here children play, vendors sell, and the neighborhood social life takes place.

Continued on overleaf

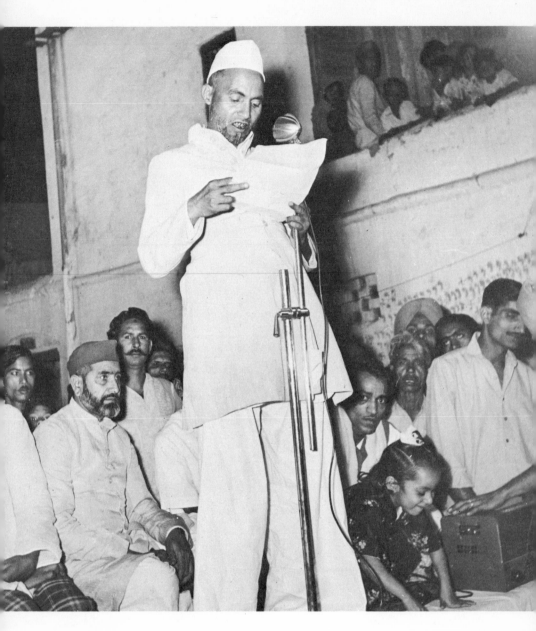

Vikas mandals (area councils), elected among the residents themselves, are designed to attack such problems. Although officers are often illiterate, their familiarity with community ways makes them effective leaders in selecting and organizing local improvement projects. This inaugural meeting is attended by the area's city councilman (seated second from left).

Continued on back endpapers

SLUMS AND COMMUNITY DEVELOPMENT

Slums and Community Development

EXPERIMENTS IN SELF-HELP

Marshall B. Clinard

Fp

The Free Press, *New York*
Collier–Macmillan Limited, *London*

Collier-Macmillan Canada, Ltd., Toronto, Ontario

Library of Congress Catalog Card Number: 66–10960

To My Colleagues,
B. Chatterjee
and the Staff of the Pioneer Delhi Pilot Project
in Urban Community Development

PREFACE

In this book I have analyzed the slum as a social and cultural phenomenon, bringing together relevant research materials about slums in Western and non-Western societies. I have also dealt with the problems and processes of planned social change, particularly through the new approach of urban community development, which focuses on building citizen participation, integrating local communities, and developing self-help. In various parts of the world today there is increasing interest in developing community feeling and citizen responsibility within large urban areas and in the possibilities of self-help as a dynamic force for change. I have included a discussion of many of these efforts as they relate to the slums. In particular, I have presented a case study of an experimental project to change the slums of India through community development.

My interest in slums and efforts to change them go back to The University of Chicago, prior to the Second World War, when I, like many graduate students in sociology, used the slums as a research laboratory. There I became intimately acquainted with the pioneer efforts of Clifford Shaw and Henry Mc-Kay to bring about, in their Chicago Area Project, social change in the slum through the slum dwellers' own efforts. This preventive approach to delinquency and other slum problems, crude as it was in both theory and method, seemed to make a great deal of sense. As an academic person, I had done research and writing on urban deviant behavior and social problems, much of it related to the slums, in which I stressed the need for active citizen involvement if prevention was to be successful. I had an opportunity to engage in applied work in 1958, when I was asked to serve as consultant to a program in urban community development in the Indian slums, which was supported by the Ford Foundation. Such a program was a logical counterpart to programs in rural community development in the villages of India and elsewhere, as it was an effort to change

vii

Indian slums through the efforts of the people themselves. I spent three years in India helping to develop the Delhi project and also to set up a similar one in Ahmedabad, beginning in 1962. The experimental project in Delhi was a part of the municipal government, supported in part by a Ford Foundation grant, and attempted to deal with slum problems by directly involving the local citizens. By 1965 it comprised forty-seven citizen development councils, representing nearly 150,000 people. These urban projects in India were among the first of this type not only in developing countries but also in the world.

The Delhi project has attracted world-wide attention to what slum dwellers can do through their own efforts. Together with the Ahmedabad project, it became the model for the national program in urban community development that was undertaken by the Indian government in 1965. Several articles on the project have appeared, and finally I decided to write up a study of urban community development. The fact that the slums of India are generally considered among the worst and the slum dwellers among the poorest and most apathetic of any major country in the world seemed to give added impetus to the possibilities of a similar type of approach elsewhere. The conceptual framework, many of the procedures, the process of change, and the methods of evaluation appear to be applicable to slums in other parts of the world, in developed and less developed countries.

I had also visited and studied slums and slum-improvement projects in various parts of the United States and Europe, in Asia and Africa, and in parts of Latin America, and in writing a book on the Indian slum I came to see the need for a broader discussion of the issues and of the slum as a world-wide phenomenon. In fact, as the book developed, it became more a general treatise on the slum and urban community development with less focus on India alone: The Indian slum serves as a case study or example. I therefore decided to include chapters on the nature of the slum, types of slum and slum dweller, and slums from an historical perspective. I also saw that there was need for a thorough discussion of urban community development, and I have therefore analyzed its background and approach, pointing out the sharp differences between it and slum clearance, welfare services, traditional community organization, and well-meaning philanthropy. I have been critical of the explanation and solution of the slum problem through primarily providing opportunities for economic and educational advancement. This approach may provide upward mobility for some slum dwellers, but it is unlikely to alter or eliminate the slum itself.

Much of this book is an attempt to apply sociology to the understanding and solution of a concrete problem, the slum. In general, the application of sociological concepts to the solutions of actual rather than theoretical problems is still limited. I have used an analytical model to examine the process of social change in slum areas. I have tried to develop a number of general principles of social change related to the slum, and I have stressed in particular the group aspects of slum life, the pursuit of self-imposed change, the acquisition of power, and the use of indigenous leadership. Above all, the development of a new self-image or change in identity through emphasis on prestige and respectability appears crucial to any effort to change the slum.

I owe a special debt of gratitude to my Indian counterpart, colleague, and friend, B. Chatterjee, first director of the Delhi project and now technical adviser with the United Nations, and to the staff of the Department of Urban Community Development, Delhi Municipal Corporation. Chatterjee and I planned the Delhi project together, but his task of administration was infinitely more difficult than was mine as consultant. He read a number of the chapters and offered helpful suggestions; several of the ideas presented here have come out of our many discussions. I have utilized reports prepared by the project staff and have included numerous extracts from community organizers' reports on slum changes that they observed. It is difficult for me to single out people on the staff, but I should like to express my appreciation particularly to V. Gopalan, R. Prasad, P. Nagpal, M. L. Kaul, and M. L. Dahr. From the beginning, Douglas Ensminger, representative of the Ford Foundation in India, has offered encouragement to the project. Nothing I have said should be interpreted, however, as representing either the opinions of the Delhi Municipal Corporation or of the Ford Foundation.

Grants from the Institute of Public Administration, New York, and the University of Wisconsin Research Committee provided me with funds, without which it would have been difficult, if not impossible, to find the time and assistance necessary in preparing this volume. Portions of the manuscript have been read by Joseph W. Elder, John F. Harrison, Leo F. Schnore, Arthur P. Miles, Leo Jakobson, Burton R. Fisher, and Vimalbhai P. Shah, all of whom offered helpful suggestions but are not responsible for what I did with them. Others who made contributions included Edward M. Lawrence, Martin H. Ross, and James B. Ramsey. I also wish to express my gratitude to Harcourt, Brace & World, Inc., and to Martin Secker & Warburg Limited for permission to reprint from Lewis Mumford, *The City in History*; and to E. P. Dutton, Inc., for permission to reprint from *Child of the Dark: The Diary of Carolina Maria de Jesus*, translated by David St. Clair (this material is also reproduced from *Beyond All Pity* by Carolina Maria de Jesus by permission of the publishers, Souvenir Press Limited). Most of all, I again find it difficult sufficiently to acknowledge the patience, the endless typing and retyping, and the editing of my wife, Ruth, who has appreciated my interest in the slums and the people all over the world caught up in their seemingly endless process of socialization and resocialization.

Marshall B. Clinard

University of Wisconsin
Madison, Wisconsin

CONTENTS

xi

Part Two. APPROACHES TO THE SLUM PROBLEM

Part Three. URBAN COMMUNITY DEVELOPMENT AND THE INDIAN SLUM: A CASE STUDY

Part Four. SOCIAL CHANGE AND THE SLUM

PART ONE

THE SLUM

The Nature of the Slum

Slums constitute the most important and persistent problem of urban life; they are the chief sources of crime and delinquency, of illness and death from disease. Slums are of all types, shapes, and forms. Bombay has its packed multistoried chawls, New York its Harlem and its Lower East Side, Chicago its Black Belt, and London its well-known East End. Families in Bangkok crowd together in "pile villages," composed of poorly constructed wooden shacks raised on wooden stilts along the waterfronts. There are the tin shacks, bamboo huts, and straw hovels along the small lanes of Calcutta, Dacca, and Lagos, which steam with the high humidity and stink from the open drains. Impoverished shanty towns or squatter shacks constructed from junk cover the hillsides of Rio de Janeiro, Lima, Hong Kong, and other Asiatic, African, and South American cities. No slums are more crowded than those of Hong Kong and Singapore, where a single room houses from ten to forty families, each with only "bed space" and no element of personal privacy. In areas of Canton, Shanghai, and Hong Kong hundreds of thousands of families live in waterfront sampan or "floating" slums.

§ *Characteristics of the Slum*

Slums vary from one type to another, but certain general patterns of slum life are universal. Although the slum is generally characterized by inadequate housing, deficient facilities, overcrowding, and congestion, it involves much more than these elements. Sociologically it is a way of life, a subculture with a set of norms and values, which is reflected in poor sanitation and health practices, deviant behavior, and characteristic attributes of apathy and social isolation. People who live in slum areas are isolated from the general power structures and are regarded as inferior, and slum dwellers, in turn, harbor suspicions of the outside world.

The word "slum" has long had a negative connotation, has been almost an epithet, implying something evil, strange, to be shunned and avoided. In fact, the word itself is apparently derived from "slumber," as slums were once thought by the majority to be "unknown, back streets or alleys, wrongly presumed to be sleeping and quiet."[1] Emotional attitudes toward the slum are still reflected in popular definitions and value-laden terms that emphasize the seamy aspects of the slum, its filth and squalor, its poor social conditions, and the presence of vicious characters. The slum, for example, has been described as a "street, alley, court, etc., situated in a crowded district of a town or city and inhabited by people of a low class or by the very poor; a number of these streets or courts forming a thickly populated neighborhood or district of a squalid and wretched character."* Because the term has been used in such value-laden and derogatory contexts, its use has often been avoided in recent years, in the United States at least. Other terms of a more genteel nature have come into use, for example, "blighted area," "renewal area," "deteriorated area," "gray area," "lower class neighborhood," "low income area," and "inner core area." Still, as Hunter has said, "slum" is a "good, old-fashioned word that carries real meaning."†

HOUSING CONDITIONS

Of all the characteristics of a slum, the physical conditions have been emphasized most often. Slums have commonly been defined as those portions of cities in which housing is crowded, neglected, deteriorated, and often obsolete. Many of the inadequate housing conditions can be attributed to poorly arranged structures, inadequate light and circulation, poor design and lack of sanitary facilities, overcrowding, and inadequate maintenance.‡ In developing countries, many cities have large squatter areas, shanty towns built of scrap materials on unauthorized land and providing minimal protection from the elements.

In terms of physical conditions and housing standards, it is important to keep in mind the comparative nature of the definition. A slum should be judged physically according to the general living standards of a country. Certainly slum housing in New York City or Chicago would be regarded as adequate, or even good, in many parts of the world. Even limited availability of running water, flush toilets, electricity, and cooking facilities may be enough to exempt

---

* *The Oxford Universal Dictionary* (1955 ed.; New York: Oxford University Press, Inc., 1955), p. 1921. The earliest use of the word "slum" is reported as having occurred in 1812 and the introduction of "slumming" as a fashionable pursuit in 1884.

† David R. Hunter, *The Slums: Challenge and Response* (New York: The Free Press, 1964), p. 6. The term has wide acceptance in other countries, particularly in developing areas.

‡ Barnes defined the older or "ancient" London slums as housing that was close together and badly arranged. He pointed out, however, that the "modern" slum is to be "distinguished from the 'ancient' slum in that the insanitary conditions result not from the construction or arrangement of the buildings but from the failure to maintain a proper sanitary standard." Harry Barnes, *The Slum: Its Story and Solution* (London: Staples Press, Ltd., 1931), p. 5.

certain "slum" areas from classification as slums, at least in the physical sense, in other parts of the world.

Attempts have been made to develop a system of rating points for determining a slum in a physical sense. The American Public Health Association system gives penalty points, for example, for land crowding; interference from nonresidential land use; hazards and nuisances from transportation systems; hazards and nuisances from natural causes like flooding, inadequate utilities, and sanitation; and inadequacy of such basic facilities as water, toilets, light, and heat.[2] Such systems, however, are always subject to the charge that they are unrepresentative of actual conditions, either through omissions or through overemphasis on certain types of factors. Other physical criteria to designate slum areas, of an administrative or quasi-legal nature, have been set forth rather arbitrarily. The United States Urban Renewal Administration, for example, has specified that one of two primary conditions must exist if an area is to be considered suitable for slum clearance:

(1) More than 50 per cent of the buildings, not including accessory outbuildings, must, by reasonable criteria, be "substandard" to a degree warranting clearance.
(2) More than 20 per cent of the buildings must be "substandard" requiring clearance, and substantial other clearance must be warranted to remove effectively blighting influences such as (a) inadequate street layout, (b) incompatible uses or land use relationships, (c) overcrowding of buildings or the land, (d) excessive dwelling unit density, (e) obsolete buildings not suitable for improvement or conversion, or (f) other identified hazards to health and safety and to the general well-being of the community.[3]

The United States Census Bureau classifies poor dwellings as dilapidated or deteriorated. Dilapidated housing does not provide safe and adequate shelter, and deteriorating housing needs more repair than would be provided in the course of regular maintenance.[4] According to the 1960 Census, the United States had 3,684,000 urban-slum housing units, of which 1,173,000 were "dilapidated urban units."[5] According to one estimate, this figure means that 12,500,000 persons lived in slum areas.[6] If slums in the United States were to be defined according to such standards as dilapidated housing, lack of adequate sanitary facilities, overcrowding, and location in extremely undesirable surroundings, it has been estimated that one-sixth of the urban population, or more than five million families, could be said to reside in a slum environment.[7]

There is a world-wide tendency to stress the physical aspects of the slum and to define it in these terms alone. A study of Houston, Texas, for example, showed that in the five census tracts with the highest delinquency rates, 65.5 per cent of the occupied dwelling units were in need of major repairs or had no private bathrooms, whereas in the five tracts with the lowest rates, only 3.9

per cent of the units were in similar condition.[8] The coefficient of correlation between delinquency rates and the percentage of poor housing was .75 ±.06; between delinquency rates and overcrowding the correlation was .85 −.04. The explanation of such a relationship, however, is more likely to be a slum way of life, which promotes deviant behavior. Careful analysis of the high deviation rates in the slums fails to show that bad housing explains them, although poor housing may encourage a slum way of life. Rather, low economic status and discrimination force people to live in low-rent areas where certain values prevail. Some studies have attempted to show that improved housing also means improved general social conditions, including lower incidence of delinquency, but this result by no means always follows. Morris found, for example, that, even after the construction of new government housing projects in an English city, the rates of delinquency remained high.[9] He concluded that an area's physical characteristics bear little relation to its crime and delinquency, except indirectly as a determinant of the social status of the area.

The importance of distinguishing the physical from the social aspects of the slum has been emphasized. One writer has pointed out that the "slum problem" differs from the "renewal problem." The latter is concerned with how to construct, maintain, and rebuild those parts of a city in which buildings have become deteriorated, or in which the facilities, although still in sound structural condition, have become so obsolete that they cannot be brought up to standards of health, comfort, or efficient operation. The slum problem, on the other hand, is "basically a problem of the attitudes and behavior of people and of the indifference of the community to the neglect and victimization of the underprivileged,"[10] Obsolescence per se is not harmful, and the designation of an area as a slum for this reason alone "is merely a reflection of middle-class standards—and middle-class incomes."[11]

In Tokyo the proportion of dwellings listed as slums is much smaller than that in New York City. On the other hand, the average Tokyo "non-slum dweller" lives under physical conditions much inferior to those of the average New York slum dweller. His home is often made of shoddy materials, is not connected to a sewage system, has no central heating, and does not have bathing facilities. Such differences in the definition of the extent of slums cannot be explained only by differences in the standard of living. As Glazer says: "the main explanation is that Tokyo does not have as large a social problem population as New York. In a variety of ways, the slums of any city will tend to equal the number of people defined as social problems, regardless of the quality of design or construction."*

---

* Nathan Glazer, "Slum Dwellings Do Not Make a Slum," *The New York Times Magazine*, November 21, 1965, p. 57. The atmosphere of most of the areas where people live in poor housing conditions in Tokyo is not that of a slum. Furthermore, Glazer points out that it is false to assume that in the United States the physical forms of communities have inevitable social consequences.

A slum may be an area overcrowded with buildings, buildings overcrowded with people, or both. Density does not always result in unfortunate social consequences; the issue is primarily one of overcrowding.[12] Congestion, however, may be so great that a judgment about the physical conditions of the buildings must often be made in terms of the high density per block, acre, or square mile. It has been pointed out, for example, that, if New York City's total population density were as high as that in some of Harlem's worst blocks, the entire population of the United States could fit into three of New York City's boroughs.[13] Whyte stressed the importance of overcrowding as a criterion for measuring slum conditions when he described how he chose Boston's North End for his well-known sociological study of "street corner society":

> I made my choice on very unscientific grounds: Cornerville best fitted my picture of what a slum district should look like. Somehow I had developed a picture of run-down three-to-five-story buildings crowded in together. The dilapidated wooden-frame buildings of some other parts of the city did not look quite genuine to me. To be sure, Cornerville did have one characteristic that recommended it on a little more objective basis. It had more people per acre living in it than any other section of the city. If a slum meant overcrowding, this was certainly it.[14]

Some Indian slum areas, like those of Delhi, have 400,000 people to the square mile. In the Bombay tenements, ten people commonly live in a room ten by fifteen feet. In Panama, slum shelters bulge at the seams with as many as twenty people in a room fifteen by fifteen feet, sleeping in relays. In Kingston, Jamaica, nine people may live in a single tiny hut six by ten feet. In Accra, Ghana, occupancy per single house in 1960 was 19.3 people, and it was even higher in Kumasi. Migration into some cities of the Far East has created living conditions without any vestige of privacy or room for motion. In Hong Kong, five or six human beings share single cubicles measuring forty square feet.[15]

People who live under such crowded conditions obviously have little privacy, a factor that may be of great importance, especially in its effects upon interpersonal relations. Frazier states that overcrowded housing probably explains why so many Negroes congregate on the streets of Negro neighborhoods. "So far as the children are concerned, the house becomes a veritable prison for them. There is no way of knowing how many conflicts in Negro families are set off by the irritations caused by overcrowding people, who come home after a day of frustration and fatigue, to dingy and unhealthy living quarters."[16] The ill effects of this feature of slum life are partially mitigated, however, through the greater use of outside space, including front stoops and sidewalks, hallways, alleys, and lanes. Most studies of lower-class and slum life have shown the importance of peer-group relations developed under these very conditions, where slum streets, sidewalks, lanes, and alleys become important places for promoting such contacts.[17] Hartman refers to this factor as an interplay of slum dwellers between "inside and outside," both in physical and social senses.[18] The middle class places a higher value on privacy, which tends to encourage orientation toward individual responsibility and achievement.

NEIGHBORHOOD FACILITIES

Poor slum housing is invariably associated with poor facilities and community services. Along with shabbiness and dilapidation, the park facilities are inadequate, the schools are of poor quality, and other public facilities are often insufficient. Streets and sidewalks often go unrepaired, and rubbish and garbage are infrequently collected, adding to the undesirable environment. These services may be especially neglected in slums inhabited by minority groups in the United States.[19] In developing countries, this lack of facilities and services is often stressed in defining slums. The slums in India have been described as chaotically occupied, unsystematically developed and generally neglected, overpopulated and overcrowded with ill-repaired and neglected structures, insufficiently equipped with proper communications and physical comforts, and inadequately supplied with social services and welfare agencies to deal with the needs and social problems of families who are "victims of biological, psychological and social consequences of the physical and social environment."[20]

Shortages of water, electric lights, and sanitary facilities are common in developing countries. Several hundred people may share one water tap, so that it is practically impossible, particularly in tropical areas, to keep water clean when it is carried long distances and kept for hours or days in exposed tubs or cans. Sanitary facilities present even more serious difficulties, for the disposal of human feces remains one of the stubbornly persistent problems of urban man. Skyscrapers may shoot up side by side with colonies of slum dwellers whose only latrine is a rarely cleaned trench shared by hundreds of families. Many slums in underdeveloped areas commonly use pail collections of night soil, and even this service is absent or haphazard in some places. Often the night soil is allowed to accumulate for weeks or even months before it is removed, and the resulting pollution is accepted as part of the way of life. In Lagos, Nigeria, for example, 85 per cent of 4,759 school children whose stools were examined were found to be infected with intestinal parasites, roundworm and hookworm being the most common.[21] Dysentery and diarrhea accounted for 10.1 per cent of all deaths in Lagos in 1960. In the same year, 54.5 per cent of all deaths in Nigeria's capital city occurred among children under the age of five.

Slums have generally been dirty and unclean places. In fact, the United Nations, which has been concerned more with the slums of developing countries, has defined them largely in terms of physical deterioration, stressing particularly unsanitary conditions and lack of sufficient facilities like water and latrines.[22] These factors have resulted in high death and disease rates, which have always been typical of slum areas where overcrowding and the presence of rats, cockroaches, and other pests complicate the problems of health and sanitation. One United States estimate is that, on the average, the slum areas of a city that contain about 20 per cent of its residential population will have 50 per cent of all its diseases.[23] The infant-mortality rate of any community is reputed to be the best single index of its general health. In 1961 this rate for Harlem was 45.2 per 1,000 live births, as compared to 25.7 for New York City, and in Cleveland's Hough area the infant deaths are almost double those of the rest of the city.[24] In the slum areas of developing countries, the rates of disease, chronic illness, and infant mortality are exceptionally high. There is little application of proper sanitation and health practices.

A high incidence of deviant behavior—crime, juvenile delinquency, prostitution, drunkenness, drug usage, mental disorder, suicide, illegitimacy, and family maladjustment—have long been associated with slum living. In the Western world, particularly the United States, the slum is closely associated with delinquency and crime. Hunter's survey of the evidence led him to estimate that in slums accommodating 20 per cent of the population of an American city there occur approximately 50 per cent of all arrests, 45 per cent of the reported major crimes, and 55 per cent of the reported juvenile delinquency cases.[25] Numerous studies made over a period of several years in Chicago, for example, have revealed that conventional crime, delinquency, mental disorder in general and schizophrenia in particular, suicide, prostitution, vagrancy, dependency, illegitimacy, infant mortality, and high death and disease rates are largely concentrated in the slums.[26] A 1960 study of Milwaukee showed that the slum, or inner-core area of the city, which had 13.7 per cent of the population in 1957, had 38 per cent of the arrests for burglary, 69 per cent of the aggravated assaults and 47 per cent of other assaults, 60 per cent of the murders, 72 per cent of the arrests for commercial vice, 22 per cent of the drunkenness, and 67 per cent of the narcotics arrests.[27] Similar findings have been reported in such cities as Cleveland, Jacksonville (Florida), and Indianapolis. A slum area in Cleveland, which contained only 2.5 per cent of the city's population in its 333 acres, was responsible for 6.8 per cent of its delinquency, 21 per cent of its murders, and

26 per cent of its houses of prostitution.[28] The rates for nearly all twenty-nine types of crime known to the police in Seattle and arrests for these crimes, during the period 1949–1951, showed a decline as one moved through six one-mile concentric zones from the center of the city. Slum areas were higher in twenty-three of twenty-nine crimes and were particularly high in robbery, prostitution, rape, gambling, and common drunkenness.[29] Two detailed studies of criminal homicide in the United States, one in Houston and the other in Philadelphia, have shown concentrations in lower-class slum areas.[30] In Houston, more than 87 per cent of all criminal homicides occurred in four lower-class areas, not far apart, located near the city center.*

Studies by Shaw, McKay, and Thrasher in Chicago several decades ago demonstrated the much higher rates of juvenile delinquency within slum districts.[31] Furthermore, the Chicago slum areas also had had much higher delinquency rates in both 1900 and 1920, even though their ethnic composition was almost entirely different. Whether slum areas were occupied successively by Swedes, Germans, Poles, or Italians, the rates were high, as they are today with a primarily Negro or Spanish-speaking population. Similar findings have been reported in the United States for eight other large metropolitan areas and eleven other cities, all widely separated geographically, including Boston, Philadelphia, Cleveland, Richmond, Birmingham, Omaha, and Seattle.[32] In 1960, ninety-seven health areas of New York City, comprising 27 per cent of the population, accounted for 51 per cent of the juvenile delinquency.[33] In a recent study of drug addiction among juveniles in New York City, the highest rates were found in the slums.[34] A study of Croydon, a large English town near London, revealed that the highest rates for delinquency were concentrated in areas populated by unskilled and semiskilled workers' families.[35] Indications are that, with the growth of urbanization, the cities of developing countries are beginning to face similar problems in the slums.[36] Studies of Kanpur and Lucknow in India showed that juvenile delinquency, juvenile vagrancy, and crime are primarily associated with slum areas.[37]

The existence of unconventional values in slum areas accounts for the high rates of such deviant behavior as delinquency. Yet it should be recognized that not all those residing in slum areas become deviant. In any slum area, there exist simultaneously conventional value systems carried through certain individuals, schools, churches, the police, and other sources.[38] The interaction of conventional and such unconventional value systems as those of delinquency and crime may have differential impacts on individuals.[39]

Research in Chicago and in seven other United States cities on the residences of patients admitted to state and private mental hospitals, particularly for

---

* In London, crimes of violence like criminal homicides and assaults, particularly those arising from domestic disputes and neighborhood quarrels, are largely concentrated in slum areas. See F. H. McClintock, *Crimes of Violence* (London: Macmillan and Co., Ltd, 1963).

schizophrenia, has revealed much higher admission rates from the slum areas of the cities.[40] A New Haven study of all patients of psychiatrists or psychiatric clinics or in psychiatric institutions on December 1, 1950, revealed that those in the lowest classes had the highest rates of diagnosed mental disorder.[41] Those in the lowest class had almost twice the expected percentage based on total population; schizophrenia was almost two and a half times as great. A survey of the prevalence of mental disorder among the adult population in midtown New York City revealed a higher rate among the lower class; in fact, 32.7 per cent of the lowest class was classified as "impaired," compared with only 17.5 per cent of those from the highest status group, for those with "severe symptom formation" or "incapacitated," 14.7 per cent compared with 5.7.[42] The validity of this and the other studies depends, of course, upon the research procedures and criteria used to determine "mental health," "mental disorder," "neuroses," and "psychoses."

THE CULTURE OF THE SLUM

Culture might be defined as a system of symbols or meanings for normative conduct standards, having three distinct properties: It is transmittable, it is learned, and it is shared. The slum has a culture of its own, and this culture is a way of life. This learned way of life is passed from generation to generation, with its own rationale, structure, and defense mechanisms, which provide the means to continue in spite of difficulties and deprivations. One writer has commented on the slum: "It is because people themselves produce blight, or more correctly, the cultural patterns operating through people produce blight. This distinction between people themselves and the cultural patterns operating through people is an important one, because people themselves produce neither slums nor well kept neighborhoods. It is the habits, customs, behavior patterns people have learned and which they hold that move them to act in particular ways."[43]

This slum culture affects virtually every facet of the lives of most of the world's slum dwellers. It is largely a synthesis of the culture of the lower class and of what Lewis has referred to as the culture of poverty.[44] Nearly all slum dwellers are of the lower class, and, with few exceptions, they live at the poverty level, but not all lower class or poor urban people live in slums. The culture of the slum has a number of characteristics that vary only in degree.[45] Although these cultural patterns are typical of the slum from an over-all perspective, they vary in detail from slum to slum, from ethnic group to ethnic group, from society to society. Each individual in the slum is influenced in different degrees by the general slum culture.[46] Furthermore, certain people may live in a slum area, and may even be poor, yet remain removed from the slum culture. Members of higher social classes, for example, may reside in a slum, as they do in some Asiatic cities, yet not become part of its way of life. Others, like students and artists, may simply seek cheap housing in the slum and never become part of it. In addition, certain groups, like the Jews in Europe and the Japanese-Americans in the United States, have often resided in slum areas but have not necessarily shared the values of most of those who live there.

Life in the slum is usually gregarious and largely centered in the immediate area, where are found friends, shops, and possible credit. There is little privacy, and confusion and noise seldom abate; life, however, has more spontaneity, and behavior, whether in the home or on the street corner, is more unrestrained than in middle-class areas. Toughness is often regarded as virtuous, and frequent resort to violence to settle disputes is common. Initiation into sexual experiences, whether by marriage or otherwise, comes early, and middle-class standards of sex conduct are not widely observed. Above all, there is a greater tolerance of deviant behavior, a higher rate of delinquency and crime, and an ambivalence toward quasi-criminal activities committed against the "outside world." Slum dwellers generally display apathy about their conditions, apathy associated with intolerance of conventional ambitions. Often accompanying this sense of resignation there is an attitude of "fatalism" toward life.*

Throughout the slums, such attitudes have led to the development of generalized suspicion of the "outside world," which includes government and politicians, welfare groups, and the upper and middle classes generally. Slum people often fail adequately to utilize those very agencies, both public and private, that could be helpful to them, such as the health department, schools, and even the police. These services are often feared as possible dangerous sources of interference in everyday living. Such fears are frequently confused by the people's own failure to understand modern health or educational services or even the proper use of such public facilities as schools, playgrounds, and parks.

Miller has outlined six focal concerns of lower-class culture, focal concerns that apply to most slum areas, particularly those of the Western world.[47] First, there is concern over "trouble," an attempt to avoid it and in other cases to seek it. The second is a concern with "toughness," in that lower-class men often feel the need to demonstrate physical powers, "masculinity," and bravery. "Smartness" centers on the capacity to outsmart, outfox, outwit, dupe, "take," or "con" another, as well as on the ability to avoid being "taken" oneself. "Excitement" and the search for thrills characterize many features of lower-class life; examples include the use of alcohol and often narcotics, gambling, and the recurrent practice of taking a "night on the town." Much emphasis is placed on "fate" or

---

* Mau recently studied urban slum dwellers in Kingston, Jamaica, and he found that a considerable proportion of them had not uniformly rejected the possibility of progress and the idea of an improved and meaningful future. See James A. Mau and Walter E. Freeman, "Political Mobilization and Belief in Progress Among Slum Residents in Kingston, Jamaica," paper presented at the meetings of the American Sociological Association in Chicago, Illinois, September, 1965. Also see Mau, "The Threatening Masses: Myth or Reality?" paper presented at the Second Caribbean Scholars' Conference, August, 1964.

luck by many who feel that they have little control over the forces affecting their lives. "Autonomy" is the final concern of lower-class culture: External controls and restrictions on behavior and authority that seem coercive and unjust are bitterly denounced, although often actually desired.

Unemployment, underemployment, and low wages are the rule in the slums. There is a constant struggle for economic survival. Work patterns are likely to be irregular, and lack of stable employment often contributes to unstable family patterns. There is an almost complete absence of savings or even of the desire to save, and there is little ability to plan for the future or to defer present gratification of the senses. Food reserves are often nonexistent, and personal possessions are frequently pawned, or local money lenders are visited. Any treatment of the slum solely as a product of poverty, however, is far too simple. "Poverty" is both an absolute and a relative term. In an absolute sense, it means a lack of resources for specified needs; in a relative sense it refers to the extent of these resources in comparison to what other individuals in the society have. As societies vary in the degree of poverty characterizing them, individuals and the slums themselves vary in the degrees to which they are "poor." Slum people in the United States have a higher standard of living than many in higher social classes in other parts of the world. For example, the radio, television, electricity, processed foods, and other material possessions that slum dwellers generally have in the United States today would have been considered luxuries years ago, and they are still not available to large numbers of people in many countries. A slum person in the Western world may have many more material goods than a slum person in India has: A poor urban family today may have technological possessions and education superior even to those of the upper socioeconomic classes in the eighteenth century. In other words, poverty must be defined in terms of the aspirations and expectations of a culture and its capacity to produce these goods, and in these terms as an explanation of slum life it has serious limitations.

The social aberration among the poor of the slums, as well as their apathy, is a product of their being the poorest, rather than of their being "poor," and their alienation, apathy, and withdrawal from the general society appear to be maximum under urban slum conditions. In rural areas, the relative effects of poverty are counterbalanced by stronger traditions and group ties. In areas of extensive urbanization and also industrialization, where traditional and primary-group ties are weakened, the lack of power and status among the poor, particularly those in urban areas, is much greater.

General categorizations of the relation of poverty to lower-class life, however, are too broad. Sydney Miller has suggested, using as criteria family stability and job security, that there actually are four types of lower class: the stable poor (both familial and economic stability); the strained (economic stability and familial instability); the copers (economic instability and familial stability); and the unstable (economic instability and familial instability).[48] Such a classification makes it possible to consider cultural variations in the lower class. In any event, the lower class, which is associated with slum living, should not be identified with, or confused with, the "working class." The working class, made up of communities of semiskilled and skilled workers, has more stability of employment, although the orientation may largely be toward "getting by." The working class is more concerned with educational improvement than is the lower class but not so much as is the middle class.[49] Organized family life plays an important role in the working class.[50] Although the working class is not concerned with manners and proper behavior to the same extent as is the middle class, it does not generally have so high an incidence of deviant behavior as does the lower class.

APATHY AND SOCIAL ISOLATION

A slum also has an image in the eyes of the larger community. There is a societal reaction to slum dwellers. The nonslum dweller often associates the physical appearance and difficult living conditions of the slum with belief in the "natural inferiority" of those who live in the slums. As a slum is an inferior place, those who live there are also inferior. This reaction has important conquences in the social isolation of slum dwellers and their exclusion from power and participation in urban society. Those who live in the slum lack an effective means of communication with the outside world because of apathy, lack of experience in communicating with outsiders, and their own powerlessness to make their voices heard. The common denominator of the slum is its submerged aspect and its detachment from the city as a whole. "The life of the slum is lived almost entirely without the conventional world."* The local politician often becomes the only "ambassador to the outside world," one who unfortunately tries to manipulate it, frequently for his own benefit.[51]

Inevitably the slum dweller's conception of himself comes to reflect the attitudes of outsiders toward the slum and its inhabitants. Slum dwellers realize that they live under conditions that are physically, although not necessarily socially, inferior to those of the middle class. Sometimes they take actions that they hope can improve their lot, but far more often they apathetically accept the situation, do what they can with what they have, and experience little or no control over their surroundings. A research study of midtown Manhattan, for

---

* Harvey W. Zorbaugh, *The Gold Coast and the Slum* (Chicago: University of Chicago Press, 1929), p. 152. As Hollingshead has pointed out in one study, the upper classes view the area populated by the lowest class in these terms: "They enjoy their shacks and huts along the river or across the tracks and love their dirty, smoky, low-class dives and taverns. . . . The men are too lazy to work or do odd jobs around town. . . . This group lives for a Saturday of drinking or fighting. They are of low character and breed and have a criminal record for a pedigree." Hollingshead, *Elmtown's Youth* (New York: John Wiley & Sons, Inc., 1949), pp. 110–11.

example, reported that lower-class tenement dwellers tend not to plan ahead, have feelings of futility, and express a fatalistic outlook on life.[52] In a New Haven study, the lower class was described as fatalistic, tending to accept what life brought.[53]

Slum people feel relatively powerless to alter their life situations.* This powerlessness is accompanied by long-standing patterns of behavior and beliefs that reflect acceptance of this weakness. As conditions of success, a person tends to see chance rather than effort, luck rather than planning, and favoritism rather than ability. One writer refers to this outlook as the "feel" of a slum, the "feel" when an outsider is in a slum, or the "feel" of things when one lives in the slum.[54] "The attitude of the slum dweller toward the slum itself, toward the city of which the slum is a part, toward his own chances of getting out, toward the people who control things, toward the 'system', this is the element which as much as anything else will determine whether or not it is possible to 'do something' about slums. This is what makes slums a human problem rather than a problem of finance and real estate."[55] A slum dweller reported: "Survival for us depends on staying on good terms with the rich people and the law. Whenever I think about myself and the kids, I am reminded what my father used to say, 'We are the ones who are told what to do, when and how' around here. This town takes us for granted. Most people think the people down here [the tannery flats] are too ignorant to do anything and don't care; I guess they're right."[56]

Not all slum dwellers feel inferior or rejected, however. Studies of the more settled Italian slums in Boston have demonstrated that the residents found many satisfactions in their neighborhood and did not want to be moved from it. Firey, for example, found that the physical undesirability of the North End was outweighed by the advantages of living with people of similar backgrounds.[57] Whyte stated that, although the North End was a mysterious, dangerous, and depressing place to an outsider, it provided an organized and familiar environment for those who lived there.[58] Seeley lived in the Back of the Yards in Chicago in the early 1940s, and he discovered that its inhabitants had many advantages not found in "better" parts of the city: possibilities for fulfillment of basic human needs and outlets for aggressiveness, adventure, sexual satisfaction, strong loyalties, and a sense of independence. When the slum inhabitants were taken "slumming" into middle-class neighborhoods, they did not envy the residents.[59] In the West End of Boston, Gans found much the same attitudes reported by Firey and Whyte for the North End. Residents were satisfied with their neighborhoods and did not want to leave them for the suburbs or central-city locations that offered "improved" conditions.[60]

---

* "Power" is used here in much the same way as Floyd Hunter uses the term, "the acts of men going about the business of moving other men to act in relation to themselves or in relation to organic or inorganic things." Floyd Hunter, *Community Power Structure: A Study of Decision Makers* (Chapel Hill: University of North Carolina Press, 1953), pp. 2–3.

§ *The Social Organization of the Slum*

As slum dwellers are largely part of lower-class culture, they develop characteristic styles of life within their environments in the same manner as does the middle class. The fact that their patterns of life differ does not necessarily imply that one is "better" or more acceptable as a "standard" of life, as many authorities on social problems unfortunately seem to suggest through their use of middle-class standards as measuring rods or "core culture" with which to compare other class cultures.[61] This tendency has led to some erroneous assumptions about the life of slum inhabitants. For example, one such belief or assumption has been that the slum is composed of a "disorganized" population whose members neither know nor care about others living in the immediate vicinity.[62] Because delinquency, violence, sex patterns, the spontaneity and enjoyment of sensual pleasure, and such various other norms of behavior as lack of emphasis on good sanitation, neat housing, and industriousness differ from the norms of the middle class, they have been attributed to or are said to constitute "disorganization."

Detailed descriptive studies of slum communities often reveal high degrees of organization, with systematic and persisting features of social behavior.[63] Rather than being "disorganized," the slum often simply has its own organization, usually a type judged by the middle class to be unconventional. Miller states that lower-class culture is a cultural system in its own right, with its own integrity, set of practices, focal concerns, and ways of behaving, systematically related to one another rather than to corresponding features of middle-class culture.[64] Whyte has pointed out that, in the American slum, behavior may be as highly organized and social controls as effective as in middle-class suburbia but that the slum resident may not always conform to middle-class standards of proper conduct and respectability.[65] Formal governmental controls may be ineffective, and police and other government authorities may be held in disrespect, but they are replaced by some degree of informal control based on age, sex, occupation, or ethnic group. Sanitation, health, and child-care beliefs and practices may also reflect a highly organized system, though one contrary to both scientific and middle-class beliefs. Delinquent gang activity in the slums can be viewed as the lower-class boys' "positive effort to achieve status, conditions or qualities valued within the actor's most significant cultural milieu."[66] In fact, Cloward and Ohlin have theorized that slum-gang delinquency in the United States has become more aggressive and violent as a result of the disintegration of traditional slum organization due to massive slum-clearance or renewal programs, which have displaced entire slum-neighborhood populations.[67] The original residents have been dispersed throughout a community, and people who are strangers to one another have been assembled in housing projects. These residents are not only new and alien, but they commonly lack patterns of social organization that might bind them in community life. In addition, traditional slum patterns change because of declines of the urban political machines, which have meant the loss of important integrating structures and of significant channels for social ascent for the urban lower class.

Although some slums lack unity, disunity cannot be assumed to be a general phenomenon of the slum. Rather, each slum neighborhood must be examined in the light of its own subculture. In each case, the particular subculture will be the dominant influence on the life patterns of the respective slum inhabitants, shaping their lives through the pressures of environmental and family backgrounds, cultural traditions, and major life concerns. Zorbaugh described the rooming-house slum as a district of little social interaction among neighbors, as people constantly move in and out without ever really becoming part of the neighborhood.[68] Ethnic slums in the United States, on the other hand, may maintain their common cultural ties through their lodges, neighborhood shops, and taverns, which serve as meeting places. As ethnic slums split up and the more upwardly mobile residents move away, a breakdown in the effectiveness of the neighborhoods as units of social control results, and the continuity of neighborhood traditions is broken.[69] Furthermore, although ethnic and racial groups may live in close association with one another, there may be considerable isolation from other ethnic groups living geographically close by.[70]

Upper- and middle-class areas in the city are, however, quite different from slum areas in ecology, social structure, and, above all, the ability to participate in and utilize effectively the resources of the larger city. Middle- and upper-class groups, particularly in the Western world, live in neighborhoods, but their actual participating areas, where they shop, visit, and pursue recreational and cultural activities, are generally much larger. The world of slum people is much more fixed. It is centered in smaller areas that tend to create resentment and suspicion of the outside urban communities. Slum dwellers spend most of their time in the immediate neighborhoods: Their friends and relatives live there, whatever recreation they have is there, and what credit they can get is also there. Slum dwellers thus remain more fixed in residence, although in certain types of slum there may be considerable mobility, mainly, however, to other slum areas in the same city.

§ *The Function of the Slum*

Throughout history, the slum has met various needs and has served several useful functions for slum residents. In particular, it has provided cheap housing for the poor, has fostered group associations, has educated people in urban ways of life, and has given some of its residents an element of anonymity. One could, of course, look at the function of the slum from the point of view of the non-residents. For example, some people believe that, were slums not profitable to absentee landlords, "slumlords," they might well diminish in extent. For some employers slums have been useful as places where employees could live at lower rentals and therefore on lower incomes.

HOUSING FOR THE POOR AND THE MIGRANT

The most common function of the slum has been to provide housing for the lowest income groups in society. Slums have been havens for penniless rural migrants and immigrants who need a first living base in the city at the lowest possible prices. In areas undergoing industrialization and urbanization, migrants to the cities in the past and today have found their first homes, at rents they could afford or as squatters, in the city slums. Living in the slums has made it possible for low-income families to save enough for other purposes, as in the case of Italian immigrants who desired to save enough money to enable their families to join them or eventually to provide better lives for themselves and their children.[71] Similarly, the Jewish immigrants to New York's Lower East Side slum tried to save in order to send money to their families to pay their passages to this country.[72] Then there are those who, by living in the slums, have managed to build up small businesses or to save enough money by renting out rooms to be able to move to more suitable neighborhoods.[73] In developing countries, however, where vertical class mobility is severely restricted, the older and more settled slums and the large colonies of squatter shacks that spring up in and around large cities often become more or less permanent habitations for the poor. With low rents or no rents at all, their meager existences can be stretched indefinitely.

GROUP ASSOCIATIONS

In many countries, the slums serve as places where group living and associations on the basis of villages, regions, tribes, or ethnic or racial groups may develop. The appearance of a slum can easily be quite misleading to an outsider. What the middle-class observer often sees as a neighborhood of filthy, dilapidated and overcrowded dwellings is often viewed quite differently by those who live there and understand the neighborhood and its residents. In the West End of Boston, for example, the low rents, the sentiments of the people, and their identification with the neighborhood, as well as their strong kinship ties, built an attachment to a slum or low-rent neighborhood that cannot be fully understood by a person with middle-class values.[74] Whyte found an organized way of life in the slums, which offered many satisfactions to its residents.[75] Firey also found a strong identification with the Italian communities and its distinctive values among many of the Boston North Enders. For those who most fully identified themselves with the Italian values, the overcrowded and run-down housing was more than offset by the advantages of living with similar people in an Italian neighborhood. The fact that many of these people could have moved out had they so desired tended to demonstrate the invalidity of the conception of the slum as a "product of compulsion rather than design."[76]

Satisfaction for residents of the ethnic or regional slum arises from the fact that, for them, the residential area is often the setting for a vast and interlocking set of social networks and from the fact that physical area has meaning for them as an extension of their homes, various parts of which are delimited and structured on the basis of a sense of belonging.[77] A feeling of belonging in or to a slum area is thus, in some cases, an important factor in the attitudes of slum dwellers toward their environments. It is especially important in the slums of Asian and African cities.

EDUCATION FOR URBAN LIFE

The slum performs a function as a type of "school" to educate newcomers to the city. It gives them a place to become oriented upon arrival, to find first jobs, and to learn the ways of city life. This function is particularly important in developing countries, where the contrast between village and urban life is often great. As many immigrants of the past lived in the slums for periods of adjustment before moving on to better neighborhoods, so today, in large cities of the United States, the slums house the migrants from rural areas, the Negroes from the South, the Puerto Ricans, and the Mexicans.

DEMAND FOR ANONYMITY

An important function of the slum is that of offering a place of residence to those who prefer to live anonymously. The urban slum has harbored both those on the way up and those on the way down, and this dual character of the slum's social function has often been overlooked.[78] The slum accepts people who may be rejected elsewhere, and this function is important in preserving conformity in the remainder of the city. Some of the deviant behavior found in the slum does not originate there but in more fashionable neighborhoods. After defeat in personal life, a person may drift to the slum.[79] The Skid Rows of the large cities of the United States provide an example of the anonymity offered people in all kinds of circumstances. Skid Row residents include migratory workers, "bums," criminals, chronic alcoholics, and workers in illegal enterprises.[80] Only in the city, where rapid change is taking place, and often only in the slums of the city, can the disfranchised and deviant find genuinely important roles.[81] In addition, the artist often finds his start here, as do the poet, the jazz musician, and the radical. The slum also satisfies certain demands for vice and illegal activities like gambling, prostitution, and black-market trades. These demands call forth supplies, and the question is not whether or not, but where, the supplies will be found.[82] This accumulation of various deviant groups in slum areas should not necessarily be viewed as serving no social function or as a highly disturbing or dysfunctional element, for deviant groups may play important roles in the introduction of innovations in any society.[83]

§ *Theories of the Slum*

Several hypotheses have been advanced to explain the continued existence of slums. Changes in urban land-use patterns and lack of housing, which lead to overcrowding and improper maintenance, have commonly been emphasized.

CHANGES IN URBAN LAND-USE PATTERNS

According to one theory, largely derived from a study of cities in the United States, the slum develops within the zone surrounding the central business district.[84] Early in the development of a city, this area is the home of the upper classes, a fashionable residential district. With the expansion of commercial and industrial ventures, the neighborhood becomes infiltrated with industrial, storage, and wholesale operations, and the more well-to-do move farther out, away from the city center. Low-income workers, including recently arrived poor regional ethnic, and racial groups, then move in and become the exclusive inhabitants of these areas. Because the owners receive insufficient rental income to maintain their buildings properly, conditions decline, and, because of overcrowding, carelessness, and destructiveness by the occupants, the neighborhood becomes a slum. Zorbaugh has described the growth of the slum on the near North Side of Chicago:

> One alien group after another has claimed this slum area. The Irish, the Germans, the Swedish, the Sicilians have occupied it in turn. Now it is being invaded by a migration of the Negro from the South. It has been known successively as Kilgubbin, Little Hell, and, as industry has come in, as Smoky Hollow. The remnants of these various successions have left a sediment that at once characterizes and confuses the life of this district. . . .
>
> It is an area in which encroaching business lends a speculative value to the land. But rents are low; for while little business has actually come into the area, it is no longer desirable for residential purposes. It is an area of dilapidated dwellings, many of which the owners, waiting to sell the land for commercial purposes, allow to deteriorate, asking just enough in rent to carry the taxes. . . .
>
> The city, as it grows, creates about its central business district a belt of bleak,

barren, soot-begrimed, physically deteriorated neighborhoods. And in these neighborhoods, the undesirable and those of low economic status, are segregated by the unremitting competition of the economic process in which land values, rentals, and wages are fixed.[85]

The slum develops into an area of high land values but cheap rents, a curious contradiction that results from the land's being held "in pawn," so to speak, on the assumption that the central business district will expand, bringing into the area new business firms, manufacturing establishments, and high-priced rental units like hotels and apartment hotels. The landowners, who seldom live in the area, do not wish to improve slum housing as it will eventually be torn down. This fact and the rather undesirable location result in cheap rentals, yet the land remains so high-priced that, when an occasional apartment hotel is erected, it must be of high-rise proportions to be profitable.

A modification of this theory based on city growth is that of the city pattern as a pie, divided into wedge-shaped sections. According to this theory, industrial areas follow river valleys, water courses, and railroad lines out from the center, and workingmen's houses cluster along them, with factories tending to locate even at the outer fringes of the city. According to the sector view, the best housing then does not fringe the entire city but only parts of it. The main industrial areas of the future may well be located on the outskirts of cities in new industrial towns and suburbs, as they are already beginning to be.[86]

It has been claimed, however, that the pattern of land distribution in which the slum is located in or near the central city represents a generalization fulfilled only in industrial cities, where centralized commercial and industrial activities are necessarily more prominent, and does not apply to "preindustrial" cities.[87] In such cities, formerly common in Europe and still common in the developing countries of Asia and other parts of the world, the central areas are generally inhabited by the elite, with the slums located on the peripheries where "houses toward the city's fringes are small, flimsily constructed, often one-room, hovels into which whole families crowd."[88] The disadvantages of distant locations are borne by the poorest, who must travel the farthest to gain access to the city's facilities. This pattern of slum development is seen today in the extensive squatter or shanty towns that have sprung up around the cities in Asia, Africa, and Latin America to which large numbers of rural people have migrated. In some instances, they are located closer to the cities on unoccupied or undesirable land. After surveying seven sociological studies of Latin American cities, Schnore found that the cities do not follow the zonal pattern that North American cities supposedly do. One of his conclusions is that "it is evident that an accretion of jerry-built peripheral slums still characterizes most of the larger cities of the region. Living conditions and levels of health and sanitation in these outlying slums are generally described as extremely low, and municipal officials seem powerless in their efforts to turn the tide.[89]

The continuing existence of slums has also been explained by the fact that "their inhabitants cannot afford good housing and because private enterprise will not supply it at prices they can afford."[90] The blame for their existence, according to Colean, must be shared by the landlords, the tenants, and the community: the landlords because of their indifference to their property and their willingness to profit from overcrowding; the tenants because they are too poor, too ignorant, or too indifferent to maintain the dwellings properly; and the community at large because it allows slums to develop and to persist and fails to support government efforts to enforce decent standards.[91] One theory of slums advanced by an English writer lists four factors: the physical surroundings of the house, the physical conditions of the house, the owner, and the tenant.[92] His suggested means of improving or eliminating the slum demonstrates emphasis on the physical environment as a perceived cause of slum conditions. The three essential tools for "slum-breaking" are foresight in construction, careful maintenance by owner and tenant, and expert supervision by the authorities.[93]

A relatively recent theory of slum growth and development emphasizes the role of current urban-renewal projects in creating new slums in areas where old slums have been eliminated. The main point of this theory is that slum clearance reduces the number of dwellings available to low-income families and that, as a result, they cannot bargain with landlords of the prospective dwellings to obtain repairs and improvements as conditions of rental. As slum clearance continues, tenants in low-rent nonslum housing will have a harder time convincing landlords to spend funds for maintenance. If economic growth, full employment, or the lowering of racial discrimination toward job applicants should raise the real income of a neighborhood's population, however, housing quality would tend to improve.[94]

§ *Approaches to the Slum Problem*

Over the centuries, many groups have lived in the slums and have left; others have stayed on. The slums of most cities, however, not only have continued for centuries but also in many instances have grown in size; or new slums have been created. In this sense slums are self-perpetuating, either replenished from within or established through migration from outside the city. Several traditional approaches have been developed to deal with the slum problem, including charity measures, public and private services to slum dwellers, and slum clearance. Considering the nature of slum life and the enormity of its extent in most major cities, these measures have often offered only limited possibilities of dealing with the slum way of life in the final analysis.

Because slums have been so impervious to change and because the slum has been regarded as primarily a physical problem, one approach has been the destruction of the slum through clearance and renewal programs. Within a new physical environment, it has been hoped, slum problems might disappear. So far slums have not been amenable to such a simple solution. In fact, the problems of slum dwellers have even been accentuated by this method. In developing countries, where urban housing is perennially in short supply, the entire scheme has always been surrounded by an aura of unreality. Social workers from outside the slums have also offered various services through settlement houses and welfare centers, as many humanitarians or liberally oriented people have believed that the slum dweller needs outside help through charity, philanthropy, or other form of "uplift." Efforts have been directed toward ameliorating slum problems rather than toward eliminating the slum. In spite of such services through the years, slums have generally continued to resist efforts to change them, and they remain largely unaffected by the multitude of agencies and services offered, even in developing countries. Quite recently, the idea has developed in the United States that the slum problem stems basically from a lack of economic and educational opportunities and that, given a chance by government agencies to better themselves, the people of the slums will individually respond and take advantage of these services.

Another approach is to place emphasis on enlisting the slum dwellers themselves in an effort to bring about more rapid and at the same time more permanent changes. Recognizing the essential nature of most slum problems, this approach involves developing greater community consciousness, participation in a wider community, and self-help on the part of the slum dweller. This approach, relying upon indigenous leadership to bring about change and supplemented by some financial and technical assistance from the outside, has been termed "urban community development." Various experiments along these lines have been undertaken recently in the slums of developed and developing countries. The nature and application of urban community development will be discussed in subsequent chapters. First, however, the slum will be viewed in its historical perspective. Then types of slums and slum dwellers will be discussed, including the best known of all, the Indian slums.

Chapter 2

HISTORICAL PERSPECTIVES ON THE SLUM

Some slums of European and Asiatic cities can be traced back for hundreds of years. They existed in the days of what Sjoberg has called the "preindustrial city,"* characterized by both physical conditions and a specific way of life. The crowded conditions in India and Hong Kong are often attributed to Asiatic norms, the filth of the slums of Lima and Rio de Janeiro to the Latin American way of life, the drunkenness and violence of Negro and Puerto Rican Harlem to the racial and ethnic backgrounds of the people who reside there. The Westerner who views the slums of, for example, an "awful Indian city" like Calcutta, Bombay, or Delhi with ethnocentric smugness may see, in an Asiatic city slum, merely a reflection of Asiatic rather than Western values. Actually, these conditions were characteristic of many European countries less than a century ago and of the tenement living of English, Irish, German, and other immigrants to the United States. Bad as the slum conditions of contemporary India and other former colonial possessions are, they merely duplicate the living conditions of large segments of the eighteenth- and nineteenth-century urban populations of their erstwhile rulers. For some perspective on contemporary slums it is well, therefore, to examine the historic Jewish ghetto, the British slums of the nineteenth century, and the American slum and the tenement house.

§ *The Jewish Ghetto*

The Jewish ghetto† was a unique type of medieval urban slum. It therefore warrants special mention in a history of slums. Its uniqueness stems from an

---

* Gideon Sjoberg. *The Preindustrial City* (New York: The Free Press, 1960). If the slum life of those days were to be compared, however, with that of the middle class, it might be concluded that the differences were not so great as in the case of contemporary American and European slums.
† Although Oscar Handlin has defined a ghetto as "a community in which like-minded people of the same ethnic origins live together in a coherent group," he has emphasized that, in the Middle Ages, the word applied only to Jewish neighborhoods. See Oscar Handlin, "Are there Really 'Ghettos' in America?" *United States News and World Report*, July 22, 1963, p. 70.

interesting and complex set of social, religious, political, and economic factors that created a unified, homogeneous group, which often lived for centuries isolated from the rest of society in slum-like conditions without adopting some of the corresponding ways of life.

Most of the ancient and early medieval Jews lived in towns rather than in rural areas, and they chose to live together in specific quarters of the towns, as did other racial and economic classes. The very requirements of the Jewish religious culture almost demanded that they live where they could be near the synagogue, special bakeries, slaughterhouses, baths, courts of justice, and cemeteries.[1] No formal edict of church or state established the ghetto, and originally it was not an arbitrary creation designed to impose segregation. The first written charter granting a particular area of the city to a local group of Jews emphasized that the ghetto was being granted as a right, which included protection and the privilege of residence and trade. The first compulsory segregation of Jews within the ghetto occurred in Spain and Portugal at the end of the fourteenth century; and, in 1516, it was imposed in the Venetian Republic.[2] Pope Paul IV established the Roman ghetto in 1556, and it was not long before almost every city with a Jewish population had a ghetto. The Jews were not allowed outside their ghettos at night, on Sundays, or on Christian holidays.

The most serious effect of the walled-in ghetto was the severe overcrowding that quickly developed as the population grew, for only rarely was the area of the ghetto enlarged. Although the ghetto was not necessarily a slum when first assigned to the Jews, it soon became a partial one because of the overcrowding.[3] In some cities, the transfer of houses of prostitution to the ghettos added to the latter's ill repute among the gentiles, and fires and epidemics often destroyed portions of the areas and their populations. The ghetto of Frankfurt was one of the most famous. Frequent fires swept through it, and even the Jewish cemetery displayed signs of overcrowding, for the graves were close together, with two or three on top of one another.[4] Goethe likened the Frankfurt ghetto to a prison, the confinement, filth, and crowding of which, he said, had depressed his youth.[5] This ghetto was vividly described in the 1460s: "It was a most gloomy street, twelve feet broad, in its widest portion fifteen or sixteen feet. . . . The *Gasse* contained 190 houses, built very close together, some of them very high and containing many souls, the 190 houses harboring 445 families. . . . On account of the extreme narrowness of the street and the height of the buildings on either side, the tops of the buildings seemed almost to touch each other."[6] By 1700, the same small number of houses held 8,000 people, four times the number that had been causing the overcrowding in 1460.

In Rome, the Jewish ghetto was established in 1556 in a few narrow, unhealthy streets along the left bank of the Tiber, some of them subject to periodic flooding. As late as 1848, an Italian writer described the ghetto as a "formless heap of hovels and dirty cottages, ill kept, in which a population of nearly four thousand souls vegetates, when half that number could with difficulty live there. The narrow, unclean streets, the scarcity of fresh air, and the filth, inevitable consequences of such a conglomeration of human beings, wretched for the most part, rendered this hideous dwelling place nauseous and deadly."*

Although, for centuries, Jews lived in the ghetto slums in many European countries, they did not adopt all the patterns of life typical of slum dwellers. There appears to have been less violence, and the rate of disease was less than those for other groups living in overcrowded slum districts. Wirth reports, for example, that the Jews suffered less from the Black Death than did the rest of the population. Crime has always been lower among the Jews. Some of the practices of their religion and their greater education helped to keep them from adopting typical slum patterns of living. Although the Jew lived in a physical slum, he was not fully a part of it.

§ *British Slums of the Nineteenth Century*

Cities of England experienced rapid growth in the eighteenth century, as the Industrial Revolution brought greater opportunities for employment in Liverpool, Manchester, Birmingham, London, and Sheffield and as the opportunity for families to earn livelihoods in the country decreased. As the factories grew with the Industrial Revolution, workers poured into the cities in much the same way as they are now doing in the cities of developing countries, with entire families living in single rooms close to their work.

A proclamation by the English government during the seventeenth century had a lasting effect on slum development. During the reigns of the Tudors and Stuarts, it prohibited the construction of new dwellings in London, except those "fit for inhabitants of the better sort."[7] The stated justification for this limitation on construction was a fear that large numbers of people would give rise to all kinds of disorders and that the plague would spread more easily if growth were allowed to continue. The result of the proclamation, of course, was not a cessation of housing construction for the poorer classes but rather overcrowding in those areas where the edict was not effectively enforced: subdivision into smaller units of existing buildings, conversions of stables and warehouses into dwellings, and patching up of tumble-down buildings and cellar additions. Buildings constructed in violation of this proclamation were wretched places, built as cheaply as possible and hidden in alleys and courts, as they might be ordered removed at any time. Some of the poorest parts of eighteenth-century London, characterized

---

* Quoted in David Philipson, *Old European Jewries* (Philadelphia: The Jewish Publication Society of America, 1894), p. 126. After centuries of subjugation, the ghetto walls in Rome were finally removed in 1885, 1,800 years after the destruction of the Temple of Jerusalem and the deportation of Jewish captives to Rome. *Ibid.*, p. 175.

by dilapidated courts and alleys and crumbling tenements, were the direct results of this proclamation.[8]

Mumford has described the situation in the slums of England and America in the early nineteenth century:

In England, to begin with, thousands of the new workers' dwellings, in towns like Birmingham and Bradford, were built back to back. (Many still exist.) Two rooms out of four on each floor therefore had no direct daylight or ventilation. There were no open spaces except the bare passages between these doubled rows. While in the sixteenth century it was an offense in many English towns to throw rubbish into the streets, in these early industrial towns this was the regular method of disposal. The rubbish remained there, no matter how vile and filthy, "until the accumulation induced someone to carry it away for manure." Of this there was naturally no lack in the crowded new quarters of the town. The privies, foul beyond description, were usually in the cellars; it was a common practice to have pigsties under the houses, too, and the pigs roamed the streets once more, as they had not done for centuries in the larger towns. There was even a dire lack of toilets: the "Report on the State of Large Towns and Populous Districts" (1845) states that "in one part of Manchester in 1843–44 the wants of upward 7000 inhabitants were supplied by 33 necessaries only—that is, one toilet to every 212 people."

Even at such a low level of design, even with such foul accompaniments, not enough houses were built in many cities; and then far worse conditions prevailed. Cellars were used as dwelling places. In Liverpool, one-sixth of the population lived in "underground cellars," and most of the other port cities were not far behind: London and New York were close rivals to Liverpool; even in the nine-teen-thirties, there were 20,000 basement dwellings in London medically marked as unfit for human occupation. This dirt and congestion, bad in themselves, brought other pests: the rats that carried bubonic plague, the bedbugs that infested the beds and tormented sleep, the lice that spread typhus, the flies that visited impartially the cellar privy and the infant's food. Moreover the combination of dark rooms and dank walls formed an almost ideal breeding medium for bacteria, especially since the overcrowded rooms afforded the maximum possibilities of transmission through breath and touch.

If the absence of plumbing and municipal sanitation created frightful stenches in these new urban quarters, and if the spread of exposed excrement, together with seepage into local wells, meant a corresponding spread of typhoid, the lack of water was even more sinister. It removed the very possibility of domestic cleanli-ness or personal hygiene. In the big capital cities, where some of the old municipal traditions still lingered, no adequate provision for water was made in many new areas. In 1809 when London's population was about a million, water was available over the greater part of the city only in the basements of houses. In some quarters, water could be turned on for only three days in a week. And though iron pipes made their appearance in 1746, they were not extensively used until a special act in England in 1817 required that all new mains be built of iron after ten years.

In the new industrial towns, the most elementary traditions of municipal service were absent. Whole quarters were sometimes without water even from local wells. On occasion, the poor would go from house to house in the middle-class sections, begging for water as they might beg for bread during a famine. With this lack of water for drinking and washing, it is no wonder that the filth accumulated. Open drains represented, despite their foulness, comparative municipal affluence.[9]

As industrialization progressed in the nineteenth century, the infamous tenement houses came into being in Europe and particularly in Great Britain and America. Mumford reported that Patrick Geddes had characterized the change as "slum, semi-slum and super-slum—to this has come the Evolution of Cities." The tenement houses were widespread, congested, ugly, and disease-productive. The classic report of Sir Edwin Chadwick in 1842 on the sanitary conditions of the working classes of Great Britain presented such vivid accounts of health and sanitation that many subsequent corrective measures were initiated, and Chadwick is often referred to as "the father of the public health movement." One physician graphically described the area of the Manchester working classes:

> That the filthy and disgraceful state of many of the streets in these densely populated and neglected parts of the town where the indigent poor chiefly reside cannot fail to exercise a most baneful influence over their health is an inference which experience has fully proved to be well founded; and no fact is better established than that a large proportion of the causes of fever which occur in Manchester originate in these situations. Of the 182 patients admitted into the temporary fever hospital in Balloon-street, 135 at least came from unpaved or otherwise filthy streets, or from confined and dirty courts and alleys. . . . Whole streets in these quarters are unpaved and without drains or main-sewers, are worn into deep ruts and holes, in which water constantly stagnates, and are so covered with refuse and excrementitious matter as to be almost impassable from depth of mud, and intolerable from stench. . . . In many of these places are to be seen privies in the most disgusting state of filth, open cesspools, obstructed drains, ditches full of stagnant water, dunghills, pigsties, etc. from which the most abominable odours are emitted. But dwellings perhaps are still more insalubrious in those cottages situated at the backs of the houses fronting the street, the only entrance to which is through some nameless narrow passage, converted generally, as if by common consent, into a receptacle for ordure and the most offensive kinds of filth. The doors of these hovels very commonly open upon the uncovered cesspool, which receives the contents of the privy belonging to the front house, and all the refuse cast out from it, as if it had been designedly contrived to render them as loathesome and unhealthy as possible. Surrounded on all sides by high walls, no current of air can gain access to disperse or dilute the noxious effluvia, or disturb the reeking atmosphere of these areas.[10]

The living conditions of the London slum dwellers in the year 1887 were equally bad and were described by Gregg as reminiscent of the middle passage of a slave ship: Poisonous and malodorous gases rose from the accumulation of sewage and refuse; sunlight, fresh air, and water for cleaning were often not to be found. The buildings, rotten and swarming with vermin, gave off an intolerable stench. The rooms, eight feet square on the average, were black with years of accumulated filth; windows were stuffed with rags or covered by boards.[11] The streets of the slum districts, where the beggars, the maimed, and the blind also lived, were labyrinths of twisting alleys and passageways, in which strangers might be seized and robbed.[12] Some old buildings were filled from basement to attic, six or seven in a room; back yards were piled with litter and offal, and sanitation facilities were minimal.

> Poverty and the environment of poverty produced organic modifications: rickets in children, due to the absence of sunlight, malformations of the bone structure and organs, defective functioning of the endocrines, through a vile diet; skin diseases for lack of the elementary hygiene of water; smallpox, typhoid, scarlet fever, septic sore throat, through dirt and excrement; tuberculosis, encouraged by a combination of bad diet, lack of sunshine, and room overcrowding, to say nothing of the occupational diseases, also partly environmental.[13]

The poverty and slums of London received much attention and became objects of study toward the close of the nineteenth century, when Charles Booth published his famous *Life and Labour of the People in London*, an inquiry into the characteristics of employment and causes of poverty in the city. Less scientific but more descriptive accounts of the slum were provided by George Sims and Robert Blatchford in 1889 and 1899 respectively.[14] Another study of poverty and particularly of slum conditions at that time was made in the City of York by Rowntree.[15] He described the type of building in which people lived in York: The three-story building had eight one-room units; dust between banisters and wall measured nine inches; room interiors were dilapidated, with woodwork broken away around the doors and deep cracks in the walls. The house had no water supply, but one tap was shared with eight other families in the next building. "The grating under this water tap is used for the disposal of human excreta, and was partially blocked with it when inspected." Sixteen families shared six water closets located in the same passage as the water tap, the passage being heaped with rubbish, broken bottles, and old rags and bones.[16]

These overcrowded and unsanitary dwellings naturally increased the disease rates in the slum districts. Various epidemics were common; diseases and deformities were regularly transmitted from parent to child. Work accidents added to these problems. With the general lack of adequate sewage systems in slum areas, disease took high tolls in suffering and death. Sickness, especially of the bread winner, was disastrous for the working-class home; what savings did exist often disappeared, and it was impossible, with as many as six people in a room, to isolate the sick person from the rest of the family.[17]

The slum environment was difficult for children for moral reasons as well. When both parents worked, those children not working or in school often spent their time in the streets, and infants were often drugged with opium.[18] Seeing crime, violence, drunkenness, and despair, they easily became apathetic and unable to raise themselves above the level of their surroundings. Children of the poor living in this environment were often taught how best to beg and steal, "schools" for this purpose sometimes being provided, as described in the writings of Dickens.

Not only poor health and unhappiness arose from such child labor but also immorality. A fairly common feature of family life then, as is characteristic of the lower class generally and has been especially characteristic of the American Negro urban lower class, was the high degree of family instability. A man lived with one woman for a period of time, then moved on, leaving the woman to find another man. Although many couples lived together quite faithfully and looked upon themselves as husbands and wives with certain marital obligations, Engels described sexual license as one of the principal faults of the English working man, after intemperance.[19]

Prostitution was often centered in slum areas; street-walkers lived more or less as a community, not so much from choice as because decent lodging houses would not take them in. Vagrants and practitioners of all sorts of odd street trades also resided in the slums.[20] The Chadwick Report contains a number of lengthy descriptions of some of the lodging houses of that time:

> Lodging-houses for the lowest class of persons abound in Birmingham. They principally exist near the centre of the town, many of them in courts; but great numbers of front houses, in some of the old streets, are entirely occupied as lodging-houses. They are generally in a very filthy condition; and, being the resort of the most abandoned characters, they are sources of extreme misery and vice. These houses may be divided into three kinds,—mendicants' lodging-houses, lodging-houses where Irish resort, and houses in which prostitutes live, or which they frequent.[21]

It has been reported that fortunes were made from the sale of gin to men and women of the English slum. "For poor housing, lack of sanitation, unemployment and low wages, the working classes could hardly be held directly responsible. . . . But even the most sympathetic of investigators invariably condemned their habits of drunkenness."[22] Another characteristic of slum dwellers in England during the latter part of the nineteenth century was a reckless spending of money immediately after obtaining it. Rowdy Saturday nights were often followed by want and trips to the pawnshop during the rest of the week. The pawnshop generally played an important part in the lives of the slum dwellers. Children brought bundles on Monday morning, often including the Sunday clothes, only to redeem them on the following Saturday night, when the week's wages had been received. The habit of pawning, once formed, was difficult to break.[23] Accompanying this thriftlessness was a temptation to trust to luck and to let the next day take care of itself. The general rule seemed to be, "What you make in a day spend in a day," with the result that many led almost penniless existences.[24] It was also noted that few had any interest in trying to move out of the slum areas, and there was general "indifference to the higher aims of life."[25]

In his study of 4,000 families, Booth distinguished several classes of poverty in terms of income and way of life. The lowest classes were described as consisting of loafers, criminals and semicriminals, and some occasional laborers and street sellers.[26] Families in this area lived in tiny filthy rooms eight feet square and infested with vermin. It was common for seven or more families to share a single water tap and closet. In hot weather, the occupants often would sit in their clothes in the least infested parts of their rooms rather than go to bed. Gambling in the street, drinking, and violence were common among this group. Such slum people resisted philanthropic efforts to help them, preferring to group together for mutual protection. The misuse of the houses in which they lived was characteristic of this group: As soon as they moved into a street, the buildings started to deteriorate.* So pronounced were the ways of living of this group that Booth erroneously thought them to be a problem of heredity to a considerable extent, with young men taking "naturally" to loafing and young girls almost "naturally" taking to the streets. Many occasional laborers of this group did not want steady work; when it was offered, it was often refused. Even when they accepted such employment, they soon left it, returning to more congenial pursuits in the slum.[27]

Laborers with irregular work in London, the next higher class, were at all times more or less "in want." They were ill nourished and poorly clad, although only a few were in actual distress. They lived from day to day, from hand to mouth, and drunkenness was common, especially among the women. Their goal was to work when they liked and to play when they liked. They enjoyed action-filled lives and would not settle down to routine jobs even when such were offered. Slightly above this class were those people with small regular earnings or with only intermittent earnings because of illness, imprudence, or drink.

Several of the leading writers on slum conditions of nineteenth-century London have commented, however, that the lives of the slum dwellers were not entirely miserable. "In the course of many years of the closest contact with the most poverty-stricken of our fellow-men," wrote Sims, "I have learnt to think better, and not worse, of human nature, and to know that love, self-sacrifice, and devotion flourish in this barren soil as well as in carefully-guarded family circles."[28] Booth stated that the children of the poor might actually have been happier than those of the rich.[29] "Their lives are an unending struggle, and lack comfort," he wrote, "but I do not know that they lack happiness."[30]

---

* Charles Booth, *Life and Labour of the People in London,* I (London: Macmillan & Co., Ltd, 1892), p. 174. An additional feature of the slums of London around the turn of the century was the prevalence of the kind of common lodging house in which single men shared a combined kitchen and living room. In his novel, *Down and Out in Paris and London,* George Orwell described a number of these common lodging houses in the London area: Without exception they were dirty and insect-infested, the air stuffy and smelling of sweat, vomit, and urine.

§ *The American Slum and the Tenement House*

The development of slums in the United States was closely related to the successive waves of immigration that swept the country. The earliest mention of poor housing in such cities as New York and Boston made note of the fact that recently arrived foreign groups were forced to live in the worst neighborhoods. Lack of housing and consequently high rents, even at that early date, were responsible for the fact that increasing numbers of immigrant families had to find accommodations in stables, attics, and damp cellars, all small and congested, with poor water supplies and inadequate toilet and washing facilities. Throughout the nineteenth century, descriptions of the immigrant slums were quite similar, all making much use of the words "miserable," "squalid," "crowded," "filthy," "foul," "deplorable," "dark," "damp," "evil," and others of similar connotation. The earliest slums in the growing cities were composed of houses originally built for the use of one family each, which had been subdivided for the use of many families as the numbers of newly arrived immigrants seeking housing increased. Diseases like yellow fever swept these areas, as in New York City in 1795, when one doctor wrote: ". . . I have, in a former letter, given you some account of the condition of that part of the town where the fever most prevailed; it is now to be noticed that it is in that district that the greatest number of the poor, especially the immigrant poor, reside. In those numerous miserable dwellings, were these wretched people crowded together; many families in one house; and not infrequently many families of different nations."[31]

It was not until the 1830s that tenement houses were started, for the purpose of crowding into one building as many people as possible. According to Mumford, the first multifamily tenement building in New York was constructed on Cherry Street in 1835.[32] In 1843, there were 7,000 recently arrived immigrants living in cellars in New York. "Typical of overcrowded cellars was a house on Pike Street which contained a cellar ten feet square and seven feet high, with one small window and an old-fashioned inclined cellar door; here lived two families consisting of ten persons of all ages. Rain water leaked through cracks in the walls and floors and frequently flooded the cellars; refuse filtered down from the upper stories and mingled with the seepage from outdoor privies."[33] It was the tenement-house slum that became the most famous, as well as the most characteristic, type of slum. It was this tenement-house slum that later received the most attention from the social reformers of the nineteenth century.

To these tenement houses in the slums came hundreds of thousands of immigrants. In fact, the Dillingham Commission, anxious to compare immigrant and native tenement conditions in 1910, could not find a single tenement in one area occupied by a native American.[34] Particularly bad slum conditions were found in New York City. Three primary forces were at work to shape slums there: geographical limitations imposed on the spread of the population throughout the city, which was largely confined at that time to southern Manhattan Island; the necessity for immigrants, most of whom were very poor, to live within walking distance of their work; and the form of subdivision imposed upon the city by the Commissioners' Plan of 1811. This plan, which divided the city into lots 25 by 100 feet, set the pattern of tenement construction for the next century. Upon such narrow lots it was almost impossible to design multi-family high-rise buildings without sacrificing light and air. It has been stated that the division of New York into such lots was the greatest evil ever to fall upon a city.[35] The earliest type of tenement, other than that converted from a previously single-family unit, was the "railroad" type, in which 75 per cent of the rooms were unlighted and unventilated, except by doors that opened onto rooms in the front or back of the building, which did not contain windows. This type became very prevalent shortly after the mid-nineteenth-century period.[36]

In 1878, the magazine *The Plumber and Sanitary Engineer* sponsored a competition among architects to develop an ideal plan for tenement houses to be constructed on an interior 25- by 100-foot lot, to be an improvement over the "railroad" type in respect to fireproofing, lighting, ventilation, and so forth. This competition had two chief results: recognition that a desirable and economically feasible tenement could not be designed for a 25×100-foot lot and proposal of the "dumb bell" tenement as the best improvement over the "railroad" type that could be found. Typically five to seven stories high, it held four families per floor and had an air shaft consisting of an indentation of the wall to a depth of twenty-eight inches. The shaft was enclosed on four sides and in effect became a well sixty to seventy-two feet deep, providing little of the light and fresh air it was meant to supply. Each apartment contained a parlor that opened onto either the front or the back of the building, usually ten and a half by eleven feet in size; a kitchen the same size, which received light only from the air shaft or from the front room; and either one or two small bedrooms, each of which was barely large enough for a bed. These rooms received only what light and air could enter through the air shaft and, except on the highest stories, were almost entirely dark. Two families shared each toilet, which was located off the public hallway opposite the stairway. Jacob Riis has described one of New York's notorious tenement slums of this era: "In the scores of back alleys, of stable lanes and hidden byways, of which the rent collector alone can keep track, they share such shelter as the ramshackle structures afford with every kind of abomination rifled from the dumps and ash-barrels of the city."[37]

Some of the earliest tenements in New York were built far back on the lots, leaving large front yards in which, not too many years later, other tenements were built, thus creating what were called "rear tenements."[38] Although rear tenements had an unsavory reputation during the era of tenement-housing reform, they often, in reality, offered better housing than did the front tenements. They were less crowded, with two rather than four families per floor, and sometimes had open spaces up to twenty-five feet in depth in front. It was where the new tenement was built adjacent to or less than five feet in front of the old tenement that the most unsatisfactory conditions were prevalent. In such cases, the buildings were called "back to back" tenements. The following extracts from the report of inspectors in the Tenement House Commission Study of 1900 describe the conditions that often resulted:

> 18 Clinton Street—5 stories in height. This rear tenement backs up against a factory at 157 Attorney Street, which is 5 stories high. The space between the back of the buildings is 3 inches; 25 windows get their sole light and air from this space; refuse covers the bottom of it. The rear rooms on the 1st, 2nd, and 3rd stories are pitch-black.

> 288 East Houston Street—4 stories high. This rear tenement backs up against another tenement at No. 6 Avenue B, which is 4 stories high. The space between the backs of the buildings is 9 inches. This space is filled 2 stories high with rubbish. All the middle and rear rooms are very dark. About 2 inches of water, and foul smell, in the cellar.[39]

The Lower East Side of New York is perhaps still the most famous slum district in the United States. It is said to have been one of the most densely populated areas in the world and has a fascinating history of nationality-group succession. The density of the ward closest to the central factory district reached 700 people per acre in 1900. In 1914, one-sixth of the city's population lived below Fourteenth Street upon one eighty-second of the city's land area. Most of the office buildings and factories were located there, employing one-half of the city's industrial workers.[40] "No quarter in the city throbbed with such inner turmoil as did the Lower East Side in the final decades in the nineteenth and early years of the twentieth centuries. No other district in New York sensed the agitation to its life rhythms so sharply or harbored aspirations so out of joint with its tenement milieu."[41]

In Boston, where they tended to concentrate, the Irish immigrants occupied disused warehouses, cellars, and the worst of the tenement buildings. "No slum was as fearful as the Irish slum," writes Woodham-Smith, "because the degradation endured for generations by the poor in Ireland produced an acceptance of conditions which no other nation would have tolerated."[42] Children in the crowded Irish slums survived with difficulty, and a high mortality rate resulted from the slum environment into which they were born. The Boston tenement slum was second in size only to that in New York City. Whole families lived in single rooms without sunlight or ventilation. Even the cellars were inhabited.

The Chicago tenement was somewhat different from those of New York and Boston. As Chicago had room for expansion in every direction except east, it did not develop the high population density of Manhattan Island. In addition, Chicago was a much newer city, which grew to industrial prominence in a short period of time.* Instead of five- or six-story buildings inhabited by twenty-five or more families each, the wooden structures were predominantly of one or two stories, each occupied by three or four families. On lots 25 by 125 feet, rear tenements were common. They were formed by moving the original frame houses to the back of the lots and building others in front of them, unlike the process of constructing rear tenements in New York City. An investigation of these tenement conditions in 1901 uncovered overcrowding, poor sanitary conditions, defective plumbing, crime, illness, and high death rates in the Chicago slums.[43] The chief unsanitary conditions in houses were found to be darkness, lack of air, uncleanliness, and poisonous gases. Basement dwellings, of which there were many, were especially subject to these conditions and to seepage from nearby outdoor toilets. Outside unsanitary conditions included badly paved and unclean streets and alleys; dangerous sidewalks; filthy vacant lots, yards, courts, and passages; offensive stables and manure boxes, uncollected garbage littered about; and all types of animals on the loose.[44] The Commission went on to report that pauperism, intemperance, and crime were caused by the general conditions that existed in the tenement house slums and that sickness and high death rates were brought about by the unsanitary conditions.[45] "The demoralization and degradation to which the people living in the filthy surroundings of these alley houses eventually descend is obvious. With all these evils combined, rear tenements make the worst possible dwellings for human beings."[46]

In her well-known social welfare study, *The Tenements of Chicago, 1908–1935*, Edith Abbott provided some vivid descriptions of the tenement houses inhabited by families of the various nationality groups in the city. Of the tenement slums inhabited primarily by Slovaks she wrote:

> Dilapidation was everywhere. The cellars, even the first floors, were damp because of the grading up of streets and alleys from three to seven feet above the level of the yards. The walls of the cellars and the floors of the first stories were often decayed and musty, with the water draining down about the foundations. Floors were warped and uncertain, plumbing generally precarious—defective sinks with soaking plaster in the ceiling below (one long-suffering Lithuanian showed our investigator the water dripping down on his bed), windowpanes broken or entirely gone, doors loose and broken, plaster cracked and grimy, woodwork splintered and long unvarnished. Yards, areaways, and passages were cluttered and untidy with accumulated rubbish and the keeping of fowls in unsuitable quarters—and other nuisances, such as the smoking of meat carried on in the rear of one lot.[47]

---

* Edith Abbott, *The Tenements of Chicago, 1908–1935* (Chicago: University of Chicago Press, 1936), p. 170. The prevalence of small frame shacks rather than high tenements in the early Philadelphia slum was also explained by the greater availability of land for expansion.

Jane Addams also described slum conditions as they were when she first started her work at Hull House in Chicago in 1889. Streets were dirty, schools inadequate, sanitary legislation unenforced, and the stables "foul beyond description." Paving was miserable and entirely lacking in alleys and in smaller streets, and many houses were without sewer connections.[48] She believed that immorality among the slum youths was actually a protest against the monotony and dullness of factory work and that outbursts of crime resulted from the need for an outlet, attempts by the people to prove that they could do things, "without being bossed all the time."[49]

The slums of Pittsburgh around 1910 were no better than those of other major cities, and in some respects they were much worse. A survey sponsored by the Russell Sage Foundation in 1914 reported: "Some of the conditions we found were as bad as could be imagined. The privy vaults were often found to be foul and full to the surface, sinks without trap or vent, the rain conductor serving to carry off waste water; damp, dark, and ill-smelling cellars used for living purposes; cellars filthy; leaky roofs causing the walls and ceilings to become watersoaked, rendering the rooms damp and unhealthy; broken and worn floors; broken stair railings and worn and broken treads; plaster broken and paper torn and dirty."[50]

Washington, D.C., and to a lesser extent Baltimore, Maryland, had a form of slum unique among American cities. It was found in the back alleys in the interior of a block. Substantial buildings often faced the streets on all four sides, with the entrances to the alleys sometimes hardly noticeable from the streets. Within, however, were found run-down shacks of the worst types.[51] Civil War Washington has been described:

> It was a Southern town, without the picturesqueness, but with the indolence, the disorder and the want of sanitation. . . . Flocks of geese waddled on the Avenue, and hogs, of every size and color, roamed at large, making their muddy wallows on Capitol Hill and in Judiciary Square. People emptied slops and refuse in the gutters, and threw dead domestic animals into the canal. Most of the population still depended on the questionable water supply afforded by wells and by springs in the hills beyond the city. Privies, in the absence of adequate sewage disposal, were plentiful in yards and dirty alleys, and every day the carts of night soil trundled out to the commons ten blocks north of the White House.[52]

Developing at the same time as many of the tenement slums in the larger cities of the country were the cardboard and tar-paper shacks of the "shanty town" slums. German, Irish, and other construction workers building roads and quarrying stone north of the City of New York, together with rag and bone pickers and factory workers, settled in a number of shanty towns, where they lived without paying rent until they were forced to move, at which time the shacks were packed up like tents and carried to new sites. The families often lived on nothing more than what could be earned from the sale of coal by the children.[53]

§ *Effects of Tenement Slum Conditions*

The deleterious features of the tenement-house system were well summarized by the New York Tenement House Commission Study of 1900: (1) insufficiency of light and air, (2) danger from fire, (3) lack of separate toilet and washing facilities, (4) overcrowding, and (5) bad housekeeping apparent in filthy cellars and courts.[54] The problems of obtaining adequate light and air in the tenement houses of New York City and Boston arose from the smallness of the airshafts. The shaft, which was often used as a receptacle for garbage and all sorts of refuse, also spread odors and noise from one room to the others and destroyed any idea of privacy in the tenement house. The tenements were built so close together and often constructed of such poor nonfireproofed materials on the inside that fires spread easily from one tenement building to the next. Such unsanitary and crowded conditions led to the spread of disease: Cholera epidemics were frequent, and infant mortality was high. In New York City, the infant mortality rate in 1810 was between 120 and 145 per 1,000 live births, and it rose to 180 per thousand in 1850, to 220 in 1860, and to 240 in 1870. It was reported that one-third of the children living in the New York tenements in the 1860s died before they were a year old and one-half before they were five.[55]

One tenement house that was investigated in the 1850s held 120 families in cubicles averaging 196 square feet each. Families used group toilets and took water from a common tap. Seventy-one families were interviewed, including 504 people. There had been 138 deaths in the seventy-one families in two years, including fifty-nine infants.[56] Outlawed unsanitary privies were in use by 40 per cent of the families in the three Chicago slum districts studied, with eight individuals (1.6 families) using each privy.[57] The 1,598 front houses had only 161 bathtubs, and the 408 rear houses had only three.[58] Basement dwellings were especially deficient in sanitation. They were without proper light or ventilation and were damp and smelly. Floors were of wood and not waterproof, and sewage from neighboring houses and yards drained under the floors and around the walls. In many of the cases observed in the study, toilets were not exposed to the outer air, being ventilated into the house. The rooms usually could not be reached by the sun, which might have dried out the floors and driven away the vermin. Filth accumulated in the dark corners, and rats overran the slum neighborhoods, spreading disease.

Overcrowding in tenement buildings was found by several studies to have resulted in "moral degradation" and physical suffering, although "overcrowding" may not have had the same meaning to people that it has today. A Chicago study in 1901 reported that overcrowding was the main problem in the tenement districts and went on to say that there was no more important test of tenement-house conditions than the amount of space covered by buildings.[59]

An example was given of a twenty-five-foot lot with two buildings covering 95 per cent of its area and holding ninety-eight people. With people of both sexes, of all ages, and of any or no relationship forced to live in close proximity and with parents and children sleeping in the same rooms, sometimes even in the same beds, there was a lack of privacy. Young children growing up in such environments were constantly exposed to the norms and values of adult slum dwellers; family quarrels could be heard by an entire building. For most families, bathing, when it occurred, had to be performed in the presence of others after water had been carried up three or more flights of stairs. Some used public baths. Because of the crowded conditions in the tenement slums, a great deal of time was spent on the front steps, the street corners, and the streets themselves.[60] Hot summer nights found many of the tenement dwellers sleeping on fire escapes and roofs.

Prostitution became prevalent in the tenement districts, both because of lax police enforcement and because of the need to earn money to support families. Gambling was also common; policy playing with small sums of money provided some degree of excitement in the dreary tenement life, and there was always the hope of winning a large prize. Pauperism, living off charity, was contagious. "All the surroundings of tenement-house life favor its growth, and where once it has taken root it is harder to dislodge than the most virulent of physical diseases."[61] Two or three families living off charity sometimes set the standard for others in the tenement, and begging children often would encourage their playmates to beg with them.[62]

The infamous "sweatshop" system of industry accompanied tenement conditions in the larger cities, recruiting as laborers the recently arrived poor European immigrants, whose fares to this country were sometimes paid by employers seeking labor at low wages. Under the "sweatshop" system, manufacturers of clothing, for example, would let out on contract to individuals work consisting of such manufacturing steps as sewing on pockets, adding buttons, and so forth. Individuals working on a small scale would bring the materials home, where the entire family would spend long hours in their dark rooms completing as many articles as possible, for which they were paid piece rates. Larger-scale contractors would hire the poorest people, including women and children, at low rates of pay. The workshop provided would often be small and dark, sometimes located in a stuffy basement, and always unclean.

The saloon became a social institution of such urban working-class areas as the tenement slums in both the United States and Great Britain. In 1896, New York City had nearly 8,000 saloons, sometimes thirteen on a single block in tenement districts.[63] The saloon's patronage was strictly male, drinking was done at an elaborate bar, and there were free meals and special "family entrances." The elaborate décor was in dramatic contrast to the squalid everyday life of the working man. Most saloons performed an important function by helping to relieve the poverty, loneliness, and monotony of tenement living. Where slum houses were cold, dark, filthy, and unhappy places, men turned to the ever-present saloons. Many of the arriving immigrants came from traditional drinking cultures, which added to the popularity of the saloons in the slum neighborhoods. Although some saloons became associated with drunkenness, gambling rackets, or prostitution, a sociological study of saloons in a slum area of Chicago between 1896 and 1897 revealed that most saloons were not centers of intemperance or vice.[64] In fact, the saloon was found to have many other, more social functions:

> It is the workingman's club. Many of his leisure hours are spent here. In it he finds more of the things which approximate to luxury than he finds at home, almost more than he finds in any other public place in the ward. . . . But his demand for even these things is not fundamental, they are but the means to his social expression. It is the society of his fellows that he seeks and must have.[65]

§ *The Legitimation of the Slum*

In the nineteenth century every urban society had its lower class living in the slums, and in earlier times the low productivity of society and the great gap between rich and poor made this distinction seem natural and inevitable. The upper classes did little to help, writing off the poor as the result of "God's will" and generally ignoring the starvation, illness, and despair of the slums. Occasionally people of the wealthy class found recreation and entertainment in "slumming" expeditions, and now and then some philanthropic individuals visited slums, judging it their "Christian duty" to make some personal contribution. On the whole, however, the slum was taken for granted, assumed to be inevitable, or ignored by most people. A contemporary account revealed how little power slum dwellers among the two million residents of the East End of London in 1882 had in civic affairs:

> Probably there is no such spectacle in the whole world as that of this immense, neglected, forgotten great city of East London. It is even neglected by its own citizens, who have never yet perceived their abandoned condition. They are Londoners, it is true, but they have no part or share in London; its wealth, its splendours, its honours, exist not for them. . . . No one is curious about the way of life in the east. . . . If anything happens in the east, people at the other end have to stop and think before they can remember where the place may be.*

---

* Quoted in Guy Thorne (Cyril Arthur Edward Ranger Gull), *The Great Acceptance* (New York: Hodder and Stoughton, 1913), pp. 1–2. The remoteness of East London was illustrated by a witness before the Select Committee on the Health of Towns in 1840, who said of social conditions in the worst districts of the East End that "none but the medical men and the parish officers knew anything about them: they are as much unknown as the condition of a district in Otaheite." Quoted in Asa Briggs, *Victorian Cities* (London: Odhams Press, Ltd, 1963), p. 326.

Even as late as the 1890s in most American cities, people were seriously unaware of the slum or the ways the slum dweller lived.[66] Post emphasized this lack of interest in slums, pointing out that several thousand people died each year in New York as a result of conditions in the slums. While this fact was buried on the inside pages of the newspapers, headlines proclaimed the drowning in a flood of a few hundred people or fewer, society became perturbed, and millions of dollars were spent to prevent a recurrence of the tragedy.

Early studies of slum districts revealed a certain aloofness, and tenement dwellers were discussed as if they were a strange species of humanity with which the writers had little in common. They were described in various American writings of the 1890s as debased and undeserving of sympathy; devoid of moral feeling and a sense of shame; "not as decent as brutes impregnated with a stench that would poison cattle"; as living in "a commingled mass of venomous filth and seething sin, of lust and drunkenness, of pauperism and crime of every sort." In fact, a federal-government report in 1894 described slum inhabitants as a "squalid and criminal population."[67]

Over the past six or seven decades, a more general conviction has gradually developed in many countries that the existence of slums contradicts important values of society. Poverty might be regarded as a personal matter, but the slums could not be so easily dismissed. Efforts made to eliminate slums have largely been inspired more by emotional and æsthetic revolt against their physical ugliness and their danger to the larger society than by full appreciation of the plight of the slum dweller himself. People first became concerned about the slum in the United States, for example, because of its effects upon the larger society.[68] Slum regions lay close to busy commercial districts and to some of the better residential areas. Rioting and brawling in the slums disturbed the more sedate life of the city. Others saw the slums as sources of undesirable citizens and warned against indifference to the slum dweller. Still others saw slums as an increasing threat to public health. The connection between the slums and epidemics of typhoid, cholera, smallpox, and other diseases became recognized. The poor of the slums might fall in greater numbers, but eventually some members of the upper strata would also succumb.

It was easy to put greater emphasis on physical property in the slum than on the people, for it is much easier to demonstrate physical deterioration than human deterioration.[69] Great Britain, for example, enacted statutory authority in 1851 to condemn unfit houses. A number of groups and individuals began to take a serious interest in improving slum conditions, and it was these people who aroused public concern and who pressed for legislation to improve housing for the poor. At the close of the nineteenth century in Great Britain, the writings of Booth and others on the slum conditions of London brought greater recognition of the conflict between the existence of slum problems and the moral values of the Victorian age,[70] and similar developments occurred in several other

European countries. In the United States, a New York City journalist, Jacob Riis, was perhaps the leader in the campaign to arouse public concern over the slums. In his book, *How the Other Half Lives*, published in 1890, he emphasized that the poor did not live in the slums because they were lazy, dirty, immoral, or intemperate. He protested very little, however, against the larger forces that consigned people to the slums, except in the cases of the women and children. "His was no cry for social justice, but a call to the propertied classes to bestir themselves lest the crime engendered in the slums and diseases bred there invade the comfortable quarters where ladies and gentlemen resided."[71] Copies of Riis's book were found in the most fashionable homes, and, largely as a result of his writings, society ladies held luncheons and benefit dances to raise money to help the poor of the slums.

The tragedies of slum life were "discovered" in part also through the literature of the late nineteenth and early twentieth centuries.[72] Dickens's novels, particularly *Oliver Twist*, described the slums as "haunts of hunger and disease" and as foul and "frowsy dens." His humanitarian writings, embellished with great realism, stressed that "every slum would visit retribution upon the community that permitted breeding places of ignorance, vice, disease and despair to exist."[73] A number of American authors tried to imitate Dickens, but they took a more lurid approach, using the slums as backdrops for stories of crime and violence. Modern slum life has probably never been portrayed more brilliantly and more savagely than by such realistic novelists as James Farrell (Studs Lonigan trilogy) in the 1930s, Willard Motley (*Knock on Any Door*) in the 1940s, and James Baldwin in the 1960s. The published diary of a slum dweller had wide impact in the 1950s on the people of Brazil.[74]

The slum situation of past centuries differs from that of the present largely in the attitudes toward it. In the past, there was acceptance of the inevitability of the correlation between slum conditions and social status.* Today there is increasing awareness among large segments of the elite of most countries that slum conditions have to be changed, not only on humanitarian grounds, but also

---

* Even today many of the members of the upper socioeconomic groups regard the slums in similar fashion, as the following excerpt reveals: "Each workday morning I drove from my home in Brookwood Hills to my office in Atlanta's business district. The concrete boulevard looped down through pleasant streets until it reached a corner of the Georgia Tech campus. . . . I always moved a little faster here, for ugliness was packed close on either side: crowded, dilapidated dwellings, ragged, dirty children, reeking outhouses—a human garbage dump—a slum. Why such an untended abscess should fester between the lovely campus of our proudest school and the office buildings in the heart of our city never consciously entered my mind. Though my business lay in central real estate, I had no connection with the Techwood slum. It was no concern of mine. Consequently, I put greater pressure on the accelerator as I drove through that slum twice a day, my eyes fixed on the downtown towering structures in the morning, and on the ivy wall of Georgia Tech's fine stadium as I headed homeward at sunset." Charles F. Palmer, *Adventures of a Slum Fighter* (Atlanta: Tupper and Love, Inc., 1955), p. 7. Palmer became a leader for federal slum-clearance legislation during the New Deal period in the United States.

to expedite the development of the entire society. A belief is also emerging among many slum residents that their situation is not inevitable and that it can be improved. In the United States, as elsewhere, slum-clearance and urban-renewal programs and, in some instances, antipoverty programs have been directed at the elimination of the slums. This awareness of a "slum problem" is only recent in developing countries, where even the physical conditions of life have not generally shocked the sentiments of those in positions of economic and political power. Even in India, however, the slum has become increasingly recognized as a subject for investigation, government planning, and possible eradication. In many other parts of the world as well, in developed and developing countries, the slum has become recognized by those in positions of power as a social area of real consequence and concern for the general society; as a problem, it has become legitimated.

Chapter 3

TYPES OF SLUM AND SLUM DWELLER

Slums are of various types, and they can be viewed in three different ways. They can be viewed in terms of the social mobility of the slum dweller and in terms of the primary reason for the slum dweller's becoming involved in the slum, and they can be looked at comparatively.

§ Social Mobility and Types of Slum

An important classificatory model of types of slums has been developed by Stokes, who uses two main variables: first, the attitude of the slum dweller toward social mobility through assimilation or acculturation in the social and economic life of the community and, second, the measure of socioeconomic handicaps and barriers to such movement.[1] Each of these two variables provides two general classifications: "slums of hope" and "slums of despair." The former are characterized by the attitudes of the residents, whether or not they expect to improve their situations and whether or not there are opportunities for advancing out of the slums. Slums of hope have been generally the homes of the recent immigrants to the community, whereas those of despair have been populated by groups of longer residence. In each type of slum, there are "escalator" and "nonescalator" classes. Slums of hope are more likely to contain escalator classes, groups of people who can be expected to move up through the class structure, whereas nonescalator classes, denied in some way the privilege of escalation, are more characteristic of slums of despair.[2] In slums of hope, people intend to better themselves. The distinction is similar to that between the employable and the unemployable. The escalator and nonescalator classes are comparable to two categories of jobs, one of which permits escalation and the other of which does not.[3]

Using these distinctions, four types of slum can be identified: slums of hope with escalator classes, slums of despair with escalator classes, slums of hope with nonescalator classes, and slums of despair with nonescalator classes. They are referred to as types "A," "B," "C," and "D" respectively. An example of the "A" type is a slum in Guayaquil, Ecuador's largest city, which has grown through immigration from the countryside and the mountains. It was built on the flood plain, and a constant process of filling in the marshes, *relleno*, is necessary. As this process is completed and paved streets are extended, better-quality houses are constructed. The "A" slum, that is, the slum of "hope" with escalator classes, is probably the least attractive of all slums because it is the most temporary. It is also the one most likely to change, for such a slum formation can be considered basic to the growth process of cities of developing countries, providing a kind of school for teaching the ways of city life, as well as a temporary home.

The "B" type of slum is often found in the United States, in an area originally "genteel" that has become the home of the castoffs and those who have been unable to complete the process of acculturation. It is more attractive than is an "A" slum but less progressive in outlook. An example is Boston's South End. "Along streets which often have parks down their center stand four-and-five-story brick houses with bowed fronts. There is a haunting charm to these elm-shaded streets. But the second impression is more lasting. Decay is everywhere. An air of hopelessness pervades the atmosphere."[4]

The Negro slum of Chicago's South Side is an example of the "C" type. Hope and aggressiveness are found there, but there is limited opportunity to move into better neighborhoods. What makes it different from the "A" type is its almost complete barrier to acculturation. The "D" type of slum (despair and nonescalator classes) is exemplified by the Indian shack settlement outside Lima, Peru, where the residents have no chance of being accepted and are largely unaggressive.

Each of these four types of slum has various social, economic, and political implications. Slums of types "A" and "C" serve necessary purposes, and are self-eliminating if society has the time to wait. The other two, however, do not pass away with economic growth. As economic skill and education become necessary to rise above the level of poverty, as is the case in the more developed economies, those in the slums of despair will have more difficulty in escaping. Although a fixed amount of ability is necessary to rise above the slum level, the slums of despair will grow at about the population rate of growth, assuming no further immigration, according to this theory. As ever-increasing degrees of competence are demanded in a growing, advancing economy, a larger proportion of the immigrants may be incapable of rising and thus destined to remain in slums of despair. Stokes concludes that "a low level of income does lead to poverty and slums, but . . . a rising income is limited in its ability to remove slums if ability barriers exist."[5]

§ A Functional Classification of Slum Dwellers

In his classic work on the slum, Zorbaugh made the exaggerated statement that the slum acquires its distinct character through a cumulative process of natural selection, which continues as the more energetic move out and the "unadjusted, the dregs and the outlaws accumulate."[6] Slum dwellers, however, can be classified according to the lengths of time they remain in the slums and the reasons for their presence there. Residents of Boston's West End have been classified, for example, into four strata or subcultures: the lower-class action seekers, the working-class routine seekers, the lower lower-class maladjusted, and the working-class mobiles, who seek to enter the middle class.[7] The first two and largest groups are characterized by particular conceptions of living, ways of responding to opportunities presented, and choices. One is based on a search for routine in life, and the other has a more adventurous approach to life. The routine seekers are likely to have stable jobs and routine life styles; for the action seekers, life is a series of episodic thrills, in card games, fights, sexual interludes, and drinking bouts. These two types result from "differences in rhythm of life, in the patterns of family relationships, work, leisure, religious behavior, attitudes toward authority, and, indeed, the very purpose of existence."[8] Whereas action and routine seekers are socially nonmobile, there are others who, although they superficially resemble routine seekers, strive to move themselves into the middle class. The maladjusted are those who are unable to control their behavior because of alcoholism or other personal difficulties.

Seeley has divided slum dwellers into the "permanent necessitarians," the "temporary necessitarians," the "permanent opportunists," and the "temporary opportunists."[9] Within each of these four types are several subtypes (see Table 1). Although derived from observation in the United States, this classification has implications for other societies.

Table 1

Types of Slum Dweller by Primary Reason of Involvement

	PRIMARY REASON FOR SLUM INVOLVEMENT	
LIKELIEST TERM OF INVOLVEMENT	Necessity	Opportunity
Permanent	I a. the indolent b. the adjusted poor c. social outcasts	III a. fugitives b. unfindables c. models d. sporting crowd
Temporary	II a. the respectable poor b. the trapped	IV a. beginners b. climbers c. entrepreneurs

Reprinted by permission from John R. Seeley, *Redevelopment: Some Human Gains and Losses* (Indianapolis: Community Surveys, Inc., 1956), p. 50.

THE PERMANENT OPPORTUNISTS

People who stay in the slums because of the opportunities offered there are the "fugitives," the "unfindables," the "models," and the "sporting crowd." The fugitives are of two types: "those whose encounters with the law or the credit agency have led them into a life of subterfuge and flight, more or less permanent; and those whose nature or experience has decided them to flee the exigencies of rigorous competition in a better area in their own business or profession."[10] The unfindables constitute a floating population that cannot be located easily, is seldom counted in the census, and lives a shadowy existence both in terms of location and social identity. The models consist of some people who remain in the slum to bring culture or religion to those whom they regard as less cultured or unsaved; they come to think of themselves as social missionaries. The sporting crowd consists of many types of people who live in the slums to save money for other things like drinking and gambling and to meet others in the same situation.

THE PERMANENT NECESSITARIANS

Among the permanent necessitarians are three subtypes: the "indolent," the "adjusted poor," and the "social outcasts." The most striking characteristic of the indolent is general apathy or immobility. "Whether from inherited characteristics, disease, mal-education, mal-nutrition, the experience of perennial defeat, religiously-founded 'resignation,' or mere valuation of other things— these are the do-nothings, who 'have no get up and go.' "[11]

The adjusted poor live in the slum from necessity but have adapted to its ways. They are the destitute, or nearly destitute, who accept poor living conditions because of low rentals. Wishing to remain independent they prefer marginal physical existences to accepting conditions of dependence. The last subgroup, the social outcasts, consists of drug addicts, peddlers and pushers, prostitutes and pimps, and others of marginal or shady activities.

THE TEMPORARY NECESSITARIANS

These people are of two types, the "respectable poor" and the "trapped." The respectable poor may live temporarily in the slum or even remain there most of their lives, yet they never become adjusted or reconciled to it. Their values and identifications, as well as most of their associations, remain outside the slum. The trapped are those who had acquired homes before an area became a slum and who thus simply happen to be there.

THE TEMPORARY OPPORTUNISTS

This group is important both because of its size and because, for its members, the slum offers a way to pursue those things that American culture has taught them are worth pursuing: self-improvement, independence, property ownership, and savings accounts.[12] This group has three subtypes: the "beginners," the "climbers," and the "entrepreneurs." The first group consists of largely unattached immigrants to the city, who live in the slum while they try to find work and become adjusted to city living. This group is largely without access to such agencies of assimilation as churches or ethnic associations, and seldom do its members have helpful relatives nearby.[13] The climbers are similar to the first group, except that they have been in the city for longer periods of time. They live in the slum, usually during periods of apprenticeship, practicing self-denial and self-sacrifice while they build up backlogs of work experience, money, and other material possessions to enable them later on to improve their standards of living.[14] The entrepreneurs have orientations similar to those of the climbers but are more ambitious, saving out of business enterprises the means for escape from the slum.

§ A Comparative Typology

Slums can be classified along a continuum. They differ in physical setting, overcrowding, permanence of the inhabitants, degree of organization among the residents, and types of problems presented. In some slums, unique circumstances affect the residents. Physically, slums may be mere shanty towns, collections of hovels made of scrap materials, hastily erected on unauthorized land and without even the basic comforts of water and sanitary facilities. Others may range from substantial multistoried tenements to palatial old houses formerly occupied by wealthy citizens. Regardless of physical structure, most slums are overcrowded far beyond the minimum standards of health and decency. Some, in fact, are so tightly packed with humanity that families must occupy "bed space" in small rooms, as is especially characteristic of slums in Hong Kong and Singapore.

> Because of its inclusiveness, the word [slum] too often obscures the vast differences between one type of slum and another. Slums may be either rented or owner-occupied, either legal or illegal. They include cabins, shanties, dens, dugouts, sheds, stalls, and other manifestations of poverty. Some are single-family shelters converted into several smaller compartments; some are one-story and others six-story tenements. . . . Others line the back alleys of mansions.
>
> Some slums are new and some the abandoned houses of those who have moved up in the economic scale. The new slum is built because it has a use at the price, while the old slum survives because there is nothing cheaper and more serviceable to replace it. The new huts built of scavenged scrap by in-migrants to Asian or South American cities are often worse than the old ones.[15]

Abrams has attempted to classify slums in the United States: (1) the "metropolitan slum," which dates from the time of the great immigration; (2) the "rural slum"; (3) the "ghetto," characterized by congestion, because of the limited range of available dwellings, and by disrepair; (4) the "company slum," homes, owned by employers, for workers in coal mines and textile plants; (5) the "perpetuated slum," shacks and cabins intended for temporary use but continued as homes for families who can afford nothing better; (6) the "depopulated slum," ghost towns and sections of cities hit by depression; (7) the "overrun slum," a once livable area invaded by factories, a highway or railroad, smoke, dust, noise, odors, and ugliness; (8) the "hand-me-down slum," once fashionable buildings subdivided into small units; (9) the "regenerated slum," kept going by occasional repairs, though many defects exist; (10) the "home-owned slum"; and (11) the "potential slum," a poorly built and designed subdivision, which will turn into a slum within a few years.[16]

Some slums are the gathering points for large numbers of recently arrived rural or village migrants. Although they may exhibit considerable heterogeneity they may also sometimes maintain degrees of unity in their ethnic, religious, or tribal backgrounds. Others are populated by long-term residents whose families often have lived under slum conditions for many generations.

Slums differ in the degrees of organization among their residents. In some, few ties exist beyond the immediate families, and even family ties may be weak. In other more stable slums, quite close group and family relationships have developed. In a sense they constitute real slum communities, with sets of norms and values that differ sharply from those of the outside world.

Certain slum groups are products of unique sets of circumstances, as in the Negro slums of the United States and South Africa. There the difficulties of slum living have been compounded by the ever-present imprint of slavery and discrimination. In the United States, the pre-existing social values of the slums to which the Negroes moved were combined with the shattering effects of their slave backgrounds; in South Africa, detribalization, apartheid, and slum living have all affected slum living conditions. In both cases, the results have been exceptionally high rates of crime and delinquency, family instability, illegitimacy, and violence.

Slums also differ in the specific problems they present. United States and European slums often are associated with delinquency, alcoholism, and similar problems, including drug addiction and illegitimacy in the United States. Although these problems are also present in much of Asia, Africa, and Latin America, they do not constitute the major complications. There the major obstacles are more physical in nature—the totally inadequate building structures, excessive overcrowding, lack of facilities, poor sanitation, and high disease rates. Although these problems exist in the United States and Europe, they do not provoke the same major concern. At one time, however, they were nearly as difficult.

SQUATTER COMMUNITIES AND SHANTY TOWNS

An ever-present phenomenon of the rapidly developing cities of Africa, South America, and Asia, particularly India and Pakistan, is the extensive communities of squatters and shanty-town dwellers that have sprung up in and around peripheral areas of cities.* Rural migrants move into these slums rather than into the older city tenement slums because space is often unavailable in the tenements whereas there is vacant land on the outskirts of the city for building shacks. The buildings erected by squatters are of various types, most being one-story makeshift dwellings of scrap materials like lumber, tin, and bricks.

Peripheral shantytowns spring up on land that is not being used for one reason or another. The occupant may simply set up a hut as a squatter, may pay a small rent to the owner of the land, or in the case of some better organized groups of workers, may obtain recognition from the Government of his right of occupancy. The land is often unused because it is undesirable or unsuitable for permanent buildings. It may consist of swamps (as in certain districts of Bangkok), steep hillsides (as in the favelas of Rio de Janeiro), low ground subject to flooding (as in the outskirts of Baghdad), or refuse dumps. Waste areas of these types may be found near the center of the city as well as on the outskirts. In other cases, the land is too arid for cultivation and outside the scope of the city water system. Many shanty-towns also occupy land that is held vacant by urban investors in anticipation of future city growth, so that the occupants face eventual eviction; these include shacks on scattered vacant lots in the inner parts of the cities.[17]

There are various types of squatter: the owner squatter, the squatter tenant, the squatter holdover, the squatter landlord, the speculator squatter, the semi-squatter, and the floating squatter.[18] The owner squatter is the most common type, owning his small makeshift home but not the land it covers. The squatter tenant rents from another squatter, a common practice among new migrants to a shanty town. The squatter holdover is a person who formerly paid rent but whom the landlord fears to evict. The squatter landlord generally has lived for a long time in an area and rents huts to others. The speculator squatter is one who squats on public or private property with the idea that he will later receive money or some other kind of benefit for leaving. The semisquatter builds his house on unauthorized land but later works out a financial arrangement with the owner. The floating squatter lives on an old hulk or a junk, either owned or rented.

Estimates have been made of the numbers of squatters in various countries

---

* In many cities of the world, particularly in Asia, large numbers of pavement dwellers live, either alone or in families, on the streets. They are "mobile squatters" without houses. (See Charles Abrams, *Man's Struggle for Shelter in an Urbanizing World*, Cambridge, Mass.: The M.I.T. Press, 1964, pp. 3–4). In Bombay in 1964, a municipal survey reported 400,000 people living on the city's pavements, and there are at least 600,000 in Calcutta. They will not be considered as slum dwellers here, as many live in nonslum areas, some are transient, and they have little distinct physical or social unity.

in 1962.[19] In Ankara, they made up 45 per cent of the population; in Istanbul, 21 per cent; in Manila, 20 per cent; in Caracas, 38 per cent; in Cali, 30 per cent; in Santiago, Chile, 25 per cent; in Singapore, 15 per cent; in Kingston, Jamaica, 12 per cent; and in Delhi, 7 per cent. The reasons for these high figures are numerous.

Squatting is triggered by many factors—enforced migration of refugees because of fear, hunger, or rural depression, the quest for subsistence in the burgeoning urban areas, and simple opportunism. Usually it is the by-product of urban landlessness and housing famine. Surplus rural labor and the need for labor in the towns combine to speed migrations. When there is no housing for the migrants, they do the only thing they can—they appropriate land, more often publicly owned land, from which there is less fear of being dislodged. Sympathy with the squatters' movements or lack of a consistent official policy encourages further squatting. Existing settlements spread, and new settlements mushroom.*

Latin American cities have many older and more permanent slums and probably some of the worst shanty towns in the world. Latin American countries generally have large urban populations; one-fourth of the population in 1950 lived in cities of 20,000 or more and 17 per cent in cities of 100,000 or more. In Argentina, one-third of the population lived in cities of 100,000 or more, in Chile one-fourth, and in Brazil, Colombia, Venezuela, Ecuador, and Paraguay about one in fifteen. Cities with more than one million inhabitants in 1960 were Buenos Aires, whose six million inhabitants make it the second largest city in the Americas; Mexico City, the third largest, with five million people; and Rio de Janeiro, São Paulo, Montevideo, Santiago, Bogotá, Caracas, Lima, and Havana. Although these large cities of Latin America are centers of fabulous wealth, of tall skyscrapers, modern residential areas, and green parks, "the overwhelming majority of the people live in primitive grass huts, hovels fashioned of mud, and long stretches of crumbling, stinking, filthy slums . . . masses of urban humanity exist through the years without toilets, water, or enough to eat."[20]

In these cities during colonial days, public buildings and the houses of the wealthy were grouped around large plazas, while, outside the city proper, semiautonomous villages of workers, Negroes, and Indians grew up without

* Abrams, op. cit., p. 14. Hong Kong's acute problem of closely packed tenement living has been aggravated by the impact of hundreds of thousands of refugees, settling in unoccupied hillside squatter settlements. A 1955 survey reported that 300,000 people lived in hundreds and even thousands of huts built of mud, wood, bamboo, sheet metal, tar paper, and other materials. See Edvard Hambro, The Problem of Chinese Refugees in Hong Kong (Leyden: A. W. Sijthoff, 1955), p. 51. Also see Hong Kong Government, A Problem of People (Hong Kong: Government Press, 1960), pp. 13–4. Today about 500,000 people still cling to the hillsides of Hong Kong, living on the sidewalks or in sampans and junks. The Government has relocated several hundred thousand in tall multistoried tenements. Although they are decidedly an improvement, they consist of one-room family quarters with joint latrines. With a large influx of new refugees and an average annual population growth of 150,000, any final housing solution appears to be difficult.

municipal services or streets.[21] Modern cities have followed this pattern, with broad avenues, great plazas, public office buildings, modern upper-class housing within the city proper and a periphery occupied by the poor, who live in shacks built by themselves or by previous occupants. In most of the urban areas, people have also crowded into the cities themselves, living in old buildings divided into small, usually one-room apartments.* Where there is waste land on steep slopes and in swamps unsuitable for permanent building, slums have grown up. Small-shack squatter communities may also be found, on occasion, near the city centers. The slums, of whatever description, are constantly being moved to the peripheries, as new roads are constructed and the city expands.

Such slums are known as *jacales* or *colonias proletarias* in Mexico; *favelas*, *mocambos*, *algados*, or *vilas de malocas* in Brazil; *callampas* in Chile; *villas miserias* in Buenos Aires; *barrios clandestinos* in Colombia and Peru; and *ranchos* in Venezuela. A study of urbanization in Latin America has concluded that perhaps "the most serious social problems of urban areas in Latin America are manifest in the relatively large and widespread 'shanty-towns.' "[22] The quality of housing varies in such shanty towns. Whereas some shacks are built of scrap materials on vacant land and occupied by very poor casual laborers and people with makeshift occupations, some settlements have fairly substantial houses, built on small regular plots of land and owned by their occupants, who exhibit pride in such ownership.

At the slum level, there is seldom any social or political machinery by which the people can improve their lot. There is no way in which enlightened leadership can percolate up from the slums. "Planning and the determination of policy, the allocation of resources, and the formation of programs for improvement, constitute a business which is limited to the ruling class; the majority of the people have no way of taking part in it or of knowing anything about it."[23]

A large proportion of Mexico City's population lives in slums of several types. Hundreds of *vecindades*, one-story slum tenements consisting of one-room apartments, are located near the center of the city. The *jacales*, shacks built of scrap materials, are found throughout the city on vacant lots and in large colonies, particularly in the vicinity of factories. The *colonias proletarias* have appeared since 1940, and they provide means by which organized groups can obtain grants of land from the government to build their own houses. The *jacales* of Mexico City were occupied in 1957 by 315,000 people, constituting 10.7 per cent of the city's population.[24] The *colonias proletarias* were populated

---

* For a discussion of the variety of lower-class housing and the nature of social integration in a Latin American city like Santiago, see Guillermo Rosenblüth López, *Problemas socio-económicos de la marginalidad y la integración urbana* (Santiago: 1963); and Richard M. Morse, "Recent Research on Latin American Urbanization: A Selective Survey with Commentary," *Latin American Research Review*, 1 (Fall, 1965), 35–74. Also see Theodore Caplow, Sheldon Stryker, and Samuel E. Wallace, *The Urban Ambience: A Study of San Juan, Puerto Rico* (Totowa, N.J.: The Bedminster Press, 1964).

in 1952 by 420,000 people, 14.2 per cent of the population. Generally the houses are more substantial than are the *jacales*. Density of occupation is low, but the localities are arid and barren of trees. Water is supplied by municipal trucks, and people wait in line with pails and containers to receive their water rations. "Most of the houses do not have electricity or sewer connections; garbage disposal is generally lacking and large mounds of rubbish accumulate; the limited public transport is provided by worn-out buses withdrawn from service in the city."*

Caracas, a city of more than a million inhabitants and the glittering capital of Venezuela, rich with profits from oil and iron ore, houses more than a third of its population in battered shacks called *ranchos*. Between 1941 and 1950, the number of *ranchos*, according to census data, almost tripled. In 1953, it was estimated that 38.5 per cent, or 311,000 people, lived in the Caracas slums, the classification of which depends upon the types of land on which they are located. Those on steep mountain slopes are called *cerros*; those in steep ravines subject to seasonal floods are called *quebradas*. *Barrios clandestinos* have grown up around major cities of Colombia and Peru. Sometimes they are built without permits on land unsuitable for development, as in Cali, where they stand on steep slopes that have been severely eroded. Lima has hundreds of thousands of occupants in its *barrios clandestinos* or *barriados*, slums that lack practically all amenities and thus constitute the principal problem faced by the city.[25] Most of them are populated by Indian migrants from the highlands of Peru. *Callampas* or improvised slum houses have developed rapidly around the outskirts of Santiago, Chile. Often located near factories, they are generally the stopping places of rural migrants and families displaced by the clearance of older slums in the city who wish to be closer to the factories.[26] About 10 per cent of the population of the Greater Buenos Aires area, or 800,000 people, have been estimated to live in *villas miserias*.

The *favelas*, or slums, of Rio de Janeiro cover a large part of the city: It has been estimated that there are 183 slums containing at least a fifth of the total population.[27] In São Paulo, there are estimated to be approximately 200,000 inhabitants. The oldest inhabitants are generally Negroes, who, since gaining freedom in 1888, have not been able to find adequate work or housing and have settled on low swamplands in São Paulo and in the high hills of Rio, which until recently had not been occupied. These hills have become the homes of more poorly paid workers whose old tenements were destroyed to make way for business establishments. Other inhabitants came from such poor areas of

---

* *Report on the World Social Situation* (New York: United Nations Bureau of Social Affairs, in cooperation with the International Labour Office, the Food and Agriculture Organization, the United Nations Educational, Scientific and Cultural Organization, and the World Health Organization, 1957). The municipal government is making vigorous efforts to improve urban services, particularly where some sort of local community organization has been established.

northern Brazil as Nordestinos, where there are frequent droughts. The *favelas* consist of shacks clinging to the hillsides by the thousands. They are viewed with pride as the occupants' very own homes, and movement to modern apartment houses is not often regarded with favor. A census carried out in Rio in 1948 revealed that only about 11 per cent of the inhabitants received more than the equivalent of $54 a month each and that two-thirds of the houses, built of clay and scrap materials, were valued at less than $108 each. Only 24 per cent had toilets or latrines, 7 per cent had piped water, and 38 per cent had electric lighting.[28] Water is carried great distances from the few public water taps. Schools are inadequate, and a large percentage of the children do not attend school. Illness is common, and many suffer from a variety of skin conditions. Everywhere there is poverty, but "it is a bustling place filled with everyday sights and sounds, one of which as often as not is laughter."[29]

It is not merely the physical conditions that make squatter communities into slums; it is the way of life also. The social conditions in the *favelas* of São Paulo have been vividly described in the diary of a Brazilian woman with only two years of schooling. A long-time resident of a *favela*, she is the mother of three illegitimate children, each by a different father.[30] She has described her filthy house, the squalid homes of neighbors, the lack of facilities, the frequent fighting, the sordid sex life, and the ever-present poverty.

I classify São Paulo this way: The Governor's Palace is the living room. The mayor's office is the dining room and the city is the garden. And the favela is the back yard where they throw the garbage. . . . [pp. 34–5.]

Sometimes families move into the favela with children. In the beginning they are educated, friendly. Days later they use foul language, are mean and quarrelsome. They are diamonds turned to lead. They are transformed from objects that were in the living room to objects banished to the garbage dump. . . . [p. 39.]

At 8:30 that night I was in the favela breathing the smell of excrement mixed with the rotten earth. When I am in the city I have the impression that I am in a living room with crystal chandeliers, rugs of velvet, and satin cushions. And when I'm in the favela I have the impression that I'm a useless object, destined to be forever in a garbage dump. . . . [p. 38.]

I went to get water and the line was enormous. What an unpleasant thing to wait at that spigot. There's always a fight or someone who wants to know all about the private life of another. In the morning the area around the spigot is covered with shit. I am the one who cleans it up. Because the others aren't interested. . . . [p. 83.]

In the favelas children of 15 stay out as late as they want. They mess around with prostitutes and listen to their adventures. There are those who work and those who just drift. The older people work. It's the younger ones who refuse to work. . . . [p. 24.]

The worst thing in the favela is that there are children here. All the children of the favela know what a woman's body looks like. Because when the couples that are drunk fight, the woman, so as not to get a beating, runs naked into the street. When the fights start the *favelados* leave whatever they are doing to be present at the battle. . . . [p. 46.]

While I was dressing I heard the voice of Durvalino arguing with a strange drunk. Women started to appear. They never miss these things. They can stand hours and hours just watching. They don't think of anything even if they left a pot on the stove. A fight for them is just as important as the bullfights in Madrid are for the Spanish. . . . [p. 77.]

BED SPACE: OVERCROWDING IN THE SLUMS OF HONG KONG AND SINGAPORE

Few slums today, even the majority of those in India, are as densely crowded as are the older, more permanent Chinese slums of Hong Kong, a city of three million people, and Singapore, a city of over a million. Some areas in Hong Kong have 2,800 people to the acre.[31]

Characteristically, the Hong Kong slum dwellers live in closely packed tenement houses, the ground floors often occupied by shops. The rest of each three- or four-story building is divided into small living quarters or cubicles. A 1957 survey showed that three-fourths of the people (75.3 per cent) had only part of a room each. The cubicles are usually lined along the walls, with a small corridor down the middle. Beds or double-decker beds take up most of the room; the adults and children sit or sleep on them, and the family possessions are kept under them. Except when at work or on the street, the family must spend its time in these restricted quarters because there is little room in the corridor. When there is insufficient room for a cubicle, bunks are installed, and, if any room remains, temporary camp beds may be put up at night. Most cubicles are clean even though cluttered. Each floor has a common kitchen, generally a single bathing facility, and a latrine, regardless of the number of families on a floor. Although common bathing and toilet facilities are features of slums everywhere, the sharing of kitchen facilities is a peculiar feature of these slums. The kitchen is usually a verandah with one wall open to the sky and the rain. The amount of floor area per head was less than five square feet in 1957. About 18 per cent of the floors surveyed were without any common bathroom for the households.

A study of a single street, consisting of 632 households and 1,814 persons, in the Chinese slums of Singapore, has given some specific information on the nature of overcrowding.* A single tenement floor had as many as twenty-four cubicles, the average size of which was 103 square feet. Ninety-four cubicles

---

* Barrington Kaye, *Upper Nankin Street Singapore: A Sociological Study of Chinese Households Living in a Densely Populated Area* (Singapore: University of Malaya Press, 1960). An extensive new housing program is now under way. Some difficulty is encountered in persuading people to move from tenement houses to skyscraper apartment houses because of their reluctance to give up the community feeling of their former dwelling places.

had an average space of less than sixty square feet, approximately the size of two rectangular double beds side by side. The mean number of persons to a cubicle was 3.3. More than five people occupied each of six cubicles; five cubicles were occupied by nine or more people each. More than half (56 per cent) of the households occupied single cubicles, 7 per cent shared cubicles, and 4 per cent had only bunks. Only 16 per cent of the population lived in family households that occupied more than one cubicle each. One-third of the cubicles had no external opening or window; in fact, the tenements were so close together that the only source of ventilation was the airshaft. The stairways were generally steep, very narrow, dirty, and dark, as there was no artificial light. The toilets were all of the open-bucket variety, with only about one-third emptied daily. On the average, twenty adults used one toilet; some toilets were used by forty or more adults each.

It has been said that Hong Kong proves that an urban population can survive and even flourish under conditions of density and overcrowding that today seem unthinkable to many Americans.[32] Part of the reason for the tolerance of these high densities lies in Chinese urban living traditions and in transportation costs. The slum dwellers have become accustomed to living in close quarters, and the cohesion of the Chinese family system imposes strict controls on the behavior of its members under such crowded conditions.

A major problem in the slums of Hong Kong is drug addiction. According to a British government report in 1960, Hong Kong had an estimated 250,000 drug addicts, or one in every twelve of the British colony's population.

RAPID URBANIZATION, CONGESTION, AND DETRIBALIZATION: WEST AFRICAN SLUMS

Africa is becoming urbanized at a rapid rate. Cities like Addis Ababa, Lagos, Accra, Dakar, Abidjan, Mombasa, Nairobi, and Léopoldville have doubled and even trebled in size in the past ten years. Dakar has grown from 30,000 in 1926 to 500,000 today; Accra from 38,000 in 1921 to more than 400,000; Abidjan from 18,000 in 1936 to 300,000; and Lagos from 100,000 in 1921 to 450,000. This growth has been associated with increasing concentration in urban centers of commercial and administrative activities, as well as with the industrialization that has come with the development of these countries, particularly since independence.

Although Africa has virtually leaped into large-scale urbanization in the past twenty years, as a whole it is still in an early and limited phase of urban development. The Yoruba of Nigeria and several other peoples of Africa have traditions of urban living, but the absence of such urban life in most parts of Africa has meant that urbanization has been accompanied by acute problems of social change. African society has been based on tribal ties; the heterogeneity of the city has reduced such influences. For example, a study of Freetown in West

Africa concluded that "within the city there are no longer districts in which all the residents belong to one tribe."[33] In tribal society, the social system is based on tradition, and social and cultural change is gradual; in the cities, where members of many tribes are thrown together, urban society is continuously changing, modifying, and adapting. Of the heterogeneity of urban areas in Africa, one writer has stated:

> One of the most noticeable features of both African periurban areas and African areas inside the towns is the high degree of tribal mixture in the population. It is not unusual to find from twenty to forty different tribes represented in such urban areas, the residents of which are thrown together without regard to their varied cultural backgrounds. This great heterogeneousness contributes substantially to a peculiar type of congestion, the formation of tribal settlements—little pockets of intense overcrowding where members of the same tribe live and find comfort in one another's presence in an otherwise alien environment.[34]

Basic to the problem of urbanization and urbanism is the decline in effective intimate communication among the members of a society and the effect of this decline on social control of behavior. In the past, as in many rural areas today, the family or the tribal group was the center of life and the focus of all economic, religious, political, and educational activities. In areas undergoing social change, such familial institutions have been greatly weakened. Many reports from Africa have emphasized the importance of this factor in the emergence of juvenile delinquency.[35] The complexity of the problem of social adjustment faced by an African worker has been well summarized in one United Nations study.

> For the African worker in particular, who has been adapted in childhood to work, comfort and recreation in a comparatively small but comprehensive face-to-face group, the transition to a series of discontinuous impersonal relations—with employers, work-mates, officials, landlords, policemen, traders and prostitutes—is abrupt indeed. The craft and other skills he acquired in early life are often useless or at least undervalued in urban conditions. The early patterns of domestic, kinship and neighborhood relations are often excluded, while the self-reliance and group-solidarity for shared production and sustenance under a subsistence economy are little guide to the foresight, economizing and bargaining required in the new patterns of wage income and the need to buy most goods, while unfamiliar modes of expenditure for livelihood and display are offered and even enforced.[36]

Urban slums are becoming major problems in most countries, as more and more of the rural population piles into the cities. So extensive are they that, except for a few modern areas inhabited by the upper classes, the cities are almost entirely slums. There is the same jumble of decrepit buildings lining narrow, winding streets, many constructed of odds and ends of scrap. In contrast are tall modern buildings symbolic of national pride, some of them more than thirty stories high, jutting up here and there among hovels and narrow streets, crowded open bazaars, and vegetable markets. Despite many modern buildings, most of Dar es Salaam's residents, for example, live in "areas of abject poverty, where streets are not improved, sewerage systems often non-existent and other facilities scarce at best."[37] Slum conditions in Lagos, the capital of the largest African nation, Nigeria, may be considered typical of much of West Africa.* One study has summarized the slum situation in this large and growing city.

> The standard of housing in Lagos is low. Most houses have neither piped water nor a sewage system. The only bathroom or lavatory may be a rough shelter of corrugated iron with a bucket, knocked together in a corner of the yard. Water has to be collected from a stand-pipe in the street, and latrine buckets collected by a service of the Town Council. There is no water-born sewage system for the city. In central Lagos the drains are open, often a shallow channel running down the middle of the lane, in which refuse and ordure float.[38]

In four streets studied, there were 3.5 people to a room, and most rooms were "small, dark and poorly ventilated."[39] But as many as ten to fifteen people, family and close relatives, may sleep in a single small room, ten by twelve feet. Customarily they hang their possessions from the walls and may even tie up the beds during the day; in good weather, they may sleep outside. During the day, one notices few women in the slums, primarily because nine of ten women in central Lagos work during the day, usually as shopkeepers, taking with them their small children. A striking feature of Lagos is the common personal cleanliness of the people, although they live under aesthetically bad conditions: The men's long robes; the women's skirts, blouses, and head-dresses; and the clothing of the children are all remarkably clean when compared, for example, to parts of Asia. One African social worker has observed that "even though slum people are clothed in rags their clothing is clean."

In spite of a comparatively high degree of personal cleanliness, the general unsanitary living conditions of Lagos seriously affect the health of the people. The most common diseases are malaria, bronchitis, pneumonia, and dysentery, which cause about half of all deaths. The death rate, especially for children, in the slums of Lagos is very high. Almost 60 per cent of the deaths recorded in 1958 were of children under five; the total average death rate is about sixty per thousand—more than ten times the rate, for instance, of the County of London. "The rate is roughly seven times as high as in London for children between five and fourteen, three times as high between fifteen and twenty-four, and twice between twenty-five and forty-four."[40]

APARTHEID AND DEVIANT BEHAVIOR: SOUTH AFRICAN SLUMS

Of all the slums on the entire earth, few are more appalling, both physically and socially, than those of South Africa. Populated exclusively by Africans, their filth, congestion, crime, promiscuous sex, and other slum conditions leave

---

* The author spent nearly a week studying the Lagos slums in 1963.

the inhabitants in a state of degradation. This degradation is partly a direct result of apartheid and partly a consequence of the demoralization that sets in when urban slum living shatters traditional tribal existence. In the anonymity of the city, tribal or group controls break down, family discipline is weakened, and individual Africans are presented with new values of sexual laxity, disobedience, and crime as a way of life.[41]

The Johannesburg African population constitutes a city within a city. It has grown from 229,122 in 1936 to 395,231 in 1946 and to 555,000 in 1959, when the total population was two million. Most of these people are still housed in squalid shacks, but vast new townships have been built in recent years, with row upon row of small houses in which life is perhaps more efficient from a physical point of view but also more regimented, segregated, and dehumanized. Reading of these townships, one can almost wish for the "old life," which was at least less drab. One slum area sixty years old situated about nine miles from the downtown area, Alexandra Township, or "Alex," had a population of 100,000 in 1961. People crowd into one-room brick and iron shanties, accommodating 90 people each on plots 80 by 140 feet. The sanitation problem is particularly difficult. Alexandra Township has been described as a place where one can find everything one finds in other African slum areas "except that one must always expect a more liberal supply: crime, cruelty, sporting achievement, business, delinquency, sexual laxity, the lot."[42] It is notorious for crime and has long been known as the "Chicago of the urban African areas." People from other areas are often afraid to visit it at night. There are *tsotsis* or toughs who stand on street corners "with guns, knives, sharpened screwdrivers and bicycle spokes, half bricks and hammers." Parents early lose control over their children, and there are serious disciplinary problems in the schools. Older children often tire of this situation and go out on their own, the girls often becoming involved in promiscuous sex relations, which result in a high rate of illegitimacy. Girls who do not wish to engage in promiscuous sex relations may be sexually assaulted by *tsotsis*, on the grounds that the girls owe them money. A young girl may have a number of "boy friends," one of whom is more or less steady and is referred to as her "rent boy friend" because he pays for her lodging. "Alexandra's sex life is as dirty as its streets and lavatories are, but I haven't heard of a brothel in the true sense of the word, perhaps because there is no need for one, as each little room and shebeen serves the purpose."[43] Drunkenness is common, and there are many houses that sell drink where women are also employed for sexual purposes.

HERITAGE OF SLAVERY AND DISCRIMINATION: THE UNITED STATES NEGRO SLUMS

The Negro migration to the slums of northern cities, which began three decades after Emancipation, was given great impetus by the First World War.

In the decade between 1910 and 1920, Detroit, for example, experienced a 600 per cent increase in its Negro population, with 35,000 people pouring in from the rural South to join the 6,000 who had arrived earlier.[44] As the Midwest was the closest industrial area to the Deep South, it was the destination of a majority of migrating Negroes.[45] Any enclosed spaces in what came to be known as "Black Belt" districts that could serve as shelters were rented out to these new-comers. Apartments were subdivided and families doubled up in single rooms, but still there was need for expansion of the Negro ghettos. The increased demand for living space led to the division of large apartments into smaller units, or kitchenette apartments. A six-room apartment renting for $50 a month could be divided into six kitchenette apartments, each renting for $8 a week, thus increasing the total income to $192 a month.[46]

The Second World War brought still another wave of Negroes to the industrial North, in answer to increased demands for labor in the war-production industries. Again there was a shortage of housing, but this time the pressure existed in the smaller as well as in the larger cities and, for the first time, in the Far West, where in some cases the migrants outnumbered the original Negro population eight to one.[47] The sizes of the districts readily available to Negroes had increased little or not at all, in most cases, in spite of the population increase. Although the Negro largely moved into old slum areas, part of the present Black Belt in Chicago, for example, was once a "quality" residential district for whites; the dwellings, subdivided into smaller units, provided housing for large numbers of Negro migrants arriving from the South. The physical changes in these houses took place primarily on the inside, and consequently the external appearance of the buildings could be deceiving: behind an ornate brick façade could be found overcrowding, filth, lack of sanitary facilities, and unsafe and deteriorated partitions and stairways.[48] The Negro slums in Manhattan, like those of other racial groups, are characterized by walk-up tenements of four to six stories, narrow courts and airshafts, dark hallways, hall toilets, and other such conditions.[49] In Harlem today, 20 per cent of the housing units are reported to be overcrowded, using one person per room as a standard; this figure compares with 12 per cent for the city as a whole.

The subculture or way of life that predominates there, however, tells the real story of the Negro slum. Centuries of living under slavery and repression have brought about pronounced patterns of attitudes and behavior that today effectively keep the lower-class Negro from rising out of the slum, and, at the same time, opportunities to leave are restricted by discrimination. Most of the areas into which Negroes moved had long been slums populated by various immigrant groups, each generation molded by the slum cultural values. What made the impact of slum life so much greater on the Negro was that he, among all groups who had resided there, had been a slave, and the mark of slavery has influenced the Negro's adjustment to urban life. As promiscuity, unstable family relations, and a matriarchal family pattern once characterized slavery, they have now been carried over into the Negro slum. The Negro, in his relations with other Negroes, had to resort to violence because appeals to the outside world of the whites were often difficult. Furthermore, the white southerner himself has been more apt to engage in personal violence than have people in other parts of the country. Patterns of violence have been carried into the slum and have become a primary distinguishing feature of the Negro slums.[50]

Among slum occupants, in the past the Negro alone had little sense of identity and pride, and this lack has made it difficult for him to rise above the slum world in the same way as have various ethnic groups. Slavery erased even his knowledge of his African homeland and all his past heritage. In contrast to other slum occupants, the Negro lost his cultural identity. "The shiftlessness and lack of ambition which characterize lower class behavior are generally associated with a lack of race pride."[51] In recent years urban lower-class slum Negroes, however, have come to experience increasing racial consciousness and pride, but the situation is still generally not comparable to those of other ethnic and racial groups in the slums.

The outstanding characteristic of the Negro slum resident is the high degree of instability in his family life. This factor is seen in the large proportion of families headed by females and in the high rates of desertion, divorce, marital violence, and illegitimacy within the Negro slums. During slavery, marriage was largely impossible, for, as slaves, Negroes could not make legal contracts, and on many occasions fathers were sold away from their families. As a result, illegitimacy and sexual promiscuity were common, and mothers rather than fathers were generally the centers of what families did exist. After Emancipation, the irregularity or absence of employment for the male Negro, together with his lack of education, made it difficult or impossible to provide regular support for a wife and family. This problem resulted in a tendency to wander from place to place and from woman to woman. The Negro woman, however, has generally been able to obtain domestic employment with relative ease, and she has thus often managed without the help of a steady male partner.[52] Unstable common-law marriages are of short duration, and the women, after dismissing the men or being deserted by them, consider themselves "widowed" and find other men. This pattern of family instability greatly impairs the normal process of socialization, which in turn contributes to the absence of sound conceptions of an adequately functioning family unit among the youth in a Negro slum.[53] In fact, a U.S. Department of Labor report of March, 1965, traced the Negro urban problem to its social roots, the splintering Negro family.

> The fundamental problem, in which this is most clearly the case, is that of family structure. The evidence—not final, but powerfully persuasive—is that the Negro family in the urban ghettos is crumbling. A middle-class group has managed to save itself, but for vast numbers of the unskilled, poorly educated city working

class the fabric of conventional social relationships has all but disintegrated. There are indications that the situation may have been arrested in the past few years, but the general post-war trend is unmistakable. So long as this situation persists, the cycle of poverty and disadvantage will continue to repeat itself.[54]

Patterns of family instability have been difficult to eliminate in the slums, superimposed as they have been upon the instability of large-scale urban migration. In a study of one New York City Negro slum neighborhood, Conant found that one-third of the pupils came from family units in which there was no father, stepfather, or male guardian. Statistics on Negro families in Central Harlem, the slum district immediately north of Central Park in Manhattan, generally reflect the instability of family life among lower-class slum Negroes, where a third of the families had no fathers and a third were on public-assistance rolls.[55] Only half the children under eighteen were living with both parents, as compared with 83 per cent for New York City as a whole. Of the Central Harlem women, 29.7 per cent and, of the Harlem men, 19.1 per cent were listed as separated, compared to rates of 6.2 and 3.3 for New York City women and men respectively.[56] The rate of aid to dependent children was 220.5 per 1,000 youths under eighteen years of age, three times the rate (72) for New York City as a whole.

With respect to illegitimacy, it was found that 44.4 per cent of the girls who dropped out of school did so because of pregnancy.[57] The lower class does not attach opprobrium to illegitimacy as do the middle and upper classes but rather seems almost indifferent toward it.[58] Infant mortality is also greater in the Negro slum; the rate for Harlem was 45.2 per 1,000 live births in 1961, compared to 25.7 for New York City as a whole.[59] The high infant-mortality rate was due largely to poor housing conditions, malnutrition, and inadequate health-care facilities. The venereal-disease rate for people under twenty-one was six times the city rate.[60]

Low levels of education also contribute to the problems of the Negro slum.[61] Children of poor slum families have not had home environments that stimulate the desire to learn, nor do they arrive in school with verbal fluency, capacities for deferred gratification, or sustained attention spans that allow them to learn as quickly as children of middle-class families generally do. Two particular handicaps are limited educational experience prior to entering school and low motivation to do well in school.[62] With such disadvantages, it is not surprising that, in 1959, 53 per cent of the Central Harlem students in academic schools and 61 per cent in vocational schools dropped out before receiving diplomas.[63] Furthermore, as these students progress in school, the proportion of them who perform below their grade levels increases.[64] One explanation for this decline is that substandard performance is expected of these students; school administrators aware of the disadvantages children of the slums suffer set lower goals for these children, which result in poorer performances.[65]

Juvenile crime in Negro slum areas has been described as the result of this depressing tangle of problems, in addition to the presence of gangs, lack of organized community controls, discrimination both in educational and employment opportunities, and family problems like divorce, desertion, and illegitimacy.[66] The Negro slum boy witnesses frequent norm violations, and delinquency seems an easy way to achieve goals. In 1962, Harlem's delinquency rate was 109.3 per 1,000 population aged seven to twenty, whereas the rate for New York City as a whole was 46.5; the delinquency rate in Boston's Negro ghetto was four times that of the city as a whole.[67] Drug addiction has also increased greatly; the Harlem rate is almost ten times that of New York City.[68] The extensiveness of Negro crime and violence in urban slum areas has been revealed by a large number of research studies. Urban Negroes, largely concentrated in the slums, have a higher arrest rate than do their rural counterparts. In 1960, the total urban Negro rate in the United States was about seven times that for rural Negroes.[69] Even if allowance is made for discrimination in arrests and the judicial process, the figures are still much larger than those for the white and general population. The incidence of murder and assault appears to be particularly high among Negroes, mostly directed at other Negroes, relatives and friends for the most part. The homicide rate in Harlem is nearly six times that of New York City, and in one neighborhood the rate is fifteen times greater. A study of 462 homicides in one large urban county in Ohio between 1947 and 1953 showed that 76 per cent were committed by Negroes, although only 11 per cent of the population was Negro.[70] Wolfgang's study of 588 victims and 621 slayers in Philadelphia between 1948 and 1952 showed that the homicide rate among Negroes was four times that of whites and emphasized the role of subcultural factors and the effects of isolation from the general norms of society.[71] Assault is another crime in which Negroes in urban areas outdo the white population. Organized gambling, particularly the policy racket, has been found to be prevalent in slum areas.

A high degree of powerlessness appears to be characteristic of Negro communities as a whole and of Negro slum areas in particular. Both middle- and lower-class Negroes are seldom on important committees, boards of directors, and other decision-making groups in the community. They are less likely to occupy positions of status or have degrees of organization that will influence community power. Studies of Harlem indicate that not only is this large community relatively powerless but the people, being aware of this fact, come to believe that they are largely helpless in controlling and directing their own lives. Negro slum residents do not participate widely in either the decision making of the larger community or in the Negro community itself. Negro communities generally have little real political, economic, or similar power, and decisions for them often tend to be made by governmental and welfare groups. Social agencies in Negro areas are generally dependent on outside white sources for funds; their boards of directors are made up chiefly of whites not living in the area. Until the civil-rights movement, Negro urban areas had little effective community organization, most organized groups being largely social rather than political or action-oriented. Handlin has explained this lack of effective organization among Negroes as being largely the result of Negro migrants, coming as they did from the southern part of the United States and never having experienced the shock of separation from the "homeland" as did foreign immigrants, who, as a result, tended to develop some unity.[72]

CULTURE CONFLICT: PUERTO RICANS IN NEW YORK CITY

The tenement-house life in the Puerto Rican slums of New York City is similar to the one that formerly characterized new arrivals from European countries. Puerto Ricans face an already difficult slum situation further handicapped by their Hispanic language and customs. Because of their mixed white and Negro racial backgrounds, however, some encounter the same types of prejudice as do American Negroes. Insufficient employment opportunities and overpopulation have driven the Puerto Ricans to seek a better life on the United States mainland, usually in New York City.[73] The 1960 Census showed 613,000 people of Puerto Rican birth or parentage living in New York City, most of them in slum areas. The largest concentrations are in East Harlem[74] and on the Lower East Side. Puerto Rican migrants who arrive in New York looking for jobs have two disadvantages: They are usually unskilled, and they often cannot speak English fluently.

The typical housing of Puerto Ricans in New York is the tenement, which through the years has housed other immigrants before they rose economically and moved to better areas. Various studies of Puerto Rican housing emphasize again and again its dilapidation, falling ceilings, dirty hallways, rats and cockroaches, poor sanitary facilities, and overcrowding.[75] Glazer and McEntire have vividly described how a neighborhood can change when Puerto Rican families move into it. The particular area is the West Side of upper Manhattan in the vicinity of Columbia University, and the buildings are large, "brownstone" houses and apartment houses in generally good condition.

> The curtains go from the windows, and one may see, in passing, dingy rooms with bare overhead bulbs, crowded with children. People of all ages are to be seen lingering around the stoop most of the day. The garbage containers are filled to overflowing and their contents spill onto the street. If there is a tree in front of the house, it is killed by the vigorous play of the children. There is no question that the block has "declined." The residents begin to wonder about the effect on the public school of the introduction of large numbers of children from such houses. The building becomes an eyesore (although its exterior remains exactly the same), and the tenants and landlords on the block are concerned with its future and the future of the neighborhood.[76]

This conversion of a "good" residential district into a Puerto Rican slum, however, is not the typical history of Puerto Rican neighborhoods. More often, the Puerto Ricans have, like all other immigrant groups, moved into the same areas that housed other immigrant groups before them: East Harlem, the Lower East Side, Williamsburg in Brooklyn, and Morrisania in the Bronx. Puerto Ricans do not create slums there but move into existing slums that are being vacated by upwardly mobile Jews, Italians, Irish, and others, thus extending for another cycle the lives of the historic tenement-house slums of New York.

The nuclear family is the basic family type among Puerto Rican immigrants, though relatives and special friends may be invited to live with the family, especially if the mother is working or sick and needs help in cleaning, cooking, and taking care of the children. The father is the head of the household, and the wife and children are expected to conform to his decisions. In Puerto Rico, the consensual marriage, without the formality of a marriage certificate, is recognized as legal, with the same responsibilities among family members. This arrangement does not meet with the same widespread acceptance in New York, and social agencies may refuse such privileges as entrance to public housing to families based on consensual marriage.

Although violent juvenile gangs are not extensive in Puerto Rico, in New York City such problems are serious in the Puerto Rican slum areas. Much of the area in which Puerto Ricans live has been termed a "disorganized slum," in contrast to the more stable slums of the older ethnic groups.[77] Such slums are often communities of strangers living in very close physical contact but with few meaningful human relationships. Often an area may be a mixture of stable and unstable slums like the Lower East Side of New York City. According to Yablonsky, the stable slum creates a more normative delinquent adjustment, whereas the disorganized slum has a higher rate of violent behavior. The disorganized slum seems to produce more violent gangs because social controls, particularly parental controls, have broken down and serious schisms between adults and youths have developed.

In comparing the investigations of the slums of Boston by Whyte and the Chicago sociological studies, Stein saw an important difference in the degree of organization. The slums of Boston were "stable," those of Chicago "disorganized," in the Twenties. This difference was attributed by Stein to a cycle of slum growth; he argued that the Chicago slums were in a "nascent" stage, the older slums of Boston more "established."[78]

Some slums remain quite stable and well organized. Although their physical facilities are substandard, they furnish reasonably adequate comfort. Such a slum, a Mexico City vecindade Casa Grande, has been described in a study by

Oscar Lewis. Most of the people live in rows of dwellings along inside court-yards shut off from the street. There are 157 neat, one-room, windowless apartments, in front of each of which a ladder leads to the roof, where chicken coops, lines of laundry, and pots of flowers are kept. "Living standards are low but by no means the lowest in Mexico and the people of the neighborhood look upon Casa Grande as an elegant place."[79] The average number of years of school attendance among the residents was 4.7, and only 8 per cent of the in-habitants were illiterate. Lewis has described the daily bustle in the courtyards:

> In the daytime the courtyards are crowded with people and animals, dogs, turkeys, chickens, and a few pigs. Children play here because it is safer than the streets. Women queue up for water or shout to each other as they hang up clothes, and street vendors come in to sell their wares. Every morning a garbage man wheels a large can through the courtyard to collect each family's refuse. In the afternoon, gangs of older boys often take over a courtyard to play a rough game of soccer. On Sunday nights there is usually an outdoor dance. Within the west entrance is the public bathhouse and a sunny garden whose few trees and a patch of grass serve as a meeting place for young people and a relatively quiet spot where the older men sit and talk or read the newspapers.[80]

The ethnic slum in the United States may also be regarded as a stable slum. Michael Harrington has called it the "old type," as distinct from newer slums of the "internal migrants," that is, the Negroes, the Puerto Ricans, and the poor whites from rural areas, which he calls the "new type" of slum.[81] He has de-scribed the old ethnic slum as a narrow world, with a single religion, language, and culture, but one that encourages movement toward the outside world.[82] Although there has been considerable movement out of the ethnic slums in the second and third generations, they are still a major slum type in American cities.

Several physical characteristics distinguish the American ethnic slum from other slum areas: foreign wording on the signs; special food shops that cater to the ethnic group; and, of course, the mannerisms and appearances of the residents themselves. An additional difference is the generally higher quality of maintenance in the ethnic slum. Because of both longer residence in the urban environment and differences in cultural background, there is a tendency among residents of ethnic slums to maintain at least the insides of their homes in better condition, as was discovered in Boston's West End by home-survey inter-viewers. In other respects, the ethnic slum is similar to those of Negroes, Puerto Ricans, and recent arrivals from the southern hill country. The buildings may be similar, having changed only in occupancy from one group to another. High density characterizes both the ethnic and nonethnic, or the "old" and the "new," slums. Use of such outside space as hallways, front stoops, streets and yards, and other dwellings are common to both.[83] The existence of the American ethnic slum emphasizes that slums are more than physical entities, areas composed merely of dilapidated buildings: They are also social phenomena with characteristic attitudes and ways of life.

Perhaps the most intensively studied ethnic slums of the United States in recent years have been the Italian slums, particularly those of Boston. Whyte, Gans, Firey, and others, through their investigations in that city, have provided many insights into the lives of residents of the Italian ethnic slum.[84] Many differences exist, of course, between the residents of the ethnic slums and the rest of American urban society; the characteristics of the former may be classified under social organization, family-life patterns, and general attitudes, including those toward the neighborhoods in which they live.

Zorbaugh's classic study in 1929 of the Italian slum on Chicago's Near North Side described it as unorganized and the people as living almost entirely outside the conventional world.[85] In criticizing this view, Whyte pointed out that, because political activity and social organization did not take the same forms in the slum as in middle-class areas, Zorbaugh had assumed that they did not exist at all and failed to see some of the significant features of this life. Whyte, on the contrary, found a real neighborhood unit, friendliness, and organized social life.[86] Most later studies of life in the Italian ethnic slums have recognized the organization that does exist there, and its importance to the resident populations. Whyte, for example, described the corner gangs, local racketeers, and politicians as building blocks of community-wide organization, satisfying important needs and providing potential means of social mobility. The major problem in ethnic slum areas, he discovered, is not "disorganization" but rather conflicts between the organized life of the slums and the values of "respectable" middle-class society.[87]

Similarly, in a later study of the West End,* an Italian ethnic slum or low-rent district in Boston, Gans found that the peer-group society was the most important element in the lives of the residents, the peer group consisting of people of the same sex, age, and life-cycle status. Boys meeting on the corner, men talking in the living room, and women conversing in the kitchen during the evening constituted the main parts of their lives, a strong form of social organization within that community. In the nearby North End, Firey found a similar identification of the Italian-Americans with neighborhood Italian groups and values. These continuing interaction patterns added to their ethnic solidarity, and patterns of association in mutual-aid societies, among *paisani*, and in extended families passing from one generation to the next, determined in large part the social structure and organization that he found there.[88] According to Harrington, the family pattern and value system found in the ethnic slum provided strong counterforces to the degradation of the physical environment.[89]

* There are conflicting opinions on whether or not the West End is a slum. Gans, who lived there during the six months of his research, believes it is not a slum, but planners and other writers have described it as a slum. It will be considered here as a slum.

The importance of the family in Boston's West End, according to Gans, extends beyond the nuclear family to include a circle of relatives and friends, that is, the peer group. The world is viewed in this subculture from the point of view of the family circle, and everything outside this circle is seen as a means either to its maintenance or to its destruction. Work is viewed primarily as a means of maximizing the pleasures of life within the family circle. An additional characteristic of the West Enders, which is perhaps typical of ethnic slums in general, is a tendency to be "person-oriented" rather than "object-oriented." They aspire to be individuals within a group, to be liked and noticed by members of a group whom they like, rather than to strive toward "objects," whether moral, material, cultural, or social.* The West Enders seek a minimum of "object goals." This orientation contributes to some characteristic working-class attitudes toward work, education, and middle-class society. A lack of motivation caused largely by ambivalence among parents toward the usefulness of education and by the absence of books and other intellectual stimuli in the homes often results in the failure of West Enders to respond to education. Other characteristic attitudes of the residents of a working-class slum are detachment from work, concern with job security, negative evaluation of white-collar workers and bosses, fear of doctors and hospitals, and general antagonism toward law, government, and politics.[90]

Ryan has described the characteristics of the West Enders as *integration*, the cohesion of a distinct sociocultural subsystem, and *expressiveness*, an orientation to human relationships.[91] The first is exemplified in the value of ethnic harmony among the West Enders, the second in the peer-group relationships that play such an important role in their lives.

Some of the disadvantages of an ethnic-slum area were described by Gans: inability to participate in formal organizations and in general community activity; general inability to understand bureaucratic behavior and "object-orientation"; rejection of certain types of caretakers, especially those whose services can be provided by the family circle; placing low value on privacy; and the general conservatism of the working-class culture, which penalizes those who deviate.[92] He concluded, however, that working-class culture is a positive response to the opportunities and deprivations it encounters and that the advantages outweigh the disadvantages.[93]

In observing the highly positive manner in which the West Enders looked upon their housing, Hartman was led to question whether or not the usual descriptive criteria of substandard living conditions are adequate indicators of either

---

* Herbert J. Gans, *The Urban Villagers: Group and Class in the Life of Italian-Americans* (New York, The Free Press, 1962), pp. 89–90. Whyte also noted this distinction. "Chick," a college boy and not a corner boy, "judged men according to their capacity for advancing themselves." "Dock," one of the corner boys of the slum, "judged them according to their loyalty to their friends and their behavior in personal relations." William F. Whyte, *Street Corner Society* (Chicago: University of Chicago Press, 1943), p. 107.

objective physical standards or subjective value preferences—whether or not the description of the West End as a "slum" is accurate.[94] A number of neighborhood characteristics was relevant to this question: One was the large number of apartments whose inside conditions were superior to the buildings' outside appearances, 32 per cent of the dwellings surveyed. Residential satisfactions of the West Enders were found to be related to an entire living pattern and not merely to the physical attributes of their buildings and apartments. The West Enders were deeply committed to the area, and apartments were only one aspect of their residential life. A conflict inevitably arose between the desire to maintain the social and personal values satisfied by their ethnic neighborhood and the desire for better housing, and consequently over-all physical quality of living space assumed a secondary role in the hierarchy of residential values.[95] Still, the stable slums are often characterized by delinquency and crime, health problems, drug addiction, dilapidation and deterioration of housing, litter in the cellars and alleys, and other typical facets of general slum life.

Chapter 4

THE INDIAN SLUM

The predominantly rural and agricultural nature of Indian society has, as in other developing countries, in effect minimized the essential role that cities have played in the past and are still playing today. Four-fifths of India's population presently resides in its half-million villages, yet the country can no longer be called "a nation of villages." Today several cities of India are huge metropolitan areas, but their significance in the total economic, political, and cultural structure of the country greatly exceeds their proportion of the total population.[1] As in any country, the cities of India have become the centers of modern technology and the hope of future progress. Among the nations of the world, India is being increasingly judged by the stature and conditions of its great cities, where lie the core of its commercial and industrial power and the strength of its transportation, distribution, and communication systems. The cities of India have played an important role in breaking away from tradition-bound social practices, and from the cities most of the modernization processes in the country radiate. Political and social reform movements have largely originated in the cities and have then spread out. Indian cities can be expected to play an even more dynamic role in the social, economic, and political transformation of the country.[2] Urban sociologists may wonder whether there is a meaningful boundary between "urban" and "rural" in Western nations, but there is no doubt about it in India.[3]

The cities of India and Pakistan have a particularly great past. They have played a major role in the development of both countries and their cultures. Among the earliest cities in the world were Harappa in the Punjab and Mohenjo-Daro to the South in the valley of the Indus River, both having been capitals of great empires of the Harappa culture from 2500 to 1500 B.C.[4] Mohenjo-Daro, for example, is famous throughout the world for its plan, its construction, and such special advanced features as its water system.

Ancient Indian cities, established between the time Buddha lived and the fourth century B.C., include Banaras, Ayodhya, Ujjain, and Patna, the last of which controlled a large part of Northern India. Later, under the Mauryan

Empire, which dated from the fourth century B.C., Ajanta and West Broach, in Central and Western India, and Conjeerveram and Virapathnam, farther south, came into being. Still later, other cities, under Muslim influence, expanded as centers of government and crafts: Delhi, Agra, Hyderabad, and Ahmedabad, for example. With the establishment of their East India Company, the British developed a flourishing trade, which contributed to the rapid enlargement and enrichment of cities they created for trading purposes. Bombay, Calcutta, and Madras were originally forts and trading centers.

§ *Urban Population Growth*

Although India's urbanization rate has been slow, compared to those of such countries as Japan and the United States, there has been a steady increase in the Indian urban population.[5] Davis believes that the slow growth rate has been the result of the slow rate of past industrial and economic growth in India,[6] itself partly the result of the British policy of restricting industrial development in colonial areas. Another inhibiting factor from the past has been the major epidemics that periodically swept the country.[7] In 1921, the urban population, population in "urban places" or places with more than 5,000 people and nonagricultural characteristics generally, was 11.4 per cent; in 1941, 13.9 per cent; in 1951, 17.3 per cent; and in 1961, 18 per cent, approximately one-fifth of India's total population.* As industrial development is accelerated, there will be relative increases in the populations of the urbanized areas.[8] It has been estimated that, in about thirty-five years, around A.D. 2000, the percentage of the Indian population living in cities of 20,000 or more alone will have risen to 30.8 per cent, with 21.2 per cent living in cities of 100,000 or more.†

Although India's ratio of urban population to total population is one of the lowest of any major country in the world, it may be a very misleading figure because of the enormous population base of 439,072,893 people in 1961. An increase of only 1 or 2 per cent adds several million to the total mass, and the

---

* In India's 1961 census, the definitions of urban and rural areas were modified. Expectations that the population increase in urban areas would break all records between 1951 and 1961 did not materialize because the rate of increase was less than that of 1941–1951, which was 37.9 per cent. It it clear, however, that the absolute increase in the rural population has been a strong factor in holding the rural–urban ratio almost constant in the last ten years.

† Kingsley Davis, "Urbanization in India: Past and Future," in Roy Turner, ed., *India's Urban Future* (Berkeley: University of California Press, 1962), p. 11. These estimates are based on the growth of urbanization in the United States, which is faster than in Great Britain or France but slower than in Japan. India's 1951 percentage of cities of 20,000 and more was equal to that of the United States in 1858–1859. One might characterize these estimates, however, as based on unwarranted assumptions that fail to take sufficient account of the differences between these two countries. For example, the United States had an extensive unpopulated frontier and has been a major industrial nation for a long time.

urban percentage growth may be comparatively small, even though, in absolute terms, urban growth is quite large. As an illustration, India's population in urban places in 1961 was more than 78.8 million people, which is higher than the total populations of most countries in the world. In fact, this figure is exceeded only by the populations of China, the Soviet Union, the United States, Indonesia, and Pakistan. Even if the urban-population percentage (based on 20,000 or more) does reach 30.8 in the next thirty-five years (compared with 11.9 in 1951), India would still not be, comparatively, a highly urbanized country—though in aggregate numbers there would be an estimated 225,000,000 to 300,000,000 people living in cities of 20,000 and more.[9] The population of metropolitan areas of more than 100,000, it is estimated, will reach 21.2 per cent of the total population by the year 2000; the median estimate is 212,000,000 people, with a range from 158,000,000 to 233,000,000.

Urban growth has been particularly great in the larger cities, and this trend will intensify. Only two Indian cities had populations of more than a million in 1941; in 1951, there were five. By 1961, there were seven, and Davis has estimated that, by 1970, there will be ten.[10] In 1951, seventy-seven cities had populations of 100,000 or more, and, in 1961, the number was 107, representing a percentage increase of 29.8. Within twenty years, the ten largest cities of India had doubled in population.

The expected migration will result in almost incalculable consequences for the country. A staggering volume of new housing, water supply, transport, and urban employment will be required to accommodate it. When this growth from migration is added to the natural population increase, the problem of accommodation in Indian cities almost defies imagination. The effects of this growth have been estimated for the ten major Indian cities in 1970 and 2000.[11] The population estimates involve predictions based on (1) the total urban population, (2) the size of the largest city, and (3) the estimated populations and sizes of all ten cities in relation to (1) and (2). The results of the highest and lowest prediction are given in Table 2. According to these estimates, Calcutta will probably be the largest city, with between twelve and sixteen million inhabitants in 1970 and between thirty-six and sixty-six million by 2000. The second largest city, probably Delhi, will have between eighteen and thirty-three million people within the next thirty-five years.

If it seems difficult to visualize cities of such size, it should be remembered that no country the size of India, with a projected population of one billion people by the year 2000, has ever before experienced a transition from a village economy to an urban industrial economy. Consequently, if India experiences the industrial development that the population projections imply and the economic plans envisage, there is every likelihood that it will have cities of such tremendous size. On the basis of the estimated one billion population, the principal city of sixty-six million will contain only 6.6 per cent of the total population, which is actually a rather modest percentage for the chief city of a large country.[12] There has been some discussion of the possibility of decentralizing urban growth in India so that people will not pile up in the large cities.[13] Decentralization could be accomplished, in part, by developing new industrial towns and by locating major industries in new areas away from the large cities. This procedure would siphon off a large number of rural migrants if carried out on a large scale. The potential volume of migration to the cities is so tremendous, however, that large cities might be expected to continue to increase, despite efforts at decentralization. Although improvements in rural life and the development of small-scale industries might prevent some migration, the

Table 2

Estimated Size of the Ten Major Cities in India in 1970 and 2000 (in millions of inhabitants)

| METROPOLIS | TYPE OF ESTIMATE OF POPULATION IN CITIES | | | |
| | Low | | High | |
	1970	2000	1970	2000
Calcutta	12.0	35.6	16.0	66.0
Delhi	6.0	17.8	8.0	33.0
Bombay	4.0	11.9	5.3	22.0
Madras	3.0	8.9	4.0	16.5
Bangalore	2.4	7.1	3.2	13.2
Ahmedabad	2.0	5.9	2.7	11.0
Hyderabad	1.7	5.1	2.3	9.4
Kanpur	1.5	4.5	2.0	8.3
Poona	1.3	4.0	1.8	7.3
Nagpur	1.2	3.6	1.6	6.6

Reprinted by permission from Kingsley Davis, "Urbanization in India," in Roy Turner, ed., *India's Urban Future* (Berkeley: University of California Press, 1962), p. 25.

consolidation of land holdings and the mechanization of agricultural procedures might drive even more people to the cities, and any restrictions on such migrations appear to be almost impossible under a democratic framework.

The Indian city offers numerous advantages to its citizens. Industries are developing, wages are often higher, employment may be steadier, and better educational facilities are usually available for children. In addition, city living is attractive to many who live in isolated villages. The noise, the electric lights, the glamor, the differences among people, the variety of articles on display, the motion pictures—all are quite different from the resources in the village. Cities also offer greater opportunities for certain depressed groups like the Harijans (Untouchables) and members of various low-caste groups. In the city there are opportunities beyond those traditionally available to such groups in the village, and the greater anonymity of the city provides greater equality. Since partition, there has also been an influx of refugees, who have congregated particularly in Delhi and Calcutta.

The extent and concomitant problems of this urbanization process have been so great that some experts refer to "overurbanization." A UNESCO seminar report stated that Asia, as a whole, was overurbanized in 1950 because only 30 per cent of its labor force was engaged in nonagricultural pursuits; when this percentage should have been 50–55 in terms of the degree of urbanization.* It is claimed that this thesis is strongly supported by the character of urban employment in India today. Industrialization and the rate of economic development have not kept pace with urbanization, and unemployment is extensive.[14] Urban services have failed to keep pace with population growth, and economic resources are insufficient to meet the demands. Consequently, the urban population is larger than can be justified by the levels of agricultural and nonagricultural productivity. Others have argued, however, that the term "overurbanization" applied to developing countries like India is based on a false assumption, as urban development represents a capital asset with a high production potential. Furthermore, urbanization facilitates entrepreneurship, disciplined work, and diffusion of new production techniques. The average income of a city laborer, even in the service trades, may be higher than village incomes. It is claimed that urban areas facilitate the spread of new ideas and promote social change, which may result in greater long-range changes even if there is underemployment.

§ *Social and Physical Conditions in the Indian Slum*

A concomitant of urbanization in India has been the continuous growth of the slum population, as most internal migration has been concentrated in the slums. Slums have a long history in India, and the physical and social conditions of today's Indian slums are generally considered the worst, and the most extensive, of any important country in the world. Although India is a large, heterogeneous country, whose diversity often makes generalization difficult, slum conditions can still be characterized in general terms. The streets, lanes, and open drains in typical slum areas are filthy, and people sleep as many as six to twelve in a room, hovel, or shack. The Indian slum, however, is far more complex than the mere aggregate of these appalling physical surroundings suggests. It is a way of life. Rates of disease, chronic illness, and infant mortality remain high, and there is little knowledge of health and sanitation, nutrition, or child care. Illiteracy is exceedingly high, and cultural and recreational activities are

---

* Philip M. Hauser, ed., *Urbanization in India and the Far East* (Calcutta: UNESCO Research Centre on the Social Implications of Industrialization in Southern Asia, 1957), p. 133. This conclusion was based on the assumption that the relationship between urbanization and industrialization in the United States, Canada, France, and Germany is normal. Sovani has concluded that this assumption is "bad logic, bad history, bad statistics all combined in one." N. V. Sovani, "The Urban Social Situation in India," *Artha Vijnana*, 3 (June–September, 1961), 215.

almost entirely lacking, except those provided by such commercial enterprises as the cinemas and gambling. Most slum dwellers are apathetic and suffer a great sense of futility. They have little community pride or even consensus, and they often blame the local authorities for their plight. They have become antagonistic toward them, seldom cooperating with municipal personnel in efforts to improve either the immediate area or the city as a whole.

The shock of the Westerner viewing the slums of India for the first time, in this case those of Delhi, is recorded in two extracts from the diary of the author:

November 5, 1958. Visited an area today in the slums of Delhi, one of my first experiences. Some 25,000 people have lived in this area for over a hundred years. Houses are one and two story, so close together that no sun comes through, everything is damp and this makes the odors of filth and urine all the more noticeable. There is an awful stench everywhere. The area was covered with hordes of flies. There are only dry latrines, many of which are uncovered, and human offal is often piled beside them because they were too foul to be used inside. Children use the gutters. Saw a man eating his lunch in front of his house a yard away from flies and offal in the gutter. Probably he has no conception of the idea that flies and disease are interrelated. I almost threw up, and the educated Indians with me put their handkerchiefs over their faces. Women were washing clothes, pounding them on the dirty streets—there was no public wash place. The children have only one small place to play, and it is in bad condition. People seem fatalistic and apathetic. There is need to re-educate the people about cleanliness as new buildings will be useless without such education. As we drove away I kept the windows up so that the hordes of flies would not get inside. I couldn't eat my lunch that day.

January 6, 1959. Visited three places in the slums. Came back overwhelmed by urban India. Had a feeling as though I had seen enough and wanted to forget the misery, open drains filled with sewage, the feces on the ridge behind the houses, the dampness of the rooms, the dirty clothing and human bodies, the apathy everywhere—people just sitting. One asks what can be done.

HOUSING CONDITIONS

It has been estimated that the slum populations in the large Indian cities run from 7 per cent to as high as 60 per cent of the total city populations.[15] If slum areas were defined by Western criteria, the percentages of slum dwellers would undoubtedly be even greater. "It is reported that more than three-fourths of the population of the city of Calcutta proper live in overcrowded tenement and bustee (slum) quarters."[16] A study group of the Bombay government reported at least 144 slum areas, with a population of 400,000, 18 per cent of the total population of that city. Indian slum areas seldom have streets; more common are narrow, winding lanes and dark passageways. Some houses are built in such a way that the verandah of one serves as a passage to another, giving the feeling that the houses were constructed first and the passageways as an afterthought.

As many lanes and alleys are unpaved and are of *kucha*, or mud, they become almost impassable during the monsoon rains. The people who live in these urban slums,* as well as the general public, usually call the slums in the various areas and cities by specific names that refer to the general housing or to the type of construction, materials used, and so forth. For example, there are lanes, *katras*, chawls, bustees, *jompris*, *juggies*, *ahatas*, and *cheris*.

Katras are small single-room tenements, normally constructed in rows within large courtyards or enclosures having single entrances. Many of the Delhi *katras* were originally parts of old Muslim homes, which were dark and dingy because they were originally constructed for security against depredations of the dacoits, or robbers, and security of the womenfolk against the eyes of all males, excepting the family. "The security was sought by a sort of fortification provided by building the walls with only a single entrance and no windows."[17] The multistoried buildings in the Bombay slums are called chawls, and they often house as many as eighty or more families apiece. In many of their one-room tenement cubicles sunlight never enters, and even at midday the rooms are dark. More than seven people, sometimes as many as two or three related families, live in each room.[18] Sleep must often be taken in shifts, as one-fifth of Bombay's population lives in tiny rooms shared by more than six people each. "For the twenty or thirty families whose lives center around a single air shaft, there may be one or two latrines and a few taps of cold running water. Cooking is done on a brazier on the floor of the cubicle; often without benefit of chimney."[19] The doors and windows are dilapidated, the plaster has dropped from the walls, many of which have never been whitewashed, and the general odor and squalor of the staircases make these buildings pathetic places. Two-thirds of Calcutta's residents live in *kutcha* (unbaked brick) buildings.[20]

Bustees are usually thick clusters of small dilapidated mud huts, often with roofs or sides made of scraps of wood, gunny sacks, scrap metal, or other waste materials.† Located in rather open areas of the city or away from the city center, usually on unauthorized land, they are of two types: *Jompris* are huts made of stone and wood, and *juggies* are huts made of wood and straw. In cities like Kanpur, they are called *ahatas* and are built within compounds or enclosing walls. These small, dingy rooms are usually extremely unsanitary and overcrowded, with as many as eight to ten persons living in each.

In such southern cities of India as Madras, Madurai, and Cochin, slums are called *cheris*, which usually consist of mud and thatched huts similar to those of villages or are built of old kerosene-tin plates. The average hut is eight by six feet and poorly constructed; it collapses easily in rain storms and admits almost

---

* Although there has been a tendency, particularly in America, to avoid the term "slum" and to substitute less valuative phrases like "urban-renewal areas," words like "slum" are commonly used in India.

† In Calcutta, the term "busti" or "bustee" applies to any densely populated slum area.

no light. Gandhi described his visit to the *cheris* of Madurai: "In all cases they are so low that you cannot enter without bending double. . . . And in all cases the upkeep of the place is certainly not even to the minimum sanitary standard."[21]

Pavement dwellers abound in many Indian cities. It has been estimated that Calcutta, where the situation is the worst, has several hundred thousand pavement dwellers, consisting mainly of families many of whose members have been born and reared on the sidewalks. They cook, eat, sleep, have intercourse, and die on the streets. Some of these families live there because they cannot find or afford housing; others live there because they want to be near their employment and thus save transportation costs. During the day, their meager possessions may be stored with nearby people, but at nightfall the sidewalks come alive with hundreds of cooking-fires and sleeping people rolled up like mummies in filthy coverings lying beside the buildings.

OVERCROWDING OF POPULATION

Indian slum dwellers live under conditions of greater population density than occur even in the great industrial centers of the West. For example, the 1951 average population density was 136,536 per square mile in Delhi, 77,300 in Calcutta, 38,834 in Ahmedabad, and 25,579 in Greater Bombay. These figures can be compared to 27,308 for London County and 11,318 for Greater London in 1950, 27,000 for Paris in 1946, 16,721 for New York City in 1950, and 15,850 for Chicago in 1950. These differences are far greater for certain areas within these cities. In three of Delhi's eighteen wards, the densities are more than 400,000 to the square mile, another four wards have densities of more than 275,000, and only five wards have densities of less than 100,000.[22] In the multistoried tenements of Bombay, a density of 873,984 was found in the Bhuleswar section of C Ward. In comparison, Manhattan Borough had the highest density (76,156) in New York City in 1950, which means that Delhi's average density was nearly twice as great as that of the most densely populated borough in New York City. These great densities occur despite the absence of tall buildings, for most of the population lives in huts or houses of only a few stories each. If an average of 2.5 people to a room is an index of overcrowding, for example, more than 90 per cent of the Bombay population lives under overcrowded conditions.[23]

UNCLEANLINESS OF THE INDIAN SLUM

Some critical observers have called the slums of India "the filthiest in the world." In fact, there are few slums anywhere that are really "clean," for the very nature of living in such areas presents problems of cleanliness. In the slums of India, however, the drains are generally open, the water is usually stagnant because of poor gradients, and the choked drains present sickening sights and offensive odors. Refuse is everywhere, and the few available containers are seldom properly used. More often trash, garbage and refuse are shoved into the drains or left on the streets. The municipal sweepers may even dump refuse into the drains, and the children usually use them as latrines. Whereas individual dwellings, even in the worst slum areas, may be well swept and clean, a sense of cleanliness or tidiness is seldom extended beyond the limits of the individual dwelling.

Throughout India, one is conscious of bodily functions. A trip through an average Indian slum area requires considerable attention and some dexterity to avoid human feces. This mess more than anything else has given India its reputation for unsanitary conditions. In all slum areas, it is customary for children, up to the age of five or six, and often up to the age of twelve, to defecate in drains, lanes, or almost anywhere outside the home. Their excreta, because of the very high incidence of disease among them, are the chief means of spreading such diseases as dysentery and cholera among the populace. Screens are almost unknown in India, except in the homes of some foreigners, and even in the bazaars practically no food is covered. An Indian public-health expert has explained the situation:

> Irrespective of whether the slums have a piped water supply and/or drainage, an invariable feature of slums is the fouling of open spaces, passages and streets by refuse, garbage and human excreta. Any visitor from abroad, with knowledge of the science of public health as now understood, cannot but be astounded by the sight of human excreta in open spaces and on streets, even in a well managed city like Bombay. It cannot be gainsaid that living in damp, insanitary, ill-ventilated and crowded houses in slums affects the health of the slum dwellers. . . . Food garbage is indiscriminately thrown in the open spaces, which serves as a breeding ground for flies. These flies have a ready access to the faecal matter, left in the surroundings by children. They can easily contaminate all exposed food. The dangers inherent in consuming such food cannot be over-emphasized. Apart from diseases like typhoid, cholera and dysentery, diseases like ascariasis and hookworm are also spread by the exposed human excreta. In ascariasis, the eggs are taken in by children playing round about, while the hookworm infection is caused by penetration of skin, in case of persons moving about with bare feet. The indiscriminate throwing about of garbage and fouling of open spaces by human excreta are thus a danger to the health of the community, particularly in slum areas where this feature is most pronounced, and where people also have a generally low vitality.[24]

Of the conditions under which the textile workers in Bombay live, one writer who has made a study of the area has reported:

> The quarters of the labourers stink with all sorts of foul smell. . . . The latrines are just cesspools and bathrooms are pools of filth and dirt. All measures of sanitation adopted so far have been a failure. . . . The ignorance of these labourers

in health matters is also a great handicap. They exhibit a lack of hygienic sense and are so indifferent to the unhealthy conditions around. There is no organization to arouse their consciousness, and the need and desirability of cleanliness. There are few facilities for recreation. . . . Small children play in dirt and themselves make the surroundings dirty. . . . Living in these chawls for years, they get accustomed to this life and gradually grow completely oblivious of the harmful effects of this type of living.*

ASPECTS OF SANITATION PROBLEMS IN THE INDIAN SLUM

It might be suggested that these unsanitary conditions are peculiar to Asia and can be attributed to the general poverty of developing countries. With the exception of Pakistan, however, there is probably no major country in Asia with sanitary conditions quite comparable to those in the slums of India. Visits by the author to city slums in Ceylon, Thailand, Singapore, and Japan, as well as in Hong Kong, have revealed nothing quite like India's predicament. Even in large West African cities like Lagos, Ibadan, Kano, and Accra, all cities without sewage systems, people live in the slums under difficult and crowded but apparently much more sanitary conditions.

Some of the factors that account for unsanitary conditions in the Indian slums are citizen apathy; indiscriminate defecation and urination; the poor sanitation practices of village India, from which many city slum dwellers have come; insufficient latrines, proper drains, and trash bins; outdoor community living; religious beliefs; the role of the Indian sweeper; and the presence of dairy cattle. One cannot maintain, however, that the high population density of Indian cities necessarily accounts for the unsanitary conditions. Japan has dense crowds of people on the main streets and in the lanes where the poor live, yet the people and their surroundings are remarkably clean.

Citizen Apathy. If all the people in a slum area, rather than an occasional few, fail to cooperate in maintaining cleanliness, it is almost impossible to deal with the problem; if people do not cooperate, the government can do little. The general attitude of the Indian slum dweller is that either the municipal government or the landlord is responsible for the provision and maintenance of latrines,

---

* P. N. Prabhu, "Bombay: A Study of the Social Effects of Urbanization," in *The Social Implications of Industrialization and Urbanization: Five Studies of Urban Populations of Recent Rural Origin in Cities of Southern Asia*, United Nations Educational, Scientific and Cultural Organization Research Centre on the Social Implications of Industrialization in Southern Asia, Calcutta, 1956 (New Delhi: Oxford Printing Works, 1956), pp. 75–6. Of the sanitary conditions in a central Indian city, Hyderabad, which has a population of one million people, one study reported that "a high majority of the citizens commit nuisance promiscuously in open spaces." See S. Keseva Iyengar, *A Socio-Economic Survey of Hyderabad-Secunderabad City Area* (Hyderabad: Government Press, 1957). Even in Bangalore, a South Indian city also of nearly a million people, which appears modern and has a good climate, a description of the life and activities of the slum people, who are largely mill workers, differs little from that of a more northern Indian city. See K. N. Venkatarayappa, *Bangalore: A Socio-Ecological Study* (Bombay: University of Bombay Press, 1957), pp. 128–30.

drains, dust bins (trash bins), and water taps. It seldom occurs to him, despite the hardships that result from the absence of facilities, to provide them for himself, and he feels little sense of responsibility for taking proper care of the public sanitary facilities. Most Indian families insist upon the cleanliness of their own brass cooking utensils, which are kept well polished, and often upon the cleanliness of their personal living quarters, yet they appear to think little of adding to the general disorder and filth in the streets and alleys.

Indiscriminate Defecation and Urination. Many complex factors are related to indiscriminate defecation among children and some adults—and to common public urination by both. Mothers of young children, for example, are accustomed to it; they have never known anything different, and they are therefore not often conscious of the necessity for or even the existence of alternatives. If children are allowed to defecate outside, the low-caste municipal sweeper will come and clean the area. Furthermore, the whole area is already so dirty that the children's feces add little to the litter. In addition, because of the association of uncleanliness with such bodily functions, caste-conscious mothers wish to avoid pollution from dealing with feces. Few households have their own latrines, and public latrines pose problems for children, as they are built to adult scale.

Another major problem in India is the failure to use fecal matter productively, either in rural or in urban areas. In various parts of the world, China, Japan, Korea, and Hong Kong, for example, feces are carefully collected in both farm and city—and even purchased—for manure. Neither in the villages of India nor in the cities are feces collected, and this fact may well contribute to the differences in the sanitation problems of the different areas. One author writing on China, for example, has commented that the preservation of fecal material and urine for use as fertilizer probably caused less pollution to the general environment than would have occurred if the dense rural and urban populations had directly polluted the ground, as is common in countries like India that do not use human excreta as fertilizer.[25] Mumford has also indicated the profitable nature of the use of human excreta from cities.[26]

Sanitation Practices in Village India. Mahatma Gandhi once characterized the villages of India, whose way of life goes back for thousands of years, as "dung-heaps." "Instead of having graceful hamlets dotting the land, we have dung-heaps. The approach to many villages is not a refreshing experience; obviously one would like to shut one's eyes and stuff one's nose, such is the surrounding dirt and offending smell."[27] Few village residents use latrines, preferring the open fields fairly near their homes. At night, however, the lanes and refuse heaps are used by adults, whereas small children practically always defecate immediately outside their homes. People are prejudiced against latrines because they are smelly and dirty, because others use them for defecation, and because they constitute a source of caste pollution. Attitudes toward human feces are intense, highly charged, and highly negative.

Gradual changes in environmental sanitation practices in the Indian villages are being brought about through various rural community-development programs, and they will undoubtedly improve the sanitation practices of future village migrants to the cities. Progress has not yet been great enough, however, to alter the situation sufficiently to affect materially the patterns of living that rural migrants bring with them to the city. The open air and sunshine of the village ameliorate some of the unsanitary conditions of the villages, whereas the damp, dark alleys in Indian cities, devoid of the drying effects of sunlight, may actually make village sanitation practices worse when followed in the city.

Insufficient Latrines, Proper Drains, and Trash Bins. One contributing factor is the absence of sufficient latrines and proper drains. Approximately two-thirds of the slums of Kanpur have no community latrine facilities, one latrine being used by an average of eighteen people.[28] Two-thirds of the slums of Agra have no drainage systems; in that city, which is the home of the Taj Mahal, an average of eighty people use a single latrine. In most of the Delhi slums, latrines are either absent or insufficient. Out of 1,724 *katras* surveyed, 27 per cent, housing 33 per cent of the population, had no latrines. Approximately four families shared a single latrine, where a latrine was available, and 85 per cent of the latrines were dry.[29] Not only are latrine facilities inadequate in the areas where the people live, but few are available to passersby in many areas. Passersby also are not provided with receptacles for trash, as municipal authorities seldom provide trash bins. Bins are not normally owned by slum families, and consequently Indian slum dwellers dispose of refuse by throwing it into the streets.

Outdoor Community Living. The dense concentration of people in these slum areas is aggravated by the heavy pedestrian traffic, the heat and the humidity. Many people spend much of the day in the streets, and such "outdoor community living" contributes to the uncleanliness of the city. The sight of many people eating, sleeping, and even urinating in the open suggests that a minor matter like throwing litter onto the streets does not bother them. Urban Indians think nothing of dropping leaves, mango peels, and orange skins wherever they may finish with them. Of this extreme tendency toward outdoor community living in the urban areas of developing countries, one writer has said:

> The inhuman densities inside the shelter might be relieved by adequate space outside, but too often the only outside space is a narrow, rutted path that must provide room for movement of people, the carrying off of waste and rain water, cooking, peddling one's wares, and sometimes space for draft animals as well. Where streets are paved and wide enough, however, the street has assumed some of the functions that the home unit lacks. In Asia, the street is often the mass dining room for family and the place where one gets his oxygen amid the miscellaneous odors of culinary activity.[30]

Another factor contributing to the clutter of an Indian slum is the tendency to keep everything for later use or eventual sale. Bits of paper, bottles, string, pieces of metal, boxes, and pieces of wood may net a few paise or a few cents. Such hoarding is probably common in slum areas everywhere because of the limited incomes, but it exists on a much larger scale in poor countries. In slums of the Western world, such items can be stored in rooms, basements, or sheds, but, in places like India where storage space is negligible, they are kept in the open, often on top of shacks if they are large, thus marring the aesthetic appearance even further.

The Role of Religion. Religious beliefs and attitudes also play important roles in the problem of sanitation. Stray cattle wander through the city streets, particularly in the slums, and effective action is often barred by public sentiments of charity and tolerance for animal life, particularly cattle. Hindus regard the cow as a sacred animal, and it is therefore not only permissible but even a religious act to feed them. Vegetable parings and refuse from fruits of all types are thrown regularly into the lanes. As Indians consume large quantities of vegetables and as prepared foods are rarely used, sizable amounts of such refuse are thrown out daily. Although vegetable and fruit parings are usually quickly consumed, the habit of throwing out all types of waste is well established.

For centuries, the Hindu religion has exhibited concern for cleanliness, purity, and the avoidance of pollution. This concern has largely involved, however, *ritual* rather than biological pollution. A pious Hindu housewife may make sure that no dirt from the street is brought into her kitchen on the sandals of family members, but she may be impervious to the contaminated drinking water in the water jug or the flies that swarm over her food. Although the individual Hindu may bathe daily before making his puja, or worship, or before going to the temple, he is seldom bothered by the unsanitary conditions around and inside the typical Hindu temple. Hindus who make pilgrimages to their holiest temple cities, Varanasi (Banaras) in the North, Puri in the East, and Madurai in the South, may not notice that these religious places are extremely unclean even by Indian standards.

The Indian Sweeper. For centuries, it has been customary for a municipal or privately hired sweeper, an Untouchable, to clean local areas in the city once or twice each day. This detailed system, in which a male or female sweeper bends or crouches with a small broom and a basket to clean the lanes or alleys, has few exact counterparts in any place in the world, except perhaps in Pakistan. Actually, the use of such a sweeper system by municipal and private authorities accounts for many inadequacies in sanitation. The system diminishes community responsibility, for the Indian urban citizen can throw things about or let his children defecate in the drains with the full knowledge that a sweeper will, if the system is operating efficiently, collect it within a matter of a few hours. Urban dwellers even litter the ground immediately behind a sweeper as he cleans an area. In this sense, the presence of the sweeper in Indian cities is one "cause of unsanitary practices," a fact that is rarely recognized by municipal officials and certainly not by slum dwellers, both of whom are apt to feel that what is needed is more and better sweepers.

On some occasions the sweepers contribute to the sanitation problem. After removing the night soil from the dry latrines, they permit it to flow into the open drains, or they clean the drains and put the filth on the edge to dry until another sweeper can later remove it. This approach in itself adds to the rubbish problem. Such problems are due to laziness of the sweepers, to failure to understand the need for proper sanitation, and to general public apathy toward the objectives that the sweeper is trying to accomplish. Some support for this view came from a "natural experiment" in Bombay a few years ago during a strike of municipal sweepers. The city government was faced with a difficult health emergency, and citizens were told that if they threw trash into the lanes no one would be available to remove it. They were asked to leave all rubbish at specifically designated corners where it could be picked up by municipal trucks. A former municipal commissioner stated that never before or since has the city been so clean.

Presence of Dairy Cattle. The problem of animal sanitation is increased by the presence, often in the most crowded areas of an Indian city, of many small herds of dairy cows or buffaloes, as well as of bullocks and horses, which are used for pulling loads of all types. It is difficult to remove these dairy herds because they supply milk, which constitutes a large part of the Indian's daily diet of protein, and because urban dwellers like to see the cows milked in their presence, as they believe that otherwise the milk will be adulterated with water. Bombay has been quite successful in removing dairy herds by establishing large municipal dairies outside the city; Delhi and Ahmedabad have tried similar methods with only partial success.

THE PROBLEM OF ILL HEALTH

Among major countries in the world today, India has one of the lowest life-expectancy rates and one of the highest infant-mortality rates. The death rates from childbirth, dysentery, cholera, typhoid fever, and tuberculosis are extremely high in the slum areas of cities.

Although urban areas have more medical and hospital facilities than do rural areas, such facilities are still inadequate. A sick or injured person may wait hours for treatment in a public dispensary or hospital. Even if these services were adequate, however, many people would not avail themselves of modern medical care or such preventive measures as vaccinations and inoculations. Slum people do not readily accept scientific explanations for death and disease. When they do seek medical care, they often go to "quack" doctors simply because they charge less for their services and drugs than do more respectable government or private clinics. Even these expenses can mount. One study revealed that nearly 10 per cent of the incomes of 827 people from 703 families in the Delhi slums was spent on illnesses.[31] These sample families incurred medical expenses during the year that amounted to R.147 per family, or about R.12 per month.

Slum dwellers generally fail to understand the importance of good health or even of life itself. Infant mortality, for example, has been so high for such a long time that people do not really expect all their children to reach normal life spans or even adulthood. Very often a Hindu child is not even named until he is one year old. Strong beliefs about reincarnation, the nature of the afterlife, and predetermined fate often mean less concern with the importance of health in this life or even of death itself. Such resignation is difficult to overcome. Not really appreciating good health, people often accept ailments like chronic dysentery, hookworm, and even tuberculosis as "satisfactory" health. A health survey in Delhi revealed, for example, that the people's own opinions of their health differed a great deal from the official health statistics.[32] Of the slum dwellers surveyed, 44 per cent said that they had "good health," 52 per cent reported their health "satisfactory," and only 4 per cent reported their health "indifferent" or "sickly." They may not even know that they have diseases like hookworm and tuberculosis; listlessness and fatigue may be attributed to environmental conditions, or illnesses may seem to be caused by changes in the weather or by eating hot and cold foods at the same meal. Even for such minor conditions as burns and cuts, they do not realize the importance of cleanliness and often resort to cow dung or tar as a remedy.

Urban areas are frequently swept by epidemics of smallpox, cholera, typhoid, and diphtheria. The region of endemic cholera is mainly in West Bengal, with its nucleus in greater Calcutta.[33] Although immunizations are available free from most municipal health authorities and such immunizations would curb these epidemics, they are not widely sought. Many people do not understand or accept the need for such precautionary measures, and some fear that they might incur the wrath of the gods if they should be immunized. Even when they are approached about immunizations, they often refuse them. In addition, people who have previously been immunized often fail to be re-immunized after several years, not recognizing that periodic vaccinations are essential in a country where smallpox, for example, is endemic.

Personal Hygiene. As one observes the slum dwellers of a typical north or central Indian city, one is struck by their poor personal hygiene, reflected in their dirty clothing and unkempt appearances. Especially striking is the condition of many children, particularly those not in school,* whose hair is matted and

---

* On a visit to one of the worst slums of Singapore, the author was struck with the cleanliness of the children's clothing, even though it was ragged, and the well-scrubbed appearances and combed hair of the children.

disheveled and whose clothing is filthy and ill fitting. Even babies may be quite dirty, covered with scabies, or suffering from other skin diseases that result from uncleanliness. This lack of personal hygiene in the Indian slum dweller is often difficult to explain, particularly when so many people, including those in the slums, seem to have some recognition that living in filth is not the proper way to live. India has been exposed to Western standards of cleanliness under several centuries of British rule, and many Indians have been educated abroad. Although it is true that the tendency in the past was to separate the so-called "native quarters" of Indian cities from the European quarters, which somewhat limited the influence of Western ideas of personal hygiene and sanitation, there is a contradiction about personal cleanliness on the Indian scene. The religious practices prescribe bathing before prayers and before attending religious rites. During religious festivals and national holidays the Indians of the slums and their children are likely to be quite neatly and cleanly dressed. It is as if the Indian slum dweller often knows the virtues of personal hygiene but does not consistently practice them.

Adulteration of Foods and Drugs. Food and drug adulteration is by no means confined to Indian cities, but there the problem is particularly acute because of its pervasiveness, the vicious nature of the adulteration, and its effects upon people who are poor, undernourished, and uneducated. These problems are of proportions too enormous for the government to deal with alone, but at the same time the consumers are too ignorant and too poorly organized to do much about them. The entire marketing system in India is conducive to adulteration practices, as all types of foodstuff are generally bought in bulk. Without packaging and labeling, the consumer is at the mercy of the shopkeeper for both quality and quantity.

One of the most all-pervasive forms of adulteration is in grains and related products. Illegal coloring is used to disguise inferior products, and insecticides and pesticides frequently have been used as preservatives. Tea, which is widely used throughout India, is sold without regard to standards, and edible oils are adulterated with white oil and even petroleum oil. Milk is extensively watered, marble powder is combined with wheat flour, sawdust is added to grains, and saturated sugar solutions dilute honey. Of 5,614 samples of milk, milk preparations, edible oils, wheat flour, spices, and so forth, collected by the Delhi Municipal Corporation Health Department in 1959, 2,420 or 43.1 per cent, were found to be adulterated. In the individual items, the percentages were, for example, honey and confectionary products 56.5, milk 52.5, and chili pepper 38.3. Shops seldom have equipment for refrigeration, and spoiled meat and fish are sold extensively. According to one Delhi estimate, 30 per cent of the meat sold daily is spoiled.[34] Drugs are frequently adulterated. Of 4,168 samples tested in 1959 by the Central Drug Laboratory, 944, or 22.6 per cent, were found to be adulterated with worthless or dangerous chemicals.

The seriousness of this situation in urban India arises from several factors other than a widespread shortage of funds for adequate inspection and proper enforcement. Because of general poverty, most urban residents cannot pay more than a certain price for any commodity, generally seeking the cheapest commodity rather than a higher-priced one that may be of better quality. If a commodity becomes scarce and the price rises while incomes remain the same, merchants may supply the same quantities at the same prices, making up the difference by adulterating the product or by short-weighting.

THE PROBLEMS OF FAMILY PLANNING

Whereas India's population increase comes mainly from the rural areas, the urban population is so large that control of urban growth in the slums would help a great deal in solving the national problem of overpopulation. In addition, the economic and social conditions of the slum dwellers could be improved if residents had fewer children. Presently there is little difference in the numbers of children urban and rural women of child-bearing age have, but studies have shown that the urban population is more favorably disposed toward family planning. In addition to expressed approval of contraceptives, other factors favor population limitation. Indians generally, for example, have no decided religious opposition to family planning. Many want higher standards of living and some relief from poverty and do not care to add to their economic burdens by having larger families. They would like to improve their children's lives by making them healthier and by obtaining more education for them. One motivation for family planning is improvement in the health of the mother.

In view of such findings, greater progress in family planning might be expected among slum people. Many social, economic, and cultural factors, however, make the widespread acceptance and application of birth-control practices difficult. Fertility worship has been a central theme of the Hindu religion for more than 3,000 years, and there is a great desire for sons. Hindus believe, for example, that funeral rites, which are essential caste prescriptions for the salvation of the departed soul and its presumed reincarnation at a higher level, cannot be adequately performed without a male descendant. A son, usually the oldest, must generally light the funeral pyre, for instance. Economic considerations are also important, as sons provide physical, social, and economic security. Sons carry on the family name and, in most of India, their marriages, unlike those of daughters, require no dowries. A man gains social status by having many living children, particularly sons, and a large family is thus highly regarded in India. Besides the presumed social advantage of a large family, it is also evidence of sexual virility.

The adoption of family planning is even more complex, in both urban and rural areas, for the women of India depend upon their children, particularly

sons, for their statuses in life. Marriage without children is considered in-
complete: A barren wife suffers humiliation. She is looked down upon if she
fails to deliver a male child. The taking of a second wife is often caused by the
first wife's failure to bear children or to bear male children. In order to gain
respect in her husband's family, especially in the elders' eyes, the young bride
should bear children as soon as possible. The mother-in-law, who plays the
dominant role in the family, can usually be expected, for this reason, to oppose
any adoption of family planning by a daughter-in-law, at least until she has
borne a son. A Hindu woman is extremely shy and modest, and open discussions of sexual matters are thus severely restricted. Although Hindu women,
especially those in villages and slums, may discuss sexual matters among themselves, they are often shy or frightened of their husbands, and intimate communication relating to sex and family planning is difficult. Wives frequently
will not tell their husbands, relatives, or friends about their desires for family
planning. They often hesitate to go to family-planning clinics because it is hard
for them to discuss such topics with strangers and also because they fear that
such visits may become known to their families or neighbors. The adoption of
family planning by slum dwellers involves changing a complex set of attitudes.

WASTAGE OF WATER

Water is an extremely important commodity in any urban community. In
most Indian cities, its importance is magnified by generally short supplies,
inadequate distribution to people in some areas, and frequent contamination.
The filtering of water is extremely costly by Indian standards and is one of the
largest municipal budget items. Even if it were more easily available, it would
be difficult to increase the supply of filtered water because of the added tax
burdens. In order to conserve filtered water, the supply is often restricted during
the day or night.

Public water taps are the chief sources of water for drinking and bathing in
the slums. In one survey of Delhi it was revealed that one-third of the *katras* had
no water taps and that water had to be carried some distance from public
hydrants.[35] The common water taps were shared by an average of eight
families, or forty people. In bustees the situation was even worse, with sixteen
of sixty-one bustees having no water taps. In the remaining forty-five, approximately 134 people used each tap, with as many as 500 people utilizing single
taps in some areas. Water in the slums must often be carried in pots by women
for long distances and is badly wasted in the process. Filth and mud accumulate
around public water taps, either because the areas are unpaved or because a lack
of civic responsibility is characteristic of those who use the taps.

Despite acute shortages and high costs, large amounts of water are wasted,
particularly in the slums. In Delhi, for example, an estimated thirteen million

gallons each day, or about 15 per cent of the total supply, are wasted, largely through carelessness. Public water taps either are not properly turned off or are left open. They may be plugged with rocks to keep them running constantly, or the taps may be stolen. In either case, water runs incessantly, thus cutting down on the available supply and wasting valuable municipal funds. With so many taps and so many people using them, it is impossible for the city administration to supervise them adequately.

In most Indian cities, the water is pure upon leaving the filtering plant, but it frequently becomes contaminated afterward. When the supply is short and the flow must be cut, a vacuum is created in the pipes, and outside impurities are sucked in through any weak points in the pipes. This problem illustrates the relationships between a pure water supply, the wasting of water, and the sanitary practices of Indian slum dwellers. Contamination of the water with dysentery, cholera, or other bacteria can result, if the impurities include human excreta that have been indiscriminately deposited near the pipes. Such contaminated water should be boiled before use, particularly for children, but it seldom is.

INADEQUATE LIGHTING

Still another problem of the slums is inadequate lighting, and many areas are clothed in near-darkness as the sun goes down. Although public lighting by electricity may be assumed to be a necessity in any area, over three-fourths of the Delhi *katras* had none. People stumble up lanes and into *katras*, they have difficulty in locating the latrines at night, and school children can seldom find places with sufficient light to study. An electric outlet generally costs too much for a single slum family; if groups of people could share the costs of common meters, lights could be installed here and there, bringing additional light into the slums.

ILLITERACY AND LACK OF EDUCATIONAL FACILITIES

Slum dwellers are usually not only uneducated but also largely illiterate. Although there is great need for a mass adult literacy program and facilities are often available, a major drawback to effective literacy campaigns has been the urban slum dwellers' lack of desire to become literate. They often see no purpose in learning to read and write, which is usually difficult for adults, as it may result in little economic advantage. Few preschool arrangements of any kind are available in Indian cities.

LACK OF RECREATIONAL FACILITIES

The constant pressure of poverty and poor living conditions, along with the added pressures of monotonous and inadequate activities, make adequate recreational outlets even more important in the Indian slums than in those of the Western world.[36] Such a need, however, has not been recognized, partly because of failure to comprehend the importance of recreation, the absence of adequate space, limited experience in assuming initiative for organized recreational programs, and the decline in importance of such traditional recreational activities of village life as dance and music in urban areas. Such traditional forms of village recreation as yoga exercises, wrestling, lathee (a form of exercise involving the rapid swinging of an upright pole), and *malkarm* (gymnastics around an upright pole) are seldom seen in the city. The songs and dances of the village are performed either by occasional small groups or not at all. Playing on the *tabla* or drum and singing religious hymns often continue in the city. Historic and attractive sites and the cultural activities of the city, however, often lie beyond the apparent capacity of the slum dweller to enjoy.[37]

Young children, particularly those who are not in school, seem to suffer the most from this lack of recreation. In the slums, hundreds of young children roam about aimlessly seeking something to do. They may stand and watch something, play in the dirt or with one or two marbles in groups, or find a board for teetering. Some parks and organized recreation do exist, but they are often inaccessible, and their limited equipment is often in disrepair. Families generally own few games themselves, partly because they do not recognize the importance of such recreation but also because of the prohibitive costs of most games in India. Such studies have shown that the men of the slums spend money they can ill afford on frequent attendance at motion pictures or on gambling.[38]

DEVIANT BEHAVIOR

As in other countries, deviant behavior like juvenile delinquency, crime, prostitution, professional begging, and the use of drugs are associated with cities, particularly slum areas.[39] These problems appear, however, even allowing for differences in the extent of reporting and arrests, to be not so serious as in the slums of the West. In fact, India presents evidence that poverty alone does not explain deviant behavior in slum communities. In Indian cities the family, and to a degree caste, operates as a social control, particularly as it affects reputation, over such behavior. It is questionable whether or not the effects of these controls will continue in the face of rising urbanization, industrialization, and urban way of life. One can expect rising rates of deviant behavior in Indian cities and particularly in slum areas.

PART TWO

APPROACHES TO THE SLUM PROBLEM

SLUM CLEARANCE, WELFARE SERVICES, AND ECONOMIC OPPORTUNITY

Some experts advocate the policy of destroying the slum, tearing it down physically, erasing its houses and shacks. Others believe that providing welfare services to slum dwellers is the best way to bring about changes in slum areas and to solve the slum problem. Still others stress providing greater economic opportunities for slum dwellers. These approaches appear, on the surface, to be sound and have been applied widely in a number of countries over many years. All, however, have serious limitations as solutions, either alone or together, to the slum problem. The various issues involved will be analyzed here and evaluated on the basis of experience in a developing country with modest economic resources, India, and in an "affluent" country, the United States.

§ *The Developing Countries: Slum Clearance in India*

Slums in the urban areas of India are legacies of the past. Although many are centuries old, a large number began to develop only in the latter half of the nineteenth century, with the advent of industrialization, at a time when there was no planning and when cheap housing was urgently needed. At that time, the policy of *laissez-faire* placed a premium on private profit and precluded ideas of social welfare. Factory labor, largely drawn from the rural areas, was herded together in nearby chawls and bustees with little or no regard to sanitation or hygiene. The state felt little obligation to provide housing for this working group, and the entrepreneur did not cater to its needs, finding it more profitable to build for those who could pay higher rents. As subsidiary industries grew up, country-to-city migration increased. The crowded housing situation, which was deteriorating gradually all during those years, became even worse with the partition of the country in 1947, when countless refugees found their way to the cities and towns in search of employment and shelter.

Numerous obstacles have impeded progress in dealing with urban slum housing in developing countries like India.[1] They include the enormous extent of the problem, the gap between shelter cost and income, national financial limitations, lack of savings, absence of a well-established building industry, backwardness in the use of materials, often lack of controls over land costs, land speculation, and transfers of public housing units to private owners. Problems of finance are particularly difficult because of insufficient capital for housing, mortgages, and cooperative savings programs.

Many experts think that the obvious remedy for such slum conditions and inadequate housing is to tear them down or "burn them," according to Nehru's sweeping recommendation for the Kanpur slums. Such destruction, however, would solve nothing, and would lead only to the development of even worse conditions on the ruins of the old. Proponents of physical destruction or slum clearance argue, of course, that they plan to build new and more suitable housing in place of the old. The logic of such a program and its feasibility need careful examination. There are four chief difficulties: the immensity of the physical problem in terms of limited government resources, the likelihood of increasing urbanization, the fact that the majority of slum problems cannot be attributed to physical conditions alone, and the fact that destruction of housing may also involve destruction of what positive human associations already exist in an area.

EXTENT AND COST

In 1958, it was estimated that as many as 60 per cent of the people in the large cities live in physical slums and that 1.5 million houses in Indian cities are unfit for human habitation.[2] The backlog of demand for urban houses has been estimated at nearly five million. At the present rate of growth, total slum clearance would require about 115 years and expenditure equivalent to at least two national Five-Year Plans. Three-fourths of the urban housing shortage occur in the four main cities of India.[3] Taking only the estimated increase in urban population for the five years ending 1966, the cost of housing, at the conservative figure of R.1,600 ($320) per unit, would amount to 2,880 crores, or $5,760,000,000.* If the cost of land were to be included, a total of 3,500 crores would be involved. The total housing-development outlay for the Third Five-Year Plan was only 1,000 crores, which was one-half the allotment for all social services in India. Furthermore, the contemplated housing would consist of only one- and two-room units of simple design. Housing of the type that Western-trained observers now consider representative of good and decent living would be available to only a tiny fraction of the people who must live in the cities of India.[4]

---

* Sachin Chaudhuri, "Centralization and the Alternate Forms of Decentralization: A Key Issue," in Roy Turner, ed., *India's Urban Future* (Berkeley: University of California Press, 1962), p. 223. A crore is equivalent to R.10,000,000, or approximately $2,000,000.

Little help toward achieving adequate housing can be expected from private investors, who built nearly all such low-cost slum housing prior to World War II. The private investor formerly received a good return on his money, even with low rents, partly because construction costs were not high. In most cases, the buildings were substandard, largely devoid of necessary facilities and poor in environmental hygienic conditions. Today few private investors are interested in building houses for low-income groups. The private rental of an average one-room tenement of high standards is R.28 ($6) a month, for two rooms R.41, a sum that is beyond the financial means of most urban households.[5] The incomes of more than 50 per cent of urban households do not exceed R.100 ($20) a month, and in only 10 per cent of the households are they more than R.300 a month. Park has pointed out that, in Calcutta, investment of about $1,200 per tenement unit, with a 5 per cent annual return, would require about $50 rent a year, or $5 monthly.[6] At present, however, the average monthly rent in most parts of Calcutta that would be affected by slum clearance is only $2. In Delhi, rents are often only $1 a month.

It is hard to believe that foreign exchange would be made available in sufficient sums to rebuild the cities of India, for large amounts of any available money are necessary for development of hydroelectric power, steel mills, fertilizer plants, factories, and military defenses.[7] As it is, much foreign exchange would have to be diverted for the importation of such building supplies as corrugated iron sheets and cast-iron pipes, cement, and other construction materials.[8]

Because of increasing urbanization, the housing situation in Indian cities has actually been getting worse rather than better, in spite of new housing programs. Although the percentage of urban growth in recent years has not been rapid, it has resulted in great increases in numbers of urban people. This fact, together with limited government resources, and the poverty of migrants, means that neither public nor private resources has been able to cope with the situation. In 1951 the total urban population of 61.9 million occupied 10.3 million houses, and the number of households was 12.8 million. It was estimated in 1957 that by 1961, when there would be 78 million urban residents, the total deficit in housing would be about 8.9 million. Even with the construction of three million new dwelling units, there would be a deficiency of approximately 5.96 million houses.[9] This estimate has turned out to be substantially correct, for, in 1961, the urban housing shortage was twice as great as it had been ten years earlier. The shortage of 5.5 million urban dwellings was again estimated as likely to increase rather than to decrease. These problems are some of those that India faces in meeting even immediate housing needs, and, with the large predicted migration to the cities, the problem of furnishing adequate housing in slum areas becomes staggering.

The Indian Third Five-Year Plan pointed out that two main problems in implementing a slum-clearance program were the slum dwellers' inability to pay even subsidized rents and their reluctance to move from the areas selected for clearance.[10] Slum dwellers often resist removal to areas of better housing, and when they do move they are often dissatisfied. This dissatisfaction arises, first, from such economic–dislocation "costs" as higher transportation expenses, from the inadequacies of most urban municipal transport, and from the loss of some "marginal" employment opportunities. Second, relocation often has grave consequences in the disruption of what community relationships have existed. Because of alterations in community ties, there may be less widespread community involvement than formerly existed, in celebration of important festivals and other activities, for example. Often people who have been living in areas where there is some uncertainty about their habitations have banded together for mutual protection, thus developing some degree of community feeling.[11] When they are rehoused in a manner that fails to take this feeling into account, the resulting disruption of some of their regional unities can result in friction. In addition to this problem, which is often too subtle to be understood by those directly involved, the slum dweller is often dissatisfied with the distance from his new dwelling to his place of work and with a lack of possible employment facilities nearby. In fact, the large-scale program of new low-rental housing projects for slum dwellers in Puerto Rico,* which has quite a difficult slum problem, has not been completely accepted by the residents.

> Housing projects are built because of the necessity of providing shelter for people who otherwise could not have adequate housing. But the people who build them always have the additional hope that the construction of these projects will also improve the general life style and living conditions. In a country like Puerto Rico, the implications of a move to a housing project are tremendous. It means moving from small houses to apartment buildings, from wooden construction to concrete buildings, from squatters' rights to tenancy, from shifting day by day to planned administration. Thus it involves not only the connotations such a move would have in a city in the United States, but a further step in the process of urbanization as well.

> The planner faces the difficulty, however, that many people are not ready for this change. They do not want to make it in this manner, and those who do make the move are frequently not those who could profit most by the change. This study has shown how strong is the fear of economic regimentation in the slum dweller,

---

* Even though large government funds have been provided for public housing in San Juan, the "decline of the slum population has recently averaged less than one half of one percent per year—a rate that, if continued, would give the Slum Belt two centuries more of existence." See Theodore Caplow, *et al.*, *The Urban Ambience: A Study of San Juan, Puerto Rico* (Totowa, N.J.: The Bedminster Press, 1964), p. 228.

even in many with a high potential for mobility. It may be well to consider whether there is not too much change at once in the system of building housing projects. Other systems for improvement of living conditions may fit better for many people. The pioneering efforts in aided self-help are one case in point, and there is room for similar kinds of experimentation.[12]

A leading authority on housing problems in the less developed countries concluded that all prevailing ideas of wholesale slum clearance and construction of costly housing must be abandoned and that new ideas must be developed to solve the shelter problem. "The provision of the bare essentials may have to be the world's sad but only reasonable alternative. Once we understand the enormity of the problem, however, there may be ways of dealing with it. It is only when hope is given up and eyes are closed to reality that crisis becomes inevitable."[13] Problems of finance and relocation do not mean that the slums of Indian cities must physically endure forever; it is suggested, rather, that the chances for their elimination are indeed remote. Along with slum clearance, there has to be a short-range approach through slum improvement. Writing about the plans being developed for Calcutta through the Calcutta Metropolitan Planning Organization (CMPO), Bose has pointed out that "for the same gross expenditure that might rehouse 7,000 people it is estimated that present bustee quarters can be made more safely habitable for 70,000."[14] In addition, properly organized, motivated, and guided people in slum areas can make substantial contributions to improvement of physical conditions and to other problems in the areas where they live. Physical improvements in slums can consist of repairing houses, both inside and outside, straightening lanes and open drains, and providing better sanitary facilities, water, and electricity in the areas.

A realistic plan has been suggested by Abrams—that improvements in slum housing in developing countries must proceed in two stages. The first would minimize slum clearance and allow for dense occupancy and increased reliance on self-help through savings and mortgage mechanisms, improved local production of building materials, and better suburban transport to bring workers into the city, thus somewhat relieving housing pressures. The second stage, to be reached in the distant future, would involve improving the general standard of living and economic development. In the first stage, slums would have to be accepted as a transitional phase of urban industrial change in the face of unavoidable mass migration. Then the slums could be guided in their development. Cheap land in less crowded parts of the city could be acquired and laid out so that houses and shacks could be improved and expanded over the years. Abrams states that a "planned slum is better than an unplanned slum when it consists of separate shelters that are individually owned. Without a program that acknowledges the inevitability of the slums, costly, permanent and unimprovable slum formations will be the product."[15]

The traditional approach to the slums problem through clearance and redevelopment with subsidized housing has been criticized in its application to developing countries.[16] As the cities in underdeveloped nations raise their standards, poor people from rural areas flock to the city slums. The subsidized housing projects make the cities all the more attractive to them, and the numbers of rural poor arriving in the cities become increasingly difficult to handle. According to this critical view, the only way to reduce the urban slum areas is to raise rural living standards to equal those of the city. Furthermore, its proponents argue, slum clearance in a "hungry nation" is unproductive in that there is no net addition to the housing stock.[17]

Slum clearance, however, is not exclusively a matter of replacing substandard housing with new tenements or even with planned slums. It is not always true that when decent housing is provided, such other aspects of community life as proper maintenance of living quarters and facilities automatically follow. Proper orientation of the residents to a better and organized way of life and to the maintenance of the entire neighborhood is essential, and this orientation requires the systematic education and motivation of all the people, men, women, and children, in the fundamentals of personal hygiene, home management, and environmental sanitation.

§ Problems of Slum Clearance in the United States

In the more affluent societies programs of slum clearance are often necessary under certain conditions like very bad deterioration or where city planning may require essential changes. In numerous instances slum clearance has brought about needed improvements both for slum dwellers and cities as wholes. In the United States in recent years, however, questions have been multiplying about many assumptions underlying the traditional slum-clearance (or urban-renewal) approach, which was incorporated into the Federal Housing Acts of 1949, 1954, 1959, and 1961 and which has been widely employed.* New public housing in slum areas has been criticized for its institutional atmosphere, too many or too few controls on tenant behavior, concentration of juvenile crime and violence, and failure to fit into the surrounding neighborhoods or even to develop senses of community within the projects. Frequently, because of local conditions calling for clearance of slum areas to which Negroes have been confined, *de facto* segregation has often resulted.

One study of the urban-renewal program in the United States concluded that many assumed benefits of the program did not necessarily materialize.[18] Tax returns had not increased after renewal, as they had been expected to do; urban renewal did not play a major role in improving the nation's housing; the

---

* Such federal urban-renewal programs are also directed at planning, rehabilitation, and conservation.

program had not helped the poor to secure better living conditions, as its advocates had promised; and it was even highly questionable that urban renewal had eliminated slums and prevented the spread of blight. Another writer agrees that the usual arguments for urban renewal are not viable because they tend to be based only on the project area and not on the entire community, because the new buildings do not represent net gains in the amount of available housing, and because any increase in property taxes is likely to be offset by losses or unrealized gains elsewhere.[19] Although urban renewal involves a misallocation of resources, as judged by the yardstick of the private market, it can be justified on social or nonmarket grounds by assessing the effects on the entire community and the role it plays as an adjunct to other policies that can stimulate improvements in both residential and nonresidential structures.

One of the most eloquent and well-documented criticisms of the traditional urban renewal approach has come from Herbert Gans, who for six months lived in the West End of Boston, immediately before this Italian neighborhood was demolished for an urban-renewal project. He argues that the area, called a "slum" by planners, was actually not a slum at all, as the buildings, though sometimes old and inconvenient, were not harmful to the health or safety of the residents. In fact, he claims that the low-rent West End was inhabited by a working-class group that did not share the values and objectives of the middle-class planners.[20] As eligibility standards stress the physical conditions of the structures, as the local agency selects the renewal area, and as the area's physical condition is not always a sufficient criterion, the image of the area in the minds of the middle-class residents may become the criterion for selection. "What seems to happen," according to Gans, "is that neighborhoods come to be described as slums if they are inhabited by residents who, for a variety of reasons, indulge in overt and visible behavior considered undesirable by the majority of the community. The community image of the area then gives rise to feelings that something should be done, and subsequently the area is proposed for renewal."[21] In addition to the failure to distinguish between slum and low-rent housing, Gans criticized certain relocation policies that forced many West Enders to move to more crowded units; the reduction of Boston's low-rent housing supply; the lack of adequate study and understanding of individuals and their needs throughout the program; and the lack of efficient communication lines between the city agencies and the West Enders. The conclusion was that traditional renewal policies benefit the developer most, the area residents least, and the public interest in an as yet unmeasured quantity.[22]

Another attack upon traditional urban-renewal methods in the United States has been made by Jane Jacobs. She sees mass clearance of slum areas and their replacement by new housing projects as destructive of the vitality and diversity of the city, which, in turn, brings about conditions far worse than had existed in the slum.

There is a wistful myth that if only we had enough money to spend—the figure is usually put at a hundred billion dollars—we could wipe out all our slums in ten years.... But look what we have built with the first several billions: Low-income projects that become worse centers of delinquency, vandalism and general social hopelessness than the slums which they were supposed to replace. Middle-income housing projects which are truly marvels of dullness and regimentation, sealed against any buoyancy or vitality of city life. Luxury housing projects that mitigate their inanity, or try to with a vapid vulgarity. Cultural centers that are unable to support a good bookstore. Civic centers that are avoided by everyone but bums, who have fewer choices of loitering than others. Commercial centers that are lack-luster imitations of standardized suburban chain-store shopping. Promenades that go from no place to nowhere and have no promenaders. Expressways that eviscerate great cities. This is not the rebuilding of cities. This is the sacking of cities.[23]

Her alternative suggestion is to encourage the present residents to stay so that the slums can "unslum" themselves. She also believes that this approach has been successful in the Back of the Yards in Chicago, the North End in Boston, and North Beach in San Francisco. The present practice of wiping out slums and relocating their residents at best merely shifts slums from one place to another.[24] At worst, it destroys neighborhoods where constructive and improving communities exist and where encouragement could bring "unslumming" without drastic action.[25]

Low-income public housing has been closely related to urban renewal as an approach to the slum problem, largely because of the need for subsidized housing for many of the people relocated from project-clearance areas. In large cities of the United States, the typical projects have been multistory clusters of buildings, which Harrison Salisbury calls "new ghettos," to replace the old. "Until my nostrils ferreted out the fetid story ... I was not aware that in too many instances we have merely institutionalized our slums. We have immured old horror and new deprivation behind these cold walls."[26] Michael Harrington has described the traumatic experiences of former slum dwellers who encounter the impersonal bureaucratic administrative procedures of such new housing units.[27] The "odor" of the slum often remains, even though its character has changed. Most of all, new housing projects often, but not always, have little community feeling and responsibility, as Glazer and Moynihan have pointed out about those in New York City, and they are difficult to develop.

A powerful bureaucracy manages the project, and, whatever its intentions, its mere existence and its large functions inhibit the development of a community. There are few churches or any other kind of organization within the projects. Social isolation of tenant from tenant is common, because after all people have been bureaucratically assigned to projects and apartments, within a limited choice, rather than having located to be near friends, family, or institutions. Suspicion is also common, in part because there is fear of having transgressed one of the many rules of the Authority, and many tenants take the point of view that the less the neighbors know of them the better. The weakness of the bonds of community within the projects is true whether they are all Negro or partly Negro.

... The improvement of the projects as communities probably depends on a host of measures that are even more difficult than affecting their racial composition: involving the people of the projects in their management and maintenance, encouraging and strengthening forms of organization among them (even when the main purpose of these organizations seems to be to attack the management), encouraging forms of self-help in them, varying their population occupationally as well as racially by greater tolerance in admissions, reducing the stark difference of the projects from their surroundings by changing their appearance, considering more seriously the impact of their design on the social life that they enfold, all this and more have been suggested.[28]

Aside from the physical characteristics of new housing projects, the frequent requirement that a family move out when its income exceeds a certain maximum level has been criticized. Such a policy leads to a concentration of poor and multiproblem families in an area with no rising middle class. This concentration might be remedied by shifting the subsidy from the dwelling to the low-income family, allowing each family some choice in its rental selection. If income should rise, it would be possible for the family to purchase a home.[29]

As objections to mass slum clearance continue to mount and as the worst slums cease to exist because of past clearance, rehabilitation and conservation of existing structures have assumed greater importance in the renewal programs of many cities. As the Biddles have stated, "Because urban renewal has often destroyed traditional neighborhood communities and produced an alienation that is difficult to overcome, emphasis has been placed more recently upon neighborhood rehabilitation."[30] Rehabilitation involves repairs and improvements to bring structures up to the city's standards of sanitation, health, and safety, and conservation involves preventing the deterioration of standard structures. Those areas most likely to benefit from such neighborhood conservation methods are those that display vitality, as evinced in the presence of neighborhood identities, with community spirit among the residents, neighborhood stability, and general recognition of the areas as pleasant places in which to live.[31]

Another attack upon the physical features of the slum has involved "taking the profits out of slum properties." Among the most important such attacks has been that of rent controls.* Suggestions along this line have also included a

---

* The use of rent controls as a solution to the slum problem has been sharply criticized. In his study of housing policies in the United Kingdom, Sweden, West Germany, and the United States, Wendt stated that the use of rent controls to deal with the slum problem has not had a desirable effect and that rent controls have magnified the problem of slum housing and rendered its solution more difficult because standards of maintenance are lower. Considerable improvement has taken place where rent controls have been discontinued. Paul F. Wendt, *Housing Policy—The Search for Solutions* (Berkeley: University of California Press, 1962), p. 60.

system of greater taxation on the owners of slum property, a better balance between the land taxes and improvements, a more restrictive policy toward tax delinquencies in slum areas (where an owner may sometimes lose his property to the city and then have to repurchase it under conditions that, in effect, eradicate tax obligations), and various rehabilitative inducements in the form of credits or deductions for improvements.[32] Under the 1962 New York City Receivership Law, for example, the city can take over a building where there are major code violations and use the rent collected for these repairs.[33] Other methods for bringing about compliance with New York City municipal codes include the right to vacate a building considered unfit for human habitation, the power to initiate criminal proceedings against parties responsible for code violations, reduction of the maximum rents on those buildings still under rent control, and referral to the Department of Welfare, which can withhold payment of rents for public-assistance families who are living in substandard structures.* Government-subsidized rent for slum dwellers has also been proposed.

What started as an attempt to provide decent, safe, and sanitary housing for the poor living in slums has often turned into a means of providing civic centers and luxury high-rise apartments convenient to downtown for the middle- and upper-income people who work there. Attempts to "save the central business district" and to raise property taxes have, in many cases, overshadowed the need for improved housing for the poor. Although many families relocated for the projects have been moved into better housing, too often the reverse has been the case. A fair evaluation of the program as it is being carried out today can be made only by recognizing its true objectives in practice, rather than by concentrating on the stated objectives in theory. Judged as an aid to the slum dweller, the traditional slum-clearance program has had only limited success. Judged as a program to improve the appearance and livability of housing for the middle- and upper-class urban dweller and to reform the central part of the city to his standards and for his benefit, the program has scored much higher.

The traditional mass-clearance approach to the slum problem involves two ethical questions: "Should government officials use the taxpayers' money and the power of eminent domain to scatter residents of rundown areas of cities, demolish the buildings they once lived in, and then guide the reconstruction according to aesthetic, social, and economic standards which they feel to be more suitable?" and "Should the individual property rights of some people be

---

* A newer and more informal device to accomplish similar objectives involves the withholding of rent by the tenants, commonly called the "rent strike." The rent strike was first staged in New York City in the last months of 1963 and then spread to such cities as Chicago, Washington, D.C., and Cleveland. A civil-court judge in New York in 1963 stated that, although it is generally illegal for tenants to withhold rent, it is justified in cases involving constructive evidence that hazardous conditions existed. "Withholding Rent: New Weapon Added to Arsenal for War on Slumlords," *Journal of Housing*, 21 (March, 1964), 67–72.

sacrificed so that their land can be appropriated and sold by the government to other private individuals who will put it to a 'higher and better' use?"[34] Anderson answers that the federal urban-renewal program has not been successful, that it has been supported by and for the advantage of the financial and intellectual elite, and that it has worked to the disadvantage of the poor and especially the minority groups.[35] What is probably needed is more judicious selection of areas for slum clearance, wider use of rehabilitation measures, and recognition that the slum is more than a physical condition and that a limited perspective may make a slum situation even worse.

§ Social-Welfare Centers and the Problems of the Slum

Despite the enormity of their urban slum problems, most developed and less developed countries today have continued to rely mainly upon "social welfare centers" to bring about improvements among the masses in the slums by providing services of various types. The social welfare centers of today had their origin in the settlement houses that were established in the nineteenth century for the poor of England and for immigrants in the United States.[36] As used here, the term refers not only to welfare centers but also to "social settlements," "settlement houses," "centers," most "community centers" operated by private welfare groups, and to the more recent United States "neighborhood centers."[37] "Centers" give slum dwellers the feeling that something is being done for them and make both the government and the wealthy citizens feel more secure about efforts to improve the life of the poor. Closer inspection, however, raises serious questions both about the philosophy behind them and about their ability to solve complex urban problems on a broader and more permanent basis.

Theoretically, a center or settlement house is supposed to change the slum by providing services and exposing slum dwellers to a different set of values and norms. Typically, centers are rooms or even separate buildings where services like sewing, handicraft, and literacy classes, as well as occasional cultural activities, are offered. Usually there is a school for younger children, and often in developing countries free prepared milk is given to children and to certain adults. The area served by a center is seldom carefully defined. Space and fund limitations, however, make it impossible for a center to serve more than a fraction of the residents in what is often a large area. The staff usually consists of a few professional social workers and a number of volunteers, most of whom do not live in the area served. These volunteers, and even some of the professional workers, are usually from a higher social class, with more economic advantages, and are almost without exception better educated than the typical resident of the area. The policy board generally consists of people who reside outside the area, although there is sometimes token participation by area residents. The number of people actively involved is normally so small that the per capita costs are actually quite high. The following is an example that illustrates the inadequacy of welfare centers as a solution for the Indian slum problem.

Two centers served an area of textile workers' chawls housing some 200,000 persons. One had a creche for 50 children, another for 100, both groups being neat and clean and supervised by experienced teachers. The area, however, must have at least 25,000 children under the age of seven who were not in school. Nearby was the only recreational center in the area, consisting of one rather large room and four small ones. The daily attendance was from 200–600 persons, the women participating in a sewing group of 30, the men playing on two ping pong tables and using two wrestling platforms. This attendance is a small percentage out of 200,000 people in the area. Most of these persons came from areas immediately adjacent to the center. The persons in charge seemed to be doing things for the people. . . . Meanwhile masses of people live in misery and do little for themselves.*

A contemporary center in a lower-class Italian area of Boston has been described by Gans:

Elizabeth Peabody House, or Peabody House as it was called, was the largest settlement house in the area, its eight floors overtowering the tenement blocks it served. Although its program had been cut sharply in the 1950's, in 1958 it still conducted activities for children of all ages, adolescents, and adults. For the children, the House provided arts and crafts, athletics, dramatics, scouting, cooking classes, and game room activities, as well as a variety of activities for sexually segregated peers who were organized into clubs formed by the House staff. For the adolescents, there were similar activities, as well as dances, and a teen-age lounge in which they could dance or play a variety of games. The women had a Mother's Club and sewing and cooking classes. The men were also invited, but, since they never came, there were really no activities for them. The policy-making board and most of the staff came from outside the neighborhood. The board itself was made up largely of upper-class businessmen, most of them Yankee Protestants. The staff consisted of professionals as well as students from Harvard and Massachusetts Institute of Technology.[38]

Very often staff members, particularly the volunteers, are interested in "doing something for the underprivileged." Such an approach tends to create dependence among the people on the center and its staff rather than to develop a desire on their own part to work out solutions to their problems. While accepting the "alms" from the center, they often resent having to depend upon others, or they develop an exploitative attitude, seeking free services and even supplies of food from as many sources as possible and often, in the case of the

---

* The author has visited many such centers in India, the United States, and elsewhere. This passage is taken from notes on one such visit in India.

latter, selling them. This practice is particularly common in the developing countries.*

The staffs of welfare centers hope to change the way of life of the slum dwellers through the limited training that can be given and through example and exhortation. Gans has suggested that settlement-house people are "missionaries," in that they want the clients from the area to adopt their own behavior and values. In that sense, they constitute "outside" character-building agencies.[39] A study of Hamtramck, a Polish-American lower-class area near Detroit, concluded that settlement houses, although often helpful, could not wreak profound changes in the way of life of the people, as they are essentially undemocratic.

> Settlements everywhere have involved the moving in on an area by people from the outside apart from any initiative from the people to be served. The assumption has been that people cannot raise themselves by their own bootstraps. Thus, the securing of funds, the making of programs, the recruiting of staffs, and all other plans are made from the outside without asking "by your leave" of the prospective clientele. It is significant that the officers . . . and the chairmen of its standing committees, include no Polish names, and assuredly no residents of Hamtramck. Though this is generally typical of American philanthropy, it is not democracy; and it is to be doubted that any profound, permanent improvement in community conditions can be effected through such methods.[40]

Because of the middle- and upper-class origins and the professional training of most members of center staffs, it is difficult for them, except in rare instances, to share the perspectives of the people with whom they work. Too often, not only in India, but also in many other countries, this type of "welfare work" appears to involve a particular channel through which the wealthier people, particularly women, are able to achieve special status or even political prestige. There is also a tendency among these people to attribute the behavior and the way of life of the slum dweller to economic deprivation, poor housing, and absence of individual initiative. Gans has said of one Italian lower-class area in Boston that the settlement-house people "could not admit that the West Enders acted as they did because they lived within a social structure and culture of their own. Such an admission not only would have required the realization that change was much harder to bring about, but also that they had little or no control over the primary causes of such change."[41]

---

* In India, for example, powdered milk obtained from a center may be sold to sweet shops, and sewing machine needles and other articles may be "lost" or broken through careless use in free sewing classes. Years ago, Zorbaugh described how social agencies on Chicago's Near North Side slum made possible a sort of "legitimate graft," through which the small incomes of people in the area were considerably supplemented. Families prided themselves on their abilities to obtain more Christmas food baskets than did their neighbors, the baskets often not being wanted for any reason other than such competition. See Harvey Zorbaugh, *The Gold Coast and the Slum* (Chicago: University of Chicago Press, 1929), pp. 152–3.

In general, center programs involve only individuals, and little may be done to improve conditions in the surrounding areas. Consequently, the effect on the total community may be negligible. Some center staffs, particularly in developing countries, are aware of this problem and often try to organize clean-up campaigns, usually with the help of outside youth volunteers, to help improve sanitation. These campaigns are seldom successful, as improvements usually do not last long. Such efforts generally fail adequately to involve groups of people in self-help efforts, and, unless a group approach is made, the effects of the programs have no permanence. In addition to failure to use a broad-based group approach, center programs are not organized in such a way that credit for programs or successes can be given to the people in the area. Because of the organization of a center, credit for any accomplishments often goes to the center itself or to its staff, whereas failures are often attributed to the people's apathy and lethargy.

A further element that makes the use of social-welfare centers to deal with urban social problems in less developed countries ill advised is their connection, either direct or indirect, with political parties. As some missionaries may use food or other free services to promote conversion to their religions in developing countries, centers often use their free services to promote particular types of political image or altruistic service. People of opposing political beliefs may not wish to use the center, and a politically oriented center is likely to fail in its efforts to change a community of adherents to many parties. Its fortunes may fluctuate with political changes.

It is therefore unrealistic to hope that conventionally oriented community centers can successfully create an impact on the large-scale problems of cities in either developed or developing countries. This statement does not imply that the centers should be abolished, particularly in developing countries, where services are limited and where all types of organization can make legitimate contributions, but rather that the approach of the centers must be re-examined and reinvigorated with new and sounder techniques to stimulate real self-help, full neighborhood participation, and indigenous leadership among the residents. Social-welfare centers may bring about more significant changes in the urban way of life if the areas served are more carefully delimited, if they can be established on more modest bases, and if they can really be managed primarily by the people who use them and tied to representative citizen organizations in the areas. In recent years in the United States, many welfare centers and settlement houses have been renamed "neighborhood centers." In general, however, the basic philosophy has been little changed. Such centers operate largely as welfare centers, areas are seldom carefully delimited, and there are generally little real management and decision-making by representative area citizens. Here and there there are exceptions to this broad generalization, areas where the work is really citizen-oriented, but on the whole it fits.

§ Welfare Services and Slums in the United States

The welfare approach to social change in the slum is exemplified by the social worker who offers services to deprived families. This approach has been attacked as entirely inadequate to meet large urban-slum needs. In view of the massive nature of the problem, such programs for change are low in yield and high in cost, and they are impossible from a long-term political and economic point of view. The inadequacy stems, not only from the large number of professional social workers required, but also from the fact that middle-class social workers cannot adequately view the lower-class "client" and his problems. Too often social casework is divorced from the lower-class culture with which it deals, and it has developed a frozen frame of reference from which to attack the problems of the lower class.[42] It has drawn heavily on psychiatric and other psychological sources, erroneously assuming that the problems that haunt slum families are produced mainly by difficulties within families or within individuals. In an era of rapidly expanding knowledge about human behavior, practitioners must continually change and adapt their practical programs as new knowledge becomes available. Despite increasing evidence that the slum is probably the result of large-scale group problems arising from the social organization of slum life and the culture of the lower class, most social workers continue to be trained exclusively in casework.*

Too often those with a welfare approach have assumed that the problems of the slum arise from failures to provide sufficiently broad or adequate services. Hunter terms this view "the illusion of services," for there is little evidence that such services seriously modify the slum environment.[43] Where the slum dweller is apathetic, the services, whether for prevention of delinquency or for adult education, have largely gone unused. Social casework has often been more successful with the middle class or the upwardly mobile lower class. Slum youths exposed to delinquency often seem not to be touched by welfare services, or at least such services have had little effect upon delinquency. On the other hand, great enthusiasm has been shown among the lower-class poor for the services they want, reflecting, for example, the desire for literacy in Mexico and Africa and the interest in the Arabic language and African culture among the

---

* Of 9,058 students enrolled in schools of social work in the United States in 1965, only 494, or 5.5 per cent, had field placements in community organization. This figure represents, however, a substantial increase since 1960, when it was only 1.6 per cent. These data are from Community Organization Curriculum Development Project, Council on Social Work Education. For a discussion of the role of social work in an urban society, see Alfred J. Kahn, "The Function of Social Work in the Modern World," in Kahn, ed., *Issues in American Social Work* (New York: Columbia University Press, 1959), and Harold L. Wilensky and Charles N. Lebeaux, *Industrial Society and Social Welfare* (New York: Russell Sage Foundation, 1958).

Black Muslims in poor urban areas of the United States. The people must be motivated to want the services offered.

Whyte has questioned the social-welfare approach to social change in slum areas in Boston's North End, where he found that the settlement-house social workers were far removed socially from the vast majority of Italian slum residents.[44] In the first place, very few of the employees of the settlement house were of Italian origin, and those who were held the most menial jobs. The middle-class social workers made little effort to understand either the Italian culture, the working-class way of life, or the predominant values in this working-class area. "The social worker's conception of his functions was quite evident," said Whyte. "He thought in terms of a one-way adaptation. Although, in relation to the background of the community, the settlement was an alien institution, nevertheless the community was expected to adapt itself to the standards of the settlement house."[45] Gans found much the same situation in the West End of Boston, where he lived as a participant observer in the same way that Whyte had done twenty years earlier in the North End. Applying the term "caretaker" to anyone who provides services to people, Gans found that the "caretakers" from the outside, those who staffed the welfare agencies, the settlement houses, and the library, were not able to see that West Enders had their own social system and culture. Nor were they able to understand the needs and perspectives of the West Enders.[46] The duties and objectives of these "caretakers" were destructive to many of the most meaningful values in the lives of these people. The "caretakers" wanted, for example, to break up the peer-group society, with its person orientation, and to replace it with an object orientation, so that the West Enders could participate in "purposive" groups within the neighborhood and city. The "caretakers" also desired to reduce the dependence of the individual on his peer group, to bring parents and children closer together, and to weaken the adult-centered focus of the household. They believed that West Enders did not accept these objectives (desirable by middle-class standards) because of the overcrowding and poor housing of the neighborhood. An admission that the West Enders lived the way they did because they had their own social structure would have required admitting also that the "caretakers" really had little or no control over the causes of change.[47]

It is perhaps unfair to leave the impression that all social-welfare efforts to change slums are like those described by Whyte and Gans, but the social-work profession has generally and unwittingly encouraged the belief that more and better social-welfare services will solve slum problems. This belief has not reflected a careful analysis of the basic causes of slums and the social problems existing there, and, in many cases, it has reflected adversely upon social work for its inability to cope with ever-increasing problems of the slums. Furthermore, the adequacy of programs of welfare services in slum areas has seldom been evaluated. Hunter has pointed out that many youth-serving agencies in the slums claim to be preventing delinquency without the slightest evidence that they actually do. "On the contrary a little digging beneath the glossy pages of the fund-raising leaflets usually shows either that the most delinquency-exposed youth are not touched by the agency, or that, if they are touched, the touch has little effect on their delinquency. They may use the gym with gusto and then step outside to violate the societal norms."[48] The ideal evaluation of welfare programs would require a detailed input–output study. In such a study, a number of comparable population groups would be selected, and they would be assigned at random to experimental and control groups. Base-line data on both groups would be gathered and a study made of the program's impact on the experimental group over a period of time: the results would be compared to those of the other group at the end of a given period.

Experimental efforts are being made to achieve broad coordination of public services to slum areas, in an effort far exceeding those of the health and welfare councils of traditional social work, which coordinate primarily private social-welfare agencies and services. In Oakland, California, various agencies of the city, county, and state governments are coordinated through the Oakland Interagency Project, and pressure is exerted to stimulate the slum dweller's acceptance of changes that these agencies feel would benefit him. The chief purpose of this organized effort is to bring about greater communication among all levels in the public agencies that had previously been working separately and unilaterally on many problems.[49] The scope of this initial program was expanded, through a Ford Foundation grant, to mobilize all governmental and some private agencies for a concerted attack on the city's numerous slum problems. The express purposes of the program are to reverse the process of slum development and associated problems of delinquency, school failure, broken homes, and declining community leadership; to help integrate newcomers into community life; and to raise the physical standards and the cultural and social levels of slum neighborhoods.[50] The neighborhood school was chosen as the most appropriate and effective medium for achieving the objectives of the project. It was believed that the major potential for change and improvement rested with the youth of the community. Through the schools, access to all students and indirectly to their parents was provided, and the school buildings also furnished physical centers and meeting places for the various neighborhood projects.

An important feature of the Interagency Project is called "social planning and interagency coordination" and is directed at enhancing the effectiveness of community institutions in resolving problems and contributing to the achievement of the other objectives. It had been observed that the problems confronting the community were not structured as the agencies were structured, and it was believed necessary to reshape agency operations to fit the problems. Unilateral and uncoordinated actions by various agencies had to be avoided, and integration of all major operations at all levels had to be achieved.* It is significant that the Oakland project does not involve the creation of an entirely new semi-autonomous agency to deal with slum problems; rather, it works through existing government bodies and private groups by encouraging mutual cooperation. The results of this approach may have importance for future projects in urban community development.

It seems apparent, however, that, regardless of form, the provision of free welfare services, without emphasis on the direct involvement of slum residents through their contributions in planning, some financial assistance, or labor, is likely to create continued dependence.† It does not lead to real self-help, and, without a determination on the part of the slum people themselves to change the norms and values of slum life, it is unlikely that a *slum* will be basically altered. At most, certain individuals will be helped, while the slum and the majority of the people who live there will continue relatively unchanged. Those affected by the slum must come to assume some responsibility for change. This question of involving slum residents in planning and services will be discussed more fully in Chapter 13.

§ *Economic Opportunity*

In many parts of the world, various groups have begun in the slum, and, as they have improved their economic positions many members have moved out. In the United States, for example, slums at various times have been predominantly populated by English, Irish, German, Swedish, Jewish, Polish, Italian, and other ethnic and religious groups. As each group has risen in the economic scale and become acculturated to the general values of society, many of its members have tended to move to better areas. Today many ethnic groups still reside in the slums, but slum residents are increasingly Negroes, Puerto Ricans, and poor native white migrants. Because the latter groups find it difficult to move up in the economic scale, the belief has developed that the solution to the slum problem is primarily one of speeding up economic and educational opportunities. The fact that *the slum* has continued to exist to socialize new migrants, however, has often escaped the attention of those who take this approach, as has the fact that many problems of the slum cannot be attributed entirely to economic deprivation.

---

* The basic philosophy of another program, Action for Boston Community Development (ABCD), is that any city's slum social problems are so intertwined that they cannot be solved in piecemeal fashion. In many ways, the Boston program is similar to that of Oakland, in that it relies heavily on special educational programs for the culturally disadvantaged and on special job training.

† The Oakland project does involve some citizen community programs, but they are not the major emphasis of the experiment.

There is no question that measures to bring about improved economic conditions will be of great value to slum people. These include more adequate wages, guaranteed minimum incomes, undiscriminatory employment policies, accessible and inexpensive credit, programs to train and retrain youths and adults, more effective training for certain occupations and improved social security and public assistance.[51] Education programs also have to be improved, so that teachers are of better caliber, reading skills can be improved, more tutoring services can be made available, and the school functions can be geared to the improvement of the community as a whole.

The lack of economic and educational opportunities, however, has resulted in one-sided approaches like that embodied in the concept of anomie, which has been used by Merton and others to explain the apparent higher incidence of such deviant behavior as crime, delinquency, mental disorder, alcoholism, and suicide among the lower class, particularly those living in slum areas.[52] According to this view, anomie reflects the inability of the social structure to provide for all members to achieve the goals of society. Deviant behavior in the lower classes, according to Merton, is the result of the clash between institutional means and cultural goals, which occurs in the striving for success goals by legitimate means. Modern urban societies emphasize such competitive goals as material gain and higher education but provide limited means for achievement of these goals because of differentials in status. The greatest pressure for deviation arises among the lower socioeconomic groups like those living in slums, where opportunities to achieve economic success are fewer and the level of education lower. Those denied access to legitimate means may adopt such illegitimate means as delinquency and crime or may retreat from the goals through such "adaptations" as mental disorder, alcoholism, drug addiction, and suicide.

This functional theory of anomie has been challenged on the grounds that it is not substantiated by empirical research findings and that, as an explanation, it is deficient in social psychological theory as well as in theory explaining how deviant behavior originates and comes to be defined.[53] It does not explain why certain deviations lead to symbolic reorganization at the level of self-regarding attitudes and roles and others do not. Such factors as subculture, urbanism, and especially the role of collective deviant adaptations are not taken into account.

Ample evidence exists, furthermore, that deviant behavior cannot be explained by poverty alone. Such groups as Japanese- and Chinese-Americans and Jews have lived in slum areas of American cities under conditions of great poverty but with little juvenile delinquency or crime. Rates of drug addiction have been found to be highest not among slum dwellers but among doctors and nurses who have ready access to drugs and know their effects.[54] Crime has been found to be extensive among such white-collar groups as businessmen, doctors, and lawyers.[55] The crime rates among rural dwellers are generally much lower than among urban residents, despite the fact that rural dwellers are generally poorer. Studies of the business cycle suggest that it bears little or no direct relation to most forms of deviant behavior other than suicide.

Cloward has attempted to reformulate Merton's theory so that deviant behavior can be explained, not only by differential access to legitimate means, but also by the differential access to illegitimate means characteristic of most slums.[56] In the slum, there are greater opportunities to acquire deviant roles, largely through deviant subcultures. Together with Ohlin, Cloward has developed a more complete statement in an explanation of delinquent gang subcultures in slums.[57] They argue that delinquent subcultures arise mainly when access to legitimate means for the attainment of the success goals of the larger society, to such means as economic and higher educational opportunities, are blocked; differential access to delinquent and criminal means plays a part, though a subordinate one. "The disparity between what lower-class youth are led to want and what is actually available to them is the source of a major problem of adjustment. Adolescents who form delinquent subcultures, we suggest, have internalized an emphasis upon conventional goals. Faced with limitations on legitimate avenues of access to these goals, and unable to revise their aspirations downward, they experience intense frustrations; the exploration of non-conformist alternatives may be the result."[58] Beside many of the criticisms directed at anomie theory in general, this reformulation by Cloward and Ohlin has been criticized for being largely culture-bound and heavily restricted to the minority situation in the Negro slums of large urban areas in the contemporary United States; for not defining clearly the success-goal aspirations of slum boys, except for economic and educational goals; for assuming that success goals are fully appreciated by people living in slum areas; and for barely recognizing the extensive violation of ethical and legal norms in the general adult society among all social classes, including white-collar crime.[59]

A number of projects in the United States have been heavily influenced by these theoretical approaches, however, and have been primarily directed at juvenile delinquency and other youth problems in slum areas from the point of view of the need for greater opportunity.* Such programs, although they sometimes have other facets, attempt to improve slum conditions primarily by increasing economic opportunity and emphasizing education, job training, and placement. For the most part, they are directed at helping slum youths to break the self-perpetuating cycle of their poverty.

Youth service corps have been created to provide work experience and

---

* For a statement of the principles involved in the "opportunity approach" see Irving Spergel, *Racketville, Slumtown, Haulberg: An Exploratory Study of Delinquent Cultures* (Chicago: University of Chicago Press, 1964), Chapter VII, "Community Action and Delinquent Subcultures." The development of citizen participation through block organization is the last of a series of seven proposals for change that emphasize economic and educational opportunities.

training for youths between the ages of sixteen and twenty-one, focusing on projects useful to the neighborhood that also afford varied training opportunities. Youth job centers have also been established to assist in finding jobs; to publicize available work-experience, training, and educational programs; and to offer guidance and placement services. Several experimental programs have attempted to break down the barriers facing "the slum child in the slum school." Special classes have been proposed to teach improved instruction methods for lower-income youngsters, and attempts are being made to raise the standards of the regular school systems. Programs planned to solve the problems of anomie and lack of opportunity have been centered in the academic and vocational schools of the slum areas.

All these programs are important to the solution of the slum problem, but there appears to be too much emphasis on providing opportunities for the "anomic poor" through vocational training, education, and greater employment opportunities. The assumption that most people of the slum will immediately grasp such opportunities is questionable, as is the view that delinquency, drug addiction, and other forms of deviant behavior arise from restrictions on opportunity. The per capita costs of such programs, even with government support, are likely to be disproportionately high for the results achieved in a given area. At most, a relatively small proportion of urban slum youth can be reached, and meanwhile there are continued additions to the area through natural increase and rural migration. Unless the slum way of life is also significantly altered, there is likely to be limited participation and a high drop-out rate from such programs. This overemphasis on free vocational services may also develop into a new form of charity, adding to the dependence felt by slum dwellers. As most slum people do not fall within the scope of these training programs, the latter are likely to have little impact on neighborhoods of the poor. The basic problem is not the acquisition of skills by a few but effecting changes in the way of life of the slum poor in general, encouraging them to assume responsibilities.

It is questionable whether or not the so-called social psychological aspects of urban poverty—apathy, powerlessness, lack of planning, and hostility to outside agencies—can be directly attributed to poverty. A given level of income does not necessarily produce certain consequences in psychological attitudes. In fact, subgroups among the urban poor may display reactions quite different from the psychological aspects of poverty. For example, very low-income families may have high levels of aspiration; leaders with high levels of motivation may be found among the poor; lower middle-class families with high aspirations and little deviant behavior may actually have lower incomes than do many poor people receiving economic aid and benefits; members of certain religious groups of which poverty is characteristic may have high aspirations; and, finally, influential intellectual leaders in Asia and other parts of the world like India may receive very low incomes.[60] Furthermore, Haggstrom claims that an increase in income among the poor in the United States has not altered these characteristics, nor has an increase in real per capita welfare and unemployment payments altered such characteristics. Differences in income and welfare payments among the various states do not appear to change the general characteristics of the slum and poverty.

Despite rural improvement programs, one can assume continued large-scale migration to cities and consequently into the slums. This migration means that job training of slum dwellers will present a constant problem but will itself not materially alter the *slum* as a social and cultural system. In the past, people have moved out of the slum, but the slum seems to endure and to be ever replenished.[61] An example of a different situation is Stockholm, a city of nearly a million people but without slums, even though it has many old buildings and continues to grow by migration. New arrivals in the city do not move into slum areas.* Finally, although the increased-economic-opportunity approach may have some merit in an affluent society, it is unrealistic for the solution of slum problems in less developed countries. The economic development of such countries is generally so inadequate and the poverty so general, the slums so large, the migration from rural areas so great that efforts to deal with the slums primarily through singling out slum dwellers for economic improvement are virtually impossible.

Fortunately, several projects in the United States have attempted to combine increased economic and educational opportunities with broader efforts to change communities. Such a combined approach has been attempted, notably by Mobilization for Youth in New York City, Harlem Youth Opportunities (HARYOU), Community Progress in New Haven, and the Chicago Youth Development Project.[62] Funds for such programs have come largely from several federal government agencies, and some have received substantial assistance from the Ford Foundation and other private sources. The projects have also stressed the development of the communities and changes in the subcultures of the areas through increasing citizen participation. The United States Economic Opportunity Act of 1964, which places emphasis on vocational training and work opportunities, also provides for community-action programs.

The services provided through the Mobilization for Youth project, which is concerned with a sixty-seven-block slum area in Manhattan containing a population of 100,000, mainly Negro and Puerto Rican, are diverse. In addition to providing extensive training and job-placement and subsidizing the initial employment of some youths by employers who normally refuse to hire people

---

* Although the absence of slums in Stockholm is partly related to large-scale economic improvements in the country, major credit must be given to adult education in the folk high schools and to extensive study circles within the trade unions, which over many years changed, through self-help, the "way of life," the norms and values, of millions of lower- and working-class Swedes.

without prior work experience, the project has an extensive "homework helper" program, preschool education, reading clinics, and guidance counselors. It also tries to bring together teachers and parents in common activities, to organize unaffiliated adults into groups concerned with their common problems and becoming politically active, and to provide such other services as legal aid to the indigent, consumer education, apartment-finding help, clinical services for narcotic addicts and the mentally disturbed, and a reintegration program for juvenile offenders released to the neighborhood from penal institutions. It is hoped that such a "saturation" program in high-delinquency areas will prove the best possible method of crime prevention.[63] In this and other projects it remains to be seen whether attempts to change the slums through the people's own efforts will eventually receive due emphasis or whether efforts will continue to be misplaced primarily on providing greater economic opportunity and services by outsiders.

Chapter 6

URBAN COMMUNITY DEVELOPMENT

It has become an intriguing intellectual exercise to seek labels for the age in which we live. Some have called it the "Nuclear" or "Space Age." Others refer to it as the "Age of Materialism." Auden has termed it the "Age of Anxiety." Perhaps a more appropriate label is the "Age of the City." At no time in the history of man have so many people lived in cities or have the social problems of an age become so linked to those of the city. Whereas the world population has increased nearly 165 per cent during the last 150 years, the urban population has risen 2,535 per cent, in what has been termed not merely a "population explosion" but a world-wide "urban explosion." Cities of 100,000 or more contained 1.7 per cent of the total world population in 1800; in 1960, they contained 20.1 per cent. In 1800, fewer than fifty cities in the entire world had 100,000 or more inhabitants; none had a million. Today more than fifty cities have populations in excess of a million. Most of the less developed countries of Asia, Africa, and Latin America are primarily rural and agricultural, but this statement tends to obscure the urban increases that have occurred in the past ten to twenty years. Between 1950 and 1960 the proportion of the population living in cities of 100,000 or more increased about one-third faster in the less developed regions than in the developed areas of the world. People will continue to swarm to the cities. Between 1960 and 1970 alone, it is estimated that 200 million people will move to the cities of Asia, Africa, and Latin America, most of them to pile up in already congested slums.[1]

The growth of the modern city has produced a complex and difficult world in terms of social relationships. Urbanism as a way of life tends to be characterized by extensive conflicts of norms and values, by more rapid social change, by increased mobility of the population, by emphasis on material goods and individualism, and by marked decline in effective communication.[2] These characteristics are generally products, first of all, of size, which, as the number of inhabitants increases beyond a certain limit, brings about changes in people's relationships and in the nature of the community. Secondary contacts largely replace primary contacts, thus increasing impersonal and superficial contacts.

Intimate personal groups like the family, caste, and tribe become less meaningful. Second, the great heterogeneity of the city is, in part, a product of the migration of many people of diverse origins and backgrounds. An urban population is a heterogeneous mass, a mixture of races, ethnic and regional backgrounds, religions, occupations, social classes, and, in Asia and Africa, castes and tribal groups. In some cases, enclaves of related groups maintain some semblance of former unity, but there are indications that unity even in these groups is breaking down with increased migration, housing pressures, and changing attitudes toward discrimination.

As a result of this heterogeneity, few common values or norms exist, and individuals are confronted with conflicting standards of behavior. Formal controls like law administered through the police become ways of enforcing uniform standards in the city. Rural people, taught as they have been to accept the supremacy of a single rule, may become skeptical of the validity of that rule when they discover, under urban conditions, that breaking it does not necessarily bring about social ostracism or censure as they had supposed. In general, the move to the city opens up a way of life called "urbanism," which is much different from that of the more traditional rural world.[3]

Basic to these problems of urbanization and urbanism is the decline in effective communication among the members of an urban society and its effect upon the social control of behavior. A report on the effects of African urbanization in the slums pointed out that, whereas the family or the tribal group was the center of life and the focus of all social activities in the past and still is in many rural areas, these familial institutions have been greatly weakened in areas undergoing social change. Reports from Africa have demonstrated the importance of this factor in the emergence of juvenile delinquency.[4]

Several recent studies, particularly of suburbia in the United States and of some urban slum neighborhoods in the United States, Mexico, India, and Africa have tried to minimize the impersonality of the city. According to Janowitz, sociologists have failed to take into consideration that "impressive degrees and patterns of local community life exist within ... metropolitan limits."[5] Certainly a degree of intimate life does exist in any city, in both the neighborhood and the place of work, but it is generally not nearly the same as that in villages or rural areas. Furthermore, in the city, a person shares almost daily many impersonal relations in which his identity is not recognized, and in which he is confronted with a variety of conflicting norms and values. To admit the need for exercising caution to avoid overstating the universal presence of urban characteristics does not minimize, however, their importance as a framework for understanding much of contemporary life and urban problems.

Comparisons indicate that increased urbanization and urbanism have been generally accompanied by increased rates of juvenile delinquency, crime, mental disorder, alcoholism, and many other forms of deviant behavior in almost all countries. With few exceptions, the rates for most forms of deviant behavior are far greater in the urban than in the rural areas throughout the world. There are also indications that tensions among certain racial and ethnic groups may be increasing under conditions of urban living. Problems involving the physical deterioration of housing, sanitation, and health are by no means confined to the cities of the developing countries, where they constitute the chief difficulty in city living. These characteristic problems of urban areas are not spread uniformly over a city but tend to concentrate in what are termed "slum" or "problem" neighborhoods. Today societies are becoming urbanized faster than urban institutions have been able to adjust.

A particular characteristic of rapidly expanding urban areas has been the ever-increasing institutionalization of society and the individualization of man.[6] Institutionalization can be seen in the scope of governmental and nongovernmental services in the city, all of which have been the inevitable results of the presence of large numbers of people concentrated in particular areas. Government has grown larger, there are more specialists to take care of varied services, and the active participation of individual people in the improvement of urban society has correspondingly diminished. Often the lines of communication among the people, the city officials, and the politicians break down, and the individual citizen ceases to feel personally involved.[7] Even private or voluntary agencies are frequently cut off from those whose needs they presumably serve. In both developed and, particularly, developing countries the rural migrant to the city, as well as the older urban resident, becomes bewildered by the impersonality of the city, the municipal government, and often the factory for which he works.

In all the cities of the world, some way needs to be found in which urban residents, particularly new arrivals and those living in slum areas, can develop a sense of community, of importance and unity within the structure of the city. The other issue is self-help, and one writer has declared that the urban social system "cannot be perfected by clever manipulation, no matter how well trained, nor by eager philanthropists working alone and from the outside. The toughest problem is that of generating indigenous leadership and the spirit of self-help."[8] Another problem is to find some way to speed up the process of change in slum areas and, at the same time, to affect large numbers of people.

Urban community development offers a new approach to some of the problems of urban areas generally and of the slum in particular. It involves two fundamental ideas: the development of effective community feeling within an urban context and the development of self-help and citizen participation, of individual initiative in seeking community integration and change. In other words, this approach relies directly on the slum dwellers themselves. If their apathy and dependence can be overcome and replaced by pride and a sense of initiative, the slum dwellers can make good use of their "millions of hands" and their own resources, meager alone but large when pooled, in trying to solve their manifold problems.

§ *The Background of Community Development*

The term "community development" has come into use mainly since World War II; it designates organized efforts to improve the villages of developing countries, most of which had been under colonial rule, and to overcome their residents' apathy through emphasis on self-help. The term has spread fairly rapidly in different parts of the world where such programs have developed, supplanting such earlier terms as "mass education," "village improvement," "rural welfare," "rural development," "rural community self-help," "community organization," and "fundamental education." A United Nations report on community development in rural areas has emphasized its components: community self-help, and technical assistance.

> The term "community development" has come into international usage to connote the processes by which the efforts of the people themselves are united with those of governmental authorities to improve the economic, social, and cultural conditions of countries, to integrate these communities into the life of the nation, and to enable them to contribute fully to national progress. This complex of processes is then made up of two essential elements: the participation by the people themselves in efforts to improve their level of living with as much reliance as possible on their own initiative; and the provisions of technical and other service in ways which encourage initiative, self-help and mutual help and make these more effective.[9]

RURAL COMMUNITY DEVELOPMENT

The poverty, hunger, disease, and other problems of villages in less developed countries like India have been difficult to master because the social environment has not stimulated self-improvement and the acceptance of technical assistance from the outside. Limited local initiative and self-help, however, have existed in a few places for a long time. In recent years, they have become more widespread, so that residents have combined voluntary self-help efforts and technical skills and have been organized as part of national economic- and social-development programs called "rural community development." A number of factors contribute to the necessity for such programs: the decline of community spirit and leadership under colonial rule; the poverty of the people and their governments; low productivity due largely to primitive methods of production; the lack of resources for investment and development; serious health problems; and high illiteracy rates. As a result of these long-prevailing conditions, the social and economic life of the village community has often stagnated. In a survey of developing countries, Poston concluded that apathy and failure to appreciate the possibilities of self-help have been the chief obstacles to village progress.

In the newly developing countries countless millions of people, the majority of whom live in peasant villages, lack the incentive to apply themselves to the task of improvement. People everywhere want better conditions and a richer economy, but after centuries of mental and physical starvation, the people have no confidence in themselves or in the idea that there is anything they can do to change the situation. The great masses are not only unaware of how to go about helping themselves, they frequently are not aware of the fact that self-help is a possibility. Ancient customs, a fatalistic outlook on life, long established attitudes of resignation and superstition, a deeply ingrained set of fears and suspicions, and rigid social and cultural patterns act as powerful blocks against the people's initiating any effective action of their own toward social or economic progress.[10]

In rural areas where individuals have been asked to assume a measure of responsibility previously assumed or seized by autocratic governments or imposed by colonial powers, the principle of self-help has seemed revolutionary. Village people have found it hard to comprehend that they should have a real voice in determining their future. "They have been exploited, lied to, and imposed upon for so many centuries that they seem unable to grasp the possibility that anyone honestly intends that they should participate in making any of the real decisions about their future. In consequence, it has been most difficult to get them involved in any fundamental way."[11] Villagers can do many things for themselves; for other things they must have government assistance. Community-development programs thus involve cooperative endeavors between government and villagers. Villagers have learned to produce more food, improve their sanitation, build their own houses, help to build schools and health centers, organize their own recreation, construct feeder roads, and improve their wells.[12] To do so, however, the local communities have often needed both technical assistance and financial aid. Such government aid, if not overdone, has stimulated community self-help efforts. In India before 1948, governmental efforts to raise agricultural production and to improve the conditions of village life had failed, in general, because little effort had been made to deal with the multifaceted needs of the village simultaneously. In addition, programs were imposed from without, with little attempt to develop the people's understanding of the objectives and methods of change. After 1948 pilot projects were launched in community-development schemes, involving self-help, which have gradually been instrumental in changing the course of India's progress in solving the multitude of village problems and helping to overcome the stupendous obstacles to its transition into an increasingly productive agricultural economy.

Although there had been, in various parts of India over the previous two or three decades, a number of community-development-type programs, a few pilot projects were especially significant in launching broader community-development programs. In 1948, a government pilot community-development project was launched at Etawah in Uttar Pradesh through the efforts of the American planner and architect, Albert Mayer, and there were also projects of considerable significance in two refugee colonies, Faridabad and Nilokheri, which "had demonstrated that village people could generate their own capital and reconstruct their own villages with their own labour."[13] In the pioneer Etawah project, the rehabilitation and reconstruction of a village were undertaken by the villagers themselves.*

A nation-wide program of rural community development was initiated in 1952 to reach all of India's more than half a million villages through a combination of self-help and technical assistance. This massive assault was to cover all aspects of village life—agriculture, animal husbandry, public health and medicine, education, cottage industries, programs for women and children, and irrigation projects. The contribution of the people themselves to the program has been substantial and has, in large part, been responsible for the progress that has been achieved. In the original program, there was an administrative organization in the Ministry of Community Development, which involved state staffs and new administrative subdivisions consisting of 100 villages each, with total populations of about 60,000 and covering 120–200 square miles each. An officer was in charge of each development block, and he was assisted by advisers in agriculture, animal husbandry, public-health, rural industries, and so forth. This staff supervised the village-level workers, or *gram sevaks*, who were responsible for stimulating self-help and, to a large degree, for "supervising" the development of five to ten villages.

Certain changes were made in the program in 1958, as the villagers had begun to feel that the program was being imposed upon them from above and they had lost some of their enthusiasm. One of the programs begun in 1957 was the training program for the *gram sahayaks*, or village leaders. A primary objective in the training of village leaders was to make sure that the cooperatives and *panchayats* were regarded as real people's institutions. "Their primary purpose in existing is to provide village people with the essential organizations to work together, first, to function as a village community and second, to make full and effective use of the resources of government, both manpower and financial, available to them."[14] By 1963, the new program, called Panchayati Raj, had been adopted by over half the states of India and was being implemented by the others.

---

* Albert Mayer, *Pilot Project, India: The Story of Rural Development at Etawah, Uttar Pradesh* (Berkeley: University of California Press, 1959). This book provides a history and discussion of the pioneer Etawah project in rural community development and of its problems and achievements. Albert Mayer had been an army engineer in India during World War II and had been invited back to India by Prime Minister Nehru to try out his ideas about community development. Similar projects, termed "mass education" and involving efforts to promote the active participation of villagers, had been launched in the 1940s in Africa. See British Information Services, *Community Development: The British Contribution* (London: Her Majesty's Stationery Office, 1962).

The new plan provided for a high degree of village autonomy in planning, decision-making, and implementation, which had previously been managed in combination with government officers. Although the latter continue under the new system, theoretically they merely advise the villagers. The elected *panchayat* has charge of all development programs for each area. A cooperative frequently handles economic functions, and the village school is being developed to undertake educational, recreational, and cultural activities. Associate organizations like those for women and youth, farmers, and artisans are linked to the *panchayat* in development activities. The cornerstone of the new system is the village *panchayat*, or council, which is elected by all the villagers.* At the block level, the *panchayat samiti* is elected by the various *panchayats* within the block. At the higher district level, covering about one million people, or about 170 villages, is the *ẓila parishad*, elected by the *panchayat samitis* within the district.

The idea of village self-help has spread throughout Asia, Africa, and Latin America, where large-scale government programs have sought to bring isolated villages into the modern era. At least thirty countries now have far-reaching programs of community development in rural areas.[15] In many less developed countries, such programs for village community development have often been initiated with great enthusiasm and with expectations of almost unlimited success. Later it is discovered that people do not easily change their practices and that years are often necessary. As Carl Taylor has written: "New ways of doing and thinking always create psychological insecurities' and sometimes create ethical and spiritual insecurities. Change automatically creates uncertainty about what is really happening and what can be expected. Furthermore, old ways practiced for generations are likely to be considered sacred. Beliefs about their rightness are taken as much for granted as the air people breathe."[16]

A development parallel to rural community development in developing countries has been the set of large-scale programs for community action and citizen initiative in planning and self-help in small towns and rural areas in the United States. Rural sociologists, community-development workers, and extension workers have made significant contributions both in technique and in theory, some of which are being applied in developing countries as well.[17] There have also been efforts to stimulate self-help with more limited problems like literacy.[18] The kibbutz, or cooperative agricultural village, of Israel represents one of the most complete forms of self-help and citizen initiative.[19]

Community-development experience in rural areas has increasingly raised the question of the possibility of a program in "urban community development."

---

* There are indications that the system of elections in the Panchayati Raj has created caste and factional disputes. See Carl C. Taylor, Douglas Ensminger, Helen W. Johnson, and Jean Joyce, *India's Roots of Democracy: A Sociological Analysis of Rural India's Experience in Planned Development Since Independence* (Bombay: Orient Longmans, 1965), pp. 569–70, for example, for a discussion of the problems of caste and class in community-development work. Also see Beatrice Pitney Lamb, *India: A World in Transition* (New York: Frederick A. Praeger, Inc., 1963), p. 217.

For example, a 1958 publication of the British Colonial Office stated that the "techniques of community development can and should be used in urban areas particularly because of the growing importance of the new towns in developing countries."[20] It has also been pointed out that cities have an importance out of all proportion to their size, for they are centers of rapid political and economic change and have the greatest political influence on the life of a country. Because of the heterogeneity of cities, people need to discover a new sense of belonging and to develop new loyalties. United Nations reports have pointed out the possibility of applying rural community development to city slums through neighborhood-development projects. "The slum is still a product of group and individual apathy which works against any effective application of local or outside resources. The task of inducing changes through the neighborhood on its own volition still has relevance to the processes of community development."[21]

COMMUNITY DEVELOPMENT IN URBAN AREAS

In addition to work in rural community development, a number of self-help projects in urban areas has also indicated the feasibility of such an approach. In the cities of the more highly developed Western industrialized countries, there has been increasing concern with the large-scale degeneration of the local community as a meaningful form of association. Cities are often characterized by considerable impersonal relations and lack social cohesion. Various possibilities have been considered as to how best to generate community feeling in such cities, and in this search efforts have been made to restructure and replan or to decentralize the city into smaller units. In other cases, there have been efforts to create new forms of primary association in the city to replace old forms. As Ross has pointed out, these efforts are aimed at developing "(1) meaningful functional communities as members of which individual citizens may have some sense of belonging and control over their environment, and (2) a new sense of neighborhood in the large metropolitan area through creation of citizens' councils and other forms of neighborhood organization."[22] In the United States, these efforts have been primarily directed at the problems of juvenile delinquency. One of the most important contributions to the development of the program came from the Chicago Area Projects, which in 1934 initiated a neighborhood self-help approach to the control of delinquency and other neighborhood problems in several slum areas there.* Developed by the state of

---

* Clifford R. Shaw and Jesse A. Jacobs, "The Chicago Area Project: An Experimental Community Program for Prevention of Delinquency in Chicago" (Mimeographed; Chicago: Institute for Juvenile Research, n.d.). Also see Anthony Sorrentino, "The Chicago Area Project after 25 Years," *Federal Probation*, 23 (June, 1959), 40–5; and Solomon Kobrin, "The Chicago Area Project—A 25-Year Assessment," *The Annals*, 322 (March, 1959), 19–29. This general approach has been adopted in several other cities in Illinois and, in 1963, by the Chicago Youth Development Project in two inner-city areas of Chicago.

Illinois, this program involved the organization of neighborhood citizen councils to enlist help from residents in planning, supporting, and operating constructive programs that the citizens would regard as their own. The program stressed the training and utilization of local community leaders to assume major roles in actually developing the program, in consultation with the professional staff. The activities were regarded primarily as devices for involving local residents in constructive community enterprises. An evaluation of these pioneer urban slum self-help projects, which are now more than twenty-five years old, concluded that the program successfully developed civic pride and stimulated the people to assume active roles in the prevention of delinquency and other local problems.

1. Residents of low-income areas can organize and have organized themselves into effective working units for promoting and conducting welfare programs.
2. These community organizations have been stable and enduring. They raise funds, administer them well, and adapt the programs to local needs.
3. Local talent, otherwise untapped, has been discovered and utilized. Local leadership has been mobilized in the interest of children's welfare.[23]

In a somewhat similar program during the 1940s, the Back of the Yards Council also made substantial changes in the neighborhood community through its own efforts.[24] This area, located southwest of the stockyards in Chicago, was a slum district made famous by Upton Sinclair in *The Jungle*. It had the highest delinquency rate, the highest infant-mortality rate, and some of the worst housing in the city. The area was characterized by conflicts among nationality groups. With the help of outside leadership, particularly Saul Alinsky, a militant citizen organization was formed with a slogan, "We, the people, will work out our own destiny." The Back of the Yards Council fought through the years the political machine of Chicago, the meat-packing companies, citizen apathy, and conflicts among ethnic groups, and it succeeded in obtaining improved services from the city, higher wages at the stockyards, recreational facilities for the youth of the area (including a summer-camp program), a credit union for the working men of the area, cooperation from the savings and loan associations in making loans for home improvement in the area, and efforts by residents to improve their housing. The area has become, in Jane Jacobs's terms, "unslummed."

In the United States during World War II, as in many other countries, the average urban citizen was widely involved in self-help activities. The United States Office of Civilian Defense made extensive use of block organizations to disseminate civilian defense information and to carry out its program.[25] In some cities, thousands of local block-committee members called upon residents to enlist their support of civil defense and to hold local meetings. Thousands of citizens were active in the Red Cross, salvage collections, air-raid precautions, defense councils, and other projects. Of particular interest were the defense councils set up by the Office of Civilian Defense in 1941 to protect the population, to facilitate citizen participation, and to aid national morale. More than 11,000 local councils were established. Some cities had block plans on a territorial basis; for example, Nashville, Tennessee, was divided into twenty districts, according to census tracts, and they were, in turn, divided into blocks, with a leader for each one. Chicago had 15,000 blocks, with a captain elected in each by the residents. Although carried on in many lower-class areas, this type of work was generally more successful in middle-class than in lower-class areas.

Indigenous citizen self-help organization in middle-class areas, particularly in the suburbs, has been increasing in the United States since World War II. Since 1954, some citizen participation in planning has also become a characteristic feature of urban-renewal programs. Although private neighborhood welfare organizations have also been trying to create more broadly based neighborhood centers, they generally continue to utilize a welfare-service approach and nominal citizen participation in planning and operation. They do not therefore represent true community development, although several social-work theorists in community organization have called for the development of more indigenous neighborhood leadership and self-help.[26] A significant neighborhood-development movement, the Hyde Park–Kenwood Community Conference, developed in the 1950s, dealt with the problems of a Chicago middle-class interracial community that was deteriorating into a slum. It made wide use of a citizen-participation scheme through a system of block organizations.[27] Since 1960, experimental efforts to develop local community feeling and self-help in slum and near-slum areas have rapidly expanded, particularly under the stimulus of the Ford Foundation and the federal government. These efforts have included, for example, Harlem Youth Opportunities and Mobilization for Youth in New York City; ACTION-Housing neighborhood extension projects in Pittsburgh; Community Progress, Inc., in New Haven; Community Progress, Inc., in East St. Louis, Illinois; the Chicago Youth Development Project and the near North Side Demonstration Area in Chicago; and the various community-development projects, using indigenous leadership, of the Industrial Areas Foundation. There are increasing indications that self-help is being recognized as an important tool for solving slum problems. Its applications ranged from a self-help project to retrain the unemployed in a Negro slum area of Philadelphia, Opportunities Industrialization Center,[28] to large-scale, self-help housing improvements in the Mexican community in Dallas,[29] to organized citizen vigilante patrols in New York City to prevent robberies and assaults.[30] Neighborhood organization for community improvement, for example, has been carried out in the Adams-Morgan district of Washington, D.C., located less than a mile from the heart of the city, with a population of about 15,000, half white and half Negro.[31] Each block in the area has been organized by a citizen self-help group. Citizen committees have been formed to deal with membership, hospitality, property maintenance, streets and parks, property exchange, police and fire problems, zoning and building matters, welfare and juvenile affairs, and legislation. Much of the activity has been directed toward the cultivation of better living habits like proper disposal of trash and prevention of the accumulation of debris in the streets, improvements in housing, and assistance to police in dealing with loitering, vagrancy, and delinquency.

These different types of projects seek to find a process to transform certain urban areas, particularly slums, into strong neighborhood communities. They have been classified into four types of approach: neighborhood conservation, social invention, self-determination, and neighborhood extension.[32] Neighborhood conservation is illustrated by the work of the government of New York City to help citizens in older neighborhoods assume more responsibility for neighborhood conservation. Social-invention organizations in such places as New York, New Haven, and Oakland seek to improve the urban establishments by offering citizens, particularly deprived ones, such improved urban services as wider involvement of citizens in community schools. Greater self-determination among people of deprived areas is encouraged by the Industrial Areas Foundation, which helps the people form power organizations capable of getting what they need. The neighborhood-extension approach, like that of ACTION-Housing, Inc., in Pittsburgh, seeks to create initiative among neighborhood people for change and then to furnish needed services to neighborhood people working cooperatively with city government and other agencies.

Many experimental slum projects of the "social invention type" however, tend to represent primarily the efforts of "outside" agencies, together with the extensive use of local public and private welfare agencies, to change the slums. Even though indigenous workers from an area are sometimes employed, funds for the program, often of considerable size, come almost entirely from outside sources, as do key personnel and the members of the boards of directors. Relatively little of the direction, planning, and credit for achievements in an area is really in the hands of those who reside in and are a part of the slum. Slum residents continue to receive many free services and make little financial contribution to programs of change in their areas. Consequently, it is difficult to term such projects really "self-help," and this factor may have considerable negative consequences for possibilities of large-scale permanent social change in the slum area.

There have also been examples of indigenous efforts at self-help in the urban areas of developing countries.[33] Probably one of the first organized community-development projects in a developing country was the Lyari project in Karachi, Pakistan, which was initiated with United Nations technical assistance in 1954. In this project in a 150-year-old slum area, an effort was made to help people to develop some community feeling and to engage in self-help activities. This project, which eventually involved 50,000 people, continues to be active, dealing, partially on a self-help basis, with sanitation, school construction, typing classes for youths, and sewing classes for women.[34] Although it was called a "self-help" project, much assistance has come in the form of donations from wealthier groups, and considerable direction has been given by professional workers. In Hong Kong, a program of self-help activities guided by neighborhood organizations called *kaifongs* has been in operation since 1950. It is supported mainly by contributions from local Chinese businessmen and receives professional assistance from the government of Hong Kong.[35]

Although the term "community development" is new and is often used with different connotations, there is an increasing trend toward adoption of urban community development in different parts of the world as an approach to the solution of slum problems. A United Nations European meeting was held on urban community development in 1959 and an Asian meeting in 1962. In 1961, the United Nations issued an important publication on community development in urban areas.[36] The International Conference of Social Work devoted its 1962 meetings to urban and rural community development.[37] In the United States, there are several large-scale urban community-development projects. By 1965, there were three major urban-community development projects in India.* Urban community-development programs, which are part of the municipal governments, were started under Ford Foundation auspices in Delhi in 1958, in Ahmedabad in 1962, and (under the auspices of the American Friends) in Baroda in 1965. Although there are no national programs for urban community development in developed countries, several are in existence in other parts of the world, particularly in India, Pakistan, the Philippines, Colombia, and Venezuela.[38] Urban community-development work has also been carried out in Ethiopia since 1964.

§ The Approach of Urban Community Development

The ingredients of an urban community-development program are the people and their problems, the government and voluntary resources available to stimulate self-help, and urban community organizers to locate and develop indigenous leaders and to translate their problems in such a way that they can be adequately interpreted by government and private agencies. In this sense, urban community development is "the collective initiative of families living in the same neighborhood and support of their efforts through services rendered to them by a higher level of government."[39] Urban community development in-

---

* Calcutta was planning another, and a national program of twenty projects, of 50,000 people each and located in a large number of cities, was begun in 1965.

volves democratic action, stressing citizen participation, self-help, and self-determination through group action, in meeting the problems created by city life. In urban community development, people become involved in responsible action directed toward solving mutual problems. Such citizen participation is a process through which individual citizens have direct roles in the physical and social changes affecting their immediate lives. The approach assumes that a community has the capacity to deal with its own problems. Even in the most "hopeless" slum and among the most apathetic residents, latent skills can be developed to alter the environment. The approach to the problems of the city slums through urban community development involves the following elements:

1. creation of a sense of social cohesion on a neighborhood basis and strengthening of group interrelationships;
2. encouragement and stimulation of self-help, through the initiative of the individuals in the community;
3. stimulation by outside agencies when initiative for self-help is lacking;
4. reliance upon persuasion rather than upon compulsion to produce change through the efforts of the people;
5. identification and development of local leadership;
6. development of civic consciousness and acceptance of civic responsibility;
7. use of professional and technical assistance to support the efforts of the people involved;
8. coordination of city services to meet neighborhood needs and problems;
9. provision of training in democratic procedures that may result in decentralization of some government functions.

The four main objectives of an urban community-development program applicable to the slum are development of community feeling, self-help, indigenous leadership, and cooperation between the government and the people in the use of services. The first requires the creation of effective community relationships, where none or few exist, for the purpose of bringing into urban life some of the organization that unites people in the villages and large family units of rural areas. Such territorial units help to induce neighborliness, to decrease the isolation of urban living, and to make possible the development of progress of community action. The establishment of effective community relationships is extremely important, as the ties that bind people together in villages often weaken or disappear in the city. Ethnic, regional, tribal, caste, and even family ties often become less meaningful, and in many cases no new ties develop to replace the old ones. People may live in close physical proximity yet still not constitute a community. In urban areas, in the absence of the recognizable communities of rural areas, it is necessary to build real communities in those areas where people have been brought together from many different backgrounds.[40] It is necessary to create small urban neighborhood units. "While family ties and caste loyalties have proved remarkably resistant to urban influences and have partially compensated against the anonymity and indifference of urban environments, it will be useful to seek leverages of change in the solidarity of small neighborhood groups and groups with linguistic affinities—social cohesions that appear to be significant."[41]

Where a community exists in an urban area, there is more than physical proximity: There are common symbols, meanings, and goals uniting the people. They have a feeling of common purpose, of belonging, of being neighbors. This feeling makes them a community, for effective communication and social interaction have been established among the members of the area. A community can thus be considered a territorially organized system of people, which shares common facilities and goals and meanings, in which there is effective communication among the members, and in which the people identify with the area in which they live.[42] These common factors and interrelationships have been analyzed in a community model. Such a community has been defined as a "combination of social units and systems which perform the major social function having locality reference."[43] These major functions are five in number: production-distribution-consumption, socialization, social control, social participation, and mutual aid. The first involves the processes of producing, distributing, and consuming goods and services necessary and desirable for everyday life. Socialization is the process by which a subgroup, in this case a community, transmits prevailing behavior patterns and social values to its members. Social control is the means by which the group enforces conformity to norms by its members. Social participation takes place through families, kinship groups, and neighbors. Mutual support during sickness and other difficulties is frequently provided by the group.

A second goal of urban community development is the discovery of "effective ways of stimulating, helping and teaching people to adopt new methods and learn new skills."[44] The "development" aspect of community development involves stimulation of self-help and active citizen participation in urban affairs among slum people. As a form of social and economic development, it uses self-help, with technical assistance only to implement this self-help.[45] As many needs are only vaguely felt and as the misery and squalor of the slum are often accepted, the problem is to help people to recognize their needs in ways that will result in the attainment of desired objectives. More permanent improvement in slum living conditions cannot be achieved by a largely apathetic collection of individuals; the people themselves desire change and are prepared to exercise their own initiative in planning and carrying out projects and programs to meet their own needs.

Many people assume that slum residents will move up the social scale merely by receiving economic and educational opportunities from outside sources of power; it is often this very dependence on others, however, that leads to apathy, further dependence, and failure to develop necessary economic and educational skills. This dependence over a period of time becomes institutionalized in habits, traditions, and organizations in the slum. It becomes "customary" to drop out of school, to reject conventional agencies of control, to scale down aspirations. Financial means, therefore, are only one of the many kinds of power source; feelings of personal creativeness among slum people may also give a sense of power.[46]

Third, without some sense of community in a heterogeneous area, it is difficult to promote self-help. On the other hand, improvement of the community itself comes through recognition of the need for change and for citizen cooperation in such self-help activities as building latrines, repairing houses, paving lanes, immunization against disease, keeping the area clean, maintaining schools, or dealing with delinquency. The people themselves need to become involved in the identification of needs, the selection of priorities, and the carrying out of activities. To bring about change successfully, potential indigenous leadership in local areas needs to be identified and developed. Such indigenous leadership then carries direct responsibility for initiating change among the people. Successful change in a slum area depends a great deal upon the motivations and interests of such leadership.

Finally, the nature of slum life makes it doubtful that people can improve their patterns of life and their surrounding environments without the aid and stimulation of government and other agencies. As in rural community development, urban citizen efforts require some financial help and technical assistance in such areas as sanitation, public health, education, and recreation. The municipal administration itself needs to make more effective use of public services, schools, and the health and recreational media. A program of self-help cannot provide a satisfactory substitute for these essential services. It can, however, by creating a functional relationship with the local authorities through self-help schemes, not only help to fill the gap in many essential services, but also to make more meaningful the proper use of these services by the public. "Urban community development is therefore concerned not only with stimulating citizen participation and self-help schemes but also with helping to mobilize public voluntary and traditional services in association with the people's own efforts."[47]

There are considerable possibilities, for example, in improving slum conditions in developing countries through self-help or aided self-help housing, in which the householder himself constructs his house. A number of such organized government programs has been carried out in various parts of the world, particularly in Puerto Rico, and there have been several such programs in India, especially in Madras and Delhi.[48] Abrams has suggested that there are many possibilities for such an approach to slum housing problems, particularly when the urban migrant comes from a rural background where houses have traditionally been erected on a self-help basis or when craftsmen in the area know how to build houses.[49] Self-help housing may be in many cases the only alternative because of lack of other resources. Such self-help efforts may also stimulate the building of roads, schools, and community facilities if the government helps with funds and materials. On the other hand, Abrams believes that self-help housing alone cannot be a solution to urban slum-housing problems. In the United States, several community projects in urban areas have involved self-help efforts to improve deteriorated housing.[50]

In this connection, another goal of community development in urban areas is to prepare neighborhood communities to share responsibility for the administration of certain basic services not adequately provided by the municipality. Urban areas have become so huge and sprawling and city administrative units so large that effective supervision of sanitation, parks, schools, and other services has become increasingly difficult. A certain degree of decentralization of civic authority in the slums might result in greater support for government and thus help to overcome some of the apathy and hostility displayed by many slum dwellers.

§ Differences between Urban and Rural Community Development in Developing Countries

Although many of the problems and goals are similar, urban community development in developing countries differs from rural community development in several respects. Both emphasize community, self-help, citizen participation, and technical assistance from government.[51] A primary goal of rural community development is the economic improvement of the villager and the nation through greater production of agricultural commodities. Efforts are made to teach the farmer improved methods of cultivation and animal breeding, the use of improved seeds and proper fertilizers, and broader projects for building irrigation systems and establishing marketing, production, and consumption cooperatives. The development of small-scale and cottage industries is also directed at general economic improvement and the reduction of unemployment. The economic goals of rural community-development projects is thus specifically related to village life. Rural community-development economic schemes cannot be transferred to the city without great modifications.* Urban community development is unlikely ever to be as comprehensive an economic program as is its rural counterpart.

An urban program has fewer possibilities for directly affecting the economic conditions of a neighborhood. One writer has even said that community development is not suited to urban areas because economic action on the neighborhood level is a practical impossibility when people work other than where they

---

* Peter Hodge has pointed out that rural community-development techniques did not work in the urban areas of Ghana because of the pronounced differences in the two settings. "Community Development in Towns," *Community Development Bulletin*, 10 (March, 1959), 26–30.

live.[52] He also questions its applicability on the grounds that the neighborhood has limited meaning for its residents and that the important role of government in various spheres of urban life diminishes chances for real community-development projects. There is much that can be done, however, to improve the literacy, employment skills, and work motivation of urban slum people through community development. Furthermore, as one of the goals of urban community development is the improvement of slum living conditions, it might be said that, with improved conditions, the city workers may well be able to perform more productive work and that their families would enjoy healthier and more satisfying lives in improved physical surroundings.

In contrast to most urban slum areas, where little feeling of community or neighborhood exists, villages in developing countries generally have long traditions and some sense of village pride and identity. Although this sense of pride and belonging is an asset in any rural community-development program, the villager's ties to tradition and his fear of change hinder his acceptance of modern technological advances, even the simplest ones. Whereas, on the surface, the slum dwellers' problems seem insurmountable, the very absence of traditional ties may facilitate more rapid social change. The village migrant to the city may feel the loss of his family, caste, and regional-group ties, but he may be better prepared for building a new identity in his urban situation.

Rural areas are less complex in social structure and consist mainly of relatively homogeneous communities with common interests. Relationships among village people are primarily intimate and personal, whereas city residents have far more impersonal relationships. There is seldom even a common occupational tie, as is characteristic of rural areas. Urban slum people often tend to live more anonymously and may not even know many of those who live in close physical proximity to them.*

Geographic isolation characterizes most villages; because of the size, density, and heterogeneity of the urban population and the extremely difficult problems of urban slum areas, however, operational units even smaller than villages must be organized if community-development work is to be successful. People who live in urban slum areas are physically less isolated than are rural dwellers and are less accustomed to relying upon their own resources to solve their problems. Water, electricity, and sanitary facilities, for example, may be available but minimal. Slum people are more likely to expect the government municipal departments, welfare agencies, politicians, and so forth to deal with these problems, despite the fact that the inadequacy of public facilities is the result of too-

---

* On the other hand, in India, the nature of village caste relations often means close physical proximity with great social distance between groups. Village social structure is fairly well organized, with emphasis on rather clearly defined caste relationships and large-family organization. With the decline of these relationships in city life, new social patterns must be found.

rapid growth of urban populations. Sometimes urban slum problems, compared to those of rural areas, are intensified by a multiplicity of available agencies with so little coordination that the individual does not feel the impact of any one of them.

Rural communities are more stable, slowly growing units. With the exception of women who have married into village families, newcomers are relatively rare. Most people have always lived in their villages. City populations, on the other hand, have often grown rapidly and include large numbers of newcomers from various rural regions. Most city slum areas contain heterogeneous masses of people brought together by chance or necessity. There is often greater distance in the city between the place of residence and the place of occupation. Community-development work in urban slum areas is thus likely to involve a more unstable population. Migrants from rural areas are poorly prepared for the life of the city, and often they have no intention of settling there permanently, preferring to keep their village ties. They do not identify with the community or with plans for community development. In most villages, councils, headmen, village elders, *panchayats* and caste *panchayats* have long been in existence, and rural community development relies on revitalizing them. In urban areas, citizen development councils must be almost entirely created through urban community-development work, even though there are often existing traditional groups.

On the other hand, because urban slum people, although apathetic, see social change all around them, they are likely to be more emancipated from traditional views and more inclined to accept some development programs than are village people. They are more exposed to outside influences and are probably less likely to be entirely satisfied with simple improvement, as is the case with villagers. They see the great contrast between wealth and poverty, between wants that have been stimulated and satisfaction of such wants, between what is and what should be, and between expectations and accomplishments.

§ *Different Approaches to Community Development*

The term "community development," whether urban or rural, has several different meanings, depending upon the way it is viewed. Sanders has suggested that it be viewed as a process, as a method, as a program, or as a movement.[53] As a *process*, it focuses on changes in social relations. People of a community may be accustomed to having their decisions made by a few leaders within or without the community; they come, through community development viewed as a process, to make decisions themselves about matters of common concern. They move from a state of minimum to one of maximum cooperation, from participation of the few to participation of the many, and from a condition in which all specialists and other resources come from the outside to one in which residents make the most of their own resources and capabilities.*

Viewed as a *method*, community development is a means to an end, a way of achieving a goal through this process supplemented in part by other methods to achieve some objectives of the national government, private welfare agency, or the people themselves. Community development as a *program* emphasizes a set of procedures with emphasis on activities as well as methods. The emphasis is on carrying out the program of activities rather than on what happens to the people in the program. Finally, community development as a *movement* involves an emotional approach that stresses the idea of community development. As a movement, "it tends to become institutionalized, building up its own organizational structure, accepted procedures and professional practitioners."[54]

§ Community Development and Related Concepts

Urban community development should be distinguished from a number of other concepts or frames of reference. It is not the same as "community improvement," which may be accomplished in many ways other than, for example, the use of citizen self-help. It is not synonymous with action taken by an agency for community improvement. "Much of the fog which sometimes impedes serious discussion is created by social workers, the medical profession, agricultural extension specialists and others who, in making use of community development techniques to achieve agency set goals, equate it with their own specialist roles in human organization and advancement."[55] Community development is not the same as economic development alone, either rural or urban, for the emphasis in a community-development program is also on the development of the people of the community and on changes in their practices. "Success cannot be measured by adding up the material projects completed . . . the product of successful community development . . . is stable self-reliant communities with an assured sense of social and political responsibility."[56] Finally, it should not be confused with either urban development and town planning or with community organization.

"Urban development," or what might be called "city" or "town" planning, concentrates on physical planning and facilities, although it may include community development. Such activities are usually carried out by govern-

---

* Also see J. D. Mezirow, "Community Development as an Educational Process," *International Review of Community Development*, 5 (1960), 137–50. The Biddles have defined community development as a "social process by which human beings can become more competent to live with and gain some control over local aspects of a frustrating and changing world." William W. Biddle and Loureide J. Biddle, *The Community Development Process: The Rediscovery of Local Initiative* (New York: Holt, Rinehart & Winston, Inc., 1965), p. 78.

mental or semigovernmental agencies and are focused on such physical aspects of the community as housing and slum clearance, improved transportation, increased water supply, more efficient industrial locations, and better-planned commercial centers. By itself, it does not necessarily involve community relations or citizen self-help, and failure to include these elements in development plans has sometimes resulted in catastrophe. "In its narrower meaning associated with the activities of planning boards, the term has little relationship to community development, although it should be noted that there is a continuous ferment within, or at least on the periphery of, the planning profession which agitates for a broader conception of planning and looks toward more consideration being given the social aspects of planning, as related both to the task objectives of planning and to the process through which plans are formulated and decisions reached."[57]

Consequently, urban problems can be viewed in either their physical or their community-development aspects. Physical situations affect in various ways the manner in which community development can be applied:

1. *Community creation.* New towns or new districts of existing towns are constructed, giving rise to new community structures and not merely to imitations of existing urban communities.
2. *Community renewal.* Areas that have become physically outdated are reconstructed, resulting in disturbance of long-established habits of work and leisure and all aspects of social and cultural life.
3. *Community rehabilitation.* Improvement of the lives of the people is sought where districts have grown up in social, cultural, or vocational isolation because of too rapid expansion or lack of planning.
4. *Community reorganization.* An area adapts to rapid change in size or in the prevailing occupations of its inhabitants, often neglecting the need both for new types of services and for changed attitudes among the people.
5. *Community integration.* Periurban areas or small adjoining districts that become absorbed physically in the spread of a city are particularly affected, and coordination of services and measures to alleviate intergroup tensions are necessary.[58]

"Community development" refers to something quite different from what is usually denoted by the term "community organization," which is widely used in social work. As generally used, the latter refers to the coordination, extension, or initiation of such existing agencies and institutions in a community as welfare agencies, churches, service clubs, and schools. More typically, such work deals with the coordination and elimination of overlapping services and planning to bring about greater efficiency among social-welfare agencies, as in the case of a health and welfare council. It is generally carried out by boards of the more educated, wealthy, and professionally oriented citizens in the community, under the guidance of professional social workers. Instead of emphasizing structural changes, community development is more functional and process-oriented. It also covers a wider field of activities. Beside emphasizing self-help by the average citizen and indigenous leaders, it "initiates a people-directed process that is based upon their own perception of their needs. It recognizes the necessity for the discovering or creating of a community, in a process that will utilize the existing social structure, but that will help to create new organizations and institutions when needed."[59] Ross, a writer in the field of social work, uses the term "community organization" in much the same way as "community development" is used.*

Sherrard has attempted to link community organization, as conventionally defined, with efforts in the more highly industrialized and urbanized Western countries to deal with problems resulting from rapid social and technological changes. In his view, community development is associated with predominantly rural, developing societies.[60] Community-organization work has been concerned with attempts to correct "social imbalances, to redress social wrongs, to achieve new syntheses and to these ends to develop new services or patterns of service and to help with the problems of those individuals and those segments of society suffering for one reason or another from the results of rapid social and economic change."[61] On the other hand, community development is an important means of inducing social change in traditional societies. It is an attempt to release the latent strengths and potentials of people in order to deal with poverty, disease, ignorance, and rigid political control. Community organization, at least in the United States, has consisted largely of private welfare activities, whereas community development has been a government concern in developing countries. From the point of view of programs, community development in emerging countries deals with such basics of human existence as food supply, eradication of disease, and elimination of housing shortages; in highly industrialized Western societies, the problems are more likely to be those of juvenile delinquency, family relations, and aging. Sherrard's distinction

---

* See Murray G. Ross, *Community Organization: Theory and Principles* (New York: Harper & Row, Publishers, 1955); and Ross, *Case Histories in Community Organization* (New York: Harper & Row, Publishers, 1958). In a meeting in Rio de Janeiro, in 1962, the International Conference of Social Work attempted, although not too successfully, to distinguish between community development and community organization. It concluded that "Community Development is a conscious and deliberate effort aimed at helping communities to recognize their needs, and to assume increasing responsibilities for solving their problems thereby increasing their capacities to participate fully in the life of the nation." On the other hand, "Within this context Community Organization is a complex of techniques designed to involve people, specialists and technical services to mobilize and facilitate the effective use of resources for community development." *Urban and Rural Community Development*, Proceedings of the XIth International Conference of Social Work (Rio de Janeiro: Brazilian Committee of the International Conference of Social Work, 1962), p. 29. In social work there is increasing recognition of the need for both greater emphasis on community organization and changes in the curriculum to develop more effective workers for community programs. An extensive study of community needs, curriculum, and other aspects of community organization was begun in 1965 through a large project grant given to the Council on Social Work Education.

seems artificial and does not sufficiently recognize the essential differences in the natures of the two concepts.

"Community organization" will probably be supplanted in urban areas in the United States by the term "community development," as it has been in Europe and in many developing countries. Warren has correctly pointed out, however, that, if community development is to be viewed as a deliberate and sustained attempt to strengthen the social ties of a community, what he terms "the horizontal pattern," then it cannot be confined to preindustrial countries, nor is it concerned solely or even primarily with industrial development.[62] Sanders has explained in part why "community development" is tending to supplant "community organization."

> More and more, people have been speaking of *community development* in preference to *community organization*. There may be two reasons for this: first, the health and welfare field has studied and publicized the techniques and procedures of community organization to the point where this term has taken on a social work connotation with many people. Where this has happened, those who were thinking in broader terms than the social welfare field found some other term more appealing. Second, *development* has a more popular appeal to most Americans than *organization* and certainly ties in much better with the economic approaches whose sponsors think of themselves as being involved in community development.*

Beginning with Chapter 7, a study of an experimental program in urban community development in the slums of India is presented. Although the discussion deals with India, the principles, procedures, and problems described have relevance to the slums of other developing and developed countries. Slums have more common features than differences.

---

* Irwin T. Sanders, *The Community: An Introduction to a Social System* (New York: The Ronald Press Company, 1958), p. 391. Dunham has pointed out that community development, as applied in rural areas, implies more concern than does community organization with the economic aspects of community life and more emphasis on integrated technical assistance. See Arthur Dunham, *Community Welfare Organization: Principles and Practice* (New York: Thomas Y. Crowell Company, 1958).

PART THREE

URBAN COMMUNITY DEVELOPMENT
AND THE INDIAN SLUM: A CASE STUDY

Chapter 7

THE DELHI PILOT PROJECT IN URBAN COMMUNITY DEVELOPMENT

Local authorities in Indian urban slum areas, like those in many developing countries, cannot provide even the basic facilities for the majority of their citizens. Accommodations are limited, many areas are congested, health hazards are great, adult illiteracy is on a mass scale, recreational facilities are minimal, and poverty, unemployment, and underemployment haunt the bulk of the population. Municipal governments and voluntary organizations, always limited in funds and competent personnel, are unable to cope with more than a fraction of the appalling problems that face them in the rapid and chaotic growth of slums in highly urbanized areas.

And, like other developing countries, India faces the great task of bringing about tremendous basic changes in the economy through rapid industrialization, increased agricultural production, and restrictions on population growth, while simultaneously increasing economic opportunities, housing, and physical facilities for urban dwellers. Such vast and basic changes cannot be brought about in a short time. In the meantime, and certainly for many years to come, the people of the slums, and urban India generally, must have substantially improved living conditions.

Any decision that little can be done to improve the environmental conditions of the urban slum dwellers until the total economy grows substantially would, in effect, condemn millions of urban people of this and a subsequent generation to continued misery and might even delay the entire developmental program. A solution must therefore be found, one that is likely to result in substantial changes not for a few but for millions of slum people, not for the future but for the immediate present. Any such plan must be realistic in terms of the enormity of the problems, the density and rapid growth of the population, and the limited financial resources available.

In 1958, Delhi became the site of the first experimental project in urban community development in an Indian slum. This city was chosen for this pilot project for a number of reasons. First, as the capital of the nation and a major city of the world, its conditions are of particular concern to the national government. The sudden expansion of the city after independence brought in its wake many civic problems. Second, the slum problems of Delhi are representative of those of the other major Indian cities; those of Calcutta and Bombay are perhaps greater, and those of Ahmedabad, Hyderabad, and Madras are somewhat smaller. Any procedures found suitable to the capital city might therefore be applicable in other Indian cities.

Delhi is one of the most historic cities of India, in fact, of all Asia, for it has been the capital of many empires. At least seven cities have been built on or near its present site. In 1911 the British government was transferred from Calcutta to Delhi because of the latter's geographic position and historic associations. Adjacent to Delhi a new city was constructed over a period of eighteen years, which became the actual capital. New Delhi, as this new city was called, became the capital of free India in 1947.

Following the establishment of British rule in Delhi the city became an increasingly important commercial and political center, and a period of slow but steady growth in population began. In 1901 the population in Delhi was 208,575, and by 1941 it had increased to 695,686; by 1951 it was 1,414,855.[1] The total population in 1961 was 2,359,408, representing a fourfold growth in twenty years. After independence, about 450,000 Hindu and Sikh refugees from Pakistan came to the city, whereas only 150,000 Muslims left (see Table 3).

Contributing to the growth of Delhi was its position of commercial and industrial leadership in north India: Chandni Chowk, the main street, has long been famed for its bazaars. Delhi's chief industries are cotton textiles, metal manufacture, pottery- and brick-making, and chemicals. Some plants are large, but much manufacturing is carried on in small establishments. Today Delhi is the third largest city of India, and it has been predicted that, by 1970, it will become the second largest, with a population between six and eight million; by the year 2000 it is expected to contain between seventeen and thirty-three million people.[2]

§ *Urban Problems*

New Delhi, with its population of 300,000, is quite European and modern. Old Delhi, however, is a vivid example of a traditional Indian city, although many parts are quite modern. Cows and bulls wander on the streets and among the foodshops; an acrid smoke pall from tens of thousands of dung cooking fires hangs over the city in the morning and evening; everywhere streets are packed with men dressed in every conceivable costume and headdress from pajamas and dhotis of *khadi* to immaculate Western dress; great varieties in height, skin color, eye structure, and facial features reflect the myriad races and ethnic groups left over from the Mongol, Persian, Afghan, and other invasions;

in front of small shops selling silver and gold jewelry, cloth, and other objects fat merchants sit cross-legged waiting for haggling customers, their short-sleeved, collarless, long white shirts hanging out; large billboards and sign carriers advertise garish and romantic scenes from the latest Indian movies; the continual squeaking of old-fashioned rubber bulbs serve motorcycle rickshaws and other taxis as horns; horse-driven tongas clatter and whips crack against tired horses pulling excessive loads; and trucks and slow, patient bullocks, the "trucks" of the East, move along in the dense traffic.

In the midst of this general confusion, Delhi's huge and dense slum population lives among a squalid chaos of tenements, hovels, shacks, and bazaar stalls scattered through narrow congested streets, alleys and lanes, where open drains are often blocked with refuse, garbage, and excreta. Many areas lack adequate

Table 3
Growth of Population in the Metropolitan City of Delhi

Year	Population	Percentage Increase Over Last Census
1901	208,575	8
1911	232,837	12
1921	304,420	31
1931	447,442	47
1941	695,686	56
1951	1,414,855	103
1961	2,359,408	67

latrines, water taps, and electric outlets. As in other slum areas, the infant-mortality rate is high, and smallpox, cholera, and other diseases harvest their heavy annual toll. Many slum dwellers do not avail themselves of modern medical care because of ignorance and reliance upon folk and religious beliefs. Illiteracy rates are high, but many adults see no reason to become literate or even to encourage their children to go to school. Many women, anxious to earn additional incomes for their families, can neither find employment nor produce sufficiently remunerative handicrafts because of insufficient training. Cultural and recreational activities for adults and children are usually lacking.

Apart from the various physical and social conditions characteristic of Indian slums, the bazaars located in or near all residential areas pose their own particular problems, beside adding to the total picture. They seem to have an infinite past and an aimless future. These colorful yet generally unattractive places, through which countless people pass and repass many times each day, are sources of chaos and confusion, as well as of filth and disease. The drains are often choked with garbage and filth, and dirty water flows in all directions. A broken water tap may continue to waste water for days without attention, and, in some bazaars, children and even adults urinate and defecate in nearby drains.

Articles for sale are indiscriminately displayed, food handlers show an amazing disregard for hygienic principles, and signboards are haphazardly, insecurely, and unaesthetically erected. Extensive and unauthorized encroachments on the pavements are chronic features of any bazaar and are a source of great inconvenience.

Despite deplorable physical and social conditions, the Delhi slum dwellers do little themselves to correct the situation. Over all hangs the deadly air of apathy, and there is an almost total absence of civic or social responsibility. The people have little faith in or awareness of their capacities to do anything and leave solutions entirely to national, municipal, or welfare institutions. They depend upon local authorities and at the same time are antagonistic toward them because solutions are seldom forthcoming. On the other hand, they do little to cooperate with the authorities. Water taps, refuse cans, electric bulbs in public places, and manhole covers are stolen, and streets and public places are dirtied in many ways. For example, the municipal authorities or some private welfare agency dispatches workers and youth volunteer groups periodically into a slum to clean it. The temporary results appear to have little effect upon the slum dwellers' way of living. One newspaper account of such a municipal "cleanliness campaign" in Delhi recorded the results:

> The Corporation's broom sweeps clean. Take the cobblers' township in Nai Basti, Jamuna Bazaar, for instance. Into this slum of tin-roofed shacks descended a horde of Councillors, officials of the DMC Health Department and "volunteers." It was June 27. The open drain running through this home of Delhi's cobblers was cleaned and disinfected. The shacks were given a spray and the one-and-a-half-foot lanes that divide one line of shacks from the next were cleaned of mango and banana peel, rubble, and dirt. The good deed done, the broom-wielders returned to their daily life.
>
> I visited the same setting on Wednesday. The open drain was filthy, the lanes were littered with peel and rubble and the occupants of the township went about their daily work. . . . And so life goes on in Basti Mochian. It will require more than an occasional broom-wielding campaign to convert the residents to cleaner living, and also greater amenities.[3]

Slum neighborhoods accommodate increasing mixtures of castes, occupations, and regional origins. Although members of a homogeneous group may live in close proximity and may even predominate in a certain area, housing pressures make it more and more difficult for large numbers of people with similar social characteristics to form exclusive groups. There is evidence that, although caste is still important, this importance is declining in Indian cities to-day.[4] Caste remains particularly important in the villages, where members of each caste tend to live in a separate section and to associate mainly with one another. Marriage barriers are rigidly observed, even among the subcastes. In most of village India, an upper-caste member cannot eat with or receive drink from a member of a lower caste; in fact, in some sections, he cannot even touch members of the lower castes. Water may be taken from one's equal or one's superior but not from one's inferior unless it is served in a brass rather than a clay pot. Each caste may have several wells and special places of worship, in order to avoid pollution.

Although such changes vary according to the particular castes and social strata of society, urban living conditions are rapidly modifying strict adherence to caste regulations. In addition, such regulations and restrictions will be further modified as city-born children experience fewer caste regulations and restrictions than did their parents. Although urban inhabitants still consider caste ties important, they tend to observe caste distinctions only to the extent of convenience. Economic conditions have also brought about caste changes. It has often been impossible in the city for each caste to follow its traditional occupation, and there are no caste provisions for certain new occupations and professions in an industrial urban society. Although it can be assumed in the city that sweepers, barbers, *dhobis* (laundry men), and butchers are of lower or outcaste groups, many distinctions are fast disappearing in a great many occupations. Even the traditional dress of a Brahmin and the *tilak* on the forehead are disappearing.

A migrant from a caste-dominated village usually finds his situation in the city ambiguous. City living makes the imposition of sanctions by the caste group cumbersome, and city living by itself involves such a complex system of social interactions that the observance of caste becomes difficult. Caste taboos on physical contact cannot be observed while traveling by bus, train, taxi, or tonga (horse carriage).[5] When people are thrown together indiscriminately in schools, offices, courts, hospitals, and cinemas, all the prohibitions on caste avoidance cannot be practiced.

The city itself seems to encourage more liberal views on caste. City dwellers do not generally care about the castes of other people eating in the same restaurants or of waiters, foodshop vendors, or street hawkers. Although caste regulations may prevent receiving food and drink from a person of lower caste, they may be modified in eating establishments or during festivals and national celebrations when the waiters and vendors are strangers. Hindu caste members, of necessity, eat food prepared by other castes as well as by Muslims and Christians. Kapadia maintains, however, that, though caste eating taboos may be relaxed in the city, people are not necessarily willing to ignore them in certain situations.[6] It is only upon return to the village home that an urban dweller must, however, comply more strictly with caste requirements.[7]

Within private circles in the city, caste obligations are observed more carefully, on the whole, and many homes may keep strict observance of caste. One writer maintains, for example, that in "more concrete terms, neighbors, friends among whom one may visit, and persons from whom one can receive aid or counsel in adversity are normally only persons belonging to the same caste or, at most, a related caste."[8] On the other hand, the Bombay study showed that 69 per cent of the respondents would be prepared to go to the houses of lower-caste people for dinner or lunch if invited, and 73 per cent showed willingness to invite lower-caste people to their houses to share meals with them.[9] Marriage within one's own caste is still almost universal in the cities, and nearly all urban marriages, regardless of education or income, are arranged by families. There is some evidence that marriage within one's subcaste is not so strictly required as it is in the villages. One study reported a weakening of the caste restriction on marriages, with 54.7 per cent of a group of urban migrants indicating little objection to intercaste marriages.*

Although these marked differences in caste observances do exist between urban and rural groups, some migrants to the cities have settled with their families in large units, in which they continue to observe their former patterns of living. Caste ties are observed perhaps even more carefully. Woodruff found, in a study in Madras, that an area populated by Harijans retained many of the characteristics of a village community, but she was reluctant to generalize about the extent to which this type of living was characteristic of the city as a whole.[10]

The impact on caste relations can be even more significant when city living is combined with factory work. In a study of 160 factory workers in Kanpur, a major Indian industrial city, Niehoff concluded that the social organization of neither Hindu nor Muslim was taken into account in factory organization.[11] The most important criterion for interpersonal relations in the village, the taboo against contact and pollution through unclean work, was ignored by most, although certain castes would not take jobs dealing with the tanning or stitching of leather. Employees were hired according to their ability to handle particular jobs, regardless of caste considerations. The demand for factory jobs was great enough for Hindus to forget traditional caste lines. "There are practices taking place in the factories that do not occur in the villages. Men work side by side, with physical untouchability, causing no inconvenience. Common water taps are used, and even the sucking cup for tieing thread is used in textile factories by men of different caste."[12]

Factory life affected intercaste relationships in three ways. In the first place, as men of different castes and religions worked together in the same factories and on the same jobs, they developed friendships outside the factories. Second, crowded housing conditions prohibited workers from carefully selecting their places of residence. "There is a tendency for the compound to be predominantly

* P. N. Prabhu, "A Study of the Social Effects of Urbanization," in *The Social Implications of Industrialization and Urbanization* (Calcutta: United Nations Educational, Scientific and Cultural Organization Centre on the Social Implications of Industrialization in Southern Asia, 1956), p. 94. About one-fourth of the sample consisted of married men who were not accompanied to the city by their wives, which may have intensified their feelings.

of high or low caste, but in all of them there will be at least a few families of the opposite pole in caste prestige. This proximity, along with the excessive crowdedness, is conducive to more inter-caste relations."[13] Finally, there was the important factor of anonymity in city living. "The larger bazaar areas and particularly the tea shops and restaurants are most important in this regard. Anonymity is used for other purposes as well. The low-caste workers can visit places to which access would not be allowed them if they were recognized."[14]

Many caste functions that characterize village living can be transferred to the city only to limited extents. Cities have become so mixed by caste, housing is at such a premium, and village migrants often feel so much stronger attachments to their villages or regions that the importance of caste social controls is minimized. Seldom is there a recognized way in the city, for example, to settle disputes between caste groups in the same manner as the village *panchayat* settles them, although occasionally city caste *panchayats* also settle them.

Although urbanism in India has erased some of the social distinctions based upon caste, it has created others based on class. Greater differences exist in the sociostructural hierarchy of the city than in those of the villages.[15] Davis has predicted, in fact, that the caste system will be transformed into a class system, depending on the degree of industrialization and urbanization achieved.[16] Relationships based on region, social class, education, income, and degree of Westernization tend to supplant the caste relationships that are paramount in the village. In Indian cities, regional and linguistic ties are also replacing caste ties.

§ *A Community-Development Approach to Delhi's Slum Problems*

The Delhi Pilot Project in urban community development was initiated primarily because it was believed that something could and must be done to alleviate slum conditions. So enormous are the problems of the Delhi slums, so limited the resources, and so urgent the time factor that, even were the population to remain static, some method would have to be found to deal with the situation. With rapidly increasing urbanization, however, it would take a far longer time for government and welfare agencies to meet the physical and social needs of the slums. The cost of any comprehensive program for slum clearance, improved living conditions, and extensive additional civic facilities would require colossal sums of money, far more than the government could ever raise. The annual revenue of the Delhi municipal government totals about $6 million (1955–1956), or about $2.50 per capita. In 1956–1957 expenditures for public instruction were about $1 million, expenditures for water supply and drainage were somewhat less than a million each, and those for medical relief and public health were about $1.5 million.[17] Because of the magnitude of the task, large-scale slum-clearance or -improvement projects are clearly beyond the capacity of the government at this time.

As an experiment, the Delhi Pilot Project was designed to stimulate citizen participation and self-help activities in coping with slum conditions and preventing further deterioration in the city, as well as in developing a sense of civic consciousness. It was designed as a realistic approach to the enormous problems presented by Delhi's slums; to attempt changes largely through the resources most readily available—the hundreds of thousands of hands and the small financial resources of the slum dwellers themselves. It was directed to-ward limited physical improvements—house repairs, improved drains, water facilities, latrines, and so forth—as well as toward significant changes in the way of life of the people, mainly through their own efforts. It was not offered as a substitute for large-scale government action in improving economic opportuni-ties, housing, and facilities; rather it was limited to those areas in which self-help programs were feasible.

Although the goals of the Delhi project were broadly to organize and stimulate community life and to identify and develop community leadership to handle problems on a mutual-aid and self-help basis, there were also some specific objectives:

1. development of communities, characterized by citizens' pride and sense of belonging;
2. development of self-help and mutual-aid programs to improve local communities and bazaars;
3. development of civic pride through stimulation of neighborhood interest in city-wide improvement campaigns;
4. preparation for democratic decentralization of some municipal services through the organization of citizen councils to foster indigenous leadership;
5. assistance to citizens in cooperating with municipal and other welfare agencies for the improvement of neighborhoods;
6. assistance to citizens in eliminating practices unsuited to urban living;
7. creation of the necessary climate for undertaking programs of economic better-ment, based on maximum use of available community resources and local initiative.

THE EXPERIMENTAL PROJECT

The Delhi project represented, both in philosophy and planning, a unique attempt to produce change in urban areas.[18] First, although it adopted philo-sophies of other programs, in particular seeking stronger communities and wide-scale dependence on self-help—which are characteristic of the rural com-munity-development program in India and elsewhere—urban problems are so entirely different that new techniques had to be devised. Second, welfare programs in Delhi areas were often loosely planned, directed at limited goals, involved only limited percentages of the people, and generally relied for leadership on the more educated and influential groups of the population. The Delhi project was designed to function as part of municipal government rather than of a private agency. Third, slum people themselves were expected to carry almost the entire responsibility for planning, financing, and executing self-help projects, with minimal help and assistance from community workers. Fourth, the project was planned as a comprehensive program involving all the problems of each neighborhood. Fifth, the program was planned to include a set of procedures to create formal organizations and systematic efforts to enlist as many neighborhood people as possible in self-help. Reliance was to be placed on creating indigenous leadership, which would be largely illiterate and poor. An effort was to be made to establish permanent citizen organizations led by average slum dwellers.

In the planning stage, the wisdom of establishing a social experiment in a municipal organization was questioned. Voluntary agencies were favored because, first, city problems arise in part from inefficient or inadequate municipal services. Second, city politicians might not be kindly disposed to the assumption of leadership roles on a nonpolitical basis by the people. Third, it was thought that the flexibility of a voluntary agency might prove to be helpful in the execution of the project. Failing help from a private agency, a semiautonomous "holding company" idea was suggested. In the course of the project's activities some of these apprehensions did turn out to be justified, yet the decision to keep the project under municipal auspices appears essentially to have been wise. Community development, first of all, is a partnership between "the people" and the government, and, as municipal government is the last link in the chain of public administration, the people do tend to have some respect for projects that have grown out of the branch of government with which they have the closest contact in their daily lives. The very "failure" of municipal government in some respects arose from lack of involvement among the people in ever-growing municipal problems, and there was a need to reorient municipal officials and policies by providing a two-way channel between them and the people. Finally, despite delays and difficulties, an urban project within the municipal organization might avoid becoming politically oriented whereas many voluntary welfare agencies are known to have succumbed to political influences, either covertly or overtly. The idea of another autonomous semi-official body was also dropped because Delhi already suffered from an overabundance of special boards and authorities to deal with urban problems.

The project was launched in 1958, with grants totaling $170,539 from the Ford Foundation to the Delhi Municipal Corporation.* This sum was allocated

---

* A planning grant of $25,000 had originally been made in 1956 to the Health Ministry, but this sum was later transferred to the Delhi municipal government. The project was an action program of the municipality and therefore was not associated directly with the Town Planning Organization, which, under a Ford grant, devised the 1960 Master Plan for Delhi. The Calcutta Metropolitan Planning Organization has been using another Ford Foundation grant for a physical plan for the city and surrounding area and for some work in urban community development.

to cover costs for a total of three and a half years, with the Delhi municipal government assuming an increasing share of the cost. The annual budget later came to about $50,000 a year. The Department of Urban Community Development of the Municipal Corporation of Delhi, probably the first of its kind in the world, was created to handle these functions as a regular part of city government, on a par, for example, with city departments of health, sanitation, and education.*

ASSUMPTIONS OF THE PROJECT

The pilot project was based on two assumptions about the nature of slum life and the problems it presents. First, it was assumed that social change can be most effectively brought about *where people live*, that is, in the lanes, *katras*, and alleys of the Indian cities—and that such social change can best be achieved by working with groups of people rather than with individuals. Most city families, particularly the women and children, live most of their daily lives in relatively limited areas. If social changes can be made within these areas and in the people's attitudes, a continuity can be established that can last for years. Second, slum life is largely a product of *group practices*, and any change must come from the group. The people's desire for change must precede any successful development program, and permanent change will come only as a community sees the need for the change and as the capacity for making such changes is developed by the group. On the basis of these assumptions, therefore, it was unrealistic to expect that the conventional approach to slum problems through community welfare centers could successfully create an impact on the large-scale slum problems of Delhi.

GENERAL WORKING PLAN

The plan for this pilot project was designed to accomplish the following concrete objectives: (1) the establishment of a department of urban community development; (2) the organization of six *vikas mandals* or citizen development councils of various types to provide self-help at an early stage; (3) the later addition of twenty more *vikas mandals*, consolidated into two large neighborhood groups or *vikas parishads*; (4) the improvement of the poor sanitary conditions and general disorder of the bazaar; (5) improvement in the community work of such traditional citizen groups as *mohalla* (existing neighborhood) committees; and (6) various civic campaigns to improve the physical appearance

* The Director was B. Chatterjee, a social worker trained at the Tata Institute for Social Sciences, who had been for ten years previously the executive secretary of the Indian Conference of Social Work. The Ford Foundation appointed the author, a sociologist, as consultant on urban community development. The author has discussed the role and function of a foreign consultant in such a project. See Marshall B. Clinard, "The Sociologist and Social Change in Underdeveloped Countries." *Social Problems*, 10 (Winter, 1963), 207–19.

and conditions of the city as a whole.* The plan was divided into four phases:

Phase I. planning the project (September, 1958—March, 1959);

Phase II. action phase—establishment of the first six *vikas mandals* (April, 1959—March, 1960);

Phase III. *vikas parishads,* bazaar project, *mohalla* committees (April, 1960—June, 1962);

Phase IV. consolidation, evaluation, and gradual extension (July, 1962 on).

The original plan called for twenty-four *vikas mandals* and two *vikas parishads,* encompassing a total population of 50,000 plus an undetermined number to be reached through the *mohalla* committees. Eventually, by the end of 1963, the project involved forty-two *vikas mandals* and four *vikas parishads,* encompassing nearly 100,000 people plus more than 300,000 people reached through *mohalla* committees. A bazaar project of 300 shops was also organized. By the end of 1965, there were forty-seven *vikas mandals* with a population of more than 150,000.

Vikas Mandals. The basic organizational unit for the project was to be the *vikas mandal,* or citizen development council, of 250–400 families or 1,250–3,000 people, approximately the size of an Indian village. These small groups were to be organized into communities by male and female urban-community organizers. Each *vikas mandal,* which would represent a somewhat artificially delimited area within the city, was to be made up of representatives of *vikas sabhas,* or zone councils, representing fifteen to twenty-five families. Each *vikas sabha* was to elect a representative to the executive committee of the *vikas mandal.* This executive committee in turn was to select officers. The purposes of the *vikas mandals* were to foster self-help and cooperation among the slum dwellers and to devise means for solving local problems and meeting local needs.

Because of the inferior status of Indian women and the important role visualized for them in self-help community improvements, plans were made to set up *mahila samitis,* or women's organizations, as almost exact counterparts to the *vikas mandals* but without their authority. Through such organizations, women would have opportunities to demonstrate what they could contribute to community improvement.

Vikas Parishads. As it is obvious that cities of hundreds of thousands of people cannot be entirely compartmentalized into such small communities as *vikas mandals* represent, the organization of larger neighborhood units, called *vikas parishads,* was planned. The population of a neighborhood would range from 7,500 to 20,000. Neighborhood councils, consisting of the officers of ten

---

* The plan also included the development of the first community chest for federated giving and the second welfare council to coordinate welfare activities in India (the first was in Poona). Although preliminary steps were taken, no really serious effort was made to implement these parts of the plan, and they will be omitted from the subsequent discussion.

to fifteen contiguous *vikas mandals*, were to coordinate self-help activities and to undertake larger self-help projects. To these councils were to be added representatives of established voluntary groups, welfare organizations, and municipal departments. Eventually some municipal services might be decentralized to the neighborhood level.

Voluntary Citizen Groups. Each Indian city already has some citizen organizations, on a local level, and the most common such organizations in Delhi are the *mohalla* committees. One aspect of the urban community-development program was to improve the effectiveness of these groups, especially in self-help activities, by conducting training programs for their representatives and by assigning community organizers to help them with organizational problems.

Bazaar-Improvement Work. Bazaars are a large and important part of any Indian city, and it would be a mistake to deal with neighborhood conditions and to neglect the unsightly, chaotic, and unsanitary conditions of most of these bazaars. Community organizers were to be assigned to bazaar areas, either to organize new groups or to revitalize existing organizations of shopkeepers, for the purpose of developing organizations that could make improvements through self-help, rather than through governmental or police action.

Civic Campaigns. City-wide campaigns to make citizens aware of conditions and to bring about civic consciousness and pride were also planned as part of the urban community-development program.

THE PILOT PROJECTS

It was decided to begin the formation of *vikas mandals* in one area, then to add five more, making six initial pilot projects. These first projects were to provide necessary experience for further expansion and were designed to furnish such experience in widely different types of slum situations. In such a small initial venture, a staff of workers could gradually be built up, the established workers passing on their experiences to the new ones. Two workers were thus employed for the first project, and ten more were added after a few weeks.

The six original *vikas mandal* areas were selected in recognition of the social differentiation and complexity of life generally prevalent in Delhi, as in most large urban areas in India. Consequently, the composition of each project varied in terms of religion, caste, and occupation; refugee or relocated status; density of the area; and the nature of its predominant problems. Each of these factors, it was felt, might be related to the ease of achieving community organization and stimulating self-help.

Although each area formed a single physical entity, there was, with one exception, little sense of identity among the residents. Even the Muslim area, which had some feeling of identity, had no area organization as such. These six areas generally were counterparts of the other *vikas mandal* areas that were later added.

1. *A colony built for rehabilitation of squatters from shack bustees.** This area included 429 families, a total population of 1,695 people, with an average of 3.9 people per family. Most of the families had been living for years in some of the worst shack bustees in different parts of Delhi and had recently been relocated in a completely new area, where the physical planning was relatively good in terms of drains, water and latrines. The colony had been built on a self-help basis, each squatter having been given a small piece of land and lent R.200 worth of building materials for a small standard-design one-room brick hut with thatched roof. The social composition of the group was complicated and heterogeneous. By regional affiliation, more than two-thirds (67 per cent) of the residents were from Rajasthan, and 16 per cent were from Uttar Pradesh. There were also some Sansis (ex-criminal tribes), Punjabis, and others. One-fifth had lived in Delhi since 1947 and one-half since 1952. The men and the women who worked were largely building workers and unskilled laborers with a high (80 per cent) illiteracy rate. Although this area had fairly new housing, the slum mentality brought from the bustees pervaded the people's lives. There was much tension and friction, and fights between groups and families were common. The municipal government's position as landlord created further difficulties.

2. *A slum area in a highly congested, low-income part of the city, with relative unity in occupation and highly traditional religious (Muslim) background.* This project involved 396 families, with a population of 2,322 people and an average of 5.8 people per family, living in an old Muslim locality adjoining a mosque in the western, extended part of the old walled city. Although the houses were situated in a planned way in a fairly compact block, they were in dilapidated condition. The single-story hut-type structures lined both sides of narrow lanes. It was a very traditional community in which certain elders tended to dominate; the women were in purdah and wore burkas when they went out. Nearly four-fifths of the residents (78 per cent) had been born in Delhi; only 6.3 per cent had come since 1952. Three-fourths of the adults (76.6 per cent) were illiterate. The chief occupation was trunk-making, and many of the houses were used as workshops. Lack of basic facilities and feelings of uncertainty were crucial factors in the neglect of the area, and particularly unsanitary conditions had caused a severe cholera epidemic two years earlier.

3. *A Hindu slum area in a highly congested part of the city in a lower-income bracket, but with relative unity in occupational and religious background.* This project area consisted of two major *katras* and one lane housing 273 families or a total population of 1,014 people, an average of 3.7 people per family. Nearly one-half (44.6 per cent) had been born in Delhi, and only 13.2 per cent had come since 1952. In regional affiliations, they were almost equally divided among Uttar Pradesh, Rajasthan, and Punjab. They worked mainly as potters or at unskilled construction jobs. The people belonged to the scheduled or lower castes, and their incomes were very low. Approximately three-fourths (72.2 per cent) were illiterate, and the level of education of the remainder was low.

---

* A real shack bustee was not taken for a project because most of them occupy government land without authorization. It would have been almost impossible for the municipal government to encourage self-help improvements in the area and then later to force the residents to leave.

4. *An area of predominantly better-paid and better-educated industrial workers.* This area housed 238 families, or 1,200 people, with an average of five people per household. The housing was mainly of the *katra* type. Industrial workers employed in two large textile mills accounted for about two-thirds of the population. Nearly half (45 per cent) were born in Delhi, but there was a large number of immigrants (30.3 per cent) from West Pakistan, which mainly occupied one part of the project area. Illiteracy was lower than in the other projects (42.2 per cent), and 11.3 per cent were matriculates or above. The average monthly earnings of a family were about R.100 ($20).

5. *A highly congested, low-income slum area, with considerable diversity in occupation, caste, and religion.* Included in this project were 265 families, with 1,428 people or 5.4 people per family, who lived along two sides of a long and fairly wide lane, with three smaller lanes shooting off. The lane had once been connected to the rampart of the old city. The population of the lane was very heterogeneous both in caste and class. Members of the upper castes tended to live at the end of the lane farther from the city wall, as was the custom long ago, with the Harijans and lower castes at the end nearer the city wall. Over half (53.5 per cent) were born in Delhi, and only 13.2 per cent had come there since 1952. The majority (56.4 per cent) was illiterate, the figure rising as high as 90 per cent among the Harijans, or untouchables. The caste and class heterogeneity of Brahmins, Khatiks, and Harijans was an important factor in social relationships, and integration of these groups was a primary problem.

6. *A housing colony for refugees, with low population density but with cultural and recreational problems.* This project involved 275 families, 1,360 people, who lived in a fairly uncrowded area. Situated about ten miles from the center of the city, this housing had been built with financial help from the government by refugees from Pakistan who had come to Delhi since 1947. The housing was fairly good, and the water supply, electric lights, and school facilities were adequate. The men were largely engaged in occupations that took them some distance from home. The problems of the area were chiefly a lack of cultural and recreational activities, a feeling among residents that they were not really part of the city despite the many years that had passed since Partition, and the possibility of further deterioration of the fairly satisfactory physical conditions.

THE VIKAS PARISHADS (NEIGHBORHOOD COUNCILS)

Beginning in 1960, three of the original *vikas mandals* were extended into three *vikas parishads*, or neighborhood councils, taking five to ten more *vikas mandals* in each case. The neighborhoods were known as "Sadar Idgah," "Shora Kothi," and "Paharganj," each representing a different combination of religious and regional backgrounds, economic statuses, occupations, literacy, and lengths of residence in Delhi. The coordination of the several *vikas mandals* was placed in the charge of a neighborhood organizer. By 1965, two other neighborhoods had been added.

1. *Sadar Idgah, a stable but very poor area with high population density, difficult physical conditions, and high illiteracy.* This neighborhood of eleven *vikas mandal* areas was located in an old, poor, and very conservative part of the city. The boundaries of these thirty-seven acres were four main roads; the social conditions and population were fairly homogeneous. There were many winding lanes, different types of house, and inadequate facilities. Drains were open, sanitation was poor, and there were few open spaces for recreation. Certain areas became waterlogged for long periods during the monsoons because of choked drains. A total of 3,315 families or 16,287 people (4.9 people per family), lived in the area. There were eight or more members in 17.8 per cent of the families. Fifty-six per cent of the population was male, and 44.7 per cent was female. More than half (55.4 per cent) the residents had been born in Delhi, and 50.6 per cent had always lived in the area. Only 16.4 per cent had come to Delhi since 1947; only 20.5 per cent had come since 1952. Most traced their family origins to Delhi (40.1 per cent), but, of the others, the largest group (19.4 per cent) was from Uttar Pradesh, and refugees from Pakistan constituted 14.3 per cent. Two-thirds (64.4 per cent) of the people were illiterate; very few had any education beyond primary schooling. There were 4,247 children between five and fourteen years old in the area; the percentage of those unable to read and write was 50.8. This figure ranged from a low in one *vikas mandal* of 33.2 per cent to a high of 73.8 per cent in another. About 20 per cent were Muslims, and one goal of the project was to make possible increased Hindu–Muslim relationships; at that time the two groups were compartmentalized in the area. About 5 per cent belonged to higher caste and economic levels, and the remainder belonged to a lower economic group, including three different subcastes: Chamars, Nais, and Julahans. The people were engaged in weaving, *thela* pulling (*thelas* are hand carts), and hawking, unskilled labor, portering, and factory work.

2. *Shora Kothi, an area with a large percentage of industrial workers, fair housing and facilities, and less illiteracy.* This area consisted mainly of a compact area of *katras* located along lanes, a factor that contributed to its selection. The locality, near Subzimandi, had six *vikas mandals* and was situated on private land, developed only about twenty-five years earlier. It had a good shopping center and fairly adequate civic facilities like water, lights, and latrines. General community life and sanitary conditions, however, needed much improvement. There were 1,223 families, with 6,147 people, an average of 5 people per family. Approximately one in nine families, or 12.9 per cent, had eight or more members. Only 17.2 per cent of the residents had been born in Delhi; most (52 per cent) had come since 1947, and, of these, 13.7 per cent had come since 1952. Slightly fewer than half (43 per cent) the adults were unable to read and write. The highest literacy rate was 51.3 per cent in one *vikas mandal*, and the lowest was 23.2 per cent in one that consisted primarily of refugees. There was considerably less illiteracy among children between the ages of five and fourteen, compared with Sadar Idgah. Of 1,690 children, only 28.2 per cent were illiterate. About half the populace was textile-mill workers, and most of them belonged to unions. The remaining work force included weavers, spinners, dyers, dhobis, small factory workers, shopkeepers, and hawkers. This neighborhood project afforded a good opportunity for developing cooperation between industrial and nonindustrial workers.

3. *Paharganj, physically a more homogeneous neighborhood, with a highly mixed population in terms of class and other factors and a generally higher economic and educational level.* This area was quite heterogeneous in terms of caste and class. Poor and illiterate people lived beside those who were better educated. It was felt that a neighborhood council representing all groups might help to improve the entire area. The area had eleven *vikas mandals*, with 12,437 people in 2,473 families, about 1,130 people per *vikas mandal*. There were twenty-five acres in the area, divided roughly into three fairly, but not completely, homogeneous sections; a densely populated section of low-income potters and construction workers; a section of dilapidated houses, formerly owned by Muslims, which held a large group of displaced persons accounting for 40 per cent of the population; and an old area of middle- and upper middle-class residents, with fairly good living conditions. The residents of the middle-class area were chiefly in business and government service, whereas the displaced persons were chiefly petty shopkeepers, hawkers, and shop assistants. Most of the houses and *katras* were arranged in a zigzag pattern on narrow winding lanes and blind alleys, which testified to the unplanned nature of the district. There were insufficient water taps, latrines, and electricity; sanitation was generally poor. Slightly more than one-third (37 per cent) of the people were illiterate, but if those with only a little primary-school education are included, the figure comes to 55.9 per cent. Four of the *vikas mandals* had more than 50 per cent illiteracy, but one had only 17.9 per cent. This neighborhood was, on the whole, considerably higher in economic status than were the other two, some 37 per cent of its residents being in small trades and business. When asked about the problems of their area, nearly half (49.4 per cent) the residents noted sanitation as their first concern, with housing problems and basic amenities next.

Combining the three neighborhoods of Sadar Idgah, Shora Kothi, and Paharganj and the three separate original pilot projects, there were, until March, 1963, a total of thirty-one *vikas mandals*. An analysis of this total group gives some indication of the characteristics of the slum population sampled in the project. In all, there were 7,980 families, or 39,355 people, with an average per family of 4.8. The *vikas mandals* ranged from 3.7 to 5.8 people per family. Of the total group, 37.5 per cent had been born in Delhi; 11.4 per cent had come since 1942, 34.7 per cent since 1947, and 14.5 per cent since 1952. Nearly two-thirds of the adults, or 52 per cent of the adult population of the thirty-one *vikas mandals*, were illiterate; in terms of formal education, only 8.6 per cent were matriculates or above.* Illiteracy ranged from a high of 80.3 per cent in one *vikas mandal* to a low of 17.9 per cent in another. Fifty per cent or more of the adults were illiterate in eighteen *vikas mandals*; the level of formal education was low in nearly all. The family places of origin were Delhi for 24.4 per cent; Uttar Pradesh for 19.2 per cent; Punjab for 13.2 per cent; and Rajasthan for 9.7 per cent. Refugees from Pakistan constituted 27 per cent of the total population and those from the other states of India made up 6.5 per cent.

---

* A matriculate is one who has had eleven years of education.

§ *The Project Staff*

The staff of the Department included a director and a deputy director (in charge of research and evaluation), who had four research officers and assistants under his supervision. There was a chief community organizer, under whom the neighborhood or *vikas parishad* organizers worked. They, in turn, directed twenty-six community organizers, seventeen men and nine women.* A chief of women's activities coordinated and promoted work on women's problems. There were eight field-program organizers in public health and recreation, who, along with eleven full- and part-time craft teachers, constituted the staff available for work in specialized self-help activities. A project liaison officer, assisted by an organizer and a film projectionist, supervised work with *mohalla* committees, relations with other departments, civic campaigns, financial grants to *vikas mandals*, and the showing of motion pictures. A clerical staff of twenty-one people handled accounts, typing, transport, and maintenance.

THE URBAN COMMUNITY ORGANIZERS

The community organizers played a crucial role in the Delhi project. In a sense, upon them fell the burden of developing "community" where little community feeling had previously existed. The staff consisted of two types of organizer: community organizers and field-program organizers. The primary responsibility of the community organizers was to create communities; the field-program organizers, trained in public health and recreation, developed self-help activities in their specialties.† In addition, handicraft and literacy teachers were hired on a part-time basis.

The community organizers generally held M.A. degrees in social work or the social sciences or had extensive work experience with large groups of people. Some had backgrounds in social education or public relations. The workers were selected by competitive civil-service examinations conducted in both individual and group interviews, with emphasis on group interviews, in which approximately eight people were interviewed together. It was believed that the best age group for this work was twenty-five to thirty-five years. After

---

* Figures are given for the period when the staff was largest, 1960–1962. All supervisory appointments, with the exception of the director and the deputy director, were made from the ranks of the community organizers, generally from those who had been the most successful. These posts were gradually filled as the need developed. Promotions within the staff did create some ill feeling.

† As members of the staff, such specialized personnel could be coordinated and given a self-help orientation. In the later Ford Foundation-supported Ahmedabad urban community-development project, such field personnel were made available cooperatively from other departments. Such arrangements were difficult to make in Delhi.

selection, the workers were given a six-weeks in-service training course in urban problems, the objectives of self-help work, the details of the project, interviewing slum people, and observation of existing projects.

Usually a male and a female organizer worked as a team, although on some projects there might be several male and one female organizers. Such teams could organize several thousand families into *vikas mandals* in a year, depending upon the methods used. The male organizer had primary responsibility for the organization of the *vikas mandal* and work with the men, while the female organizer worked closely with him in organizing the area through interviewing the women, offering advice, and coordinating her work with that of the male community organizer. The woman organizer had the sole responsibility for organizing the women into *mahila samitis*, or auxiliary women's groups.

Some duties of the male and female community organizers were quite similar, the differences being chiefly in emphasis. Both tried to identify indigenous leaders and to develop the idea of self-help. They suggested procedures to accomplish community objectives and were familiar with the technical staff and the agencies available in the city to assist with community problems. The organizers helped the community to clarify, summarize, and reconcile conflicting opinions by furnishing assistance and encouragement to citizen groups, without actually leading or directing. Where slum areas were fragmented into small groups with little coherence among them, their job was to develop a new sense of community. They also helped to guide citizen officers in procedures at meetings. The chief criteria measuring whether or not workers were accepted by the people were (1) frequency of consultation with the workers in the planning and execution of the *vikas mandal* programs, (2) consultation with the workers over serious conflicts in the community, and (3) the tendency of the workers to share perspectives with indigenous and other leaders.

It was also important that the worker understand the local social system, so that he could use it effectively. He had to know who were the important people in the local area and to understand the nature of the local conflicts. With this knowledge, the community organizer could help to solve basic conflicts and to bring various groups together to achieve common goals; he could avoid being caught in power struggles between contending groups that might nullify his efforts. The community organizer tried to identify with the entire community and to avoid becoming primarily associated with a particular religion, class, or caste. At the same time, he had to avoid becoming an indispensable prop upon whom the group depended.

One of several important problems involved the differences in social background, education, speech, and dress between the community organizers and the slum dwellers and the possible effects of these differences on the formation of citizen organizations for self-help. The cultural gulf between an educated middle-class community organizer and an uneducated lower-caste or -class person could not be overestimated, and the organizers tried to diminish this gulf in the words and expressions they used. An organizer had to be particularly careful at all times to see that his own personal background, particularly his social class or caste, and his generally superior education did not interfere with his ability to relate well to others. The organizers had to hide their own personal feelings or antagonisms, for example, toward unsanitary conditions or totally different modes of behavior.

At the beginning one had to expect, particularly in India, that an urban community organizer and particularly the field-program organizers, would be approached by members of the community with all kinds of personal and family problems. Should the community organizer have taken up such problems, he never would have been able to organize the community effectively. For this reason and in spite of the importance of establishing individual rapport, it was necessary to concentrate on group problems and objectives, on long-range prevention and not on the immediate application of palliative measures. A paternalistic worker cannot be an asset in self-help work. Urban community-development projects are designed to improve the group and, through the group, the individual. In concentrating on group objectives, the community organizer therefore had to make his purpose clear. In certain selected cases only could he possibly deal with individuals and then only for the purpose of seeking a broader objective.

Organizers could never be completely withdrawn from an area, although their work could taper off as projects became organized and as indigenous leaders assumed more responsibility. The transfer of a worker from one project to another, in order to equalize the work load, did present problems as the work expanded. It was often impossible for an organizer to have all his projects in one area, and commuting is time-consuming in any Indian city. Community work is quite different from work in a welfare center, as there is a tendency for the entire community to identify with the particular worker. It was found that the first worker in an area was generally well liked, but if he replaced someone in another area he was sometimes disliked.

Initially, salaries for organizers were about one-third higher than those for comparable positions, on the grounds that competent personnel were necessary to devise and apply effective techniques in an experimental project under difficult urban conditions. The working conditions were strenuous, there were no offices, and organizers had to be out of doors much of the time, exposed to the intense summer heat as well as to the monsoons. It was also important to hire people capable of preparing records suitable for evaluation and research. In addition, salaries had to be sufficient to ensure staff stability, as some members would otherwise be tempted to take other positions because of the uncertainty of their own. This policy resulted in outside criticism, and efforts were made later to reduce the salaries as the project developed and new workers were added.

A handicap the male staff members faced was the demands on their time, as most men in slum communities were available only late at night or very early in the morning. As far as possible, the worker tried to reach them at their convenience or leisure, but he often then had to crowd many meetings into a limited period of time. Fortunately, women workers did not face this problem, as women are more likely to be available when the men go to work.

THE PROFESSIONAL SOCIAL WORKER IN URBAN COMMUNITY WORK

The urban community-development worker must be oriented toward groups of people rather than toward individuals, toward prevention rather than toward treatment, and toward behavior change through manipulation of environmental forces rather than toward the resolution of intrapsychic conflicts or other individual approaches. Such orientation requires the development of curriculum programs in social work, extension, adult education, and similar fields to equip people with the necessary knowledge and skills to be effective in this broader approach.

The professional worker has an important role to play in community work, but it appears that this role can also be played by nonprofessionals. Experience in the Delhi Pilot Project has given some evidence about the performance of professional social workers in urban-community development work. Of thirty-four organizers in any capacity in the project in 1962, fifteen had M.A. degrees in social work, and nineteen had no professional training.* The director and deputy director of the program were both professional social workers. When promotions to supervisory positions within the Department were made on the basis of results and success in working with communities, however, it was found that, of seven appointments, only two came from the professionally trained group. At the time the study was made, two of the workers with the lowest performance levels were professionals, despite the fact that all workers were selected competitively from a large number of professional and nonprofessional applicants. Criteria for selection included training, recommendations, and group and individual interviews. There are several possible explanations for this situation. First, the nonprofessionals, an older group, came from a variety of fields, including social education, public relations, cooperatives, and so forth and had gained maturity and understanding about urban life and social relations that could not be provided by the younger professionals' courses and limited experiences in field placement. Second, professional workers are often status conscious, which prevents them from relating effectively to the various types of people found in slum communities or from meeting effectively

---

* The word "professional" applies to those with degrees in social work. "Social work" is broadly defined in India to include a large number of untrained people doing social-welfare work. The survey discussed was carried out by Chatterjee, whose unpublished paper has been used extensively here.

the varying situations that arise in day-to-day community work. In many ways, these people have the normative values of junior executives in industry. Third, professional workers, because of their degrees and the demand for them, have greater alternative employment possibilities and do not strive so hard under the exacting conditions required in community-development work. Fourth, work in slum areas demands much more devotion, humility, understanding, and tact than professionally trained workers often expect, even though their field training is usually received in centers. Fifth, they are often isolated from ordinary men by their style of dress and their mode of speaking, yet their positions demand that they maintain a certain level of dress and speech. It was observed, however, that women community organizers experienced much less social distance on these grounds, probably because they are still objects of identification as members of a lower-status group. Sixth, successful urban community workers seem to exhibit such qualities as faith in self-help, dogged determination, some form of organizational experience, sensitivity, and the ability to bring about social change in people. These assets are not necessarily acquired in social-work or other professional schools. Seventh, the schools of social work do not appear to train people for urban work as intensively as experience does. Many professors of social work lack real firsthand experience with the complexities of urban life—and are unfamiliar with the relevant literature. Training is deficient in providing understanding of the effects of rapid urbanization and urbanism through such concrete courses as urban sociology, deviant behavior, social stratification, and municipal government. Also students do not receive sufficient training in the broad field of producing social change and in effective public-relations work. In reality, their training is not focused on the neighborhood level but is concerned instead with welfare centers, in which doing something for someone has overbalanced the idea of self-help.

Two definite roles seem possible for the social worker in urban community development. One is that of planner and supervisor at higher levels, provided the training program is appropriately altered. The other involves identifying, recruiting, and training people with less education to carry on the actual interviewing and close relationships required in effective community work. On the basis of the Delhi experience, it is proposed that future fieldworkers should be largely nonprofessionals drawn from similar, or only slightly higher, educational, social, caste, and regional backgrounds as those of the people with whom they are to work. Their training should be supplemented with intensive in-service programs.

§ Programs in Less Developed Countries

Comprehensive organized governmental programs of urban community development stressing self-help in the slums were in effect by 1965, as part of municipal government, in Delhi and Ahmedabad in India; were being expanded into a national program in India; and were operating as active national programs in Pakistan, the Philippines, Venezuela, and Colombia. In the United States and Hong Kong, such programs were directed by private or quasi-governmental agencies, as was a special group, ACCION, in Venezuela.

India began a national program in urban community development in 1965 with a series of pilot projects. A committee on rural-urban relations was established in 1963 and, after careful study of the Delhi and Ahmedabad projects, decided to start twenty additional pilot projects covering 50,000 people each, located in a number of cities. These projects are patterned after the Delhi and Ahmedabad projects, with each pilot project divided into eight *mohallas* of 1,200 families each and further subdivided into *vikas sabhas* of 100 families each. Each project has a director, a project officer (one or the other must be a woman), and eight urban community organizers, four men and four women. All are given two-month training in urban community development at selected schools of social work, with additional field experience. The direct administration of each project is under the municipal government, and there is an advisory committee, of which the mayor is chairman. The work is under the Ministry of Health, which gives a grant of R.50,000 plus R.15,000 in contingencies for each project. The basic grants are to be matched by the state governments and the municipalities.

The Pakistan national program has most frequently been compared with the Delhi and Ahmedabad projects. It was preceded by the first important pilot project, the Lyari Project in Karachi in 1954, by a project in Dacca in 1955, and by three other projects in Lahore. The First Five-Year Plan (1955–1960) embodied recognition of the importance to the nation of a program of urban community development and recommended beginning with seventy projects. The Plan stated that town dwellers must be helped to achieve an active sense of neighborhood, so that they can perceive positive value in cooperating with one another and with the government for the common good, in recreation and education as well as in health and physical protection. The Second Five-Year Plan gave a particularly important role to community development, stressing the need for development programs in both rural and urban areas. Although there is a national program of urban community development, certain variations reflect the administrative and other differences between West and East Pakistan. Whereas the government agency ostensibly in charge of urban community development in Pakistan is the Ministry of Health, Labor, and Social Welfare, the Directorates of Social Welfare counterparts in West and East Pakistan actually direct the entire range of social-welfare programs, including urban community development.

The Second Five-Year Plan provided for two or three social workers, one to be a woman, for each project of approximately 25,000 people. This project was to "help the community operate much needed services effectively on a self help basis." The worker would concentrate on obtaining, through the cooperation of basic democracies, the political subunits of Pakistan, the active participation of the communities in the mobilization of resources, the organization of necessary services, and the assessment of needs. The role of the workers in a self-help program was clearly stated in the Plan. "The workers stay in the background and act mostly as professional consultants, coordinators and guides. Thus enabling the community to build up confidence, meet its own needs, and organize and maintain its own services. These services include community sanitation, medical clinics, general health and fundamental education centers for adults, family planning and recreation. The urban community development projects do not duplicate the efforts of the program of Basic Democracies, being rather demonstration experiments which work in cooperation to stimulate self help."

The Pakistan program has four objectives: to stimulate social integration and cohesion among people living in compact geographical areas and to promote healthy practices and new values as regulators of life; to encourage the development of a spirit of self-help, initiative, leadership, and cooperation in order to improve physical and social conditions in communities; to provide opportunities for people to acquire literacy and the fundamentals of modern knowledge for healthier and happier family life; and to help people to give expression to their needs and aspirations and to bring them closer to the governmental machinery for securing mutual understanding, respect, consultation, and cooperation in the planning and execution of development plans.*

Pakistan urban community-development projects generally involve units of about 25,000 to 50,000 people. The projects are divided into *mohallas* or sectors of about 1,000 families, or 5,000 people, each. These sectors constitute the

---

* A. U. Akhtar, "Urban Redevelopment and Community Development—Common Elements," *Urban and Rural Community Development*, Proceedings of the XLth International Conference of Social Work (Rio de Janeiro: Brazilian Committee of the International Conference of Social Work, 1962), p. 183. The Government of West Pakistan provides, for each project, the salaries of two welfare organizers and their auxiliary workers, along with limited funds for office furniture and supplies. The development work is left to funds collected from the people or from other developmental agencies. In East Pakistan, on the other hand, each project receives a contingency fund from the government of R.4,000 to finance small projects or supplement available funds. In West Pakistan, the projects are financed either by the provincial governments or by the West Pakistan Social Welfare Council.

smallest units, which are considerably larger than the Indian *vikas sabhas*.* In each *mohalla*, there is an elected community council; it is elected by an organized membership, which generally constitutes from 20 to 40 per cent of the area residents. Beside citizens, private welfare organizations are often represented on the council. As such groups usually receive some government subsidy, they are nonpolitical and must be registered with the government.

In actuality, the organizational arrangement is much more complex because all Pakistan has been subdivided into decentralized units of administration called "basic democracies," which make possible a certain amount of coordination between these groups and the urban community-development projects. A basic democracy consists of about 5,000 people, and groups of eight or ten basic democracies constitute, in the cities, union committees of 25,000 to 40,000 people, comparable to political wards.[19] In the basic democracies people are elected by local residents to administer and plan community affairs and to represent them at a higher level. Every basic democracy is the first stage of an ascending hierarchy of councils—district, division, and, finally, provincial. In each higher institution a proportion of the membership comes from the next lower council.

A male and a female worker, usually with some social-work training, are assigned to organize each project.† In addition, there are three to five lower-level workers in health, crafts, and recreation for each project. For the most part, leaders in the urban community-development councils tend to be better educated and wealthier; greater emphasis was placed in India on the identification of indigenous leadership. The community council plans the self-help activities. Most such activities are concentrated on schools, adult literacy, libraries and reading rooms, immunization, dispensaries, and maternity and child-welfare centers. Considerable emphasis is placed on such economic projects as tailoring, cigar making, leather work, and other crafts. As only a relatively small number of people is involved in these projects, the costs per person are quite high, even though sewing machines are often donated. Relatively few self-help activities involve physical improvements, and relatively few are related to cultural activities.

Although self-help is stressed in Pakistani projects, the definition is not the same as, and is less complete than, in Delhi. For example, self-help may consist of simply paying the rent for a maternity and child-welfare center or a vocational training school. But even a little self-help may awaken in people feelings of community responsibility. The Pakistani program is more conventional in its approach than is that of Delhi, as it is patterned more on the community-center

---

* In 1963, the author made a tour of urban community-development projects in West and East Pakistan.

† Two technical consultants in urban community development are provided by the United Nations, one for West and one for East Pakistan.

approach. Emphasis is on small community centers with which nearly all self-help activities are associated. Such centers bear the names of particular projects and serve as symbols of area activities or as demonstration projects. It is easy for the people and visitors to see what is going on, and this sight is impressive, even though the vast majority of the people may not be involved in center programs. In addition, the Pakistani projects, being in an Islamic country, can rely a great deal on the Koran to support self-help efforts. Verses from the Koran can be carried on banners and used as slogans in other ways, for example: "Indeed, God does not change the conditions of people until they change it [themselves]."

THE PHILIPPINES

The Presidential Assistant on Community Development (PACD), whose office is in charge of implementing the integrated national community-development program, has included cities in its operations since 1959.[20] With the exception of Manila, all Philippine cities have both urban and rural sectors, with parts of the population living in the cities proper and the remainder in the open country, which in most cases is farming land. The country is divided into *barrios*, which, in turn, have *barrio* councils as the cores of local government. Of the thirty-nine chartered cities in the country, twenty-six were covered by PACD up to 1965, although Manila had no urban community-development work. A city is in the operational coverage of PACD when there are regular community-development workers assigned to its *barrios*; the number of *barrios* in a city ranges from thirty to as many as sixty, but not all *barrios* are covered. Normally there are three to five community-development workers on a city team, the head of which is an urban-development officer.

In each city, there is a city community-development council composed of the mayor, two councilmen, the heads of the different services and technical agencies of the city, and two private citizens. This body plans and coordinates the city's community-development program. The mayor is the chairman, and the urban-development officer is executive secretary. Activities include the training of local leaders, including members of the *barrio* councils. Most of the community-development activities in the city are, however, actually in its rural areas.

COLOMBIA

The emerging urban-community development program in Colombia stems from a 1957 postgraduate, practical training course in Cali, which was sponsored by the Inter-American Housing Center. The local government and university cooperated with CINVA (Centro Interamericano de Vivienda y Planeamiento, or Inter-American Housing and Planning Center) to provide experience for students in conducting social surveys to ascertain local conditions, in providing technical aid, and in applying community-development techniques to urban slum areas.[21] Legislation in 1958 authorized both rural and urban community-development projects throughout the country.[22] The nation's largest project was established at Bogotá in 1959, on the basis of the national legislation and the experience gained at Cali.

The over-all goal of Colombian urban community development is social integration of uprooted people. Special emphasis is put upon converting "disoriented squatters" on the urban fringes into responsible citizens by enlisting their participation in projects and community organization. A second goal is to enlist voluntary manpower from the slums to supplement the resources available through the government for physical development of the city. Finally, it is believed that the organization of the *barrios* would provide for a two-way communication between the government and the people, so that the government can better establish a priority schedule for local improvements.

Specific objectives have been formulated to achieve the larger goals. The people are brought into setting local priorities, planning objectives, and carrying out projects. The Office of Urban Community Development is responsible for coordinating public and private agency efforts.

Local legislation provides that a community-action council be established within each *barrio*; the council consists of local leaders, a priest, two politicians from each party, the police inspector, a teacher, and the social worker assigned to the *barrio*. Committees of *barrio* residents are to be formed and the chairmen appointed by the council, but in practice it has been found more effective to let each volunteer committee elect its own chairman. The people are encouraged to look at both short- and long-range objectives. If they undertake short-range physical improvements, the municipality will undertake the major costly projects intended as permanent solutions.

VENEZUELA

The urban community-development program in Venezuela was intended, not as simply another program among the many social- and economic-development programs that were being undertaken at that time, but as a coordinated effort that would begin at the local level and would spread gradually to the entire nation at all levels of government, "stimulating local initiative with a view to achieving the active and effective participation of the people in carrying out the programs."[23] The expressed long-range objectives of urban community development are to change people's attitudes, to achieve fuller community integration, and to obtain better yields from material and technical resources provided by government. Responsibility for urban community development in Venezuela is officially placed with the Central Office of Coordination and Planning. The program is designed to be implemented throughout the country in three successive stages.

A private binational organization, ACCION (Americans for Community Cooperation in Other Nations), founded in 1960, has been attempting to develop self-help among Venezuelan slum dwellers in more than fifty slum communities in Caracas, Maracaibo, and other cities. It involves a combination of American and Venezuelan community workers, which receives funds chiefly from corporations and private individuals in Venezuela, in addition to some help from American corporations with branches there. Although funds and supplies come largely from elements outside the slums, the emphasis is on self-help work contributions from the residents. Self-help projects include installing sewers, sidewalks, and water systems; building community centers, recreation areas, and sanitation facilities; and adult education classes and volleyball teams. Emphasis is placed on developing community spirit and indigenous leaders. In a Caracas slum, Barrio La Linea, with 25,000 people, 199 residents contributed nearly 2,000 hours of voluntary labor on sewer lines, water pipes, pavement of streets, and home improvements. Leadership was developed among seventy-two people in the community, and still others represented La Linea on meetings with outside agencies. A community center was constructed. Contributions of materials and supplies by outsiders totaled $16,750.

Chapter 8

Organizing Slum Areas

Problems of urban slums in developed and developing countries are so large, affecting as they do as many as several hundred thousand people in a given city, that any program of planned social change involves a mammoth task. The development of communities where little community feeling had previously existed, the enlistment of widespread citizen participation and self-help, and the development of indigenous leadership cannot be accomplished for such numbers of people with loose organizational procedures. One can, of course, claim that "some" organization and "some" activities have arisen in a given area, as is often the claim in urban projects, but such accomplishments may not be equivalent to basic or extensive changes affecting large numbers of people through an organized program. Effective urban community development requires a mass program, which must be approached with techniques that will affect a large number of people.

A detailed set of systematic procedures was developed in the Delhi Pilot Project to organize *vikas sabhas*, or zone councils, *vikas mandals*, or citizen development councils, *mahila samitis*, or women's organizations, and *vikas parishads*, or neighborhood councils. Through such procedures, by 1965 nearly 150,000 people were involved in more than forty-seven *vikas mandals* and more than 300,000 in *mohalla* committees. It was expected that such procedures, when tested and revised, could be used to organize large numbers of people in other Indian cities, as well as in the cities of other countries.*

§ *Vikas Mandals (Citizen Development Councils)*

A *vikas mandal* bears a superficial resemblance to the "block" form of organization that is widely employed in the United States.[1] It is generally,

---

* Under a Ford Foundation grant, with the author as consultant, the procedures developed in Delhi were applied, beginning in 1962, to a much larger-scale and more rapid organization of *vikas mandals* in Ahmedabad. By the end of 1965, a total of fifty-two *vikas mandals*, with more than 150,000 people, had been organized.

however, much larger (encompassing originally about 250 and later as many as 1,000 families, as compared to fifteen to 100 families in the typical block), it attempts to involve a larger percentage of the residents, and it is usually more formal in its organizational structure. The unit is smaller than some of those in Pakistan, which encompass as many as 1,000 to 5,000 families each. It was believed that too large a basic unit would not provide an effective focal point for the development of meaningful community relations. The size of the original basic unit was increased as time went on from a range of fifteen to twenty-five families to one of forty to 100 families in the *vikas sabha* or zone, and from 250 to as many as 1,000 families in the *vikas mandal* area. Experience showed that, given the density of Indian urban living, such increases did not interfere with organization. They also reduced costs, which are a paramount consideration in developing countries. In retrospect, the pattern appears to have been sound: to start with smaller organizational units and to expand them if necessary, rather than to start with larger experimental units that might have to be reduced in size.

In the organization of a *vikas mandal*, the staff was carefully trained to follow a set of prescribed procedures, generally involving eleven steps (some of these procedures occasionally had to be abridged into what was termed a "rapid" method of organization):

1. survey and observation of the composition, characteristics, and problems of an area and preparation of a map;
2. door-to-door interviews with all heads of families, conducted either by organizers or by citizen volunteers;
3. identification of indigenous leaders;
4. propagation of the idea of self-help;
5. division and organization of the area into *vikas sabhas*, or zone councils;
6. *vikas sabha* meetings of residents to discuss constitution of citizen development councils;
7. preparatory meetings of executive committees to prepare inauguration of the *vikas mandals*;
8. inauguration of citizen development councils;
9. implementation by the councils of specific action programs devised by the community;
10. working to make zone and development-council meetings effective;
11. merging the *vikas mandals* into the neighborhood councils, or *vikas parishads*.

DEMARCATION OF A PROJECT AREA

The characteristic straight and uniform blocks of most Western and modern cities are seldom found in the older parts of an Indian city. In a crowded and poorly planned city like Delhi, it is often difficult to demarcate areas that will eventually form *vikas mandals*. Actually, a few physical landmarks must be used to distinguish the areas, as there is hardly a break in the streets, alleys, lanes, and packed houses. In the Delhi experiment, a majority of the projects was artificially carved out of densely populated slum areas. Most project maps thus came to resemble clusters of ink blots rather than of squares.

The preliminary area demarcation was made by the evaluation and research unit, which surveyed an area and prepared a map for the proposed project. The following factors were used in demarcating an area: physical and geographic compactness; social composition; existence of, or possibilities for, cultivating relationships; common community facilities like schools or *dharamshalas* (community inns or halls); historical identification; and, finally, population size, which was in the range of approximately 250 to 1,000 families. In Chicago's Hyde Park-Kenwood Community Conference, boundaries were usually decided by each block organization on the basis of common problems. Sometimes a group would spread over a larger area as its interests expanded. Most organizations, however, involved residents of buildings facing one another on opposite sides of the street.[2]

Many problems arose because the political, social, and geographic contours generally did not coincide. If one sought homogeneity, questions arose as to which criteria should be used. In general, the physical structure of an area took precedence over other considerations. The question of demarcating an area on such a basis, however, raised such problems as whether to take houses that were side by side or those on both sides of a narrow lane and how to deal with multistoried structures housing different numbers of families. These difficulties were aggravated when lines of communication were either not clear or blocked. The dilemma was whether to demarcate an area on the basis of its social relations or according to more concrete physical realities. Another problem was the advisability of demarcating an area merely on the basis of its organizational viability without considering geographic and social cohesion. The inclusion of a particular lane whose residents had little communication with those of the rest of the area, for example, might affect political composition and give overwhelming weight to an existing power group.

As one basic objective of urban community development is over-all community feeling based on territorial lines, conforming to religious, caste, class, or political feelings in the area or acceding to the demands of a particular group sometimes militates against this objective. It was, however, found advisable as much as possible to keep together in a project area those of the same caste, occupation, or religion, provided that they lived in geographically contiguous areas and had some degree of geographic unity. The criterion was a combination of geographic entity, population composition, and common problems. As an illustration of these difficulties, one area of 300 families, which was physically homogeneous because of its location on a single lane, was selected for one of the first six *vikas mandals*. Later, the dominant caste clamored for the inclusion of an adjoining area with another 150 families, so that its strength and influence over the organization would be unassailable. Such expansion would also have protected traditional community identification and would have indirectly effected the domination of the caste *panchayat* over the entire area. Because of this difficulty, when a larger area was later organized, the area was split into two *vikas mandals*, one of homogeneous caste and the other mixed, by adding adjoining areas in two different directions. In another case, an area where several fairly equally homogeneous groups were contending for power was divided into three *vikas mandals* along group lines, and thereafter the projects worked more satisfactorily.

Although the optimum size of a *vikas mandal* was planned to be approximately 250 families or 1,250 people, after the area was demarcated considerable variations occurred. The mean size of the thirty-one *vikas mandals* in 1963

Table 4

Number and Percentage Distribution of Thirty-One Vikas Mandals *by Size of Population*

	Number	Percentage
500 = 999	9	29.0
1,000 = 1,499	15	48.5
1,500 = 1,999	5	16.1
2,000 and more	2	6.4
Totals	31	100.0

was 1,270 people, and the median was 1,259 people, which came very close to the planned size. The range, however, was from 504 to 2,322, with 29 per cent having fewer than 1,000 people each and 6.4 per cent having 2,000 or more people each (see Table 4).

SURVEY OF THE AREA

Before an area was organized for community development purposes, its location and boundaries, types of housing structures, history, social agencies, population composition, general physical environment, basic facilities (water, electricity, latrines), sanitation, health, literacy, education, and social relationships were scrutinized. Information was secured through observation and through informal interviews with local residents. Often long-time residents furnished valuable information about history and social composition. Additional data were occasionally obtained from various departments of the municipal government.

This initial survey was exceedingly important. In the first place, most areas of a city have some distinctive social and cultural patterns and differ in religious, regional, caste, and occupational composition. Even where the population composition is similar, differences often exist in the relationships among the groups.

Information about area "power structures" were also important, as they might affect the people's participation in the affairs of the community. The nature of both formal and informal groups and their interrelationships had to be ascertained early in the work. Attitudes toward health, sanitation, and recreation had to be determined. For example, many members of a community had no comprehension of the relationship between flies and disease or of the true causes of dysentery, cholera, and other diseases. Existing beliefs had to be recognized before any attempts could be made to change prevailing practices. The physical condition of the area, the amount of litter, and the condition of the children were good indices of the sanitation practices and general cultural level of the area. Detailed descriptions of such initial observations were often of great value later in planning and evaluating the progress of the program.

The preparation of such a community profile had to be rapid—usually taking only one or two weeks—and it had therefore to be somewhat superficial. Too detailed a survey of conditions might have had little practical value. The goal of the experimental project was organization and not merely data collection. In addition, experience showed that it was unwise to antagonize an illiterate slum population and to arouse suspicions and hostilities by too detailed questioning. Such antagonism could interfere with the effective organization of an area.

ORGANIZATIONAL PROCEDURES: INTENSIVE METHOD[3]

Two general types of method for organizing citizen development councils were evolved in the Delhi project: an intensive, or slower, method and an extensive, or more rapid, method. In the former, two organizers, a man and a woman, were assigned to a group of 200 to 600 families at a time, organizing it over a period of approximately six to twelve weeks. This approach called for door-to-door interviewing of male and female heads of households, with the organizers taking the initial responsibility for setting up *vikas sabhas*. In the rapid method, the organizers selected certain volunteer area leaders who could carry out the organization of the project with some guidance from the organizers. This added manpower, together with approaching people in groups, made the organization proceed more rapidly.

In the first three years of organizational work, emphasis was placed on the intensive method. Although slower and more costly, it was originally believed to be necessary because of the great apathy of slum dwellers, the hold of traditional and other conventional leaders, and the power of the local politicians. By going directly to the slum dweller, the organizer could hope to inspire independence and initiative that might make him more self-reliant and less dependent on the blandishments of the politicians or the traditional caste or regional leadership. Furthermore, the slum dweller's importance and self-esteem were enhanced when the appeal was made directly to him.

In view of the experimental nature of the project, it was decided to begin with intensive interviewing, with a higher degree of saturation in paid organizers, methods, and cost. If the project worked satisfactorily, the more intensive procedures could be relaxed. If a looser method had been employed first and if it proved to be unsuccessful in overcoming slum apathy and bringing together people with diverse backgrounds, it would then have been necessary to increase the number of paid organizers to make the project work.* The intensive method also made it possible to acquire more complete knowledge of problems in organizational work and enabled the workers to assemble useful research material, examples of which can be seen throughout this volume.

The intensive method is particularly appropriate to situations in which traditional or political leadership is well entrenched or in which leadership is so weak that it is necessary to deal directly with individuals in order to initiate change. In areas where environmental and health situations are extremely bad, it may also be necessary to use more thorough organizational methods to alter conditions, even though this type of procedure may require more time.

Stimulating Self-Help. The community organizers worked systematically to stimulate self-help and to involve the people in formation of the *vikas mandals*. The male organizer called on the male head of each household, and the female organizer called on the woman. The female head of the family was defined as the mother of the children of the family. If the mother-in-law, who is traditionally the woman head of the Indian household, was present, she was courteously treated, but the interview was held with the daughter-in-law. Although in the joint family the mother-in-law is the traditional head, it was believed that more rapid and more significant changes could be made by working through the daughter-in-law. At the same time, this approach would enhance her status and help to change her image of herself and her responsibilities. Sometimes a "fake" interview with the mother-in-law was conducted first in order to give her a sense of importance and to minimize her hostility to an interview with her daughter-in-law.

Although each organizer invited men and women to participate in the *vikas mandal* itself, it was assumed that the organization would be primarily male and that the women would form a largely auxiliary group through their own *mahila samiti*. As the unit of participation was to be the family, it was often discussion between the husband and wife, even though they were interviewed separately, that made possible a favorable decision to cooperate in the project. In many cases, it was found that the wives persuaded the husbands to participate actively

---

* Later, when this approach was found to be more rapid and less costly, it was often difficult to convince those critics of the project that the original methods were no longer being used. Actually, the success of the later, more rapid method was made possible by experience secured from the intensive approach. Although the rapid method was later more generally adopted, new workers were trained to organize areas with the intensive method.

in the *vikas mandal*; by interviewing wives, one had, in reality, interviewed husbands twice.

In these interviews, the community organizers asked six key questions, which were phrased to stimulate self-help, to discover indigenous leaders, and to reveal the extent to which individuals could be relied upon to participate in *vikas mandals*.

1. What are some problems in the local community that you think the people here may be able to do something about?
2. How long have these problems existed?
3. Would you like to do something about them?
4. Have you had any experience in any mutual aid, cooperative, welfare, or voluntary organization?
5. To whom in the area do you turn in times of crisis?
6. Would you be interested in attending a group meeting to discuss neighborhood problems?

To the slum dweller, this personal interview represented perhaps the first time he had been asked how *he* felt about problems of his area and what *he* thought the people *themselves* could do to solve them. This innovation was significant and had a marked effect in generating hope among many that their own views meant something and that a new approach to their problems was being attempted. Typically, slum people had relied upon others for decisions: the government, politicians, the castes, religious or regional group leaders, or self-appointed community leaders with selfish or personal interests, whose reputations might even be questionable. People often appreciated the respect given to their individual opinions.

A limited amount of background data was secured in the initial contact interviews and entered on cards that could later be used for planning, research, and evaluation. The background data included age; sex; occupation; marital status; size, ages, and interrelationships of the family group; region of origin; duration of residence in the city; literacy; and economic status. Interviewing slum residents presents many problems, however, as such data as ages and marriage dates are often unknown and sometimes can only be roughly calculated in relation to particular historical events or celebrations. Even such simple questions, particularly those about the number of people in the family, aroused suspicions of the interviewers' real motives and fear that the answers might bring trouble. In order to avoid unnecessary duplication, certain questions were asked only of the male heads and others only of the female heads. In the initial stages, interview cards were often kept hidden and the data entered temporarily in brief notes or recorded later.

Identifying Indigenous Leadership. Primary emphasis was placed on identifying representative indigenous leadership to stimulate self-help and to lead the organization rather than on relying upon traditional leaders who might resist change and were not typical of the community. Leadership was not sought among caste, religious, and political leaders, whose interests might lie in objectives other than changing the community. Every slum area was assumed to have some residents with leadership qualities, and it was important that they be properly identified. During the interviews with the residents, the organizers tried to find such people and to encourage them to assume leadership. This process is described in more detail in Chapter 12. It was hoped that they would, on their own initiative and with the encouragement of the organizers, assume social responsibility and later qualify to be elected as representatives of their *vikas sabhas* to the executive committees of the *vikas mandals*.

Of equal importance was the identification of those who would be hostile to the project.[4] Sometimes such hostility was based on misinformation; in other cases, existing leadership status in the community was threatened. Sometimes such individuals, by spreading rumors, could do irreparable damage to the development of the community. If they could be identified and tactfully handled, they could be either turned into assets to the organization or neutralized.

Vikas Sabha Meetings. The cornerstone of the work was the *vikas sabha*, representing from fifteen to 100 families (generally from twenty-five to fifty-five), and considered by some the most important organizational contribution of the Delhi project. This unit encompassed the small world of the slum dweller, in which he was most likely to take an active part. Following the completion of the community profiles, minor adjustments were made in the area boundaries. Later, after scattered residents had been interviewed, the organizers divided each project area into *vikas sabhas*. The division of an area into smaller areas was based upon the general physical structure of most Indian cities and the limited area of daily social interaction typical for Indian urban families. Most Indian cities, developing as they have with almost no planning, have grown in such a way that, even in the densely populated areas, the physical structures are clustered in fairly distinct small groups, usually along small twisting alleys and lanes, or *katras*. Even in the tenements ten to fifteen families are often isolated from the main streets. *Vikas sabhas* were shaped to follow, as closely as possible, such natural geographic boundaries of an area as *katras* (squares of houses), lanes, streets, or tenements. A long lane was not split into parts, but where alleys or lanes were small both sides were included. It was found that closer relations exist across an alley or lane than between those living side by side in the alley or lane.

The primary world of most urban Indian families is a small one, limited to a collection of families, whether they live on lanes or even in tenements. It is at this primary level that problems of sanitation, water, and child care have most meaning. In fact, a small area often constitutes, in terms of the relationships of the people, "one big family." Women who are not employed outside the home seldom leave their areas except to shop. They spend much time gossiping and watching the small children. Men also usually spend most of their free time in this small area.

The purposes of the *vikas sabha* or zonal organization were, therefore, quite specific. First, in order to elect the executive committee or governing body of the *vikas mandal* in the most efficient manner, representatives were chosen from each *vikas sabha*. An executive-committee election conducted among several hundred families probably would have developed eventually into a struggle for power. Executive-committee members would not necessarily then even be responsible to particular zones. In fact, the entire executive committee could conceivably come from one geographical part of the community, representing one section of the population, or from one political party. There is likely to be much less in the way of politics among a small number of families. When the *vikas sabha* represented fewer than fifty families, as it usually did, it elected a member to the executive committee and a woman to the women's auxiliary.* No officer of the *vikas mandal* or the much larger *vikas parishad* could be elected without first having been selected by his *vikas sabha*. The system provided for real "grass roots" representation.

Second, by dividing the area into small zones and by doing some gerrymandering, it was possible to see to it that the executive committee was representative of the area. In one project involving 300 families, for example, twenty Harijan (Untouchable) families lived on a single lane. By designating this area as a zone, it was possible to ensure that a Harijan could be elected to the executive committee, which might not otherwise have been possible.

Third, the *vikas sabha* made possible the election of more representative "small men" who had had no previous leadership experience. An indication of what would probably have occurred if elections had been carried out only among several hundred families is the frequently observed fact that *vikas sabha* lower-class and caste representatives, although usually more numerous, sometimes tended to nominate people who were already involved in the leadership structure and who were of higher caste or class positions as officers of the *vikas mandals*. There would also have been a tendency to elect only traditional leaders in a Muslim area or in an area of a single caste. The small election unit made it much easier to include women in the larger organization, as they were chosen at the *vikas sabha* level rather than for the area as a whole where these capabilities might not have been recognized. Finally, by having an executive-committee representative for each small group of families, communications could be rapidly relayed from the people of the executive committee by word of mouth and vice versa. This consideration is important in urban India, where a large proportion of the people is illiterate.

---

* In a later system, after *vikas sabhas* were increased to 100 families and *vikas mandals* to 1,000 families, five members, one of whom had to be a woman, were elected from each *vikas sabha*.

The optimum number of *vikas sabhas* in a *vikas mandal* was planned to be ten to fifteen. In a later study of twenty-one *vikas mandals*, eleven had from seven to nine zones, five had from ten to twelve, and four had thirteen or fourteen. One *vikas mandal* had fewer than seven because the dominant caste group did not favor much fragmentation of the area. Similarly, there was considerable variation in the number of families in each *vikas sabha*. Although originally envisaged as a unit of fifteen to twenty-five families, it actually was usually somewhat larger; approximately one-half of 201 *vikas sabhas* had from twenty-five to fifty-five families each. Such variations can perhaps be expected in slum areas because of different physical and social patterns (see Table 5).

Table 5
Numbers of Families in 201 Vikas Sabhas *in Twenty-One* Vikas Mandals

Number of Families	Number of Vikas Sabhas	Percentage
up to 15	29	14.4
16–25	68	33.8
26–35	39	19.4
36–45	36	17.9
46–55	16	8.0
55 and over	13	6.5
Totals	201	100.0

When the boundaries of each *vikas sabha* had been set and a large number of the residents interviewed, the next step, beginning about the third week, was to start calling meetings in each area. At least two meetings were conducted each week after interviewing had been completed. The organizers kept a chart of all such meetings, including dates, decisions made, and the progress of activities of each *vikas sabha*. There were two types of meeting at this stage. In the first both men and women participated. The male community organizer was in charge, but the female community organizer worked closely with him. This type of meeting had several purposes: (1) to bring the people of the area together into zones, (2) to bring to the people's attention some zonal problems and to plan possible solutions based on self-help, (3) to develop a feeling for the larger area to be covered by the *vikas mandal*, (4) to discuss the prepared constitution, and (5) to elect a committee of three members, one of whom would be the chairman and representative on the executive committee of the *vikas mandal*.* The following is an extract from a community organizer's report of the initial meeting of one *vikas sabha*.

---

* The *vikas sabha* representatives were required to be residents of the zones, as much of their work was to improve the living conditions not only of the areas but of their own families as well. In fact, the wives carried considerable responsibility. Furthermore, if residence had not been made a prerequisite for office, a way would have been opened for the election of nonresident "honorary

At about two o'clock the community organizer came and both the workers went to the place where, with the help of a local man, they had arranged for a room for the meeting and spread a carpet on the floor. The community organizer was joined by a group and all of them started visiting each house, calling people to come out soon. At about 2:40 P.M., people started to come. They were received by the worker, and a copy of the *vikas mandal* constitution was handed to each of them. Thus by the time everyone reached the group, they were ready to discuss the program of organizing a zone group in the locality.

The proceedings started exactly at 3 P.M. and continued until 5. The following agenda was carried out:

1. election of the chairman for the meeting;
2. opening speech by the chairman;
3. community organizers' introductory speeches;
4. election of members of *vikas sabha*;
5. self-introduction of every member of the group;
6. lady community organizer's proposal for organizing a separate *mahila samiti*, or *vikas mandal* auxiliary for women;
7. concluding speech by the chairman.

The second type of zone meeting was exclusively for women, under the charge of the woman organizer. The purposes of this meeting of the women's auxiliary, or *mahila samiti*, were similar to those of the *vikas mandal* zonal meetings, except that the emphasis was on the problems of the women and what they could do about them. They were (1) to bring together the women of the zone, (2) to identify the needs of the community and to plan possible solutions based on self-help, (3) to develop some feeling for the larger area to be covered by the *vikas mandal*, and (4) to elect three women zone-committee members, one of whom would be the women's chairman and presumably a representative to the executive committee of the *mahila samiti*.

The Constitution. The model constitution of the *vikas mandal* (see Appendix A) was discussed at each *vikas sabha* meeting, and to most slum dwellers such discussion was a new and exciting experience, which gave them a sense of importance. This model constitution, which was prepared for the use of the *vikas mandals* and translated into Hindi and Urdu, set forth the names, aims, objectives, duties and powers of the various officers and representatives, as well as procedures for the collection and disbursement of funds.* It reflected much ex-

---

persons," such as important political figures, caste leaders, and staff members of welfare organizations, who might have been inclined to take over the *vikas mandal* meetings. It was precisely this typical Indian "patron" who often was elected to head voluntary welfare groups in the slums as "voluntary chairman," a pattern that had to be avoided if self-help was to be stimulated. Such a pattern, unfortunately, frequently occurs in other countries as well, where the majority, or often all, of the members of the boards of directors of welfare projects in the slums consists of outsiders.

* As the organization was sponsored by a municipal department, it was important that the constitution provide such safeguards as a provision that *vikas mandal* funds be deposited in a bank.

perience with the problems of such self-help organizations, and it helped to keep the objectives of self-help clearly before the people, listing the duties of the officers in order to serve as guidelines to minimize the manipulation of the organization by certain individuals. It gave poor and illiterate people an opportunity to gain experience in the democratic process. It also lent an air of permanence to the organization and, by its very nature, made it difficult for the organization to become involved in religious or political controversies. In fact, it stated that the *vikas mandal* was "non-partisan, non-sectarian, and a non-profit making organization."

The Executive Committee. The next organizational step was to bring together members of the executive committee for one or two meetings in order to discuss what a *vikas mandal* could do, to nominate the officers of the organization, and to plan the program for their inauguration. The officers included a president, a vice-president, a secretary, and a treasurer. The executive committee consisted of representatives of each *vikas sabha* (usually one from each but possibly more, depending upon the size of the zone) and two or three women's representatives chosen by the zone representatives of the *mahila samiti.*

The inauguration meeting of the *vikas mandal,* the first formal meeting of the people in the area, was planned, with some guidance by the organizers but in such a way as to try to make the slum dwellers believe that it was *their* meeting. In one instance, for example, the executive committee wanted to include a rather lengthy program of devotional songs by some of the younger people. When the organizers intimated that the songs would take more time than could be allowed at such an important meeting, several members pointed out that it was *their* decision. The community organizers had done a better job than they had anticipated in stimulating self-help and responsibility.

Inauguration of the Vikas Mandal. The inauguration ceremony marked the beginning of the full work of the *vikas mandal,* for it was then that the officers who had been nominated by the executive committee were elected, the constitution adopted, and a name picked for the group.* Following Indian custom, the meeting was generally opened with religious singing by children, in the case of Hindus, or by a reading from the Koran, in the case of Muslims, the recitation of poetry by young men, the presentation of a "chief guest" or a dignitary like the local councilman, a speech by the convenor or temporary president, and the singing of the national anthem. The meetings were usually held at night under artificial lighting, with several hundred people present, crowded into small areas, hanging from walls, and peering in through nearby windows and rooftops. In probably all cases, such meetings were the most exciting events ever to have taken place in the areas.

---

* The names embodied, in most cases, names of conspicuous streets or lanes or historic figures like the Emperor Asoka. After Prime Minister Nehru's death, some *vikas mandals* wanted to change their names to "Jawar Vikas Mandal."

The inauguration of a *vikas mandal* in one Muslim area, which observed strict purdah and in which three-fourths of the adults were illiterate, has been described by the organizer. The inaugural meetings of some *vikas mandals* did not always proceed this smoothly, because of clashes between individuals or groups with vested interests and because of difficulties in the physical arrangements. Under the circumstances, however, despite untrained, largely unsophisticated groups, meetings generally proceeded quite smoothly.

This area, which had been leaning so heavily on the traditional leadership, which was of a more or less paternalistic order, was to have a democratic organization of its own. Furthermore, the members had to adopt the constitution and to elect officers. The meeting was a great attraction for people living in an area surrounded by dirt, disease, and ignorance. The participation of women in purdah was also a problem. With all these points in view, the worker held a series of meetings with the woman community organizer. Long before the meeting, the worker met important people, discussed the program, helped in organizing the meeting, addressed small groups, talked informally, moved from one end of the area to the other. Everything was set for the meeting.

Before the scheduled time for the meeting, a *shamiana* (large cloth tent) was erected to cover half the open space. A ladies' enclosure was especially made, to allow privacy. The dais was well decorated and covered with pillows and white sheets. Eight carpets were arranged for the meeting: Electricity was available only in the small nearby mosque, and the electric connections were made to that source. The wiring and the bulb were especially arranged for the meeting. These preparations were an entire community project.

Everything was ready by 9 P.M. Very old people helped to keep order. Everyone in the area seemed to have come to the meeting. Men, women, children, young and old, in large numbers were in the meeting place. There was a gay carnival atmosphere, and the children enjoyed it the most. Exactly at 9:30 P.M. the "before the meeting" program started, and some of the young men read Muslim poems. The chairman came at 10 P.M. and had a brief talk with the worker. The proceedings started with a recitation from the Koran. The worker then gave a brief talk, more "matter-of-fact" than anything else. One of the residents presented the constitution, article by article, and proposed its adoption. Another seconded the motion. The chairman asked for comments. There was none. The chairman declared the constitution adopted.

In accordance with the provisions in the constitution, the chairman announced the various offices and asked the audience to suggest names. One person wrote down the names and gave them to the chairman. The name of the president had been changed. It was not the same as that decided on in the preparatory meeting of the executive committee. Then there were arguments and counterarguments. In fact, the original name was of a person who had left the city temporarily two days earlier. The constitution was silent on this issue, and the chairman suggested that the convention not elect absent members. It took some time for the people to calm down, and then the list of names was again read and proposed. Another person seconded the motions. The officers were then congratulated, and the worker put his own flower garland on the president. The chairman then gave his blessings and asked the people to make the program a success. The meeting came to a close.

Formalizing the Vikas Mandal. After the officers had been elected, committee meetings were held, and at these meetings the community organizer sought to motivate the officers and to develop their feelings of importance. The duties of each officer and of the executive-committee members were explained, both to the group and to the individual officers. It was unlikely that any of the slum dwellers had had previous experience of the type required for their new duties. The organizer often gave a full report on the area demarcated as the *vikas mandal* and a summary of the work there. This report was followed by a report from each *vikas sabha* about the work already started or completed. The organizer then suggested that the responsibility for all further activities be transferred to the executive committee, as he and the woman organizer had been carrying out this work only pending the establishment of the *vikas mandal.* The transfer of activities either already underway or completed often gave the new officers initial feelings of confidence and accomplishment, particularly if there were such tangible results as a new sewing machine, trash bins, or the whitewashing of some zones.

The community organizer occasionally discovered that an elected leader was too politically motivated, was too interested in possible personal gains from his position, or behaved in an unacceptable manner. In such cases, it was the organizer's responsibility to try to change his attitude toward his new duties and the objectives of the organization. Usually this help was accepted, as the local leaders needed assistance and, once elected to office, might recognize their responsibilities to the entire local community. Some people who caused trouble were only trying to gain status, and, by involving them in decisions on what would be good for the entire area, it was possible to give them parts in setting up standards they could themselves follow while at the same time gaining status.

All *vikas mandals* operated without organized centers.* Meetings were held, and activities were usually conducted in alleys and lanes or in improvised quarters. Still it was essential that a small office for each *vikas mandal* be secured as soon as possible. A subcommittee of two or three people was appointed in each area to locate an office with the help of the organizer. It was often difficult to find office space in the *vikas mandal* area, and someone usually lent a room for temporary use. Even in the most crowded areas, office space sooner or later turned up, primarily because the entire communities were interested in having offices. Such an office filled a number of functions—as a gathering place for the officers, as a symbol to the community of its common goals, as a center for communication of problems and activities, and finally as a place to store things

---

* In 1963, one area was organized around a municipal center.

like dried milk for free distribution and organization records. If it was large enough, it could be used for sewing, literacy, and health classes.

The *vikas mandal* paid the office rent, which usually did not exceed R.5–10 per month ($1–$2). The Department lent such equipment as a desk and chairs, and usually the executive committee arranged to have the name of the *vikas mandal* painted in large letters in front of the office. Beside the office with its desk and chairs, a *vikas mandal* needed such various supplies as, for example, one or more bulletin boards to display notices and activities of the organization and receipt forms printed with the name of the *vikas mandal* and numbered to avoid any difficulty in soliciting funds. All printing was done in Hindi, Urdu, and sometimes English. Stationery was also considered important, as it gave a sense of prestige to the officers and was useful in communicating with the city government or with other agencies. If the president could not write his own name, a rubber stamp was obtained for him. Register books were used for keeping accounts and for recording minutes of the meetings. Later, other equipment like utensils for boiling milk and athletic equipment was added by the community. A successful *vikas mandal*, starting with nothing, eventually had quite a list of property items for which it was responsible.

The constitution of the *vikas mandal* provided for two types of membership, contributing and noncontributing. For purposes of the *vikas mandal*'s work, all residents of the area became members of the organization. Those who became contributing members, however, could vote and seek office. The annual membership fee was R.1, the equivalent of 20 cents, payable in two semiannual installments.* Following the formal inauguration of the *vikas mandal*, each zone representative approached the families in his particular area asking them whether or not they wished to become contributing members. Two of the officers visited each family together. They explained the purposes of the organization but seldom exerted undue pressure on an individual to join. The number of contributing memberships, which indicated active interest in the organization, increased with the success of the *vikas mandal* over a period of time. Assuming one contributing member in each family, the percentage of families from which at least one paid membership was obtained for all the first six pilot projects in Delhi came to 78. Each *vikas mandal* was required to keep the membership funds in a bank. The organizer usually accompanied the president and treasurer when the account was opened, and all accounts were open to public inspection.

The president usually discussed the project committees at an early meeting of the executive committee. Ordinarily there were five such committees, responsible for physical improvement, health and sanitation, education and literacy, recreation and cultural activities, and economic improvement. Each committee consisted of from one to three members, depending upon the size of

---

* In the second project, in Ahmedabad, the annual dues were 25 *naya paisa*, or 5 cents.

the *vikas mandal*, and each was responsible for examining the problems carefully before suggesting improvements.

In certain selected areas, *vikas mandals* were organized by more rapid methods. These projects were larger, generally consisting of 100 families each, and the *vikas mandals* of 1,000 families each. This method not only was more rapid but also required a much smaller staff, relying upon citizen leaders for most of the interview work. The organizers did not do door-to-door interviewing on a routine basis; rather they used various methods to locate potentially effective area leaders, who were then trained to make contact with the residents. They also distributed pamphlets explaining the project.

In order to communicate the self-help idea to the people, free film shows were organized in each proposed *vikas mandal* area. After each film show, the nature and objectives of urban community-development work and the idea of self-help were explained to the people. They were told that an attempt was being made to organize a citizen development council and that their help was needed.

The help of local councilmen was also solicited through individual contacts. The objectives and importance of community-development work were explained, and councilmen were asked for the names of people in their areas who, regardless of political considerations, could be relied upon to help in the formation of *vikas sabhas* and *vikas mandals*. Those whose names had been suggested by other sources were carefully considered in terms of motivation and ability, and, in this way, the organizer gained some knowledge about the quality of potential leadership. In addition, the organizers interviewed a 10 per cent sample of the people of the area about their problems, which enabled them to learn more about area conditions, as well as to find additional potential leaders. As the workers went about the area, some citizens also came forward to offer their services. As a result of these various procedures, the organizers usually located about ten to twelve key people in each *vikas sabha*, although later experience showed that only two or three people actually did the work.

These potential leaders were invited to a large orientation session, at which the goals and purposes of the project were explained, as well as the methods of work, techniques of organization, and their own roles in organizing the community. They were asked to help with door-to-door interviewing to present the program to the people, to prepare a list of all heads of families in their zone, to assume responsibility for calling general meetings of their *vikas sabhas*, and to help make them successful.

In order to explain the aims, objectives, and activities of urban community development, a printed brochure was prepared to explain in simple terms the range of activities that would be possible through area development councils.

This brochure, along with a circular about the inaugural meeting, was distributed to all the heads of families by the local people helping in the area. Those who could not read had the brochure explained to them by neighbors who were literate. From this point, the organization method was similar to, but not exactly the same as, the intensive method.

The less intensive method has obvious advantages. It saves time and energy and enables the community to assume responsibility for development work much earlier and on its own initiative. With some improvements, this method could be made more efficient and economical, and at the same time it could more firmly implant the objectives of urban community development and citizen cooperation in the minds of the citizens. Still, the method has several shortcomings. The very speed of organization does not permit this new idea of responsibility to simmer long enough. In the Delhi project, initial activity projects at the *vikas sabha* level were omitted because of time. As a result, people sometimes began to think of the organization as an additional tier in the existing political structure of the area rather than as a new self-help device. The main shortcoming of this method was that it did not always allow time to select good, well-motivated leaders who would be unanimously accepted by all the members of particular zones. Sometimes political or caste divisions conditioned the attitudes of the population toward certain leaders and worked against the success of the project.

§ *Vikas Parishads* (*Neighborhood Councils*)

Some difficulties are encountered in accomplishing many self-help programs within a unit as small as a *vikas mandal*. Densely packed slums are so interdependent that one separate small area cannot work out its destiny alone, even under the most favorable conditions. *Vikas parishads*, or neighborhood councils, each encompassing several *vikas mandals*, made greater coordination possible. Such a neighborhood organization could eventually be viewed as coterminous with, or as a large part of, an administrative ward, opening up greater possibilities for coordinating political units with citizen self-help efforts. There was also a need for a larger unit if any practical decentralization of municipal services was to be accomplished.

As it was obvious that city living could not be entirely compartmentalized in small communities, the problem of integrating them into larger communities had to be faced. The next step, therefore, was to set up neighborhood councils each representing between 1,500 and 4,000 families, or 7,500 to 15,000 people. It was envisaged that each such council would, in turn, be part of a political ward of 25,000 to 75,000 people, so that eventually a ward would be broken down into several neighborhoods.*

---

* This plan was carried out in the later Ahmedabad project in urban community development, and similar procedures are also followed in Pakistan (see pp. 161–2).

There has been much discussion of the theoretical assumptions underlying the determination of the proper size of a neighborhood.[5] In the Delhi project, the population of a neighborhood was determined mainly on three considerations: general physical and social characteristics, population density, and the maximum number of *vikas mandals* that presumably could be effectively coordinated—ten to fifteen. There was no implication that a neighborhood was a unit, or could be developed into a unit in which people were well acquainted with one another or generally did things together. This type of relationship was to exist in the small units, that is, in the *vikas sabha* and *vikas mandal* communities. Furthermore, in Indian cities, unlike in the West, it is virtually impossible to delimit the size of an area in terms of functional units like schools and shopping centers. The neighborhood units in the Delhi project turned out to be somewhat larger than those recommended by planners in the West or in the Soviet Union, which generally have included from 5,000 to 10,000 people.[6]

This extension to neighborhood units properly took place when people began to think, for the first time, in terms of geographic communities, as they learned to participate in their *vikas mandals*. The neighborhood councils could not have been promoted until the *vikas mandals* had had opportunities to consolidate their organizations and to develop some community identification in their respective areas. If the larger geographic entities had been proposed prior to the establishment of primary-area loyalties, they would have been meaningless and confusing to the people.

Efforts were made to create the *vikas parishads* in the same manner as attempts had been made to build strong *vikas mandals*, first integrating the smaller units by formally bringing their representatives into councils.* Each neighborhood council consisted of representatives, the presidents and secretaries, of ten to fifteen *vikas mandals*. The *vikas parishad* territories were established on the basis of natural boundaries and the composition of the population. In addition to delimiting them, several other steps were carefully planned and carried out. They included preliminary discussions with officers of the *vikas mandals* and a series of neighborhood-wide programs of similar self-help activities to establish a sound communications network among the *vikas mandals*. These programs were designed to show the advantages of larger units.

These investigative and organizational procedures required time, as all possible complications had to be considered before the organization of a *vikas parishad*. The constitution for the organization was carefully discussed by each community organizer with the officers of the various *vikas mandals*, particularly

---

* The Chicago Hyde Park-Kenwood Community Conference had a block steering committee made up of members chosen by the block groups. In theory the chairman of the block steering committee and the professional staff were the communicating links between the block groups and the board of directors for the project. See Julia Abrahamson, *A Neighborhood Finds Itself* (New York: Harper & Row, Publishers, 1959), particularly pp. 105–8.

the representatives to the neighborhood council, and their reactions were transmitted to the neighborhood organizer. In each neighborhood, the oldest *vikas mandal* was usually asked to issue a printed circular in Hindi and Urdu, proposing the *vikas parishad*, including a copy of the proposed constitution, outlining boundaries, and mentioning some of the proposed activities. The neighborhood organizer then personally held meetings, noting which *vikas mandals* were most favorable and most hostile to the idea, their feelings about the constitution, and who might make good officers.

Throughout this period, ideas were gathered for possible joint activities of several *vikas mandals*, which might improve communications among the groups. A number of activities was arranged by representatives of the *vikas mandals*, for example, neighborhood child-health competitions and celebrations of national holidays. The community organizers also reported to the neighborhood organizer on the feelings of such other groups in the area as *mohalla* committees, caste groups, and welfare organizations. In cases of hostility, the benefits of a common approach were presented, with assurances that the new organization would have a strengthening effect and would neither duplicate other work nor infringe upon other groups. When the time was considered suitable, regular meetings were arranged and the officers elected. The constitution provided that the governing body should consist of two male representatives, the president and secretary, from each *vikas mandal* and a woman representative from each *mahila samiti*. The two male representatives, who were supposed to be the best-informed and most active officers, could make firm commitments on behalf of their organizations.

Those selected as officers, in contrast to the typical officers of *vikas mandals*, were usually those officers present of higher class and caste, partly because they were likely to be more educated and therefore better able to carry out the functions of officers of larger groups. Beside the chairman, there were also a first and a second deputy chairman and usually two secretaries and two treasurers, which helped to spread both the work and the prestige. Though the organization was a possible arena for political opportunism, the administrative structure of the *vikas parishad*, with its representatives elected from ten to fifteen separate groups and those groups elected in turn from *vikas sabhas*, made political exploitation difficult, for there was broad representation of political parties. Funds for the *vikas parishad* came from an affiliation fee of R.10 ($2) from each *vikas mandal*, with additional funds to be raised at the neighborhood level as the need arose. Social agencies in the neighborhood could also send one representative each to the council, if they were properly registered agencies and providing their officers lived in the neighborhood. They were also required to pay an affiliation fee of R.10 each, although this requirement was seldom really enforced. *Mohalla* committees in the neighborhood could also send representatives. Ex-officio members included the municipal councilmen, zonal health officers, sanitary inspectors, principals or headmasters of area schools, and the Department neighborhood organizers. Only the representatives of the *vikas mandals* were eligible to run for office, however.

In general, activities that involved more than one *vikas mandal* became the concern of the *vikas parishad*; a neighborhood unit did not engage in the type of activity common to the *vikas sabhas* and *vikas mandals*. For example, whereas a *vikas parishad* could cooperatively purchase trash bins for an entire neighborhood, such a project was not considered advisable because of the danger of theft or misuse in the absence of close personal supervision. The paving or repair of lanes was also inadvisable for a neighborhood, as lanes in some *vikas mandal* areas were satisfactory and the people in those areas might resent paying for work in other areas. Much could be done by a neighborhood, however, in the coordination of health programs and similar activities, not only permitting wider coverage but also stimulating more smaller-unit activities. Consequently, neighborhood immunization and vaccination programs were common. Family immunization cards, on which records could be kept, were distributed in neighborhoods, and mass immunization programs were carried out.* Large health and other exhibitions like those held in connection with Cleanliness Week or the annual Health Week could also be presented in neighborhoods, whereas they would have been virtually impossible at the *vikas mandal* level. One feature of neighborhood programs was the opportunity for *vikas mandal* constituents to become better acquainted with one another and to gain a broader perspective on their obligations to larger population units and the city itself. *Vikas mandals* sometimes represented fairly homogeneous groups. Through its activities, the neighborhood council often brought Hindus, Sikhs, and Muslims together, as well as people of different castes, regional origins, and social classes. In this sense, greater opportunities were offered for intergroup relations than through the *vikas mandals*. A popular neighborhood activity was the common celebration of Indian Independence Day; Diwali, the Hindu religious feast of lights; and such events as India Plan Week. *Bal divas* or children's fairs were also held. They served to dramatize children's activities and health, as well as to furnish entertainment for both children and adults. Trips were arranged on a neighborhood basis to such places as the All-India Radio station and Parliament. In one neighborhood, the women arranged joint bus trips to such distant places in the Punjab as Dehra Dun, and the men made a trip to see the Taj Mahal. In the summer, neighborhood programs in *khadi* work, paper crafts, and making plaster models were also arranged for children. Neighborhood competitions were arranged among *vikas mandals* on a systematic basis. Sports competitions like track meets and cricket matches were held. The *vikas mandal* winners in

---

* A report for one month, for example, showed that inoculations had been carried out in all *vikas mandals* in two neighborhoods and 1,700 people had been vaccinated. In another neighborhood, 2,800 people had been inoculated.

various child-health competitions often competed against one another in all-neighborhood contests. These activities strengthened ties in the *vikas parishad* and enhanced the prestige of the *vikas mandals*.

§ Civic Campaigns

A major weakness of urban India is the lack of pride that most urban dwellers have in their cities. The development of such pride is essential to provide a better climate for the work of *vikas mandals* and *vikas parishads*. A common complaint of the *vikas mandals*, for example, was that when they tried to improve sanitation in their areas passersby invariably littered indiscriminately and also urinated in their lanes and alleys. In order to make the citizens aware of conditions and to bring about pride in the city, a limited number of city-wide campaigns was incorporated into the urban community-development program. Posters* and newspaper advertisements were used to improve cleanliness, health, and use of public facilities and to create awareness of civic problems and the responsibilities of all Delhi citizens. Exhibits on the idea of urban community development were presented at civic festivals. A city-wide conference on civic improvements was held, to which all *vikas mandals* sent representatives. Other programs, a poetry contest, for example, helped to stimulate emotional attachment to this ancient and beautiful city. Most of these programs in themselves were too limited to affect a large city very profoundly, especially when the magnitude of the problem of civic apathy was as great as it was in Delhi, but they served as examples.

§ Mahila Samitis: The Role of Women in Social Change

In spite of increased activity among certain upper-class women, Indian women in general have only recently made gains in their legal status. Except for those who have become Westernized, the Hindu woman is "still bound by ancient traditions of behavior that emphasize her submissiveness, obedience, devotion and absolute dedication to her husband and his every wish. Her husband is almost a god and the home is her life and career."[7] Practically every marriage is still arranged, usually without requiring the woman's consent, and the dowry system involves factors that may be detrimental to her happiness. In most cases, the betrothed do not see each other, except perhaps briefly, prior to marriage.

---

* These posters were selected from annual prize contests conducted by the Department on an all-India basis.

The lives of Indian slum women are almost endless routines of domestic chores, with little diversion. The traditional Indian pattern does not include recreational activities for such women, and their plight is thus made particularly difficult. Although they live in cities where there are numerous movie theaters, many women have hardly seen a motion picture. They cannot take advantage of the city's recreational offerings, but they no longer have the village cultural life to enjoy. The city slum woman may miss the group songs and dances, the meetings around the village well, and the gatherings with other women in the village. Her life is hard, and her leisure time is spent in idleness or gossip.

The active participation of the women was recognized as essential to bringing about change in the Delhi slums. As they play key roles in training the younger generation, they must be effectively involved in the process of social change. The continuity of any new practices, like that of traditional family culture, depends largely upon the acceptance of such practices by the women of the community. The backgrounds of slum women and the prevailing social conventions made it almost impossible, however, for them to be elected as representatives of the *vikas sabhas* and in this way to serve on the executive committees. Such elections did occur in two or three cases, however. For this reason, a liaison arrangement was set up between the *vikas mandals* and separate women's auxiliaries called *mahila* (meaning woman) *samitis* in all the projects, Muslim and Hindu. Three elected members of each *mahila samiti* served as ex-officio members on the executive committee of each *vikas mandal*.*

The *mahila samitis* were organized for the purpose of planning and executing self-help programs for women and children. They were established in much the same way as were the *vikas mandals*, with women organizers helping with the organization and stimulating self-help among the women. The woman community organizers often became, in terms of Indian family tradition, *bahinjees* or the emancipated elder sisters of the area. In each zone, a *mahila samiti* was organized, representing between fifteen and 100 women, generally around forty. Representatives were elected, discussions of zonal conditions were held, and decisions were made regarding the self-help activities to be undertaken. The representatives of an entire area, usually ten to fifteen, formed a council of women, the *mahila samiti*. They, in turn, chose three representatives, one of whom was a convenor or chairman, to serve as liaisons with the *vikas mandal* executive committee, as well as to represent the *mahila samiti* at special meetings. In this way women came to play an active part, and in an official capacity, in the improvement of slum areas.

---

* In each of the later and larger *vikas sabhas* of 1,000 families each, there were four representatives, one of whom had to be a woman, who then also became part of the corresponding *mahila samiti*.

Chapter 9

The use of voluntary groups

The active participation of the citizen is the very essence of any community-development program. This participation involves group deliberation and decision-making, as well as cooperative action to meet civic needs and to solve problems of the neighborhood and the city as a whole. In the task of getting people to work together to improve local conditions and community life, the strengthening of any existing citizen group is exceedingly important.

§ *Voluntary Self-Help Groups in Urban Areas*

Here and there throughout most cities of the world, particularly in the slum areas, some programs of self-help are already in existence. Often these associations are based on village, tribal, ethnic, religious, regional, or caste ties, and in other cases on geographic proximity. Some are fraternal and benevolent groups like burial societies, whereas others are church groups, labor unions, and parent-teacher associations. Although they do carry out some self-help programs, much of what they do could be done more systematically, and they could perform additional functions. It is important that any community-development program identify such groups and use them in their own programs.

Self-help activities may be made possible by the fact that some people who migrate to cities tend to form associations with people whom they have known before. In a United Nations report on cities of developing countries, it was pointed out that there is a "tendency for migrating individuals to choose neighborhoods where they have connections, i.e., relatives, friends or simply members of their home-community, and as a result there are sometimes well-defined regions and zones inhabited by communities which previously had well-defined relationships in areas from which they migrated."[1] For example, most people who live in the slum areas or *barriados* of Peruvian cities are Indians from rural areas.* Many are able to maintain some of their close village ties and to form organizations to cooperate in self-help improvements in urban areas.[2] The people of the *kampongs* in Indonesian cities also keep up some rural community ties despite their crowded living conditions. "They cling to vestigial remains of Goton-Rojong or communal labor and community responsibility and often rely upon the authority and direction of the kampong head and community sanction rather than upon individual decision and autonomous activity."[3] In other cases, certain ties may develop among urban people even without the strong kinship ties carried over from rural areas. Such ties may be formed during the celebration of traditional festivals or during certain calamities, or they may arise from joint protests to the municipal government.

In the cities of many countries, there are voluntary organizations of some kind, for example, the tribal and village mutual-aid groups so common in West African cities.[4] Sometimes self-help associations may not be formed on neighborhood bases but may cut across the city. In Accra, for example, recent migrants tend to form tribal or home-town associations for mutual self-help. There are more than 100 such associations with a total membership reported to be equal to about one-half the male population. Sometimes new arrivals look to tribal chiefs residing in the city who have traditional powers for settling disputes.[5] In Lagos, city-wide tribal associations are also quite important. They have common loan funds, help to settle disputes, secure employment for their members, and also help individuals with financial difficulties. In Freetown, Sierra Leone, though migrants no longer congregate in tribal sectors, there is a system of tribal headmanship and voluntary association, which Banton has concluded is of "considerable influence in the life of tribal people settled in the city and . . . might be utilized more systematically as a means of organizing self-help in the immigrant communities and training the newcomer in citizenship."[6] The tribal headmen are able to perform many of the same functions that they performed in rural areas where the political structures of the tribes were centered around them. The network of relationships among members of a tribe can be considered a secondary system within the larger urban social system. In Freetown, headmen help with the control of crime and furnishing bail and with the administration of estates of deceased people, as well as with other matters. Banton describes how such societies operate:

Before the 1920's bereavement clubs and entertainment societies had been

---

* One writer, speaking of the shanty towns or squatter settlements of Latin American cities, has stated that they can be viewed in two different ways: "(1) that they are slums, blighted areas, belts of misery, incubators for disease, crime, social disorganization and personality disorder; and (2) that as semirural enclaves they make available new possibilities for urban social reconstruction on the basis of neighborhood communities, regional and kinship ties, mutual-aid associations, and small-group political activity." Richard M. Morse, "Recent Research on Latin American Urbanization: A Selective Survey with Commentary," *Latin American Research Review*, 1 (Fall, 1965), 51; and Acácio Ferreira, *Lazer operário, um estudo de organização social das cidades* (Salvador: 1959).

separate, but then the Mandinka started two new voluntary associations that served both functions. Each society had its own characteristic dance rhythm, its songs, and a limited number of members who were required to attend regularly and contribute money to help any other member who had been bereaved. These societies became very popular among the youth of many tribes, and numerous branches sprang up in different parts of the city. . . . A company provided a member who was bereaved with a contribution toward his expenses, and its members were obliged to attend the wake if the burial was held in the city. In the tribal village the lineage would have been there to help at the most important event; in the city a migrant may be on his own. Consequently the wake, and honoring the member's dead kinsman, may be even more important than the material support. Another benefit deriving from company membership was the opportunity to join with other young men and girls for dancing and entertainment in relatively exclusive groups which protected themselves against attacks from the troublemakers who thrive in the new urban centers.*

Close ties have been reported among some of the *vecindades* or slum neighborhoods of Mexico City. Some *vecindades* are small, whereas others may contain several hundred people. Oscar Lewis found one *vecindad* of 700 people to be quite stable, two-thirds of the residents having been born in Mexico City and the rest coming from twenty-four of the thirty-two Mexican states. This community had undertaken on its own initiative a number of self-help activities.

Partly because of stability of residence, the *vecindad* has taken on some of the characteristics usually associated with a small community. About a third of the households were related by blood ties and about a fourth by marriage and *compadrazgo* (godparent relationship). . . . On Sunday nights there is usually an outdoor dance in one of the patios organized by the youth and attended by people of all ages. Groups of neighbors may buy a lottery ticket co-operatively, organize raffles and tandas or informal mutual savings and credit plans in an effort at self-help. They also participate in religious pilgrimages and together celebrate the festival of *vecindad* Saints, the Christmas Rosadas and a few other holidays.[7]

Ward citizen committees have a long history in the cities of Japan. Wards were semiself-governing in Tokyo as far back as Tokugawa times.[8] In those days, they were socially, politically, and economically more self-contained than they are today, employing their own gatekeepers and fire chiefs with personnel and equipment. They had ward secretaries and offices with registries of all inhabitants. Each ward governing association actually consisted of the landlords, who were supposed to look out for the tenants. Down a hierarchical chain to the

---

* Michael Banton, "Social Alignment and Identity in a West African City," in Hilda Kuper, ed., *Urbanization and Migration in West Africa* (Berkeley: University of California Press, 1965), pp. 141–2. Mutual-aid societies are often continued into subsequent generations in the somewhat modified form of "companies," one difference being that the latter place more emphasis on competition than on age or status, although membership is still on a tribal basis.

wards came a series of edicts on crime, rents, and vagrants and warnings against too much waste.

During World War II, ward committees played an important role, almost to the point of serving as self-contained units of civilian defense. During the Occupation, they were ordered abolished as elements of the totalitarian administrative setup, but ward associations were so useful that they were revived. Vestiges of this system remain today. They have been helpful during natural disasters and in relaying governmental information on health and other matters to the people. In the ward studied by Dore, a president, a vice-president, and other officers are now elected annually, and each householder pays a contribution. The money is used for incense offerings for households in which deaths have occurred, for street lighting, for night watchmen, and for ward festivals. Half the money is given to bodies dealing with such activities as crime and fire prevention, traffic congestion, mothers' aid, and refuse collection. Some of the organizations provide hot food for the night shift of the police, gifts to retiring members, and so forth. The revival of ward associations in Tokyo has been aided by the existence of a traditional model, the inadequacy of such city services as street lighting, and the existence of a still considerable proportion of self-employed workers who spend most of their time in the wards. It may be, however, that, as the urban situation changes, there will be a decline in ward sentiments. One of the functions of such committees is to develop feelings of belonging among the people of the wards.

> Many people develop informal ties with their neighbors which are of emotional and material value to them, only because the formal institutions of the ward association and the tonari-gumi give them a means of breaking the ice. The insecure new immigrants from the country, faced with the emotional shock of the death of a child or a husband, may find great comfort in the assurance of help from neighbors and even from the formal gesture of a ward official's visit with a condolence gift from the ward. Though attenuated, some sense of "belonging" to the ward, annually stimulated by the gaiety of the two-day festival celebrations, may well enrich the lives of some people and help to counteract the generally deplored psychological effects of the increasing atomization and depersonalization of city life.[9]

§ Self-Help Groups in Delhi

An effort was made to stimulate and to encourage existing voluntary citizen organizations in Delhi in order to broaden the scope of self-help activities. Such an effort is not so easy in urban India as it is in the West, where many voluntary groups based on educational, religious, and occupational interests work for civic and community improvement, although these groups are not so frequently found among, or participated in, by lower-class people in slum areas.[10] There is no equivalent of the Parent-Teacher Associations in Delhi public schools, and there are few close associations among the schools, the parents, and the communities. For this reason, in addition to the fact that not all children go to school or stay in school for any great length of time, it is difficult to involve parents in self-help activities. In Western societies like that of the United States, church groups and church leaders often play important roles in achieving civic improvements. Such roles are not common in India, where religious groups like the Hindus, Muslims, and Sikhs, perhaps like the Christian churches of centuries past, are interested primarily in matters of the spirit rather than of the immediate environment. In Delhi, labor unions are primarily interested in working conditions and in politics rather than in the conditions where the members live, although elsewhere in India there are exceptions. Small-business associations are also not sufficiently strong or community-oriented to work for civic improvements, although one project did involve self-help changes in the business section itself.

Where their members resided together, caste and occupational groups comprised logical working groups, but, unfortunately, most were usually too small. Despite traditional leadership in such groups, they were encouraged to become more interested in the wider issues of self-help and to become more actively concerned with such problems as literacy, nutrition, and health. On occasion, a caste group was encountered that had already undertaken wider self-help activities, and in such cases the groups were sometimes helped to make their activities more effective.

Here and there in *katras* and other places small-scale self-help groups, which met to discuss their problems, were encountered. Their activities were usually restricted to collecting funds for water taps or providing games and prizes for the children on Republic Day or some other celebration. These activities were broadened when the groups joined in *vikas mandal* activities. Certainly much more could be done to identify other informal groups and to develop some working arrangements. Where such groups are squatters on unauthorized land, a problem is presented for a municipality, as encouraging squatters to make improvements involves tacit recognition of squatter rights. Later it becomes difficult to move them. In Mexico City, where a different policy is followed and where there are extensive squatter colonies, a law provides that, if 50 per cent of the people in an area of fifty to 100 families organize themselves and present a plan to the city, the city will install sanitary services and electricity, for which the people will pay over a ten-year period. A further advantage of this system is that the procedure encourages slum people to build better houses for which more recognition of permanent occupancy rights is shown.

Among the most extensive and traditional self-help organizations in Delhi were the *mohalla* committees and the *vyapar mandals*, or organizations of shopkeepers in the bazaars. The Delhi project attempted to improve the efforts of these traditional groups.

§ *Mohalla Committees*

Mohalla committees originated in Mogul times as part of a system called "Mir Mohalla," in which a certain person was designated as "chief of the locality" for an urban neighborhood. The help of the heads of families in a neighborhood was enlisted by authorities to assist with keeping law and order and sometimes to serve in the actual defense of the city. Such organizations have been carried over into present-day India under different names and with different functions but with a variety of self-help programs. They needed strengthening, however, in order to become effective.

There are probably more than 400 of these committees in Delhi, claiming several hundred thousand members, and the Delhi project eventually helped to improve the work of 149 of them. The *mohalla* committees are located in various parts of the city, and generally they are very loosely knit organizations. The names of the older groups are derived from the original communities like Basti Julahan, a particular group of weavers living in a closely knit area; prominent personalities like Chatta Pratap Singh; particular historical structures like Matia Mahal; or religious institutions like Kali Masjid. Newer *mohalla* committees, known as *mohalla sudhar sabhas*, or residents' welfare committees, have developed when leaders have become aroused by such specific situations as community crises on which the people's attention has been focused. These committees often seek the aid of government or semigovernment agencies in providing such facilities as public hydrants, dispensaries and other medical assistance, street lighting, improved schools, and paved lanes. Sometimes they are ready to share the expenses, which are not normally assumed by such agencies. Their chief functions, however, have been the settling of disputes, the institution of cultural programs, and arrangements for common night watchmen.

It was believed that these existing committees and similar organizations could help with vital civic problems like sanitation and preventing food adulteration, thus serving to relieve the hard-pressed Delhi municipal departments. Consequently, efforts were made to identify such groups and to explore ways and means of assisting them to function more effectively. They could thus serve on a par with the *vikas mandals*, which were sponsored directly by the Department as agents of planned change, and in this approach a traditional institutional pattern would be given a new focus.

It was difficult to discover the names and the locations of the *mohalla* committees, as no lists were available. Although the large associations were generally officially registered as organizations with governmental agencies, the smaller committees and *vikas mandals* were not registered. Initially thirty-two such organizations were located. Seven were found to be merely paper organizations with few activities, and five were found to have been inactive for more than two years. The remaining twenty committees were studied in order to gain some insight into how they worked.

The *mohalla* committees were found to vary considerably in size, coverage, and membership.[11] Some attempted to represent as many as 16,000 people, whereas others represented fewer than 200 families. More than half the organizations represented fewer than 500 families, or 2,500 people. One-fourth, however, had constituencies ranging between 2,000 and 16,000 families. All the organizations operated in particular areas. The guiding factor in defining such an area seems to have been simply geographical entity; the nature of social relations, for example, was not taken into account. Thirteen of the organizations were located in the older parts of Delhi and seven in new housing colonies. Only one-fourth had been formed prior to 1955, which would suggest that some *mohalla* committees, even though outgrowths of an old tradition, have fairly transitory existences.

Often the groups were so loosely organized that membership lines were not clear; in fact, some people who were not even residents of the proper areas were given membership. From the point of view of participation in activities in each area, however, little distinction was made between members and nonmembers. Most of these organizations levied nominal annual dues. The total number of members enlisted during 1961 in all the twenty *mohalla* committees came to 2,661 people of about 46,000 eligible families. This figure represented an average of 132 members per *mohalla* committee. The total membership figure, however, conceals the variation among the *mohalla* committees. In a large number of *mohalla* committees, the percentage of membership was low; 65 per cent of the committees had less than 40 per cent of the total population in their areas. In only one organization was the percentage outstanding, 81 per cent in an area that had an arrangement for night watchmen.

When a comparison is made between the percentage of eligible area residents who are members in the traditional *mohalla* committees and that in the newer *vikas mandals*, it is evident that a much larger proportion of residents became members of *vikas mandals* than of *mohalla* committees. According to the first evaluation study of the *vikas mandals*, which was carried out in 1961, the total number of contributing members enlisted in all twenty-one *vikas mandals* studied was 3,325 people, out of 5,780 families. This figure represented an average of 158 members per *vikas mandal*, or 57 per cent of the families, assuming one member for each family. In a majority of cases (twelve of twenty-one *vikas mandals*, or 57 per cent) the membership ranged between 41 and 60 per cent of the resident families. Membership was outstanding in five *vikas mandals*, in which it exceeded 80 per cent (see Table 6).

The reasons for the differences appear to be that the *vikas mandals*, unlike the *mohalla* committees, held meetings and delegated responsibilities to small units or *vikas sabhas*, held regular membership drives, undertook a variety of activities on a systematic basis, involved larger numbers of indigenous leaders, and constantly interpreted the programs to the people.

All the twenty *mohalla* committees had executive or managing committees, the size of each committee ranging from five to thirty-six members; in sixteen of them, the sizes of the executive committee were between ten and twenty. Comparisons of 304 *mohalla* committee executive-committee members and 351 *vikas mandal* executive-committee members showed that there was considerable similarity between the two. In both, members between thirty-six and fifty-five years of age predominated, with the next largest group being between twenty-six and thirty-five. Great differences existed in educational backgrounds, however; in contrast to the *vikas mandals*, the more educated members predominated in the *mohalla* committees, suggesting that, in more traditional organizations, leadership is less representative and, in a sense, less democratic. In

Table 6

Membership as Percentage of Total Families in Mohalla *Committees and* Vikas Mandals

Membership as Percentage of Total Families	Percentage of Mohalla Committees	Percentage of Vikas Mandals
0–20	50	4.8
21–40	15	9.5
41–60	20	57.1
61–80	10	4.8
81–100	5	19.0
101 and more	0	4.8

a largely impersonal organization like a *mohalla* committee, people tend to elect those with higher status, those with education, political position, or some other form of success; in the more intimate *vikas mandal*, people seem to elect those whom they know well enough and believe are educationally similar to themselves. The percentage of 293 executive-committee members from eighteen *mohalla* committees with eleven years of schooling was 37, and with more than eleven years, 38. One-fifth were college graduates. In all, the more educated constituted two-thirds of the total, whereas a different picture was common in the *vikas mandals*. Those with little or no education among 351 members constituted around 31 per cent, whereas those with only primary or middle-school education constituted another 32 per cent, which means that two-thirds were people with modest education. A comparable difference was discovered in occupational distribution. In the majority of the *mohalla* committees, the executive-committee members were in service, trade, and business occupations. Workers, both skilled and unskilled, were seldom included. The over-all figure was 66 per cent for service and trade, 32 per cent for business and skilled labor, and only

1.4 per cent for unskilled labor, a composition almost the reverse of that of the *vikas mandals* (see Table 7).

Regular annual general meetings were not a common feature of most of them; in only five *mohalla* committees had annual meetings been held in the previous three years. In five others, only two meetings were held a year, and in the remaining ten only one meeting a year was reported. It was also noted that the officers of the *mohalla* committees retained office year after year. Although it was explained that other competent people did not generally come forward to offer their services, in actuality most of these organizations were dominated by select groups of people. They were not truly democratic in nature, with management and control open to the community at large, and had not developed second tiers of leadership that could replace the incumbents.

Table 7

Educational Levels of Executive-Committee Members of Mohalla *Committees and* Vikas Mandals

Education	Mohalla Committee Members*	Vikas Mandal Members*
None	2.4	19.9
Below primary	9.2	11.1
Primary (five years)	5.8	15.1
Middle-school (eight years)	7.8	17.1
Matriculated (eleven years)	36.8	19.1
Intermediate (thirteen years)	6.5	5.4
Graduate (fifteen years)	23.9	9.1
Post-graduate (seventeen years)	7.6	3.2

* In percentages.

In contrast to the *vikas mandals*, in the *mohalla* committees women were rarely involved either in auxiliary groups or as members of the executive committees.* Of all the twenty *mohalla* committees studied, only one had a separate unit for youths.

There was considerable latitude for improvement in the quality and quantity of the work of the committees, and it was this purpose that the Delhi project tried to accomplish. A community organizer with the special title of "liaison officer" was assigned to work with the *mohalla* committees, and eventually he was assisted by two other part-time organizers. Three training programs for *mohalla* committee representatives were conducted; a periodic newsletter, *Vikas Van*, was prepared to disseminate news and suggestions among the *mohalla* committees; and technical advice for changing and improving its work was given to each committee. The presidents and the secretaries of these

---

* There was a tendency, however to encourage women to participate in the executive committees in the more educated localities, in the new colonies, and in the *mohalla* committees of younger age groups.

organizations were invited to a meeting to discuss their activities and how the Department might be helpful to them.

Beside training in technical skills, an important need was the coordination of the work of the various *mohalla* committees. As they expressed interest in knowing what others were doing and planning, training sessions were organized to which each *mohalla* committee was asked to send representatives. These training programs emphasized the organization and work of the *vikas mandals* as demonstration units, much in the same manner that cooperative extension services have been used in the United States. In addition to detailed explanations of the work of the *vikas mandals*, there were discussions of the structure and functions of the city government, the slums of Delhi, the Delhi Master Plan for town planning, health and sanitation problems, programs for women and children, family planning, food adulteration, and small savings programs. A standardized constitution was prepared, help was given with official registration of the groups, and other information about various community-development programs was supplied. Arrangements were also made for posters, film shows, and dried milk for distribution among the poorer children of the areas. Workers visited *mohalla* committee officers in an attempt to effect some improvements in these efforts. These improvements ranged from official registration of the organization to more effective executive meetings or annual meetings, larger membership drives, increased women's participation, and wider variation in activities.

In a general way, work with these *mohalla* committees resembled that of the Secretary for Chinese Affairs in Hong Kong, whose staff of organizers, or "liaison officers" as they are also called, helps to improve the work of the *kaifongs* or neighborhood associations. These *kaifongs* represent a revival of the traditional neighborhood mutual-help organizations that had existed in Canton and elsewhere in China for a long time. The Hong Kong government revived these traditional organizations after a disastrous fire in 1947 had resulted in much property destruction, many refugees, and great pressures on the authorities. *Kaifongs* now number fifteen, covering the entire island of Hong Kong, and thirteen more take in the entire area of Kowloon. Each neighborhood corresponds approximately to a police district. The *kaifongs* are run by a president, a small supervisory committee, and an executive committee of ten to twenty members, whose unpaid officers are generally important local businessmen. Each *kaifong* pays for the support of a secretary and often also for school teachers and health workers. It raises money through membership dues, subscriptions from well-to-do residents of the area, and charging admission to plays and other events. Services rendered during 1958–1959 included emergency help for 16,000 victims of twenty disasters, arbitration and conciliation in about 1,000 family disputes, treatment of 300,000 patients by 246 medical practitioners, provision of 263 free classes for 9,800 pupils, twenty-nine ambulance classes for 800 trainees, forty-five homemaking classes for 460 women, and organization of seventy-three sports teams. The Hong Kong government maintains liaison with, and furnishes guidance to, the *kaifongs* through the Secretary for Chinese Affairs. Sometimes departments of the government give grants-in-aid for particular services like education, preventive medicine, and emergency relief. In general, however, governmental services are not channeled through these completely autonomous nongovernmental associations.

§ Bazaars and Their Vyapar Mandals

In the bazaars of Indian cities flows the very lifeblood of the Indian people. These colorful and exciting market places are of various types. In the northern part of the country, they are usually situated in the residential areas and consist of rows of all kinds of shops on both sides of narrow streets or lanes, behind and above which often live the shop owners and their families, as much a part of the neighborhoods as are other residents. In some, usually small, cities, the bazaars serve the entire communities.

Most bazaars are chaotic at best. Shopping is often difficult because of the confusion caused by heavy and disorderly traffic of pedestrians, pushcarts, cycles, cars, tongas, bullock carts, and stray cows. Vehicles carrying uncovered refuse pass through these districts at all hours of the day. It is common to see drains around bazaars choked with filth, leaking hydrants, and dirty water spreading everywhere. Alongside the shops children may defecate in the drains, and adults urinate indiscriminately. Apart from the bazaars' general disorderliness and chaos, they are breeders of disease. Food and milk shops, as well as small eating places, present acute problems, for their owners seldom display even the most rudimentary knowledge or practice of sanitation.

Civic authorities do little about bazaar conditions except through very occasional checkups, which seldom result in any punitive action. The situation is regarded as rather hopeless in view of the immensity of the problem and the lack of cooperation from shop owners. The people are unconcerned, the number of sanitary inspectors is pitifully small, and political repercussions are likely if attempts are made to punish shopkeepers severely for various infractions of the law. If the shopkeepers, the municipal authorities, and the public were to cooperate, even to a limited extent, many bazaars could be transformed into far better shopping centers.

Some bazaars have had their own associations, known as *vyapar mandals*, which are concerned with the commercial interests of the shopkeepers. Such associations are often of long standing, with much useful work to their credit, but their approach has usually been to seek greater concessions from the Municipal Corporation or other authorities rather than to do anything for the public. In old bazaars, *vyapar mandals* are interested in maintaining encroachments on the sidewalks, in licensing, in problems of the sales tax, and in similar issues. The sanitary conditions of the bazaars as a rule are not considered by most *vyapar mandals*. Although some individual shopkeepers may try to keep their own shops neat and clean, they are seldom concerned about the cleanliness of the adjacent places.

A major function of most bazaar associations is the planning of group celebrations of important religious festivals like Diwali and Holi. Most shopkeepers are willing to spend lavish sums on decorations for these celebrations and on gifts of sweets to one another. The *vyapar mandals* invariably use these events to invite important officers of the city government or politicians to take part in the functions, at which time they often ask for special concessions or favors.

A bazaar project involving self-help was planned early in 1960, and a typical bazaar with about 300 shops was selected. This particular bazaar was located on both sides of a street and consisted of all types of shops, with an emphasis on "cut cloth," for which it was well known. It was shabby and dirty, and it also had a reputation, whether or not deserved, for short weights, short measures, and improper charges. One of the community organizers assigned to the project wrote that the first day he was "disheartened with the magnitude of the work in making this shopping center really attractive and beautiful entirely through self-help."

The shopkeepers in this bazaar had organized themselves into a *vyapar mandal* in 1954, primarily to resist efforts by the municipality to remove sidewalk encroachments. Because of a dispute, a second, smaller organization was later formed. The *vyapar mandal* had not been an active organization. Even though its officers had been serious and had made great plans, little had really been done to improve the area. The shopkeepers were critical of the activities of their organization, which was known largely for its annual function, at which, they claimed, money was wasted on free tea and snacks.

The organizers were advised to be extremely careful to state the objectives of the project in terms of self-help and to clarify their relationship with the other municipal departments; they were to point out that they were not connected with health and inspection, had nothing to do with the issuance of any type of warrant, and would in no way interfere. Initially, the shopkeepers did not appreciate the role of the Department, regarding it as a channel for obtaining more and better facilities from the municipality rather than as an instrument of self-help. They identified their problems as mainly unsanitary conditions; lack of water taps and urinals; such nuisances as roaming cattle and the selling of fruits, vegetables, and other articles by pavement squatters; and the blocking of their shops by improperly parked cars and horse tongas.* Such problems were blamed

* The consensus among bazaar sellers was that improvements in the appearance of the shops were not appreciated, as disorder appeared to be an accepted way of life. The organizers pointed out that the

upon the health department, the police, licensing authorities, shop inspectors, and all other governmental functionaries, whom they tended to regard as corrupt and inefficient. Each talk with a shopkeeper became an opportunity for him to complain about the authorities. Although the shopkeepers had some appreciation of the idea of self-help, the problem was to turn this recognition into practice.

Gradually, some shopkeepers began to understand their own responsibilities for making improvements in the market. The community organizer helped the secretary to set up more permanent and systematic records of the organization, and new stationery with an insignia for the organization, as well as account books, was purchased. Although it was six years old, the organization had never before had a list of the shops or members, and it had thus been impossible to collect dues systematically. Although the appeal was made largely in such economic terms as increased profits, it was hoped that improvements would foster local pride and a recognition of the necessity for better sanitation measures. The response was encouraging, particularly in the attitudes of the shopkeepers toward mutual cooperation. Among some of the specific bazaar-project accomplishments were the organizational strengthening of the *vyapar mandal*, the erection of a large notice board for its activities, the erection of a billboard map of the area showing shop locations, a monthly news bulletin to inform members on various matters, and four subpostal locations for the sale of stamps. Members paid their electric and meter bills and their license fees cooperatively, to save time and effort. A major achievement was a "best-kept shop" contest during Diwali. The *vyapar mandal* organized subblock contests by dividing the area into three sections, giving a group prize to each, as well as to the best shop in each section. The sections were judged on general neatness and cleanliness, the number of shops painted sky blue (the traditional Diwali color), the quality of work done, general orderliness and display of the shops, facilities provided for shoppers, and Diwali decorations. An electric clock was jointly contributed by the *vyapar mandal* and the Department as a section prize. It was placed in a conspicuous place so that customers could see the time, but it did not keep time and later was shelved for three nonelectric clocks in each zone. The best shop in each block was given a decorative electric ceiling lamp with a glass shade, on which the name of the contest winner was inscribed. For another Diwali, the shopkeepers had their shops whitewashed and the doors painted a uniform light blue.

A subcommittee was set up to help the shopkeepers renew their licenses, and another was formed to deal with quarrels among the shopkeepers, the settlement of dues, and the payment of debts. Development of community feeling among

---

better shops in the city relied upon neat and attractive displays to sell more goods and that movie houses and similar businesses attempted to draw patrons through attractive displays and clean surroundings.

the shopkeepers was evident in a three-day bus trip they took to see the Bhakra Dam and another that same year taken with their families to another distant area. In the final analysis, it is difficult to say whether this experiment in changing a bazaar was a success or a failure. Probably it was at best a partial success, and much more time and effort will be required to produce the profound changes that are needed. Like the *mohalla* committees, it has been a useful experiment in attempting to improve a voluntary organization through the application of community development.

Chapter 10

SELF-HELP ACTIVITIES

"Self-help" means the improvement of a person or group by his or its own contributions and efforts and largely for his or its own benefit. Self-help is thus the opposite of charity. A citizen group that solicits contributions or gifts from well-to-do outsiders or secures them, with no contributions of its own, from the government is not engaging in self-help, even though it might be complimented for its industry.* Such services as sewing, child-care, and literacy classes can be considered self-help if the group contributes some share of the money for the teachers, the equipment, or the building facilities. They may also be considered self-help if they are sponsored by the group and arranged for and carried out at its invitation.

Self-help should be accompanied by a feeling of ownership, sponsorship, or involvement on the part of the group. It should instill some sense of personal pride in achievement. Even if people contribute only a small percentage of the cost of an activity, it is assumed that this contribution will give them pride in "ownership." The group's sponsorship and arrangement of an activity that is entirely financed by outside sources may have the same result. People learn by doing; those engaged in successful self-help activities often become a reservoir of community leadership in the area. Self-help activities in these terms can, of course, take unusual forms. One *vikas mandal*, for example, successfully collected sweets and candy during the celebration of Diwali for the residents of a nearby area who were even poorer than its own citizens.

One might well be skeptical about the possibilities of self-help in a country like India, where slum conditions are difficult and the resources are limited. Actual experience has revealed a wide scope for such activities, arising largely from group initiative and the pooling of financial and other resources. Even though a lengthy list of possible self-help activities had been prepared in advance, citizens constantly suggested new types never originally contemplated.

---

* Some readers might argue that, as citizens should expect some personal returns on the taxes they pay, this activity is a form of "self-help."

These activities ranged from physical improvements in sanitation, health, educational, recreational, and cultural programs and economic improvements to the control of such deviant behavior as delinquency, gambling, and prostitution. Based on the experiences of the Delhi project, the largest concentration of projects undertaken by thirty-one citizen councils was in the areas of recreational and cultural activity, with sanitation and health second. Physical improvements and facilities were third. In terms of the number of participants, health and sanitation was first and physical improvements second (see Table 8).

Table 8

Self-Help Projects and Participation by Major Activities in Thirty-One Vikas Mandals, *to March, 1963*

	Number of of Projects	Percentage of Total	Number of Participants	Percentage Total
Physical improvements and facilities	194	14.4	69,708	29.8
Health and environmental sanitation	307	22.8	71,429	30.5
Educational programs	87	6.5	4,226	1.8
Recreational and cultural programs	522	38.8	37,898	16.2
Economic improvement	167	12.4	5,658	2.4
Miscellaneous	69	5.1	45,303	19.3
Totals	1,346	100.0	234,222	100.0

The order of activities ultimately undertaken did not always correspond to the order of problems that bothered people in the slum areas. In most cases, initial inquiry revealed that physical improvements and facilities were at the top of the list of needs, health and environmental sanitation came second, and recreational and cultural activities third. Educational needs were hardly mentioned. In actual accomplishment, physical improvements and basic facilities were third and recreational and cultural activities second, if measured by the number of programs undertaken. When initially interviewed, the heads of households in twenty-one *vikas mandals* responded as follows about their needs:

physical improvements and basic facilities	37.8%
health and environmental sanitation	25.7%
recreational and cultural activities	10.0%
antisocial activities	4.1%
economic conditions	3.9%
educational facilities	3.8%
group tensions	1.5%

In Delhi, as in any city, certain municipal departments and voluntary agencies handle sanitation, health, physical improvements, recreation, and educational problems and programs. A relevant question, therefore, was the extent to which self-help duplicated government and private-agency efforts and was then, in a sense, unnecessary. As most cities have inadequate facilities to meet these overwhelming problems, there is really no area in which duplication of effort can be said to have existed in any strict sense. Plenty of room was left for self-help activities to supplement what was already being done to provide adequate facilities in underserviced areas. Furthermore, the activities were conducted in response to citizens' demands. It is unlikely that many of these activities would have been carried out otherwise; most citizens, because of lack of motivation or time, would probably not have gone to welfare centers or taken part in conventional programs managed for them by outsiders. In addition, it was difficult to limit the areas of citizen participation in order to avoid duplication. It was almost impossible to say to a citizen development council that the people could not do things for themselves in certain areas like recreation simply because a municipal department already existed to deal with this need. With self-help among the citizens, the pressure of demands on the city administration for various services presumably lessened in some cases while increasing in others.

Self-help programs were organized on a locality and group basis rather than on an individual basis through welfare centers or agency programs. The activities undertaken were sponsored by citizen groups and had more lasting effects. The introduction of such new ideas as improved sanitation practices would become part of the way of life of the group. Furthermore, when people contributed financially to an activity, they were likely to want more from it or at least to show greater concern for its proper direction.

§ *Recognized and Induced Needs*

Most activities resulted from citizen recognition of certain needs. Much has been said about these needs, which are the core of community-development work. Although the project workers did not approach the community with a ready-made program and allowed programs to be developed around the expressed "concerns" of the community, in the slums one was often faced with hazards whose correction could not be long delayed. For instance, the annual outbreaks of cholera and smallpox warranted quick action. In the initial stages, very few people "felt the need" to be inoculated, even during such an emergency, so that the workers deliberately fostered or induced the recognition of such needs. Although organizers tried not to force their own value judgments on the local community, they sometimes had to quicken the pace of community understanding.

Most self-help activities, however, were outgrowths of already recognized needs or "overt concerns" of the people, rather than of inducement by community organizers. They were even on occasion related to goals the people actively wanted. Under such conditions, the people were likely to show more enthusiasm for their work and to regard the accomplishments as their own. As an illustration, many groups readily took up such tasks as putting names or numbers on their houses, color washing the areas, paving lanes, and cooperatively purchasing sewing machines.

It was found that people should not undertake projects, even though they are aimed at recognized needs, that are too ambitious for them. Often the people in an area wanted to start, for example, with a large-scale program to improve their housing. The organizer would suggest that, though it was an important project, it would require more planning and time; in the meantime they might start with something that could be done immediately, to which people would readily respond and that would ultimately contribute toward larger projects. It was more feasible to involve people in smaller and simpler activities first, so that the results of organization and group cooperation would be visible sooner. A common initial program was to whitewash an area or to purchase a sewing machine cooperatively. Then, with the feeling of achievement gained from this experience, a better climate could be created for dealing with more basic changes like immunization, sanitation, child care, and illiteracy.

> A meeting of the residents of Vikas Sabha 9 was held. The members discussed purchasing common utensils for use in marriages and other ceremonies. The worker explained that the meeting had been called to discuss more immediate needs and that, although no doubt the idea of purchasing common utensils was a good one, they should start with smaller things that they could immediately accomplish. Then they discussed the problem of smallpox spreading in the area and decided that they wanted the community to be immunized. The worker told them that they could approach the municipal authorities and could have themselves immunized.

§ *Moving from Simple to Complex Activities*

Self-help activities generally moved from the simple to the more complex. Most projects started with a few simple self-help activities like acquiring common water taps or establishing women's singing groups, and later the activities became more complex, for example paving large lanes, child-care competitions, and provisions for reading rooms. Probably the most complex activities were the organization of a few *vikas mandal* schools, dispensaries, and cooperative food stores. A number of cooperative preschools for children aged three through six was organized, which meant finding suitable sites and hiring teachers, as well as dealing with intercaste problems. Some *vikas mandals* organized dispensaries: One obtained a large supply of medicines and bandages, arranged office space, and secured the voluntary services of a doctor in the area for two hours each week. Even more complex endeavors were the cooperative food stores, for which the people raised funds, located sites, arranged financial management, and installed cooperative supervision. Neither cooperative schools, dispensaries, nor cooperative stores could presumably have been achieved without previous experience in simpler self-help activities and the establishment of mutual trust among the people. As the *vikas parishads* developed, activities became even more complex, often representing greater involvement and coordination over a wider area. Such *vikas parishad* activities included child-care competitions, track meets, and celebrations of national events.

§ *Educational Aids*

In order to stimulate self-help projects, some financial grants were given to citizen groups. These "prime the pump" grants were termed "educational aids," for they served as stimulants to cooperative self-help efforts and demonstrated what the pooling of modest resources could accomplish. As an example, groups of fifteen women interested in learning how to sew were often given assistance in the purchase of sewing machines, each member paying R.1 a month for six months, the contributions totaling up to R.100 for the purchase of machines that cost R.180. These machines, in whose ownership the women took great pride, belonged to the *vikas mandals* and could be rented out to other women. In other cases, literacy teachers might be furnished, provided that the residents supplied the necessary materials. In general, the grants did not exceed 50 per cent of the cost of each project, and most were far less. About a third of the grants were for sums below R.25 ($5), and 31 per cent involved sums between R.25 and R.50. Much depended upon the type of activity and the economic level of the community. The larger grants went toward subsidies for major physical improvements like paving large lanes and constructing latrines. In these cases, the *vikas mandals* might not be able to undertake such large expenditures without assistance, or, if they could, to allocate large amounts of their limited funds to single projects when many other projects were also important.

In the beginning, the numbers and types of projects for which grants were available were not announced to each *vikas mandal*, as such announcements might stimulate interest in areas in which the projects were not really appropriate or might lead to undue financial dependence on the Department, thus defeating the purpose. In addition, the various groups expressed widely divergent needs. This type of stimulation of self-help projects presented a number of problems, and a considerable amount of money set aside for educational aids remained unspent. At first, grants were given on receipt of applications from the *vikas mandals*, and thus there were considerable time lags between applications and grants. Later another system was tried, in which quarterly grants on a matching basis amounting to R.250 for a *vikas mandal* and R.500 for a *vikas parishad* were given experimentally to a number of groups. This system did not work out satisfactorily either because the people tended to use these funds for other projects than those they had originally planned or because they spent the funds in response to local pressures rather than according to priority of needs.

Although aid was given to start several hundred educational self-help projects, it was not necessary in most of them. Three-fourths of the first 531 self-help projects were organized without any educational aid. Still such aid performed a very valuable function not only in starting but also in keeping up their momentum. For example, one of the original six projects was, after five years, still moving constantly ahead with self-help activities. Its leaders had the feeling, as did many others, that they should not pass up opportunities to acquire some funds for nothing, even though they had to put up as much as 90 per cent of the remainder themselves.

Contrary to original expectations, educational aid had to be continued rather than tapered off because of the static financial resources of poor communities. Sometimes red tape in the municipal government delayed its arrival beyond the appropriate time for the most effective use; in other cases, communities did not make use of it after it had been appropriated. In order to ensure the proper utilization of educational funds, each *vikas mandal* had to maintain a system of accounts, submit monthly or periodic reports, maintain bank accounts, and have the accounts audited annually.

§ *The Communication Chain in Self-Help Activities*

Problems of effective communication in an urban community-development project are complex and can be summarized as communication between the Department and its workers; between the Department and *vikas mandal* executive committees; between the Department and *vikas mandal* residents; among organizers; between organizers and residents; between organizers and executive committees; between executive committees and residents; between executive committees and other departments of the municipality; among *vikas mandal* residents; and between the Department and the councilmen.[1]

An effective and rapid communication system between the Department and the executive committees of the *vikas mandals* and *vikas parishads* was vital to the success of self-help programs. Despite general success, answers to self-help proposals from citizen groups were frequently delayed because formal channels had not been followed or because such proposals had to have organizers' or supervisors' comments. Sometimes these delays arose because the *vikas mandal* secretaries sent requests directly to the Department without consulting the workers who would, in turn, have consulted supervisors. Such delays often led to frustration among the officers of the *vikas mandals* or *vikas parishads*, who felt let down by the governmental agency. The most pressing problem faced by the slum residents, then, was the delay in implementation of self-help projects they had initiated for their own benefit. The length of the channels of communication was the main factor responsible for such delays.

Communications about activities among the *vikas mandal* constituents suffered for a number of reasons: lack of proper or adequate media of communication between the *vikas mandal* executive committees and the people; limitations on written communication because of lack of education among the people; great poverty, which resulted in such preoccupation with jobs that little time was left for other interests; and basic mistrust of cooperative ventures, bred of the anonymity and individuality of city life. Failure to use established channels of communication within their own hierarchies harmed the *vikas mandals* in two ways: first, by keeping most of the residents ignorant of the activities planned or executed by the *vikas mandals* and, second, by making it possible for false rumors about the work to spread. The executive committees' failure to communicate self-help decisions was sometimes the result of misunderstanding the need for constant communication with area residents. In other cases, it arose from the assumption of unwarranted power by the executive committees. Such failures often led to indifference among average slum residents toward self-help projects in which they were neither recognized nor included in decision-making.

§ *Improvements in Physical Conditions*

Self-help improvements in the physical conditions of slum areas were of several types: construction and repairs of houses, paving lanes, erection of latrines and urinals, improvements in drains, installing name plates on houses, and putting up bulletin boards. There were also cooperative efforts to secure improved water and electrical facilities. Until March, 1963, after an average thirty-three months of existence,* the thirty-one *vikas mandals*, with a total population of 39,355 people, had completed a total of 201 physical-improvement projects affecting 69,453 people.

IMPROVEMENTS IN HOUSES AND COURTYARDS

Some *vikas mandals* made concerted efforts to encourage all the people in their areas to repair their houses or to fix the courtyards. In the thirty-three

---

* The lengths of existence of individual *vikas mandals* ranged from twenty to forty-three months; the average was slightly lower than thirty-three months.

months (average) before March, 1963, house and courtyard repairs were conducted in twelve *vikas mandal* areas affecting 2,046 people. Such self-help efforts were more successful where the houses were made of mud and bricks than where they were of more substantial construction. In one particularly shabby area, all 400 houses were repaired cooperatively by filling in bricks and rubble that had fallen out and replastering the bricks with mud. In other cases, repairs were made to the bricks in the courtyards and the stairways in multistoried buildings.

In still other cases, deteriorated areas were cooperatively whitewashed. "Color washing," as it is called in India, is the more appropriate term, as the color of the wash may be tan, white, or blue. Sometimes this work was done individually; in other cases, private workers were engaged to do the entire area on a contract basis. Color washing of all the houses and walls of the lanes by a *vikas mandal*, especially if the houses of the surrounding neighborhood were dirty, made the residents proud, showed what they could achieve, and gave them an inexpensive start toward more substantial improvements that might alter the physical appearance and cleanliness of their area. Often a number of *vikas mandals* color washed their houses for celebration of the important religious holiday Diwali, which is associated with cleanliness. Color washing was carried out over three years in fourteen *vikas mandals* affecting 16,366 people.

In the first week of October, some of the dwellers approached the secretary of the *vikas mandal* and stated that the color-washing project should be taken up as early as possible. The secretary included this subject in the agenda of the executive committee meeting. The officers of the *vikas mandal* prepared plans for this project and started asking the dwellers to participate in the project. They approached the Department for a grant of R.50 with which to purchase ten maunds of lime and some yellow material to mix with it. The dwellers themselves did the job of color washing the houses. The work was done by lanes, and representatives of each lane were responsible. Ten empty drums, which could afterward be used as dust bins (trash bins), were used to mix the color wash. This project would have cost not less than R.300 if done on a private contract basis.

In some areas, bushes and flowers were planted, or green pots were put around to beautify the area. Housing improvements were also encouraged by competitions sponsored by the *vikas sabhas* or *vikas mandals* for the best-kept houses and sometimes for the best-kept *katras*. As the programs were planned by the communities and the prizes were given by them, competition was often intense and did much to improve the appearance of the area both outside and inside the houses. Altogether, there were eleven reported competitions conducted in eight *vikas mandals*, affecting 1,137 people in all. In one Muslim area, dirty, ragged, burlap purdah doorway curtains were replaced cooperatively in more than 300 houses, thus greatly improving the appearance of the area.

PAVING AND REPAIRING LANES AND CONSTRUCTION OF DRAINS

Narrow, winding lanes, either unpaved or in poor condition, and inadequate drains constituted major problems, especially during the rainy season. These conditions had often existed for years, and nothing had been done to repair the lanes or to pave them. During the first three years of the Delhi project, thirteen *vikas mandals* repaved or repaired lanes affecting 2,340 people. There were also fairly large-scale projects involving the construction of new drains of cement or brick. In some cases, new feeder drains were made with drainpipe. Other instances involved the repair of drains, particularly through improving the gradients so that they would not become clogged. Construction or repair of drains was handled in fourteen projects by eleven *vikas mandals*, affecting 1,980 people.

The major problem in such self-help efforts was obtaining the cooperation of everyone concerned, as none of the residents "owned" the lanes. The removal of obstructions that had been built by residents was extremely difficult to accomplish. Where the people themselves successfully worked out such problems, much time was saved. If legal action had become necessary, as would always have been the case had the work been undertaken by the municipality, it might well have forced politicians to take positions against such encroachments, thus widening the issue and stirring up citizen suspicion of authority.

The following case history describes the lengthy process, including the problems, of carrying out such a self-help project among slum dwellers. This large-scale paving effort was undertaken only after the successful completion of a simpler project.

The first major physical-improvement project undertaken was brick paving and improved drainage of the courtyard in Lane No. 7. The project was initiated in September and was accomplished in November. The total cost, excluding labor contributed by the community, came to about R.400 (about $80) for paving a courtyard 9 by 110 feet and for laying a drain about 200 feet long. The people contributed voluntary labor. An educational-aid grant of R.125, or about half the cost, was granted by the Department to accelerate the pace of the work undertaken.

The lane was one of the worst of three in the area. It was known as "Chamaran-ka-Katra" because it was so dirty and possibly because of some past association with people living in the area. The lane was uneven both horizontally and vertically. In some places it was ten feet wide and in others only five. After the rains, the courtyard was filthy with mud and slush. The drains were of dirt and unlined. During the monsoons, refuse floated into the houses.

The worker recorded on October 7, after the residents had successfully installed a water tap, "They have been approaching the community organizer and *vikas mandal* to help them in undertaking brick paving and a cement drain project in their lane." The officers of the *vikas mandal* convened a meeting of the residents. At this meeting, plans and estimates were placed before all of them, and, when they showed enthusiasm, it was decided to collect R.11 per family. The people were also made aware of the fact that the project would entail their removing obstructions and housing extensions from the lane. To this proviso all but one member agreed. A subsidy from the Department at this stage proved a very effective incentive.

The residents collected their share of R.125 and agreed to do all the labor and to spend more if the project needed any more money. They wanted R.125 from the *vikas mandal* because, for a majority of families, it was not possible to contribute as much as R.11 each. Four people went together to purchase the material.

Even the very few uncooperative residents were converted by the time actual work started on the project on Sunday, October 20, 1959, when 6,000 bricks were delivered. The work began at 5 A.M. and continued nonstop for twenty-one hours. All adults and children, men and women came out and worked. There was a skilled worker living there who helped with the project. Concrete drains were constructed along the sides. They were cleverly designed with one side higher than the other to make it difficult for children to use them for defecating.

One resident was trying to avoid work, but, when he noticed a number of children helping in the project and talking about him among themselves, he felt ashamed and joined them. Another head of a family created trouble and refused to remove his obstruction on the lane to allow the new pavement and drains to pass in front of his dwelling. The worker suggested to the local leaders that they make this man chairman of the meeting at which these and many minor problems were to be solved. He was convinced. He proved to be amiable as chairman of the meeting. He not only agreed to do what was necessary but also requested the secretary of the *vikas mandal* to write all the decisions down and secured signatures of all those present so that they could not disagree again later.

In the last phase of the project, the worker was painfully surprised one morning to find that a small wall had been erected across the lane toward one end. The person who had built it wanted compensation for his encroachments. Other families complained about this man. The secretary of the *vikas mandal* met the man and requested him to remove the wall, but he would not. At last, the residents tried a boycott. They did not speak to anyone in his family and pointed to the wall whenever any visitor came to their lane. The man was much annoyed with this behavior and complained to the *vikas mandal*. He first requested that they demolish the wall and then asked permission to keep the wall. The *vikas mandal* allowed him to keep it, as his obstruction was built on a separate portion at one end of the lane.

After the project was completed, the festival of Diwali came. All residents built their outer walls in a singe straight line, and after whitewashing and color washing, had the names of the heads of families written on the outer walls. The lane then looked better than any other lane in the area.

CONSTRUCTION AND REPAIR OF COMMON LATRINES, URINALS, AND BATHING FACILITIES

Many areas had insufficient latrines, or the existing ones were in poor condition. Much of the odor and some of the indiscriminate defecation in the area could be traced to this source. In some *vikas mandals*, this situation was partially remedied by the voluntary construction of latrines and urinals, which were often simply cement walled and floored structures with soakage pits attached. One *vikas mandal* proudly constructed one with a marble floor. In all, during this period, there were four latrine- and urinal-construction projects by four *vikas mandals*. Some were quite extensive self-help projects; one project alone involved the construction of twelve latrines by a *vikas mandal*, with an outlay of R.3,000 ($500), the most expensive self-help project undertaken by any single council. In some cases, special latrines were constructed so that children could use them, in order to prevent their indiscriminate defecation.

A major problem in building a latrine or urinal was the opposition of nearby residents. One might expect some opposition because of possible odors, but with Hindus opposition to things "unclean" is enhanced on religious or caste grounds. In some cases, efforts by the *vikas mandals* initiated municipal construction of badly needed latrines whose locations had been opposed by nearby residents. The following case illustrates an instance of the cooperation between the people and the authorities in the provision of latrines.

> The area near the *vikas mandal* was a heterogeneous one consisting of about 3,500 families, mostly in the low-income group. A large proportion of the people was illiterate. Most of the houses were single-room tenements with few such facilities as water and latrines. Hardly 10 per cent of the houses had private latrines. The bulk of the population therefore depended upon forty public latrines, which were said to be insufficient for a population of 18,000. The main handicap was that the locality was so overcrowded that there was very little open space for the construction of additional latrines.

> The people had been very much concerned about this problem. Earlier, they had approached the municipal corporation many times. The health authorities visited the area several times, but suitable sites for the latrines could not be located, as in every case a few of the residents living nearby objected. There was no organized public opinion or pressure to overcome the individual objections raised.

> The secretary of the *vikas mandal* approached the local councilman and the health authorities. A suitable place in the neighborhood was selected for a block of latrines. The site was approved by the authorities, and the work of construction was started at the beginning of May. There was again an objection, raised by one of the influential residents in the vicinity of the proposed block of latrines. He was supported by a few others, and they would not allow the construction to progress. This problem came to the notice of the secretary of the *vikas mandal*, who, along with other block representatives, met those who objected and discussed the issues with them. It was pointed out to them that, as the latrines would be the flush type, they would not cause any nuisance. Furthermore, the block of latrines was situated thirty yards from their residences. It was also emphasized that they should look to their own larger interests, as latrines had been a long-felt need of the community. This argument seemed to appeal to them. One of the main objectors went to the contractor's house and requested him to resume work. The block of common latrines was constructed in October, after having been held up for five months.

Latrines and urinals often were in poor condition, as the people vainly looked to the landlord or municipality for help rather than making repairs themselves. Commonly, the doors became broken or unhinged, causing much embarrassment, particularly to the women, and some had no cement flooring. These conditions, coupled with smells caused by careless use, often meant that others would not use them, preferring the surrounding open areas. Repairs were made, through self-help, to latrines and urinals in eight cases in which 1,615 people were affected. Probably more could have been done except for the refusal of orthodox Hindus to be personally associated in any way with the repair of facilities that they regarded as unclean.

Common bathing facilities, usually in the form of enclosed water taps or showers, were also repaired. Such repairs usually meant putting in cement flooring or repairing the walls. In one neighborhood, there were, for example, two such projects affecting 1,014 people.

ADDITIONAL WATER SUPPLY

One of the most successful self-help activities was providing additional water supply. Frequently the areas had insufficient public outlets, and the residents had to carry water some distance. As it was impossible for individual families to secure additional water outlets, the only possible solution lay in cooperative ventures. Numbers of *vikas sabhas* and *vikas mandals*, consequently, did join together to request additional water taps from the municipality, indicating their willingness to assume the installation cost and pay for the water cooperatively. Altogether thirty-seven water taps were installed in sixteen of the thirty-one *vikas mandal* areas and 7,234 people were able to use this additional water.

Although the existing and new water taps did furnish needed water, they caused some additional problems in slum areas. From heavy use for drawing water and also for bathing, the area around a tap often became quite muddy and dirty, particularly if the area was not paved. A fairly common self-help project was the building of cement flooring around the water taps. In all, there were six projects of this type affecting 1,769 people.

One area was inhabited by some 2,000 people who, until last year, depended on two wells for their water supply. Because of a cholera epidemic spreading through the well water, two public water taps were installed in the area. There was no cement platform around one of the main taps; all sorts of mud and refuse collected there. One of the local leaders suggested that the people were willing to collect R.5 if the Department would give the rest. This suggestion was agreed to, but the residents wanted it done in a certain new way; they wanted the flooring to have an edge, so that the water could run off. This type called for more contributions from the residents. The cement flooring was then provided by the municipality. The community voluntarily arranged to guard it until it was dry, which meant they could not use it for twenty-four hours. This action was unusual, as in many cases the communities do not cooperate with the city government in waiting for the platforms to dry.

The accomplishment of this early project gave a feeling of success to the community. The organizer wrote: "This cement flooring is kept clean. The tap is not left leaking as in other public taps." Subsequently the residents cooperated in paying part of the costs of additional taps and in each case had a cement platform installed, a substantial part of the cost of which they paid.

The organization of the *vikas mandals* helped to prevent theft and damage to water taps, which result in much waste of water. There were often hundreds of pairs of eyes watching the facility instead of only that of an occasional municipal official; when the slum people had contributed to the water tap, they were even more protective. In several cases, the people themselves paid for the repairs of water taps; in one case, 107 families benefited from the repair. In some instances, water was obtained from wells, and some self-help projects involved the repair and improvement of these wells.

ADDITIONAL LIGHTING

Slum areas are generally poorly lighted. To improve this situation, some residents joined together to install lights in the courtyards, stairways, and *katras*. In one case, the problem was quite simple. A *katra* in which twenty-two families had resided over a period of thirty years had never had any light at night, and the people always had trouble in finding either the latrine or their own houses. After the formation of a *vikas sabha*, they agreed to purchase a small kerosene pottery lamp cooperatively for R.2 (40 cents), and each family agreed to maintain it for a week at a cost of 2 cents. For the first time, the area had light at night. After a year, an electric light bulb was installed through their joint efforts, giving more light and enabling children to study at night. Another project report stated that: "The people of this *katra* have collected R.25 and will be paying the advance as a deposit to the electric department. Six families will be benefited by this scheme, as one meter will supply 250 watts. The remaining people are not yet prepared for the project." There were twelve cases involving 1,705 people, in which the residents had electric lights installed on a cooperative basis, sharing the installation charges, the monthly light bills, and the replacement costs of electric bulbs. Where lights already existed, the *vikas mandals* helped to protect the bulbs from theft and breakage.

OTHER PHYSICAL IMPROVEMENTS

Many other types of physical improvement were carried out by the people on a self-help basis, including the provision of dust bins, clearing space for recreational pursuits, construction of reading rooms, the making of name plates and house numbers, and the erection of bulletin boards. These activities will be discussed later in more appropriate sections. There were still other, more limited types of self-help effort; one small but significant project, for example, was the construction of a common mailbox for the area.

§ *Improvements in Environmental Sanitation*

Various self-help programs were undertaken by the *vikas mandals* to deal with the age-old problem of poor sanitation. Changing centuries-old sanitation practices is the most complex and difficult problem of all as people are accustomed to poor conditions and as it requires complete cooperation from all the people if it is to be successful; its solution will take a much longer time. The efforts were directed principally at improving the general standards of cleanliness, providing dust or trash bins, and preventing indiscriminate defecation.

As an area could be kept clean only if all families cooperated, each *vikas mandal* appointed a small committee to improve the general sanitation. This program was also usually emphasized by the *mahila samitis*. These efforts, together with those of the community organizers and the field-program organizers in public health, did much to emphasize that current sanitation practices had to be changed. Sometimes there were discussions of the role of the municipal or private sweepers, how they could improve their work, and how the slum dwellers could cooperate with them. Some slum dwellers came to appreciate the need for assuming greater responsibility for the sanitation of an area; the sweeper was encouraged to do a more efficient job rather than merely to float refuse and excreta in the drains to get rid of them. Several self-help projects were initiated to correct the problems of indiscriminate defecation by children in the drains. Special latrine facilities were adapted for children. Special seats were made of bricks laid one on top of another, with boards on top, the excreta later being suitably disposed of. For example, in one *katra*, the residents decided that children "will not ease on the drains but a temporary place for this purpose will be provided by the *katra* itself."

In many instances, clean-up campaigns were organized by area citizens themselves to remove accumulated refuse and debris. Environmental sanitation was most effective where an attitude of censure developed toward transgressors. A particularly dirty area became remarkably clean partly through such an approach. "While coming from the main door of the area, the worker was shown mango skins and seeds thrown by a person after eating mangoes. The person who showed the heap to the worker took great pains to humiliate the other person for creating dirt and disease in the area. Other people also joined in and discussed the possibility of avoiding such things in future."

Although environmental sanitation and its relation to health were not fully appreciated by the men and women of the Indian slum, flies did disturb them by getting on their faces and eyes, particularly while they were sleeping. Often flies could be used as a direct approach to the more complex sanitation problem and the relation of flies to the spread of disease, especially dysentery. Discussions about flies were held at the request of residents; they took up their sources of breeding in the slum filth and their control by improved sanitary practices, the use of chemicals like D.D.T., and the enlistment of children in programs of fly extermination. Consequently, the authorities were frequently asked by the *vikas mandals* to spray the areas, and fly-killing campaigns were conducted by children. In several instances, the area residents themselves cooperatively purchased disinfectants to kill flies.

Indian cities very seldom have public trash bins or what Indians call "dust bins." Such trash receptacles are too expensive for public agencies to furnish; they are often stolen for scrap metal, which has considerable value, and it was even questionable that the local residents would use them. Individual dust bins would have been prohibitively expensive for most slum dwellers and their usefulness doubtful. Consequently, trash, vegetable refuse, and excreta were all dumped indiscriminately about the alleys and lanes, breeding flies and causing disease and bad odors. To correct this situation, a major self-help effort was directed in all project areas toward installing dust bins. Large used asphalt or kerosene drums and tins were secured from the engineering department of the municipality by the *vikas mandals*, were straightened out, were painted, and were put in the areas, with the *vikas sabha* number painted on them. Where they were used, each *vikas sabha* usually had two such containers. In the early days of the projects, such large containers were popular, but as time elapsed they were found to have some disadvantages. Some sweepers avoided emptying the bins, as they were quite large and heavy when filled. It was later found more feasible to have a smaller number of residents share each dust bin or to secure individual dust bins. Other dust bins were small box-like affairs, which were hand-made of concrete. In twenty-seven *vikas mandals*, there were forty-two dust bin projects, involving 11,985 people.

§ *Health Programs*

Self-help activities in the field of health included immunization programs; classes in child care, personal hygiene, nutrition, family planning and first aid; purchase of first aid kits; child-health competition; establishing dispensaries; milk distribution; and celebration of health week.

IMMUNIZATION

Indian slum dwellers do not readily accept immunization programs, although smallpox, cholera, diphtheria, and typhoid fever are common diseases in India.

Many believe in fate; many believe that protection against smallpox is guaranteed by making puja (prayers) to the goddess Mata, or Sitala Mata. Others are suspicious of injections, inoculations, and vaccinations. Even those who do have single vaccinations, believe that they have received lifetime immunity rather than for only two years. Widely believed rumors circulate periodically that inoculation of children against diphtheria, cholera, and typhoid fever can cause death, that it is part of a government plot to reduce the population, or that it is given in a painful spot like the throat. Consequently, epidemics have come repeatedly to the Delhi slums, killing large numbers of adults and children, despite the fact that free inoculations are given by the municipality. The fears of slum dwellers about immunization are clearly visible in the following description of attitudes at the beginning of work in a project area, one in which later practically every child had received the necessary immunization.

Two deaths from diphtheria have occurred in the new municipal-housing area whose 400 slum families have been relocated. When the municipal doctor, accompanied by an attendant, came to immunize the children against diphtheria, he was hooted by the slum dwellers. The community organizer took the doctor to the nearby school where the teacher tried to force the children to be immunized, but many of the boys escaped. Mothers came to take away their children. The organizer gathered a few leaders of the area while injections were being given. He also collected the educated boys and had them take their younger brothers to school for injections. This example encouraged others. The teacher of the school was asked not to force the children to take the injections.

The next day a number of people were found taking children away from the area on bicycles. When the organizer stopped one of the cyclists to ask him why they were taking their children away, he burst out that the municipal authorities were sending people to suck the blood of their children and thus to reduce the population of the country. They could kill the children of poor people only because it was an easy affair to trap the poor with various excuses.

The organizer was surprised and asked the people to accompany him to see what the facts were, saying that, of course, nobody could touch their children without their permission. Almost all followed, except one lady who took away her children, pretending to take them with her to work.

A dozen or so doctors were in the area, and there were many cars, jeeps, and trucks standing outside "A" block. The organizer discussed the matter with the person in charge of the doctors and stated that, under the circumstances, he wished they had told people they were coming. With some remarks, the doctors left the colony. After the doctors had gone, the residents said that they were prepared to beat all the doctors for forcibly taking away their children for their experiments. Vaccination could not be done because of rumors. The people of this colony had two objections: that the injections were given in the throat (a false apprehension) and that they were given by Sikh doctors who wanted to kill the Hindus. The community organizer listened to some ladies saying that people who came for the purpose of vaccination should be killed.

One of those present asked the organizer why all the doctors should "raid the area." The community organizer had a chance to speak to the people about how destructive diseases are in India and also how they could be fought with the co-operation of all. This topic was discussed during the whole day in the area, and the organizer had to discuss the matter at a number of meetings. The idea of having a film in this connection was appreciated by many.

Educational programs in which citizen groups assumed responsibility for immunization appeared to be one way to deal with these fears. Large-scale immunization programs against smallpox, cholera, typhoid, and diphtheria were carried out by the *vikas mandals* and *vikas parishads*, and they proved to be more successful than the previous reliance upon the constant prodding of governmental campaigns, particularly during epidemics. In fact, the immunization program was probably the most successful of all self-help activities in the Delhi project. There were seventy-nine immunization programs involving twenty-eight *vikas mandals* and participated in by 24,128 people. In some *vikas mandal* areas nearly everyone was immunized as a result of campaigns and the services of municipal vaccinators. In one *vikas mandal* area of 400 families, for example, 850 people were vaccinated in a single day. The incidence of smallpox and cholera in some project areas of 10,000 people became less than would normally be expected for a few hundred people. People were encouraged to be immunized well in advance, rather than to wait until epidemics broke out. A simple record card, to be kept by each family, was devised for recording vaccination and immunization data for each adult and child, so that inoculations could be followed up periodically.

HEALTH CLASSES

Mahila samitis were assisted by women community organizers and by a small staff of public-health nurses or health visitors, who conducted various classes on health and sanitation in the areas, at the request of the *mahila samitis* and with the consensus of the people. These classes covered prenatal and postnatal child care, prevention of diseases, sanitation, nutrition, and family planning. The public-health classes were a major interest of the *mahila samitis*, and it was hoped that through them many health and sanitation practices could be changed. When a woman organizer found a group of women interested in health topics, she would ask the public-health nurse or health visitor to conduct a class. In most cases, it was the organizer who aroused the women's interest in the activity. In a study of seventy-nine participants, fifty-three reported that they were stimulated to join by her, seven by the women representatives, and sixteen on their own initiative.

Classes were also held on such topics as general cleanliness, care of the eyes, first aid, and home nursing. Discussions included the relation of personal cleanliness, adequate sleep, clean clothing, and sufficient exercise to health in general. Everyone was encouraged to develop better personal hygiene and to understand its relationship to general good health. In two years there were 8,686 participants in thirty-one *vikas mandal* areas in health classes sponsored by the *mahila samitis*. The breakdown of participation among 4,990 women in 1962 in classes sponsored by the *mahila samitis* was 30.2 per cent in maternity and child care, 29.2 per cent in knowledge about diseases, 21.3 per cent in general cleanliness, and 9.7 per cent in classes on other aspects of health.[2] The most popular single topics included cleanliness, family planning, and child care.

Health classes met in lanes, alleys, members' small houses and huts, and occasionally the *vikas mandal* offices. A sample survey of seventy-nine women in five *mahila samitis* revealed that only married women attended the classes, three-fourths of them between eighteen and thirty-five years of age. About half the women attended classes regularly.

Child-Care Classes. The most popular classes were those on child care, which included discussions of infant feeding, weaning, teething, proper diet, and minor ailments. In these classes, the care of children's teeth was also demonstrated, as well as the importance of daily baths and the care of hair. The public-health staff also tried to spread ideas of general good health and to introduce new ideas of child health care. In a two-year period 1,754 women in thirty-one *vikas mandals* participated in such programs.

First-Aid Classes and Kits and Dispensaries. Because of cost and ignorance, the typical slum family has no medicines or bandages available to handle such injuries as cuts or bruises. They often do nothing, thus risking infection, or use such traditional but largely worthless remedies as putting cow dung or tar on wounds. Sometimes they go to free municipal dispensaries, which may be quite far away and where they usually must wait in line, or they consult private doctors, which is expensive, the minimum charge often being almost equivalent to what a man makes for a day's work. Some even resort to "quacks" whose remedies may do no good, may make the situation worse, and, in any event, are also expensive. Several *vikas mandals* adopted plans to remedy this situation. The staff health worker trained certain designated individuals in the use of first aid or held first-aid classes, usually for young people. A *vikas mandal* cooperatively purchased a first-aid kit, containing essential medicines and bandages, for about R.20 ($4). Half this cost was paid by the Department, on the assumption that replacement costs would be borne by the *vikas mandal*. In one case, a very poor husband and wife served as the *vikas mandal* "doctors" by keeping the kit in their own home, along with a bedpan and bed urinal, which were also purchased by the *vikas mandal*. In their first two weeks they had seventeen "patients."

As originally planned, each *vikas mandal* of approximately 300 to 600 families was to have a first-aid kit, but fewer than half had them prior to the 1962 national emergency with China. At that time, first-aid kits became popular and were made available through the Indian Red Cross as part of civilian defense. Practically every *vikas mandal* then secured a kit, and generally each kit was used about thirty times a week. The kits were kept in central locations and refilled by the *vikas mandals*. Obviously they did not solve all the minor health problems of the slum dwellers; they did help protect some injuries from infection, alleviated the load of already overcrowded municipal dispensaries and hospitals, and saved the afflicted individuals both time and money.

In spite of all the advantages, first-aid kits were never so popular as one might imagine they would be. The availability of a kit was insufficiently publicized, and, as it was kept in a central location, it was still some distance from many possible users. Trained personnel were also a problem, as only literate residents were supposed to be in charge. Although medicines were sometimes designated by colors so that illiterate people could identify them, this method was not a sufficient guarantee of proper use. Use depended in part therefore upon whether or not trained personnel were available and whether or not a municipal dispensary was nearby. It had been hoped that people who had learned first aid would in turn teach others, but they rarely did, although in two *vikas mandal* areas, the *mahila samiti* representatives were taught first aid and they in turn taught the women of their areas. There was evidence that people had little reluctance about coming to the trainees for first aid.

At least three *vikas mandals* set up programs to provide medicines, which were more ambitious than merely supplying first-aid kits. They purchased larger supplies of medicines, bandages, bedpans, and similar equipment and kept them in the *vikas mandal* offices. Then they secured the free services two mornings a week of doctors living in the areas. A charge of R.1 was often made for the medicines used.

Home Nursing. Because of inadequate hospital facilities, women in some areas were encouraged to learn the basic principles of home nursing, enabling them to administer such care. Under the sponsorship of one *vikas parishad*, a group of interested women from various *vikas mandals* were enrolled in a home-nursing class. Instruction was given by a staff health worker. Upon successful completion of the course, each woman received a certificate from the Indian Red Cross and was eligible to administer first aid and to perform limited nursing duties for her family, for those in the area in need of help, and during general emergencies.* Several *vikas mandals* in one area, for example, were hit by severe floods, and a group of these home nurses became highly useful, particularly in first-aid work. The *vikas parishad* purchased all such necessary equipment as pans, bandages, soap, and simple medicines, which were usually kept in the

---

* These courses, like those exclusively on first aid, became popular after the national emergency was declared following the Chinese hostilities in 1962.

home where the classes were held. Individually, the women purchased simple white cotton saris as nurses' uniforms.

Family Planning. In the traditional clinic approach to family planning, the wife goes alone to a clinic, and usually she is required to return several times. Often there is an element of secrecy and fear that the husband, the mother-in-law, or a neighbor may become displeased about these visits. Attendance at the clinic may consequently be too brief to be entirely successful. The woman may not return, and in any event it is unlikely that much of the information secured will be communicated to others.

In the Delhi project, it was assumed that individual women living in an area could be brought together for a group family-planning class sponsored by the *mahila samiti* and indirectly by the *vikas mandal*.* Such discussions took place in the area where the women lived, usually in a lane or in someone's home, and they were led by a staff public-health nurse or health visitor. The typical class met three times altogether, for two hours each session. During this time, the reasons for family planning were explained, the physiological problems were discussed, and an explanation of contraception was made. The women were then sent to a public clinic to obtain the contraceptives free of charge.

This community approach had a number of advantages. First, the motivation came largely from the women of the area, with the women community organizers, staff public-health nurse, or health worker serving as catalyst in bringing them together. Second, the women were able to give each other mutual reinforcement to overcome their fears. Third, meeting in a group helped to overcome objections from the husbands or mothers-in-law. As other women were involved and the group was sponsored by the *vikas mandal*, there was less opposition from the husbands, and they were more likely to become involved. The mothers-in-law were often led to believe that the group was discussing "health problems" generally. Fourth, holding group meetings in the area lent prestige to the idea of family planning and helped to spread the idea to other women. Fifth, as the discussions were held near their homes, the women were less shy about discussing such an intimate topic than if they had attended a distant clinic. Sixth, the women knew the woman organizer and the health worker, making the situation more personal than a clinic, and often these professionals could introduce an outside volunteer health worker to talk to the women with their full confidence. Seventh, the dates and times of classes could be adjusted to meet the needs of the women, rather than being fixed as in a clinic, and the women could go to classes from their household chores, taking their young children.

---

* The author recalls having seen a nurse's family-planning kit kept in a cabinet in the office of an all-Muslim *vikas mandal* whose men had originally been opposed to women in purdah learning anything about family planning.

In one thickly populated area, people were totally against family planning. Even the mention of this topic was inviting trouble. After a few months, when they started coming to self-help health classes sponsored by the *mahila samiti*, some young women started taking the help and guidance of the public-health worker attached to the Department. Later they told their friends, and thus the idea of family planning spread. After a year or so, the young women of the area asked the worker for classes in family planning, but they specified that the worker not mention it to the older people, especially their mothers-in-law. The daughters-in-law and married daughters attended family planning classes, and later they were referred to a nearby clinic to secure the necessary contraceptive materials.

From a quantitative point of view, the family-planning classes were successful, both in numbers and attendance. Their success was the result of efforts by the workers, whom the women had come to trust, and of sponsorship by citizen groups. Where women followed their religion strictly and were less educated, this process took more time. During the two-year period, 1961–1962, there were forty-nine family-planning classes held in thirty-one *vikas mandal* areas with 1,435 women participating. Qualitatively the results were not good, although possibly little different from the general experience of family-planning clinics in India. The women who attended the family-planning classes were usually those who had already had several children, at least one or two of them sons. If a woman was in particularly poor health, she might come even though she had fewer children. The newly married or those with only one or two children each were seldom interested, with the exception of an occasional woman from the higher social classes who had one or two children and wished to space her additional children.

Child-Health Competitions. To emphasize the need for proper child care, as well as to offer education in this field, child-health competitions, popularly known as "baby shows," were held. These contests might involve the selection of the three healthiest children in a *vikas mandal* area or competition among the winners of *vikas mandal* contests for the healthiest babies in the entire *vikas parishad*. Competitions generally were held for infants under one year of age, but others were planned for various age groups up to five years. Often nearly every child in the particular age group was entered, which meant almost full participation of the women of the area, as nearly everyone had a young child. During an average period of thirty-three months, there were fifty-six contests run by thirty *vikas mandals*, involving 2,145 mothers.

Arrangements for a competition were made by the officers of the *vikas mandal* and the *mahila samiti*, with the help of the organizers and the public-health nurse. Cooperation was also sought from the city health-education department. A doctor was asked to judge the contest, and arrangements were made for the first, second, and third prizes, which usually included such important articles of child care as soap and baby oil. Sometimes every woman entering a child was given some candy so that she could report some "success" to her husband. At the judging, the doctor and nurse discussed the need for proper food, cleanliness, and other important aspects of child care. There was often a child-care exhibit, and it was suggested that child-care classes could be held in the area if the mothers so desired.

Milk Distribution. Another common activity was the distribution of powdered milk. Although such distribution is a characteristic activity of charitable centers, this project marked one of the few large-scale examples anywhere in the world in which the people themselves assumed responsibility for preparation and distribution of milk. The milk was obtained from various international agencies and was supplied to each *vikas mandal* that desired it. Practically every *vikas mandal* was involved in this program; twenty-four of thirty-one *vikas mandals* regularly distributed milk to 5,139 constituents.

The executive committee of each *vikas mandal* usually appointed one or two people to keep records of the milk received and distributed; to measure, prepare, and warm the milk in large metal kettles that they purchased; and to distribute it daily to those eligible, each of whom had a monthly record card. Generally, the order of priority was children under school age, pregnant women, the sick, and the aged. Most of the milk was distributed to children under school age, as others usually received milk at school. The powdered milk was delivered to the *vikas mandal* office, where the stacks of cardboard boxes were in a sense "guarded" by the people of the area. Ordinarily a nominal charge of about 25 *naya paisa* (5 cents) was made by the *vikas mandal* to each recipient to cover the cost of the record cards and the fuel for warming the milk.

This method of milk distribution had a number of advantages over the traditional center distribution method. First, it eliminated much of the degrading element of charity, as people distributed the milk themselves. Although most people in the *vikas mandal* area knew that the milk was given to the Department, which in turn gave it to them, they generally believed that it was not charity because the final distribution involved a server and receiver who were both local citizens. In fact, at the formation of one *vikas mandal*, the question of receiving free milk was brought up. Although at first some objected to accepting the free milk because theirs was a self-help organization, they changed their views when the method of distribution was explained to them. Second, as those who handled the distribution knew who was eligible to receive it, there was not much chance of people receiving it who were not entitled to it. Third, the milk was safeguarded from theft and from black-market resale to sweets makers. Although thousands of boxes of milk were handled by citizen groups, only two boxes were ever "lost" or misused, and the local group in these cases even tried to fix responsibility and recover damages. Fourth, in this way, the milk was freshly prepared and served warm.

The *vikas mandal* provided powdered milk for free distribution to children, expectant mothers, the old, and the infirm. Previously no milk had ever been distributed in this area by any agency; only the school children had received milk, in the school. A meeting of some of the local leaders of the area was held. Only one person agreed to undertake the responsibility for distribution. The objections were that no one had time to distribute it. The community organizer then informed other members of the community about the reluctance of their leaders to help in the distribution. One *vikas sabha* representative found that several volunteers were available to distribute it.

For the proper distribution of milk and the maintenance of records, individual record cards were printed to be issued to the children between the ages of two and seven years; eighty such cards were distributed. Each child was nominally charged 25 *naya paisa* (5 cents) per month, this amount being used for printing cards and purchasing firewood to prepare milk according to the instructions of the Department. The participation of the people was very encouraging as every family receiving milk paid its subscription regularly. The total number of people receiving milk was 350.

There had been difficulty in one *vikas sabha* between two caste groups who wanted their milk distributed separately. The *vikas mandal* executive committee insisted on only one distribution center, which would also help the children in the area to become better acquainted. After four or five months, however, a new difficulty arose. The volunteers who had been preparing the milk refused to continue because of the secretary's behavior. Then the executive committee formed a subcommittee, headed by the vice-president of the *vikas mandal*. He also failed to find other volunteers for this work because of the winter cold. The executive committee approved the appointment of a widow in the area and sanctioned a sum of R.15 ($3) per month as her salary.

Celebration of Health Weeks. There were concerted efforts to make local communities health-conscious, and an annual "health week" afforded an opportunity to combine citizen self-help efforts with the work of the various municipal departments. The following record is an example of how a *vikas parishad* celebrated a health week and the way in which the people were involved.

Each *vikas mandal* was asked to nominate a member to be its representative on the neighborhood health committee, which also included one of the community organizers and the sanitary inspector of the area as members ex-officio. Meetings of all the *mahila samitis* in the different project areas were also organized, and subcommittees of women were formed. The chief function of these subcommittees, each consisting of three to five members, was to visit in their respective areas and to talk to the women about keeping their houses and lanes clean. Film shows exclusively for women were also organized, and attendance on both days of the showings ranged between 200 and 250. Admission was by passes distributed to the members of the *mahila samitis*. One feature of these passes was the printing of some thought-provoking questions on health prevention on the backs. The *mahila samiti* of one *vikas mandal* also undertook to make two big banners with the motto "Swasthaya Saptah (Health Week)—7th to 14th of April," which were hung in the neighborhood. Posters were put up on the walls, and handbills were distributed during Health Week by *vikas sabha* representatives and *mahila samiti* members. The health-committee members also went on rounds and talked to the men to enlist their help in keeping the area clean. In the promotion of better health measures, the municipal sanitary inspector visited each *vikas mandal* area, accompanied by the appropriate health-committee member and community organizer. A number of *vikas sabha* representatives helped to make the program of vaccination a success. Contact with the vaccinators had been made at an earlier date, and they were assigned fixed places in the office of the *vikas parishad*.

§ *Self-Help Educational Programs*

Slum dwellers carried out programs in the field of education, including adult literacy classes, schools for young children, libraries, reading rooms, lectures, organized discussions around such important national issues as the Five-Year Plans, and planned competitions to encourage education among the youth.

ADULT LITERACY CLASSES

Illiteracy was widespread in all the projects, varying from 80.3 per cent in one *vikas mandal* to 17.9 per cent in another. Illiteracy was particularly high among the women in all projects. In a number of areas the *vikas mandals* and the *mahila samitis* tried to encourage more adults to learn how to read and write. In fact, one *vikas mandal*, which was two-thirds illiterate, made a pledge to have all adult members literate within a year. Although it did much work toward achieving this goal, it was never completely successful.

Altogether, by March, 1963, thirteen literacy classes, with 231 participants, had been held in ten of thirty-one *vikas mandal* areas. A part-time teacher was engaged by the *vikas mandal*, the Department paying all, or part, of the initial expenses. All such supplies as pencils, writing boards, and books were provided by the participants. As these classes were held in lanes or alleys, often around lamps, individuals who probably would not have gone any distance to a center were attracted by the sight of others learning to read and write. Furthermore, each class member was supported in his efforts by the others in the group.

SELF-HELP SCHOOLS

Because of overcrowded conditions, it was not always possible for the Delhi authorities to provide adequate preschool and primary-school facilities. There are no public nursery schools. Even when facilities are available, the education of slum children poses difficult problems, as some parents see little

advantage in having their children learn to read and write, particularly the girls.*
They would rather have them work and earn money for the family or help with
the housework. In the absence of adequate facilities, some communities
mobilized their resources to establish preschools or primary schools to give
young children some education. These schools not only furnished necessary
training in literacy and elementary subject matter but also afforded opportunities,
particularly for the younger children, to replace idleness and aimless wandering
in the streets with something constructive. They and their families also were
helped with problems of health and personal hygiene.

Generally the teachers came from the areas and were paid about R.75
($15) a month. The *vikas mandals* paid these salaries, often charging each child
20 cents a month; or they were partially subsidized by the Department. Space
for the classes was furnished by the *vikas mandals*. In all, twelve *vikas mandals*
established preschools with a total enrollment of 262, and one set up a primary
school with approximately 100 students. The following passage describes a
nursery school established by one community and some of the problems
encountered.

This *vikas mandal* is situated in the walled-city area behind a main road. The
area is inhabited by long-time residents of Delhi, with a very small percentage of
displaced persons from West Punjab. There are about 300 families, and they represent a mixture of castes, classes, and occupations. When the community organizer
made contact with the individual heads of families, the problem of educating
children was frequently mentioned. He gathered that, of a total of 400 children in
the age group between five and fourteen years, about half were illiterate and not
attending school. A large number belonged to the Khatik and Chamar communities,
which are considered low caste, and the rest were from the upper castes. Difficulties
in enrolling children arose from overcrowded conditions in the schools; lack of
proper information on correct admission procedures; inability to pay the extra expense of schooling; and a feeling among the lower castes that the schools dis-
criminated against their children.

The problem of educating children was discussed with individuals, groups, and
area leaders and particularly with parents who had mentioned it. It came out during
the discussions that a general desire to educate children was not wanting. Some
parents were willing to contribute nominal sums to engage a teacher and to prepare
their children for admission to public schools in subsequent years. The community organizer wanted to make sure of the extent of interest in the community.
He asked one of the leaders to prepare a list of the children between five and twelve
years who were not attending school and to ascertain how much the parents would
be willing to contribute.

It was necessary to go slowly with this program, as the *vikas mandal* had not
yet been formed and difficulties in making satisfactory arrangements to ensure attendance of children and collection of monthly contributions from children were pos-

---

* In Ahmedabad, members of the *vikas mandals* helped the community organizers make house-to-
house contacts in efforts to persuade parents to send their children to school.

sible. Furthermore, the self-help project, if launched in a hurry and not successful, would have a bad effect on other programs. The worker in the meanwhile prepared the ground so that the *vikas mandal*, when formed, could assume responsibility. As a first step, he talked to the *vikas sabha* representatives, who had been elected by the middle of September, about the program of preschool education for children. These representatives decided that the class for children not already in school should first be run on an experimental basis to test the seriousness of parents. The class was therefore started with a group of twelve in November, 1959. The female community organizer started teaching the class. Meanwhile, the secretary of the *vikas mandal* arranged with a local girl to take the class. In the third week of November she started taking the class regularly for two hours daily.

The children were required to pay R.1 (20 cents) a month each, and the amount collected was paid to the teacher. The *vikas mandal* office was used for the class. In the meantime, the number of children increased to thirty, and the accommodations were found inadequate. Furthermore, there were objections to the classes being held in the *vikas mandal* office, which was for office use only. After deliberations, the executive committee shifted the class to the *dharamshala* (meeting place) owned by members of the Khatik caste. This move presented a unique situation, for children of upper castes willingly attended a class held in a place traditionally belonging to a lower caste.

A subcommittee of the *vikas mandal*, consisting of two members, was appointed to look after the nursery school. During the academic year of 1960–1961 about twenty children who were attending it were helped by the teacher and the area leaders to gain admission to the nearby primary school, a great help to parents who had earlier experienced difficulties in having their children admitted to the schools.

The preschool continued with a part-time teacher. The children were all under five years old, and the average attendance was twenty-five. The *vikas mandal* raised R.100 ($20) and, with a matching grant from the Department, purchased equipment worth R.200. The equipment made the school more attractive to the children, and the *vikas mandal* gained considerable prestige for having successfully managed this program.

LIBRARIES, NEWSPAPERS, AND READING ROOMS

Some slum dwellers are able to read, but they cannot afford to purchase books or even daily newspapers, and it may be almost impossible to arrange for books through the public library. For those who had recently become literate this problem was particularly difficult. There was often no adequate place for reading and studying, an acute problem for school children. Several *vikas mandals* tried to remedy this situation. A number of them purchased books cooperatively for a small lending library of twenty-five to 100 books.* Other

---

* In Ahmedabad, a set of 150 children's books was purchased by the Department of Urban Community Development for each of six neighborhood councils. At the end of six months, the books are rotated among the neighborhoods, making a considerable number of books available at minor expense. To help students from low-income families secure necessary schoolbooks, *vikas mandals* have raised local contributions, which are matched by the Department.

vikas mandals subscribed jointly to one or two newspapers each. Several reading rooms were made by constructing simple shelters or converting rooms that the *vikas mandals* had secured either free or on a rental basis. Table and chairs were often obtained, and sometimes electrical connections were installed if necessary. Some "reading rooms" were quite simple. One *vikas mandal* purchased a *charpai* (Indian rope bed) and located it near a shop in the area. It subscribed to a Hindi and an Urdu newspaper, which were kept by the shopkeeper. The people sat on the bed to read the paper; those who were literate often read the news to those who could not read.

DISCUSSION AND STUDY GROUPS

Some *vikas mandals* and *vikas parishads* arranged study, debate, and discussion groups around such important topics as the various Five-Year Plans. The selection of appropriate topics depended on community interests. When twenty television sets were made available in 1960 for the first experimental broadcasts by the government in India, the Department secured one set for the *vikas mandals*, and later a second television set was made available. The citizen groups were responsible for the care of the set and for audience arrangements for the weekly programs. As many as 1,000 people packed closely together used to watch a twelve-inch screen, the men sitting on the ground—or on one side, with the women on the other. A special discussion group was organized to prepare comments to transmit to the government. These activities continued for more than two years, but interest eventually declined.

STIMULATING EDUCATION AMONG THE YOUTH

A number of *vikas mandals* tried to encourage children and young people in their educational work by giving direct assistance to young people in some cases and by promoting various types of competition. Two *vikas mandals* helped to hire teachers to conduct tutoring classes for some of the young people, in order to help them to do better in competitive examinations. Another had a painting class. Five *vikas mandals* held essay competitions involving 225 students; nine had competitions in drawing, in which 226 students participated; and two held "general knowledge" competitions, with seventy-three students participating.

§ *Recreational and Cultural Activities*

Community-organized recreational and cultural programs supplemented limited municipal and other programs. They also provided recreation where the people lived and encouraged them to assume as much of the responsibility for recreation as possible. Other recreational and cultural programs in the city were, for the most part, located some distance from where most slum families resided; visits to public parks, playgrounds, and centers often meant long walks. The facilities were therefore used by only a small proportion of the city's people, most of whom lived near them. In addition, as the maintenance of recreational and cultural equipment was generally the responsibility of the public authorities, playgrounds were often misused and the equipment stolen. The self-help program was instrumental in making the citizens more responsible for public facilities.

Indirectly, self-help recreational and cultural activities represented means of developing, sustaining, and increasing the organization of the people of an area. People had opportunities to become acquainted with one another, and through common participation they were helped to overcome differences based on religion, region, and caste, which tend to divide people. Recreation afforded possibilities for indirectly bringing about increased social organization of the community. For example, children's athletic teams, from as many as ten or fifteen *vikas mandals* competed in cricket or track, with the winners becoming the neighborhood champions. The adults of the various *vikas mandals* often became interested in supporting their community teams, even going so far as to attend matches some distance from their own areas.

Only two to four field-program organizers were generally available for this work. With the assistance of the community organizers, they helped to develop interest and skill. Self-help recreational activities were limited by lack of space, and often nearby parks and playgrounds were used. The recreational program was often tailored to such available space as a small lane. Weight lifting, for example, a sport for both youths and adults, required relatively little space, and equipment was provided cooperatively by a number of *vikas mandals*.

COOPERATIVE PURCHASE OF RECREATIONAL EQUIPMENT

When members of a *vikas mandal* wished to engage in certain games, they purchased the equipment, and one of the recreation organizers would instruct them in its use. Sometimes equipment was purchased by the *vikas mandal* as a whole or by contributions from those actively interested in a given sport. The Department often gave a small financial subsidy to help pay for the initial equipment, provided the group itself financed maintenance. Recreational equipment was purchased by sixteen *vikas mandals*, involving an estimated 1,315 participants. In this way, equipment for volleyball or cricket was acquired. The equipment was kept in the *vikas mandal* office or in the home of one of the participants. Competition was often developed by organizing more than one playing group in the area or by challenging groups from other *vikas mandals* or even from outside. Here is a description of the activities of one volleyball club and of some of the difficulties it faced:

> Through the efforts of indigenous leaders, a group interested in volleyball was enlisted. This group was composed entirely of Sansis, or members of the so-called "ex-criminal tribes," whose behavior is frequently deviant and who are looked down upon by other groups. Within a period of eight days, sixteen people joined the volleyball club, and they contributed 50 *naya paisa* (10 cents) each. The total contribution was supplemented by the Department, making a total amount of R.27 ($5.50). Some of the members also contributed nets and poles. Other necessary equipment was purchased, and the group started to play. The game attracted many other people who wished to play, which eventually created confusion and disorganization. The contributing members complained to the community organizer, who suggested that they call a meeting and frame rules and regulations. This group was also faced with the problem of space, as the place it had been using was a primary-school yard. Anyway, the group managed to locate another site in the colony. After an informal meeting, the game was scheduled regularly. Later, the members arranged a friendly match with an outside team.

> During the next month, other people from a different regional and caste background became interested and formed another group (Group B) with the help of the worker. They had already collected R.8, and they wanted a subsidy of R.30 from the Department. Group B was encouraged to join Group A in a single volleyball club, which Group A refused despite the requests from Group B.

> Gradually members began to lose interest, as was apparent in poor attendance, nonpayment of contributions, and neglect of the equipment. This slackness was discussed by the community organizer with the captains and other group leaders. Within a few days, contributions had been made, and a new ball costing R.8 had been purchased. The game was again in full swing. Previously there had been no proper record of income and expenditures. The community organizer then drew the players' attention to this problem, and responsibility was entrusted to one person. Afterward the captains of the teams agreed to maintain records. In a meeting, the members decided to raise the dues to R.1 per month and also that unemployed members need not pay dues. Participation would otherwise have been restricted to the contributing members. After this decision, the games ran smoothly and were highly disciplined.

CONSTRUCTION OF PLAYGROUND EQUIPMENT

In some cases, more permanent play equipment was constructed by the *vikas mandals*. Sometimes, they built simple affairs like parallel bars; in one case a *vikas mandal* constructed a children's slide of concrete, which Indians call a "slipping slide." The *vikas mandal* proudly put its name on the slide in large letters. Hundreds of children who had been without anything to do were able to use this slide daily. Although people had lived in this area of refugees from Pakistan for more than ten years, constructing this slide was their first major undertaking on a cooperative basis.

ORGANIZATION OF BAL SABHAS AND YOUTH CLUBS

With the help and initiative of a number of *vikas mandals*, children's clubs, or *bal sabhas*, and youth clubs were organized to furnish opportunities for organized recreational activities and participation in local improvement efforts. Youth groups often had volleyball, cricket, or football (soccer) clubs and played similar groups from other *vikas mandals*. Sometimes members cooperated in the purchase of athletic equipment. They served as volunteer junior police for special events in the area, helped with sanitation programs, and learned first aid. It was hoped that boys who took an active part in such local clubs could eventually be entrusted with greater community responsibility.

DEVELOPMENT OF LOCAL YOUTH RECREATIONAL LEADERS

There generally were only four trained recreational workers on the Delhi staff, to work with more than 50,000 people in the projects. The budget called for two additional workers, but there was a shortage of trained personnel. One method of supplementing manpower was to train volunteer workers in the areas and then to turn over much of the organization and teaching to them. Certain young men were designated by their *vikas mandals* for neighborhood training courses in recreational leadership; one such training program involved forty-five youths from a number of *vikas mandals* located in three neighborhoods. Space was found in a building in one area, and a four-weeks training course was given by the recreational workers. After receiving certificates, the youth leaders helped the recreational leaders to organize and recruit people interested in recreation and assisted with some sports events and educational film shows. They did little, however, to organize children's recreational activities in their own areas, as they had been expected to do. Several factors accounted for this failure: difficulties in finding suitable space for activities, the desire of many only to receive the certificates, and the fact that most were not strictly volunteers but had been chosen or "forced" into being representatives from their areas. It might have helped had they been given some paid employment as part-time recreational workers. Another possibility might have been the recruitment and training for part-time service of adults in the area who had had previous experience with such sports as the popular Indian wrestling.

SPORTS MEETS

Regular activities of nearly all *vikas mandals* and *vikas parishads* were the sports meets in which children and youths participated and prizes were given. They were usually held in conjunction with some such celebration as those for Independence Day or Children's Day. When space was insufficient, they were held in such nearby open areas as parks and playgrounds. Many had large numbers of participants. Generally a meet consisted of various such competitive events as foot races. Winners of *vikas mandal* contests competed at the *vikas parishad* level. There were twenty-nine sports meets organized by *vikas mandals*, in which 3,388 children and youths participated. Competitions in cricket and volleyball were often held between *vikas mandal* teams of children, youths, or adults. All these meets helped to generate interest in sports in the areas.

The preparation for the sports meet on November 18, 1962, began with a meeting of the presidents and secretaries of the three *vikas mandals*. An *ad hoc* committee was formed to run the sports meet. Handbills were distributed among the people of areas, giving them information on the purpose of the meet, available events according to age group, and the rules governing the meet; entries were also collected by going from house to house. The total participation was 232. The entry fee was put at 5 *naya paisa* (1 cent) per event for each age group, and the total collected through entry fees amounted to R.11.6. Most entries were in the age group eight to twelve years.

CULTURAL PROGRAMS

Cultural programs of music, dance, and drama were also arranged by the *vikas mandals*, and indigenous singing groups like the *bhajan mandalis* were encouraged. The singing of *kirtans*, or Hindu devotional music, was widespread; there were fifteen such groups in fifteen of thirty-one *vikas mandals*. As most of the localities in the city were inhabited by heterogeneous groups from different regions and of different religions, each with its own music, songs, and folk dances, such programs provided "cultural transfer" and could help the groups to overcome the social distances among them. For example, in one area of three *vikas sabhas*, occupied respectively by Punjabis, Harijans (from different parts of Uttar Pradesh), and Rajasthanis, each group in turn put on its own folk dances.

EDUCATIONAL AND CULTURAL TOURS

Group visits were made to various places of historical interest. A group would hire a bus and various members usually assumed specific responsibilities. Such visits in Delhi included Government of India buildings like Parliament and the Secretariat, the All-India Radio building, the zoo, the airport, and historical monuments like the Quitab Minar and the Red Fort. Places of historical and religious interest in other cities or areas were also visited; there was one long trip from Delhi to Agra to visit the Taj Mahal. In fact, nine of the ten *vikas mandals* in one neighborhood alone made thirteen joint excursions outside Delhi, involving 541 people. The total educational tours and sightseeing trips both in and out of Delhi were 111, arranged by twenty-seven *vikas mandals* and involving 2,231 people.

These sightseeing tours and picnics too served as releases from the monotony of urban living and also created "we" feelings that helped to stimulate cooperative action. A group almost always stopped during an excursion for a picnic lunch. Some *vikas mandals* went on such joint picnics without sightseeing. Although picnics are popular among Indians and a common form of recreation among the middle class, they are difficult for the lower classes to arrange. On a number of occasions, groups of young men from various *vikas mandals* formed bicycle parties to visit historic sites and have picnics. This description tells of an all-day trip taken by seventy-five members of one *vikas mandal* to see the sights around Delhi.

> Sunday, October 4, was the date decided on for the scheduled all-day trip to several important places around Delhi: Birla Mandir, Jantar Mantar, India Gate, the Secretariat building, Quitab Minar, Okhla, the zoo, Raj Ghat, and Safdarjang Aerodrome. Contributions were raised at the rate of R.1.25 (30 cents) per adult and 62 *naye pais* (12 cents) per child. By the evening, forty of fifty seats on the bus were booked. On seeing the bus some of those who had not been in favor of the trip wanted to join the party and asked for tickets, but only a few of them could be accommodated. At 9 A.M., when the bus was about to start, all seats were occupied. The bus had a seating capacity of fifty adults, and, in all, seventy-five people, adults and children, were accommodated. The bus was hired for R.80 ($16), out of which R.63 were contributed by the people; to meet the deficit, a sum of R.13 was donated by the Department. The community lunch at the Quitab Minar was enjoyed. Some of the children recited songs and gave folk dances. The party was back at the place at 6 P.M. Writing about the visit the lady worker recorded, "The trip was too long and strenuous, but still the people were enthusiastic to see more places."

CELEBRATION OF NATIONAL HOLIDAYS AND FESTIVALS

National holidays and important religious festivals are easily celebrated in villages but difficult in the packed slums of cities like Delhi. Except for massive observances involving perhaps several hundred thousand people at such public places as temples or mosques or watching parades, individuals can seldom actively participate. The *vikas mandals* furnished mechanisms for planned community observances of such important events. In all, there were 130 such celebrations recorded in twenty-eight *vikas mandals* involving 16,335 people. On national holidays like Republic or Independence Day, the citizens might gather around flag poles, often permanent ones, which had been erected in central places. There they would have a few speeches and sing patriotic songs. These celebrations helped to weld the people together and to develop greater nationalistic feeling. Religious holidays like Dussera (Ramayana Epic) and Diwali (Feast of Light) and the Muslim holiday of Id were also often observed with local celebrations. Diwali was an appropriate time to color wash and clean up the area. The Hindu holiday of Holi (spring celebration) was an occasion for people to throw color on one another. Often there was other "horse play" and things could become completely uncontrolled. Women might be abused, and tempers might fly. The *vikas mandals* did much to keep this celebration in check by cautioning the people in advance.

§ *Programs of Economic Improvement*

Self-help economic programs in slum areas present difficult problems. Yet providing an economic aspect of any program for improvement in a slum area may often be essential for the area's sustained growth, particularly in the poorer communities. There usually is no primary occupation in a slum such as exists in a village; rather there is a marked diversity of occupations, and many people are self-employed as hawkers or as skilled or unskilled laborers and are thus reluctant to try measures of unknown benefit. Poverty and illiteracy are so extensive that self-help efforts can be only modest undertakings, and the population is so dense that there are limited physical accommodations for major production units. It is difficult to promote economic development in an urban area where community feeling and relationships are often absent. A high priority must be given to the crystallization and integration of community feelings with the hope that this effort may lead to more cooperative economic endeavors. It is also extremely difficult to develop specific self-help economic programs in an area if only a few may actually benefit, although urban community development in Pakistan seems to have been reasonably successful on a fairly wide scale.[3] Furthermore, there may be duplication of effort as most cities have employment exchanges, vocational-training programs, handicraft boards, and small-scale industry corporations. Although much can be done by the average person in an urban context, it must be recognized that major economic improvements in the city will necessarily come from city-wide or national plans for expansion and intensification of employment opportunities. These purely economic schemes will be far more ambitious and consume more capital than anything that could be attempted through self-help measures in small citizen groups.

Although there was constant pressure from the slum people for programs of economic improvement, economic programs in the Delhi project involved only those areas where there was real scope for self-help or mutual aid. Most of the economic-improvement efforts were carried out by the women, the most popular attempts being to augment family income in small ways through craft training and the cooperative purchase of sewing machines or through the improved use of limited economic resources. The latter involved programs of education in family nutrition, budgeting, and home skills like soap-making and the preservation of foods.

As many women wished to learn how to increase their incomes, craft and other self-help classes were conducted by part-time instructors. Like the health classes, they were under the sponsorship and leadership of the *mahila samitis*, and for the most part represented efforts to promote new economic "skills." They included tailoring; hand and machine embroidery; knitting; making powder puffs, neckties, and handbags; making paper bags, paper flowers, and brushes; weaving mats and handbags of jute or nylon. After some women had expressed desire for such a class, the organizer usually asked the *mahila samiti* representative or another woman to organize a group. The participants often contributed some small sums toward the project and furnished necessary materials. The Department paid for a craft teacher. Handicraft exhibits were a common activity of *vikas mandals* and *vikas parishads*. There were seventeen such exhibits held in thirteen *vikas mandals*. At these exhibits, women displayed the handicrafts and clothes they had made, which not only gave them prestige but also aroused the interest of others in the work they were doing. Knowledge of these crafts serves an educational as well as an economic purpose. An opportunity was provided for women to meet together, which in turn helped to create friendliness and community feeling. Even women belonging to very conservative and orthodox families learned to do such work and to supplement their monthly incomes.

A discouraging aspect of such self-help work, however, was that the initial enthusiasm of the women was often dampened by difficulties in obtaining raw materials and in selling the finished products. Women with meager financial resources found it difficult to spend the money for such raw materials as silk for ties, cloth for embroidery, nylon for bags, and wool for knitting. The Department was reluctant to purchase the raw materials, as it was already furnishing the craft teachers. The sale of these and other products was sometimes quite discouraging. Many of the products made during the training period were obviously inferior and therefore difficult to sell. Most women, being illiterate, could not even read a tape measure. The most satisfactory arrangement was to take orders for items and then fill them. Women sometimes took direct orders from merchants, as in the case of children's garments, which were made in one area. In another instance, the women of several *vikas mandals* were making jointly a large number of cartridge belts for the army in 1964. Cloth was furnished by the government, and the women were given wages for their work. The Department could not, however, help out much because there was insufficient staff for soliciting orders, and at the same time it was nearly impossible to rely on untrained, illiterate women to perform this task. Difficulties in disposing of the products quickly discouraged women who had made investments of time, materials, and hope.

Sewing and tailoring classes were very popular among the women, and twenty-seven classes were held by twenty-one *vikas mandals* involving 457 women. Whenever a group of fifteen women was organized, a teacher was furnished for the first six months by the Department. The participants usually contributed R.1 each as an initial fee. A sewing machine was obtained either by cooperative purchase during the first three years of the project or, later, by loan from the Department. For cooperative purchase, each of the women contributed R.1 a month for six months, totaling approximately R.100 ($20) toward the purchase of a sewing machine; the Department paid the balance of R.80. At the conclusion of the six-month period, the machine became the property of the *vikas mandal*, which then lent it to women in the area. Sometimes the *vikas mandal* either paid or advanced the R.100 from its treasury. When there was a default in payments, the Department reclaimed the machine, but such action was seldom necessary. These self-help arrangements were limited to two machines per *vikas mandal*. A by-product of the cooperative use of sewing machines was the purchase, in some instances, of additional machines by groups of women on an installment, or, as it is called in India, a "lend-purchase" basis. The machines were kept in the homes of the women participants. As the maintenance of the machines, including supplying the needles, was the responsibility of the group of women, there was seldom loss or damage to a machine, and needles were rarely stolen, as they often are in social welfare centers. Later the Department purchased a few sewing machines to lend in the areas. CARE also gave twenty machines for this purpose. The *vikas mandals* and the women of the areas were responsible for safety and maintenance. This procedure allowed the machines to be moved from one area to another according to demand, rather than being used exclusively in one area or remaining idle.

FOOD PRESERVATION AND SIMILAR ACTIVITIES

Little home food preservation is done in India, largely because of lack of knowledge and experience. Although fresh fruits and vegetables may be cheap and plentiful at one time of the year, they may be scarce and expensive at other times. As canned or packaged products are prohibitive in cost for all but the wealthiest people, the average urban Indian would benefit immensely from knowing a few simple household methods of food preservation. Classes were held for interested women, at which they were taught how to preserve certain foods. The making of pickles, mango chutney, fruit jams, carrot preserves, and squash or fruit syrups for cold drinks became quite popular and resulted in considerable savings. One report stated: "As ginger and lime are now very cheap in the market, the worker gave them a demonstration of making pickles. They liked it very much."

Soap-making was another widespread activity. As soap is too expensive for the average slum family and is often of poor quality, many do not use it, which affects both their appearances and their health. In connection with soap-making and nutrition classes, budgeting could also be discussed, and families could be encouraged to make the wisest use of their meager resources. In one case twenty women cooperatively purchased an electric iron so that they could iron the clothes of their families for the first time.

COOPERATIVE FOOD STORES

Slum women in India generally buy only small quantities of food at a time. In a few instances, women join together in "buying clubs" to buy their food and thus receive cheaper bulk rates. It was hoped that there would be more such group purchasing than actually turned out to be the case; perhaps it will increase as women gain more status and confidence.

> There are two buying clubs working at present in this *vikas mandal*. These clubs were started by two different groups of people. In the one club the membership is thirty, whereas in the second fifteen members are participating. These clubs were intended to make bulk purchase from the wholesale market for distribution among the members according to their needs. At the end of each month, all the members are requested to submit their necessary requirements for the following month. After having received all these lists, two women go to the wholesale market and purchase all the necessities and distribute them among the members.

A major self-help achievement, however, was the development of cooperative grocery stores sponsored by *vikas mandals*, which by 1965 numbered eleven. These stores, which were established to maintain fair prices and to prevent food adulteration, sold Indian staples such as sugar, flour, grains, pulses, and spices, as well as fats and kerosene. Not many Indian stores carry tinned goods or prepared products. The Indian government makes it possible for citizens to organize cooperative stores, but it has not been easy to establish them in urban areas. There must be at least 100 members of a cooperative. The *vikas mandals* decided that one membership share should amount to R.10 ($2). Some people acquired more shares, but it was generally discouraged, although more than one adult member of the family could buy shares. The total amount raised was usually R.2,500 ($500). In one *vikas mandal*, 105 families purchased 250 shares at R.10 a share. The Indian government then matched the sum collected and, in addition, gave a grant of R.500 as a reserve fund.

Each cooperative store was located in a regular shop in the nearby bazaar and had its own president and other officers. It was run entirely by the officers, who appointed one person to make purchases and to keep accounts and hired clerks from the *vikas mandal* area. In practice, the officers' responsibilities tended to overlap. Anyone could buy from a cooperative, but only members could share in the profits. The stores turned out to be quite profitable ventures and probably did more than any other project to show urban people the advantages of cooperation and organization.

§ Self-Help Activities in Assuming Civic Responsibility

Two important objectives of urban community development are to intensify citizen participation in community affairs and to broaden awareness of available community resources. *Vikas mandals* learned to acquire information about municipal and voluntary services in their areas that could offer specific aid or technical assistance. The communities also learned about the organization of the municipal government, how it dealt with certain complaints, and how municipal and other agencies could assist with area problems.

Citizens participated in a wide variety of municipal, state, and national programs to commemorate certain events. The *vikas sabhas*, *vikas mandals*, and *vikas parishads* also helped to promote various national projects that affected daily living. They arranged programs for India Plan Week, Harijan Week, Anti-Tuberculosis Day, Red Cross Day, Family Planning Day, Small Savings Week, Children's Day, and many national festivals.

Emergency relief is generally the responsibility of the Indian government and various municipal departments. An attempt was made, however, to establish a standing corps of volunteers in each *vikas mandal* area, which could be mobilized during such emergencies as floods and fires. Such preparations later included a civilian-defense program, which was begun at the time of the Chinese invasion crisis in 1962. With the help of appropriate officers of the Department and the municipal administration, a nineteen-point program of civilian defense was carried out by nearly all *vikas mandals*. Similar programs were used during the dispute with Pakistan in 1965.

Some project areas had problems with juvenile delinquency and crime, and, although outside agencies usually dealt with them, some work was done by a number of communities themselves. Citizen committees discussed problems with the juveniles or the families involved, attempting to discover what conditions in the community might have given rise to the delinquency. The community dealt with delinquency as a community problem.

Gambling was a common activity among the youths and children in this *vikas mandal*, inhabited primarily by displaced persons from West Punjab. Initially, they started gambling in a small way on bus-ticket numbers, with stakes of old bottle caps, empty cigarette packets, and old bus tickets. In the course of time, however, they switched to cards and coins. Some children started gambling with their pocket money, and others misappropriated money given to them by parents for making purchases. Small thefts at home by children were also reported. The problem thus attracted the notice and concern of the residents. It was the consensus that children should be given opportunities to spend their leisure time constructively, to keep them away from gambling. The worker and local leaders organized an informal meeting, in which twenty-five children between ten and fifteen years of age participated. The worker explained the possibilities for organizing some play activities. The children were in favor of organizing a football club. Through voluntary contributions, they raised R.3. They purchased a football for R.7.50, the balance having been contributed by area adults. The help of the recreation field-program organizer was sought to organize the game. As a large number of children and youths evinced interest in sports and games, a cricket club was also formed as a part of a larger youth group, which resulted in extensive involvement of children and youths of the area in the planning and execution of recreational programs.

Another case involved citizen efforts to deal with the illegal manufacture of alcoholic beverages and with traffic in women for prostitution by other residents of the area.

This area was selected as a pilot project, and efforts were made to organize the people. After a year, however, it was determined that more direct efforts by the local residents were necessary if certain antisocial behavior was to be controlled. An action group of about fourteen members was then created in the citizens' development council, and meetings were held to plan strategy. The illicit distilling of liquor was most common among a particular group known as Sansis (members of one of the ex-criminal tribes as they are called), which consisted of about forty-eight families. This group had its own spy system, as well as close alliances with some officials, and was thus able to operate with virtual impunity. The action group of the citizens' development council encouraged the residents themselves to inform the police of the most opportune times to carry out raids. Furthermore, the group sponsored or encouraged secret meetings of residents, at which participants took oaths on scriptures to boycott liquor brewed in the area. The emphasis at all these meetings was more against the brewing rather than against the consumption of liquor. Later, the Municipal Department of Prohibition was asked to help in a prohibition campaign, and a number of well-known political leaders from Delhi was asked to participate. The twofold drive of police raids and resident-sponsored prohibitionist activities had the desired result, and the illicit manufacture of liquor ceased almost immediately.

The traffic in women for prostitution was somewhat more difficult to eliminate, as it was controlled by a smaller but more dangerous group. In spite of many warnings by members of the action group and the citizens' development council, the traffic continued unabated. The decisive action came at last in a public fight between the deviant group and the citizens' group. After the clash, which lasted nearly an hour, the members of the antisocial group were overpowered and handed over to the police for eventual trial. The group was thus broken up. Its leader was sentenced to several months' imprisonment, and the others were dispersed. The sale of women was halted.

Chapter 11

Evaluating social change

Evaluation studies are essential tools in determining the effectiveness of programs of social change. Citizens and public officials are generally skeptical of the results of such programs, for claims are often made that cannot be substantiated, and objective evaluations are seldom carried out. The aims and functions of a given program may be described, but the goals are often not stated in a way that makes evaluation possible. All too often evaluation is conceived as merely an impressionistic or descriptive procedure, involving reports of meetings, statements of activities with little by which to judge them, and opinions of key personnel.

As used here, the evaluation of social change is considered a much more clearly defined and rigorous procedure, with the use of quantitative measures or standards to test the actual achievement of stated objectives. It should be "objective, systematic and comprehensive," as distinguished from other forms of assessment that do not satisfy these criteria.[1] "Evaluation refers to the procedures of fact-finding about the results of planned social action which in turn move the spiral of planning ever upward. It is the proper methodological accompaniment of rational action. . . . The theme has always been with us; it is the performance that is different."[2]

The purposes of an evaluation program in urban community development are to determine the degree to which the objectives of the program are accomplished, to test the assumptions and theories on which the program rests, and to serve as a check on the efficiency of the methods used. In addition, evaluation studies furnish data about expectations and reactions of the people involved in the program, about their awareness of and attitudes toward the activities sponsored, and about their reasons for accepting or rejecting the new practices or programs.

§ *Evaluation in Urban Community Development*

Evaluation work in urban community development may be divided into three main areas: the impact of the program, its content, and its organizational aspects.[3] Evaluation techniques should provide evidence of changes brought about in project areas, and these changes can be studied in terms of knowledge, attitudes, and practices. Evaluation studies should attempt to determine, for example, the extent of changes in general sanitation, community functions organized, contacts and understanding among various groups, and leadership patterns.

Program content includes progress of various plans, types of activity initiated and their relationships to the recognized needs of the people, the degree of the people's association in planning and carrying out programs, the implementation and maintenance of the facilities provided, and the degree of participation among the people.

Organizational aspects include the extent to which the administrative setup and procedures are effective and whether or not there is a clear division of responsibility among the various staff categories, coordination of working fields and the nature of contacts with other departments at different levels, and the functioning of the staff and its roles.

COMPARISON WITH RURAL COMMUNITY DEVELOPMENT

Although the evaluation procedures of rural community development have much in common with those of urban work, there are differences in detail. Evaluation is generally easier in rural than in urban community development because indices of change can be more readily devised and a "base line," *i.e.*, data on certain specific indices like agricultural production against which to measure future changes, can be more easily prepared. A large part of a rural program can be evaluated by the extent to which the people have utilized fertilizers, seed grains, and improved cultivation methods. The miles of new roads constructed, number of new schools built, and number of new wells drilled also serve as indices of change. In urban work, the measures are less clearly defined. Although self-help paving of lanes and repair or whitewashing of houses may not be difficult to measure, the degree of community feeling behind an artificially created citizen council, changes in sanitation and cleanliness practices, and improved care of children are not easily measured.

IMMEDIATE AND LONG-TERM RESULTS

Immediate, concrete results of an urban-development program are often less significant than are long-term developments. Concrete achievements in a given year do not always constitute the final test of an urban community-development project's success. The ultimate test should be the results of continuing and expanding activity. Will the new methods of training be incorporated into the normal lives of the people in the community? Will there be more scientific attitudes toward health and sanitation problems extending beyond immediate inoculations? Has the people's apathy been overcome, and do they believe in the possibility of achieving success through their own efforts? Finally, have the people developed community loyalties and loyalties to one another?

Such questions raise the problem of how to measure such items and of the time needed to produce measurable results. Obviously, in urban areas of most developing countries one would not expect much impact on centuries-old practices and conditions within a few months. It is difficult to know whether a period of one or two, three to five, or even five to ten years is long enough to produce major change. Continuous growth toward the assumption of citizen responsibility is perhaps the best indication of successful change.

EXTERNAL OR INTERNAL EVALUATION

Evaluation can be carried out in two ways: by an internal unit or by an agency not connected directly with urban community development. Both are useful, and both may be used in complementary fashion in certain cases. An external evaluation is as fully independent as possible of the agency dealing with the actual execution of the development work. In its favor is the view held by some experts that the comments of a built-in evaluation unit are apt to be "self-criticism," a process distrusted by many. In India, for example, the Program Evaluation Organization of the Planning Commission is a body organized independently to evaluate rural community development. Although an extensive evaluation is carried out annually, selected issues are taken up each year because of the wide scope of the program.*

It may be unnecessary to set up a separate agency for evaluation, as it can often be carried out by the project organization itself. In the case of internal evaluation, the observations can be reliable and valid if conducted by a competent staff with a measure of freedom. Many administrators in charge of social-action programs prefer concurrent evaluations, rather than periodic evaluations. Although questions may be raised about the objectivity of internal evaluation, it has the advantage of being able to measure progress more closely. Also the observations tend to be somewhat more sympathetic and the agency concerned more open to the evaluation findings, depending, of course, upon the design, study analysis, and interpretation of the data.

---

* Such evaluation is practical in orientation, as its purpose is to help the administrator. This method implies some measure of rapport between the evaluator and the administrator, for otherwise the former will have little impact upon the latter. See, for example, Carl C. Taylor, Douglas Ensminger, Helen W. Johnson, and Jean Joyce, *India's Roots of Democracy: A Sociological Analysis of Rural India's Experience in Planned Development Since Independence* (Bombay: Orient Longmans, 1965), pp. 181–90.

In the Delhi project, evaluation was carried out internally, but the evaluation and research functions were kept separate from the program operations. The evaluation and research unit was under the administrative control of the project director, although there was an independent staff for observation and collection of field data for evaluation purposes. A deputy director had over-all charge of the unit. Although he enjoyed full autonomy in research and evaluation work, administratively he was under the supervision of the director. Such details as sampling designs, questionnaires and schedules, and tabulation and analysis of data were handled by the evaluation and research staff.* Although there was no expert committee to guide evaluation, experts in the field of evaluation were generally consulted on an informal basis while studies were being planned.

STEPS IN EVALUATION

The following steps are important in the evaluation of any urban community-development program: (1) specifying the goals of the project, (2) deciding what data to use to measure the project results, (3) collecting the necessary data, and (4) analyzing and interpreting the data so that it is possible to see whether or not the objectives are being achieved.[4]

Formulation of Objectives or Goals. The objectives or goals of an urban community-development project are extremely important, for, unless they are fairly clear, evaluation becomes impossible. For example, the goal of "improvement of the local community" is impossible to evaluate because it does not specify what is meant by "improvement." The goals should be formulated in such a way that they can be measured.

Deciding on Measurement Criteria. Once the objectives have been stated, measures for achieving them must be devised. If the objective is "community integration," the problem is how to measure it. Some measures might be the number of community meetings or community projects, how many people participated in them, and how many people in the area know about and identify with the local citizen council.

Collecting the Data. Once the criteria to measure objectives have been determined, the next steps are to ascertain the sources of data and how they are to be obtained. Data needed for evaluation purposes can be collected by several methods, including the study of available records, systematic observation of several features of the program, and interviews with the residents.

---

* In addition to the deputy director, the evaluation unit consisted of one research officer and four research assistants, two men and two women. All the research-staff members held postgraduate degrees in social science or social work and had two to three years of research experience each. The evaluation staff was familiar with more than research methods and procedures. It was also oriented toward the philosophy, approach, and method of urban community development. This orientation helped to minimize possible misunderstandings among the people of the project areas or among the program personnel as surveys were initiated from time to time.

Generally speaking, the last is the most appropriate source of data. These interviews may be conducted with either ordinary residents or such selected, more informed people as the officers of citizen-development councils. As it is generally impossible and even unnecessary to interview all residents, representative samples should be selected.

Analysis and Interpretation of the Findings. The final step in evaluation involves the analysis of the data, using, for example, various statistical measures. These results may have little meaning, however, unless they are interpreted in terms of program objectives. Conflicts may exist between the administrator and the evaluator, who is usually a social scientist. The administrator generally has these criticisms: The urban community-development program may not have been correctly interpreted; the administrator, whose understanding is acquired through actual administration, may find it hard to see how an evaluator, often a person without practical experience, can judge adequately; and, finally, the administrator may not find the evaluation useful.

These criticisms may arise from misunderstanding of the evaluator's role, which is to ascertain the extent to which a program of planned change is actually achieving its objectives. He must state the facts as he finds them, regardless of the administrator's attitudes. "If it so happens that in the course of serving a large, and rapidly expanding program, the evaluator comes across more pleasant than unpleasant facts, he must report them in the proportion in which they occur. He cannot highlight the fine success against the many failures without destroying reality. This is one of the reasons why the average administrator is allergic to the use of statistical techniques in evaluation."[5] An evaluation report tends to deal with the total, rather than with selected aspects, of a particular program.

§ *Evaluation in the Delhi Project*

The Delhi project has been presented here as an example of the possibilities of urban community development, not only in less developed countries, but in developed countries as well. The slum problems of Delhi in many ways are no less serious, comparatively, than are those of New York, Chicago, London, and Rio de Janeiro, for example. What was achieved in Delhi under conditions of extreme poverty and illiteracy, great heterogeneity, and often governmental confusion suggests the possibilities of such an attack on the slums of other countries. This evaluation of this project represents both substantive findings and an example of the different facets in evaluation of an urban community-development project.

Despite many difficulties, by December, 1965, the Delhi project consisted of five *vikas parishads* and forty-seven *vikas mandals*. The total number of people was over 150,000. In addition, there was one *vyapar mandal* of 300 shops. Several hundred thousand people had been affected by the improved work of the *mohalla* committees.

In every case, some improvement had taken place, but there were many problems remaining. Some *vikas mandals* did not perform up to project "expectations," as set by the Departments, but expectations about the level of a successful community-development program often differed in the minds of municipal government officials, councilmen, Department administrative personnel, and residents of the areas themselves. The expectations at all levels were important determinants of the eventual outcome of the work. Some expectations had more important consequences than did others. If a community organizer had high expectations and the work had not quite reached those levels, he might well become discouraged. There was, furthermore, a tendency for outsiders to put far more emphasis on some factors like improved sanitation than did the people themselves or those on the project staff.

A number of evaluation studies was carried out to determine the extent to which the goals of the Delhi project had been achieved and the degree of change that had occurred.[6] The aspects evaluated included the degree of social integration of areas into communities and the development of a sense of belonging to the areas; the extent to which citizen councils were effectively organized and their ability to foster local leadership; and the extent and nature of the self-help and mutual-aid programs designed to improve the communities.

THE VIKAS MANDALS

Two major evaluation studies of the Delhi project dealt with the formation and operation of citizen-development councils, all organized by the intensive method. The first study was made in 1961 of twenty-one of twenty-five citizen-development councils and two neighborhoods, representing 5,780 families, or 27,931 people, all of which had been formed by November, 1960.[7] It included the six original projects and fifteen other *vikas mandals* formed before the middle of 1960 and located in two *vikas parishads*. The *vikas mandals* had been in existence between four and fifteen months. For purposes of analysis and comparison, the twenty-one *vikas mandals* were grouped into "pilot projects," *i.e.*, the original six projects, the *vikas mandals* then formed in the Sadar Idgah and Shora Kothi neighborhoods. The second evaluation study was made in 1964 and covered the thirty-one *vikas mandals* and their *vikas parishads* that had been formed before March, 1963, or after an average (mean) of thirty-three months had elapsed.[8] This study included three neighborhoods, Sadar Idgah, Shora Kothi, and Paharganj, a total of 7,980 families, or 39,355 people. The *vikas mandals* ranged in size from ninety-eight families, with a population of 571, to 396 families, with a population of 2,322. The mean was

279 families and a population of 1,270 and the median was 268 families and 1,259 people.

Data were collected from the records available from the Department and the citizen councils, including weekly reports of the workers; contact cards; proceedings of the staff meetings; minutes of *vikas mandal, vikas sabha,* membership, and executive-committee meetings; educational aids; and income and expenditures. Interviews were conducted with all members of the executive committees and with the community and neighborhood organizers. Several schedules and questionnaires were used: the background-data schedule for *vikas mandal* areas, covering such aspects as population characteristics, available facilities, leadership patterns, work of voluntary agencies, and caste *panchayats,* if any; the questionnaire for executive-committee members, seeking information on problems of the areas, accomplishments, functioning of the executive committees, programs organized, and views on the impact of the program; the questionnaire for the community organizers, covering such aspects as problems of the areas, accomplishments, details about executive-committee meetings, leadership participation, cooperation from other departments, work load, and so forth.

In the second evaluation study a 5 per cent random sample, chosen from the record cards, of the male heads of households in the areas was interviewed by the research and evaluation unit to determine its knowledge of the *vikas mandal,* the impact of the program, and acceptance of the new programs. The random sample was proportionately distributed among the six pilot projects and the three neighborhoods.* In 43.6 per cent of the cases the respondents were between the ages of eighteen and thirty-five, 42.9 per cent were between the ages of thirty-six and fifty-five, and 13.5 per cent were fifty-six years of age and over. Nearly one-half were classified as illiterate (197). Respondents from the six pilot projects and Sadar Idgah neighborhood were 58 and 65 per cent illiterate; from Shora Kothi and Paharganj neighborhoods they were 33 and 37 per cent illiterate. Two-thirds (63.8 per cent) were from the so-called "upper" castes (Brahmin, Kshatriya, Vaishya, and Rajput); the balance was from the backward and scheduled castes. One-fourth, 23.4 per cent, had always lived in the area, and 56.6 per cent had come there after 1947. Of the latter, 11.6 per cent had come to Delhi after work had started in the projects. Some difficulty was found in interviewing the male heads of households because of unavailability, largely because of their work. In addition, twelve had left the area, and eight had gone away for indefinite stays. Consequently, substitutes were found for sixty, *i.e.,* 15 per cent of the male heads of families.

Most of the analysis presented here relates to the second evaluation study, as it covered more *vikas mandals* and made possible comparisons of trends.

* Individual interview cards for each family were available in the Department office. The total sample was drawn by taking every twentieth card from each *vikas mandal.*

A number of observations, derived largely from group interviews with organizers, have been added by the author. Some variations in the performance of the various *vikas mandals* and neighborhoods will be discussed in a later section. The original evaluation studies presented only percentages; the author made a more detailed analysis of the data using Chi squares, correlations, and regression analyses.

Membership. An important index of any voluntary organization is the strength of its membership. In their efforts to enlist members, the executive committee members were required to meet individual residents, and, in the process, they were able to interpret the nature and scope of the *vikas mandal* organization. Membership campaigns were sometimes conducted right after the inauguration of the organization; at other times, they were delayed. Those that organized their membership campaigns on decentralized bases of *vikas sabhas* succeeded in enlisting larger numbers of members.

The dues-paying membership figures for the *vikas mandals* in the first year were quite impressive. In the first year after their formation, five *vikas mandals* reported the percentage of membership was above 80 per cent, nine above 60 per cent, and nineteen above 40 per cent. In only one case was it below 20 per cent. In the first year, Shora Kothi neighborhood had the highest membership, 76.5, Paharganj 48.3 per cent, and Sadar Idgah 41.9 per cent. The participation in membership appeared, however, to decline over the next two or three years, but the *vikas mandals* still seemed to maintain considerable proportions of the residents on their rosters. Although complete figures were not always available because of different periods of membership campaigns for all of the *vikas mandals*, the twenty-nine reporting showed membership of 55.3 per cent the first year, fourteen reported membership of 44.9 per cent the second year, and eight reported 44.4 per cent the third year. If the same eight *vikas mandals* are compared between the first and third years, the figures are 70.2 per cent and 40.7. In the same older pilot projects, the figures are 77.6 per cent the first year, 77.2 per cent the second, and 49.2 per cent the third. The first evaluation study showed, however, that membership was not spread evenly over an entire *vikas mandal* area, and at the *vikas sabha* level it was not so encouraging. In some the percentages of membership were extremely poor. Nearly one-half, 107 of 201 *vikas sabhas*, were found to have memberships of less than 10 per cent of the families. Efforts were made to remedy this situation, but, unfortunately, the results were not included in the second study.

The lower membership or declines in membership in the *vikas mandals* was explained by the community organizers (in order of importance) as lack of organized effort on the part of the executive-committee members, conflicts among executive-committee members, factions in the communities, inadequate programs of activities, and dependence on the organizers.

Self-Help Activities. Up to March, 1963, thirty-one *vikas mandals* had carried out 1,346 self-help activities involving a total of 234,222 participants.* This figure amounted to 12.2 self-help projects per 1,000 people per year and 2.1 self-help participations per person in each project per year. There was an average of forty-three self-help projects per *vikas mandal*. Of the self-help projects, 38.8 per cent were in recreational and cultural activities, 22.8 per cent in health and sanitation programs, 14.4 per cent in physical improvements, 12.4 per cent in economic improvement, 6.5 per cent in education, and 5.1 per cent in miscellaneous programs. (See Chapter 10, Table 8.) Slightly more people were affected by the health and sanitation programs, 30.5 per cent compared with 29.8 for physical improvements.

There was relatively little emphasis on economic activities. With the meager resources of the *vikas mandals*, major projects in economic activities could not be undertaken, and there was little emphasis in this area in over-all Department planning. Programs of education were limited because of the increasing enforcement of compulsory primary education in Delhi. There were a few self-help schools, but most self-help education work consisted of organizing adult literacy classes and setting up reading rooms and libraries.

Contributions. In the thirty-one *vikas mandals* the total value of the work accomplished over an average period of thirty-three months came to R.81,240, an average of R.2,621 for each *vikas mandal* up to March, 1963. This total includes educational or grant aids from the Department. It does not include the value of free labor, as in the milk distribution programs, as well as related programs involving simply contributions of labor. It also does not include the value of the free powdered milk and other items obtained without cost. The percentage distribution of the value of the total work accomplished was 29.8 per cent in economic activities, 20.6 per cent in cultural and recreational programs, 19 per cent in physical improvements, 9.9 per cent in education, and 8.2 per cent in health and sanitation.

The people of the *vikas mandals* contributed R.50,167 ($10,000) of the total amount, or nearly two-thirds (61.7 per cent), an average of R.1,618 per *vikas mandal*. The people's contributions, in percentages, were nearly the same in all the neighborhoods, ranging from 61.9 per cent in Sadar Idgah and 64.8 per cent in Shora Kothi, to 65.8 per cent in Paharganj. The self-help contributions amounted to 80.3 per cent of the cultural and recreational programs, 76.3 per cent of the physical improvement programs, 66.9 per cent of the education programs, and 35.6 per cent of the economic programs. The contributions by the Department to the economic programs included the salaries of the craft teachers for the first six months and payments for the purchase of sewing

---

* The number of activities was compiled from the self-help cards that were filled out when an activity was completed. The number and distribution of the activities given here are somewhat less than in the published second evaluation report. Some activities were excluded here as it was believed they did not fall in the category of self-help as defined here.

machines. The first evaluation study of twenty-one *vikas mandals* showed that membership fees constituted 15.8 per cent of the total self-help income of the *vikas mandals*, the remainder coming from voluntary contributions for self-help activities.

The number of projects for which educational aids were given in this period amounted to 377, or a little more than twelve per *vikas mandal*. This figure does not include seventeen activities for which grants were given on a neighborhood basis. Most grants were small. Nearly two-thirds (63.9 per cent) were less than R.50 ($10); one-fifth (20.2 per cent) ranged between R.50 and R.100. Grants exceeding R.100 were mainly for subsidies for craft classes.

Effectiveness of Executive Committees. Slum people seemed to take their official responsibilities, an indicator of the degree of community integration and responsibility achieved, more seriously the first year than thereafter. The prescribed number of executive-committee meetings was set at one a month. During the first year, among twenty-nine *vikas mandals* reporting, this number was apparently either met or exceeded. In nine, meetings occurred from six to eight times a year; in only four were they held fewer than six times a year. In the second year, however, in all but five of the seventeen *vikas mandals* for which information was available, the number of meetings declined. Two of the seventeen were still meeting eight or more times a year, and only two were holding meetings fewer than four times a year. The organizers generally attributed failure to hold meetings regularly to the indifferent attitudes of the secretaries of the executive committees.

During the first year the executive-committee meetings in nineteen of the twenty-eight *vikas mandals* for which information was available were regularly attended by more than 50 per cent of the members; three had more than three-fourths regular attendance. In the second year the sixteen *vikas mandals* reporting showed 50 per cent or higher attendance in only seven, or slightly less than one-half.

The executive meetings generally were taken seriously by the members, as shown by a study of the topics discussed at 216 executive-committee meetings.[9] Organizational matters like appointments and reports of subcommittees, office accommodations, membership, and meetings were the main topics of discussion in 76.4 per cent of the meetings. Next in importance were health and sanitation, which were discussed in 43.1 per cent of the meetings.

An annual election of officers was provided for in the *vikas mandal* model constitution, and elections were generally carried out during the first year in twenty-four *vikas mandals* studied. In the second year only fifteen of them held elections, and the delay in most cases was more than six months. Several reasons for this failure were given by the community organizers: In nine *vikas mandals* the officers had no time; in six too much dependence was put on the community organizers; in six there was friction among members of the executive committees; and in five there were membership-enrollment problems. With few exceptions, the organizers believed that one solution to these problems would be largely solved if elections were held every two years. Then there would be less difficulty in carrying them out, and more permanence would be given to the officers, although this belief was contrary to the original position that offices should be more widely held. Other suggestions were that there should be a fixed membership period, as the annual enrollment of members was linked to the elections, and that financial grants should be withheld from any *vikas mandal* not holding an election.

Understanding the Objectives. In order to find out how well the executive-committee members understood the aims and objectives of the *vikas mandals*, each was asked the question, "What has the *vikas mandal* been trying to accomplish?"[10] The responses were grouped in three categories. Those who mentioned the self-help principle and cooperative action toward betterment of community life were regarded as having "good understanding." Others who listed a variety of activities directed toward meeting common needs of the area people were classified as having "fair understanding." Those who mentioned only one or two activities were viewed as having "poor understanding." An understanding of the aims and objectives of the *vikas mandals* by the members could be considered generally satisfactory: 44 per cent had "good understanding," 38.3 per cent had "fair understanding," and the percentage of members with "poor understanding" was only 17.3. There was, however, variation among *vikas mandals*, and this variation could be explained partly by differences in the educational level of the executive-committee members and in the workers' efforts.

Most executive-committee members seemed well aware of their own functions. They viewed their contributions as chiefly attending meetings, explaining the workings of the *vikas mandals* to people, enlisting members, and collecting funds (see Table 9). There was a variation, however, in the proportions of members reporting different types of duty. Executive-committee members appeared, furthermore, to have good understanding of their duties as *vikas sabha* representatives.[11] Of those who replied, 63 per cent said that they were to perform liaison work with the *vikas mandals*; 40.7 per cent said that they were to tackle zonal problems; 13.9 per cent said that they were to explain the principles and workings of the *vikas mandals*; 11.1 per cent said that they were to persuade the people to cooperate; and between 5.5 and 3.7 per cent said that they were to raise funds, to settle disputes, and to organize community gatherings.

A 5 per cent sample of 406 residents of the *vikas mandal* areas, of whom 175 were dues-paying members, were asked in 1964 what the *vikas mandals* were trying to accomplish. Those who mentioned self-help and cooperative efforts toward the improvement of the community were regarded as having "good understanding." Those who were regarded as having "fair understanding" mentioned a number of activities directed at dealing with common needs in the area, without emphasizing self-help. Those with "poor understanding" mentioned only one or two activities. Of those who replied, 48.6 per cent had good appreciation, 34.1 per cent fair, and 17.3 per cent poor.* A total of 159 of 406, or 39.2 per cent, however, could not mention any objective. The over-all picture looked favorable, but if the latter group is added to those with poor understanding, the percentage with a poor understanding increases to 58 per cent of the total.

Residents' Knowledge of Officers and Executive Committee. The residents' knowledge of the names of the officers or the executive-committee members

Table 9

Views of 115 Executive-Committee Members of Their Roles in the Twenty-One Vikas Mandals

Work Done	Total Percentage Reporting	Maximum Percentage	Minimum Percentage
Attended meetings	97.1	100	84.6
Explained the working of the *vikas mandals*	93.3	100	85.7
Enrolled members	82.8	91.4	71.4
Collected funds	78.1	95.7	43.5
Supervised work	57.1	92.8	33.5
Contacted departmental staff	47.6	92.8	30.5
Organized meetings	39.1	64.3	11.1
Supplied materials	35.2	61.5	11.1
Helped in getting accommodations	21.9	35.7	7.1

was considered a possible index to the effectiveness of a *vikas mandal*. On the whole, the results showed that most of the 406 area residents could not name an officer, but those 175 residents who were actually members of the *vikas mandals* did much better. As a group, one-third (32.2 per cent) of the total sample of residents interviewed was able to name a president; 29.3 per cent a secretary; and 10.3 per cent an executive-committee member. On the other hand, 57.8 per cent of the dues-paying members could name a president, 52.6 per cent a secretary, and 23.1 per cent an executive-committee member.

Development of Community Feeling. The creation of community feeling or integration in largely artificial physical areas was one of the chief objectives of the Delhi project but also one of the most difficult to measure. Community feeling was developed partially by the creation of formal organizations but more effectively through self-help accomplishments like the paving of lanes, the whitewashing of areas, and the common celebration of national holidays.

---

* Tables dealing with this sample study are contained in the *Second Evaluation Study.*

In addition, the name, the local *vikas mandal* office, area demarcation signs, competition of groups, and similar factors served to encourage community feeling in an area. Writing about the experimental projects during the first year, the author noted the beginning of community feeling:

> In our projects one senses an incipient community feeling. When one considers that most of these projects are artificially created one gets something of the feeling of being among a community of people whose officers, together with other individuals, go out of their way to show off the project area. One *vikas mandal*, the most artificially created of all, even refused to allow a woman from an adjoining project to participate in the joint purchase of a sewing machine, as she was not "in our group."

Large numbers of the people in nearly all *vikas mandals* came to identify themselves with the often artificial geographical boundaries laid down at the time of the demarcation of the areas.* In a few project areas, people had identifications with wider caste and historical backgrounds, and these identifications presented difficulties in developing area unity. The very fact that these artificial entities have all continued to exist and to carry on their activities over a number of years is some measure of the degree of the development of community feeling. The people in the programs generally became more conscious of their duties as well as of their rights. They came to know one another better. Although the expectations of the people for more effective municipal-corporation services were never fulfilled, they began to feel that they could solve many of their problems through joint efforts. More specific measures of community feeling would undoubtedly reveal considerable variation in the degree of community integration recognized by individual members.

An attempt to ascertain more specifically the impact of the program on community life was made in the 1964, 5 per cent random sample of the 406 heads of households and all of the organizers about the impact of the program on quarrels and disputes, interpersonal relations, intensification of group life, and attitudes toward children mixing with other groups.[12] One-third (35.3 per cent) of the residents reported an increase in intensification of group life and group activity, 22.9 per cent believed there had been no change, 1.2 per cent thought there had been a decrease, and 44.4 per cent had no opinion. A larger percentage of the respondents in the older projects reported an increase; 45.6 per cent in the pilot projects, compared with 37 per cent in the later projects in the Paharganj neighborhood. According to the organizers' views, there was an intensification of group life in 70 per cent of the *vikas mandals*, in 23 per cent

---

* When the first project was about to start in February, 1959, the author recorded: "I am pessimistic about the result; my only hope is that I will be pleasantly surprised. Will people see the advantages of self-help on a neighborhood or locality basis instead of caste, region, occupation, or politics? Perhaps the skill of organizers can overcome this difficulty."

there was no change, and in 7 per cent there was a decrease in group life after the work had started.

Changes in relationships among the various groups living in the areas were also an index of the degree of community integration. One-third (33.5 per cent) of the residents thought that there had been an increase, 23.7 per cent said no change had occurred, 1.2 per cent thought that there was less integration, and 41.6 per cent had no opinion. A large proportion of the residents of the older project areas generally believed that there had been increases within the more recently organized areas. More than one-half (55.9 per cent) of the heads of families were favorable to their children's participation in group activities with children of other castes, religions, or regions. Only 2.2 per cent were not in favor. The organizers reported that 70 per cent of the *vikas mandals* showed increases in interpersonal relationships, and in a little less than one-third (30 per cent) the situation was unchanged. About one-third of the residents (30.3 per cent) believed that quarrels and disputes in the areas had decreased, 24.6 per cent indicated no change, and only 2.5 per cent believed that there had been increases. On the other hand, the organizers thought that there had been decreases in disputes and quarrels in 53 per cent of the thirty-one *vikas mandals* and no change in 37 per cent. In 10 per cent they reported increases since the inception of the work.

Among 115 executive-committee members interviewed in 1961, 95.7 per cent believed that the problems of their areas could be solved largely by group action, and 88.7 per cent believed that people could work together successfully despite differences in caste, class, and politics. Three-fourths (74.8 per cent) thought that the relationships among groups and families in the areas had improved to some extent, although the members of individual *vikas mandals* who thought so varied from 42.8 to 91 per cent. In this connection there was considerable other evidence that the organization of people on an area basis appeared to be an effective way to establish communication among groups and to change narrow caste and regional loyalties. In fact, there is considerable evidence, although still inconclusive, that community activities and service on an executive committee representing an entire area helped to resolve caste difficulties and to promote intercaste amity.* Joint excursions, sewing classes, and other activities helped to overcome caste barriers and to improve communication among the residents. One evidence of such improvement was the fact that apparently later more members of different castes were invited to weddings in the communities.

---

* As an example, a mixed community of Brahmins, Sudras, and Harijans had existed on a small lane for many years, nearly two centuries, in fact. Few residents had much to do with one another. At the first executive-committee meeting the single Harijan zone representative sat alone some distance from the table. The Brahmin president finally asked him to join the others, on the ground that "we can do nothing unless we all participate."

Impact on Sanitation of the Areas. It was anticipated that changing the poor sanitation practices of an Indian slum area, because of its age-old complexities, would be an overwhelming task. The problem had always been too difficult for municipal authorities and welfare organizations. Although evidences of success or failure through an urban community-development approach were somewhat contradictory, it is clear that to change such practices will take considerably more effort and time.

Information about changes in sanitation practices was obtained from three sources. In 1964, after an average (mean) of thirty-three months, a study was made of project area residents' opinions about changes that they had noted since the beginning of the project in the general cleanliness of the area, the condition of drains, the problems of defecating by children, and indiscriminate urinating by children and adults.[13] This study involved a 5 per cent sample of male heads of families from thirty-one *vikas mandals* (406 respondents). In addition, a random 3 per cent sample of seventy-seven women residents and all seventy-two of their elected leaders from six *vikas mandals* were interviewed in 1962[14] (see p. 265). The community organizers were also asked their opinions of the extent to which changes had occurred in areas with which they were familiar.

One-third (34.5 per cent) of the heads of families felt that there had been an increase in the general cleanliness of the area, 44.6 per cent said that there had been no change, 3.2 felt it was less clean, and 17.7 per cent could not say. In the older project areas (six pilot projects), however, the record was somewhat better: One-half (55.6 per cent) of the residents felt that their areas were cleaner. Women took more positive positions about improvements in sanitation. A substantial proportion of women in all six areas believed that area cleanliness had improved; the over-all figure was 61 per cent of the women respondents and 68 per cent of the elected representatives, with the difference representing no change or couldn't say. Again, the older the project the more change was recognized. The difference among residents was found to be statistically significant (.05) with a range from 81 per cent for the older projects to 50 per cent for the newer ones. The community organizers took an even more positive view. In 83 per cent of the *vikas mandals* they felt that there was an improvement in area sanitation. In the remaining 17 per cent there was no change.

Choking of drains posed a threat to community health, largely because residents or municipal sweepers put garbage, feces, and other refuse into these open drains. About one-half (49.1 per cent) of the male heads of households in 1964 saw no change in the drains, and 24.6 per cent thought that the situation had even become worse. Only 8.4 per cent thought that there had been an improvement. On the other hand, two-thirds of both groups of women in 1962 found the drains less choked with refuse than before. The frequency of the women residents' positive evaluation was even slightly higher than that of their representatives. There was a significant statistical difference among the six *vikas mandals*; the longer a group had been organized the more improvements were recognized. The organizers, like the heads of families, however, took a less positive view: In 63 per cent of the *vikas mandals* they reported no change, and only 37 per cent reported a decrease in the frequency.

According to heads of households, the practice of children defecating in the drains either had not changed (47.7 per cent) or had increased (32.1 per cent). Only 3.7 per cent thought that it had decreased. On the other hand, a surprisingly large percentage of women thought that children defecated less frequently in the drains than before the formation of the *vikas mandals*. Sixty-one per cent of the residents and 59.7 per cent of the representatives noted such improvement. The older the *vikas mandal*, the greater the recognition of improvement among residents, 74.4 per cent of the older areas compared with 42.7 per cent of the newer, or a significant difference at .05. The reasons given by those who thought that there had been no change were the mothers' carelessness about their children and their lack of proper supervision and interest. The organizers thought that indiscriminate defecation had decreased in 60 per cent of the *vikas mandals*; in the remaining 40 per cent there was no change. Again, 51.4 per cent of the male heads of households reported that there had been no change in the practice of people urinating in the drains; 29.4 per cent said that it had increased; and only 2.7 per cent felt that it had decreased. About one in six had no opinion. The organizers thought that there had been improvement in 63 per cent of the *vikas mandals* and no change in 37 per cent.

If it is assumed that these figures represent the real opinions of the respondents, how can the differences among male heads of families, women, and community organizers be explained, particularly the increases reported by the heads of families in choking of the drains and the indiscriminate defecation and urination in the area? A significant statistical difference at the .05 level using Chi squares was found between the responses of illiterate and literate people about changes in the cleanliness of the area, defecating in the drains, urinating in the lanes or drains, and blocking of the drains. Generally a larger proportion of literate people thought there had been some improvement. While the organizers generally noticed that certain sanitation aspects had not improved in a number of *vikas mandals*, they reported no deterioration in conditions by area. One conclusion might be that, as the heads of households were men, their judgments of the situation might not be so accurate as those of the women. Perhaps the most valid conclusion is that an increased emphasis on sanitation had made the men more conscious of it, which could make for more positive changes in the future.

Acceptance of "New Practices." It seems evident that people in the projects more readily accept "new practices" like immunization against communicable diseases, family planning, and maternity and child-welfare services than they respond to changing old habits of sanitation. Every family head of the sample of 406 residents was asked, in 1964, whether or not all family members had been immunized against smallpox and cholera. The data were then classified as "all," "some," or "none" immunized. More than four-fifths (82 per cent) reported that all members had been vaccinated against smallpox, 12.8 per cent reported some, and 5.2 per cent reported none. The range of those reporting "all" members varied from 74 per cent in one neighborhood to 94 per cent in another. Immunization against cholera was a more difficult matter; 71 per cent reported all members, 12.5 per cent some, and 16.5 per cent that none had been immunized. In one large *vikas parishad*, the Paharganj neighborhood, with a higher rate of literacy, not only were 94 per cent of the families vaccinated, but 93.1 per cent were also immunized against cholera. This acceptance of the need for immunization was also supported by the views of the women: All but one of the residents interviewed in 1962 and all of the representatives favored immunizing children against diseases. This near unanimity was a significant achievement, for seldom do Indian slum women attribute smallpox and cholera to the true causes. In all, seventy-one of seventy-seven sample residents surveyed and sixty-nine of seventy-two representatives definitely thought that more people in the area were being immunized than before the area was organized. Furthermore, 90 per cent of the residents and 67 per cent of the representatives thought that there were fewer epidemics than previously.

Acceptance of vaccination and immunization was slightly associated with the literacy of the head of the family; 84.1 per cent of the 209 literates accepted vaccination, against 82 per cent of the total respondents. Similarly, 76.6 per cent of the literates accepted inoculation against cholera, compared with 71 per cent of the total respondents. The relation with the degree of education is much clearer when those with fewer than six years of education are compared with those with six or more years (see Table 10). Approximately three-fourths (78.2 per cent) of those with fewer than six years of education were vaccinated, compared with 90.4 per cent of those with more than six years of education; for cholera immunization the figures were 70.2 per cent and 83.5 per cent.

The Department provided for some guidance in family planning by public health nurses and lady health visitors who arranged talks and demonstrations in the areas. Two-thirds (64.2 per cent) of the male heads of families were not favorable, however, to family planning; the remaining 35.8 per cent were favorable. The opposition to family planning ranged from 53.6 per cent in one neighborhood to 73.5 per cent in another. Literate heads of families appeared to respond more positively to family planning than did the illiterate. Among the women surveyed, on the other hand, 59 per cent of the seventy-seven residents were in favor of family planning. None of the seventy-two representatives expressed an unfavorable opinion, but 24 per cent did not know how they felt. Opposition among the women residents came mainly from an all-Muslim area, where the majority of the women continued to maintain that children are the "blessings of God."

Half (48.7 per cent) of the family heads were in favor of their women using the services of maternity and child-welfare centers, and the neighborhoods ranged from a low of one-third to a high of four-fifths in favor. On the other hand, the support was greater among women, for the survey showed that 84 per cent of the women residents and 98 per cent of the representatives favored the use of maternity and child-welfare centers.

Over-All Performance. In connection with the second evaluation study of the thirty-one *vikas mandals*, and after an average three-year interval, an attempt was made in 1965 by the research and evaluation unit to classify *vikas mandals* into those above average, average, and below average, on the basis of the strength of the organization and the impact of the community development work.[15] The first included such items as membership, attendance

Table 10

Percentage Distribution of Literate Respondents by Education in Relation to the Extent of Family Immunization Against Smallpox and Cholera

| | | EDUCATIONAL CLASSIFICATION | | |
		Below Six Years	Six Years and Above	All Educated People
	Members of Families Immunized			
Smallpox	all	78.2	90.4	84.1
	some	13.9	4.3	9.2
	none	7.9	5.3	6.7
Cholera	all	70.2	83.5	76.6
	some	14.9	6.6	10.9
	none	14.9	6.6	12.5

at the executive-committee meetings, activities undertaken by the *vikas mandals*, and the average contributions per family. Impact was measured by the responses of residents to questions about interpersonal relationships, group life, cleanliness of the area, and other changes. As a unit, ten of the thirty-one *vikas mandals* were rated "above average" in organization and fourteen in impact; nine were rated "average" in organization and one in impact; and twelve were rated "below average" in organization and sixteen in impact. In the first evaluation report in 1962, the twenty-one *vikas mandals* were classified six "above average," nine "average," and six "below average."[16]

Efforts were made to find out whether or not each *vikas mandal* ranked in a particular category on the basis of organizational aspects received the same rating on impact of its work. For thirteen *vikas mandals* the ratings were the same; for ten the rating for impact was higher than that for organization; and for eight the rating for organization was higher than that for impact. A study of the six above average and the six below average *vikas mandals* would probably best reveal some of the factors accounting for the differences. Such a study has been undertaken but has not yet been completed. In lieu of this evaluation, the only available judgment about the reasons for a poor impact of the program was that of the community organizers. It was judged that the four most significant reasons were the transfer of the workers from one project to another, the fact that specific programs either were not undertaken or were not directed at recognized needs, and lack of interest or time by executive-committee members. More specifically, the percentages of the workers reporting particular reasons were:

transfer of workers	89.6
specific programs not undertaken	62.1
programs not related to the recognized needs of people	51.7
lack of time and interest among executive-committee members	34.5
major problems of people not solved	31.0
few economic programs	24.1
friction and groupism among the people	24.1
lethargy among the people	24.1
no cooperation from other departments of the Municipal Corporation	20.7
illiteracy among the people	17.2
departmental procedural delays	17.2
no common place or office	13.8*
no open space for self-help activities	13.8
frustration among people because of nonexecution of programs	10.3
"educational aid" policy of the Department not clear	10.3
overdependence on departmental workers	10.3

Both the first and the second evaluation studies stressed the negative aspects of the transfer of workers from projects with which they were initially associated. "It has been commonly observed that the transfer of workers from one area to another adversely affects the work. Since the transfer of workers is inevitable, the Department should devise ways and means by which transition is made smooth and easy without causing any dislocation of work. Transfer of workers should be made only if it is inevitable, otherwise in the interest of the work it should be discouraged. There should be a period of induction of the new worker at least for a fortnight, so that he or she becomes familiar with both the area and the people."[17]

---

* In order to deal with the difficult problem of space for citizen councils in Ahmedabad, the Department of Urban Community Development has developed inexpensive small multipurpose cabins at a cost of R.3,700 each for use as the headquarters of neighborhood projects. Each contains a sink and a place for a projector to show pictures outside. The *vikas mandal* in the area also uses it as a headquarters, and classes in nutrition and child-care are held there. There is room for a small library, and the walls are designed for the use of charts.

Poverty and Self-Help. The wisdom of basing self-help projects on contributions from the poor of the slums can be questioned on the grounds that they can do little to help financially with their problems. The poverty of the Indian slums did not seriously interfere with self-help efforts in the *vikas mandals.* Most slum dwellers seem to have money available for such purposes, providing the individual contributions are small, that is, R.1 for annual dues, R.1 per month for a sewing machine or a literacy class, or a few *naya paisa* for a water tap. Slum dwellers, even in the poorest localities, showed willingness to contribute to programs that concerned them intimately and that assured direct benefits to them or to their communities. In fact, on the average, more than three-fourths of all self-help activities were carried out without financial subsidies or grants from the Department. Actually, slum people in India and elsewhere are not so poor as one might assume. The average monthly rental for slum habitations is only a few rupees in Indian cities, representing probably less than 10 per cent of total incomes. Many people spend money on gambling, alcohol, and motion pictures. In addition, several members of each slum family work, adding to the total income. These facts do not imply that there is much money available individually for self-help but rather that a small contribution from each member makes it possible for a *vikas mandal* or a *vikas sabha* to raise a fairly substantial amount of money for a cooperative project. There is, however, a financial limitation to the scope of self-help; when larger projects like the construction of a dispensary are planned, it is likely that substantial financial subsidies will be necessary to keep all available area funds from being channeled into such efforts, to the detriment of other self-help projects.

Indigenous Leadership. The formation of *vikas mandals* gave opportunities for leadership experience to many residents for the first time. About two-thirds of thirty-five executive-committee members of twenty-one *vikas mandals* had had no previous leadership experience.[18] The composition of the *vikas mandal* executive committees reflected, to a great extent, the types of people who live in slum areas, as demonstrated by the fact that people generally classified as low caste represented about one-third of the membership and non-Hindus (Muslims, Sikhs, and Christians) accounted for 17.4 per cent. Nearly half the executive-committee members had had no formal education, and several council presidents could neither read nor write.

Although it has often been assumed in the Western world that illiteracy is a serious handicap for indigenous leaders, in the Delhi project people with less education were elected to the executive committees. They often reflected the community's feelings and aspirations and appeared likely to work energetically for community betterment. Although in all project areas educated people were available, slum residents selected leaders from the less educated groups. Five per cent of 351 executive-committee members of twenty-one *vikas mandals* were totally illiterate, and almost half were either illiterate or semiliterate.

The quality of citizen leadership among the officers of the executive committees seems to have been highly associated with successful *vikas mandal* and *vikas parishad* development programs. Successful leaders were distinguished by a number of characteristics. They were generally not young people because in India age engenders respect. One study of twenty-one *vikas mandals* showed that executive-committee members were usually between thirty-six and fifty-five years old. A leader was often an older man whom the people respected and whose ideas were accepted by the younger people. This age criterion was particularly notable among the presidents of *vikas mandals,* who were likely to be fifty years of age or older, whose views might not always be accepted, but whose status positions were accepted. Successful secretaries, on the other hand, were younger and were always literate.

Effective leaders were generally those who were respected and accepted because they showed desire to improve the communities rather than to gain what personal status might accrue from leadership activities. Such people would find time to help the communities to achieve their objectives. At the lowest level, people usually selected leaders from castes similar to those of the majority; at the neighborhood level, higher-caste leaders were more frequently successful. Many successful leaders were of the dominant castes. In general, the effectiveness of a leader in working with people, however, seemed to take precedence over solely caste, religion, or regional considerations. In one *vikas mandal* area, for example, where Sikhs were greatly outnumbered by Hindus, a Hindu secretary was much more effective than a Sikh who succeeded him.

In mixed political areas, the successful leaders were generally those who did not have strong political affiliations. Some of the reasons were that politically oriented people were less likely to secure the cooperation of other political groups and that their political activities left little time for community affairs that were primarily nonpolitical in nature. In a few cases, however, where predominantly one-party areas existed and where the councilmen were particularly interested, people from the party were elected over those of different political parties who might have been more effective leaders. This problem occurred in only one of three neighborhoods, however.

In the beginning, the officers of *vikas mandals* took much active interest in the program. Later, in some cases, the secretaries had to assume more initiative to keep things going, which in turn fostered disinterest among the executive committees and dependence upon the secretaries. There were some *vikas mandals* in which, after some time, frictions and rivalries broke out among the officers. It is likely that this problem can be anticipated in such work, and efforts must be made to find methods to avoid such situations.

VARIATIONS IN PERFORMANCE

As in any operation the size of the Delhi Project, some *vikas mandals* and *vikas parishads* responded to the goals of community participation and self-help better than did others.* In an attempt to discover some of the factors that might account for such variations, an analysis was made of the performances of twenty-eight *vikas mandals* in six pilot projects and three neighborhoods up to March, 1963.† Two criteria for "success" were separately employed, each adjusted to the age of the *vikas mandal*: the number of self-help projects per 1,000 population and the number of times people in an area participated in self-help projects per 1,000 population. These criteria were measures of activity; indices of community integration might have been equally appropriate measures of "success" but were not available for this analysis. The variables considered as possible determinants of success were the size and age of each organization, the age composition of the membership, its homogeneity by regional groupings, the literacy and educational levels of the population, and the occupations of the heads of families (see Appendix B, Tables B2 and B3). Total self-help projects and total self-help participations per person were analyzed, as were variations in activities according to type: physical, sanitation and health, educational, recreational, cultural, and economic. The analysis was made on electronic computers employing regression analysis.‡ Because the ages of the *vikas mandals* varied from twenty-one to forty-four months, with a mean of 31.5 months and a standard deviation of 6.6, rates were adjusted to projects and participations per month.

Correlations between the two measures of "success," participation and projects (see Appendix B, Table B4), were calculated for the totals and between various types of activity. These correlations show the degrees of variation in the "sizes" of projects when size is measured by the number of people participating. The over-all correlation between the two indices was 0.53, but there was considerable variation in the amount of participation that cannot be explained by the number of projects. The variations in the sizes of the projects, as measured by the numbers of participants, were largest with the physical projects and least with the educational projects, although in neither case were the differences great. The age, or length of operation, of each *vikas mandal* explains some of the variations; participation tends to increase with age, whereas number of projects does not, that is, projects tend to become less numerous but larger in size.

---

* The study of variations in a number of smaller projects is important in evaluation. One study, in reporting negligible results for a large-scale community delinquency-control project as a whole, indicated that some groups in the project showed positive results and that there was differential vulnerability to change among groups. See Walter B. Miller, "The Impact of a 'Total-Community' Delinquency Control Project," *Social Problems*, 10 (Fall, 1962), 190.

† The total number of *vikas mandals* studied was thirty-one. The analysis was made by the author using a CDC 1604 computer. Three of the six original pilot projects had to be excluded because of differences in the class intervals of age composition. This exclusion did not, of course, affect the neighborhoods. (See Appendix B, Table B1.)

‡ Appendix B contains a more detailed discussion of the assumptions made, the procedures used, the results obtained from the statistical analyses, and the limitations of the analyses.

Regressions were run for both participation and projects per 1,000 population per month of operation of the *vikas mandals* (see Appendix B, Table B5). The over-all effects of these independent variables were the same for the absolute numbers of participations and projects as for the relative numbers. Participation thus increased absolutely with the age of the *vikas mandal*, and the number of participations per month also increased. The total number of projects and the number per month, however, did not change significantly with the age of the *vikas mandal*. In interpreting this result, it should be remembered that the ages of the organizations varied from about twenty-one to forty-four months; for a wider range in age the effect of this variable might be more significant.

The regression results, in general, show that participation increases with the age and literacy of the *vikas mandal* and that the number of projects decreases with the size of the *vikas mandal*. As a *vikas mandal* matures, the types and sizes of projects undertaken change from small projects involving less effort on the part of the participants to larger projects involving more intensive participation. The degree of explanation by these variables, however, never exceeded 59 per cent in any of the equations, although in cross-section analysis of this type the results are probably reasonable.

The independent variables considered were, in general, not significant in explaining the number of participations or the number of projects, both variables on a per-month-of-operation basis. Occupation had little effect, with the exception of participation in physical activities, which increased with the occupational level. Homogeneity was a significant variable only for participation in sanitation and health projects, on which it had a negative effect. Age structure of the population had a slightly greater effect and was more pervasive: The older the age group the less was the tendency to participate in sanitation and health projects but the greater the number of recreational and economic projects.

The three variables with general effects were the age and size of the *vikas mandal* and the literacy of the population. The effect of size was to decrease the number of projects of all types, except economic ones. This variable also reduced the number of participations in sanitation and health projects but did not affect participation in other projects. In general, as the age of a *vikas mandal* increased so did the number of participations. With types of activity, however, the effect of age is to shift the emphasis from recreational projects to economic and physical projects. In general, self-help participation increased with literacy.

In summary, "successful" *vikas mandals* appear to be the smaller ones. As illiteracy is highly related to success, initial emphasis should be placed on self-help efforts in the area of literacy, with the expectation that such efforts may be accompanied by greater self-help efforts in other areas. The number of self-help projects does not increase proportionately with the age of a *vikas mandal*, but participation does. Other variables like occupational skills, homogeneity of the population, and the age composition of the *vikas mandal* are not so important.

The three *vikas parishads* (Sadar Idgah, Shora Kothi, and Paharganj) were quite different in many characteristics, so that it was possible to ascertain whether or not certain social characteristics affected the performance of the areas and the views of the residents (see pp. 153–4). Sadar Idgah was much poorer than the others. In literacy they varied from 35.6 to 58.2 and 66.0 respectively, which represented a significant statistical Chi square difference beyond the .05 level. There was also a significant difference in Chi squares beyond the .05 level in occupations and in the proportions of refugees, with Shora Kothi being generally higher than Sadar Idgah and Paharganj having a higher proportion than either of the others.

Table 11

Numbers of Self-Help Projects and Participations per 1,000 People per Month in Three Vikas Parishads *to March, 1963*

Neighborhood	Projects	Participations
Paharganj	20.8	2,700
Shora Kothi	15.6	3,300
Sadar Idgah	10.9	2,100

In over-all performance those neighborhoods with higher literacy and economic development had more projects per 1,000 people per month. For projects, the figures were 10.9, 15.6, and 20.8 respectively (see Table 11). Participation per 1,000 people per month was higher in the more literate neighborhoods, but the performances did not vary directly. Sadar Idgah had 2,100 participations per 1,000 per month, Shora Kothi 3,300, and Paharganj 2,700. The more literate neighborhoods tended to concentrate on recreational and cultural activities, whereas the less literate neighborhoods did more in physical, educational, and economic activities.

A 5 per cent sample of 316 heads of families (part of the sample of 406 discussed on pp. 246–7, with the six pilot projects excluded) was analyzed with Chi squares to determine whether or not there was a significant difference at the .05 level in the responses of the residents of the three neighborhoods. In most items, unfortunately, the expected frequencies fell below accepted standards in sufficient cells to preclude reporting whether a significant difference existed or not. Significant differences were found, however, in answers about the extent of defecation and the frequency of choking in the drains; in general, the more literate neighborhoods found that these problems had increased. As already indicated, this view may have been the result of greater awareness of the problems. There was also a significant difference in the extent of immunization against cholera, with total percentages in the neighborhoods ranging from 59.1 to 93.1, and of vaccination for smallpox in families, varying from 74 to 94 per cent of the total families. There was a pronounced significant difference in the acceptance of family planning, those from the more developed neighborhoods tending to favor family planning. In percentages the acceptance of family planning varied from 26.5 in the poorest and least literate neighborhood to 46.4 in the most advanced. On the other hand, there was no significant difference among the respondents from the three neighborhoods, whether merely residents or members of the *vikas mandals*, in knowledge of the names of officers and other executive-committee members.

Table 12

Numbers of Self-Help Projects and Participations per 1,000 People per Month in Five Original Pilot Projects to March, 1963*

Hypothesized Rank	Projects	Participations
Poor area, high density	64.1	1,300
Refugee colony	29.4	1,200
Muslim traditional	25.8	2,300
Industrial area	23.3	1,000
Relocated squatter colony	1.53	200

* The area with mixed class and caste was omitted because of alterations in the territory covered by the project.

THE PILOT PROJECTS

There was considerable variation in the performances of the original pilot projects up to March, 1963 (see pp. 150–2). The project with mixed caste and class had to be excluded from the analysis because the original physical area had been extended. In terms of self-help projects per 1,000 people, the poor area with high density had the largest number (64.1), followed by the refugee colony, the traditional Muslim area, the industrial area, and the relocated squatter colony (see Table 12). Participations per 1,000 people were highest in the traditional Muslim area, followed by the poor area and the refugee colony.

The poor, high-density area approached community integration and self-help with a high degree of morale and effective leadership. Although it was originally expected that the Muslim community, because of its traditionalism and high degree of illiteracy, would tend to resist change, it did not turn out to be the case. Actually, this community became one of the most successful in developing new leadership and engaging in varied self-help activities, many of them quite ambitious. The refugee colony with low density became organized into an effective area capable of doing things on its own. Initially there were indications that industrial workers would not readily respond to the idea of community integration and self-help because of their preoccupation with factory and union activities and because of other difficulties in the area. Over a period of time, this expectation proved false, and eventually the project was built into a relatively strong and effective organization. The squatter colony, relocated in an area administered by the municipal government, presented difficulties. There was often more interest in complaining about rents, municipal facilities, and problems connected with relocation than in self-help. By providing several facilities the city reduced some of the initiative for self-help. Later, after additional *vikas mandals* had been added to the area and as it continued to expand, the project showed considerable improvement.

THE MAHILA SAMITIS

By December, 1961, thirty-one *mahila samitis* had been organized. Six areas were selected for study, and all seventy-two elected women leaders and a 3 per cent representative sample, or seventy-seven of the women residents were studied.* The selection of the areas was based on the following criteria: the presence of significant women's activities; diversity among areas; and variation in the ages of the organizations. Two areas were part of the original six "pilot" projects and had been in operation about a year and a half. Two, which had been organized for a year, were called "old *vikas mandals*," whereas those that had been active for only six months were termed "new *vikas mandals*." The pilot and older areas were more conservative and illiterate. One of the pilot areas was all Muslim, and three-fourths of its residents were illiterate; the other consisted of a colony of bustee dwellers. The two "older" areas were *katras* in dilapidated condition housing 277 families, 51.9 per cent of which were illiterate, and an area of migrants from Pakistan and the Punjab, 47.5 per cent of whom were illiterate. The two "newer" *vikas mandals* consisted of one area, three-fourths of whose residents were refugees from Pakistan, with only 23.8 per cent illiteracy and a heterogeneous area where 35 per cent of the residents were illiterate.

Although these areas were substantially different in caste and social status, as well as in religious and regional composition, the study was concerned primarily with the changes in opinions and attitudes of the leaders and members of the *mahila samitis* and with variations among the areas according to project duration. The women's representatives were more likely to perceive greater change, as they were better informed than the ordinary residents of the area. The

---

* *A Study of Women's Attitudes and Practices and the Working of Mahila Samitis* (Delhi: The Department of Urban Community Development, Municipal Corporation of Delhi, 1963). A panel study or more frequent detailed studies would have been more appropriate, but they would have presented problems among a largely illiterate female population, which tended to be suspicious of many investigations.

answers of the residents served as a partial check on the representatives' opinions. It appears that considerable reliance can be placed on the answers; Neither representatives nor residents evaluated everything favorably, pointing out that in some areas little change had occurred.

Although most of the women knew about the existence of *mahila samitis* in their areas, 40.3 per cent did not know the names of their local representatives, and two-thirds (64.9 per cent) reported that the local representatives had not approached them. On the other hand, thirty-four of fifty-seven residents responding and fifty-one of sixty elected women's representatives thought that there was need for separate women's associations. The reasons they gave were the needs to discuss common problems, to gain knowledge, to plan sewing programs, to develop better communications among women, and to promote cleanliness of the areas.

Women Representatives. Women usually elected representatives who had fairly similar characteristics, except for age. Slightly more than half (55 per cent) the representatives, compared with 30 per cent of all the women residents of the areas, were over thirty-five years of age.* Only 10 per cent were under twenty-five years of age, compared with 21 per cent of the residents. The leaders had a slightly lower rate of illiteracy, two-thirds (62 per cent), compared with three-fourths (74 per cent) of the residents. Ten representatives, compared with only one of the women residents, had a middle-school (eight years) or higher education. The caste membership of representatives was almost identical with the residents. Comparative figures for representatives and residents from the upper castes were sixty-three and fifty-seven from the lower fifteen and twenty-three, and from other groups, including Muslims and Sikhs, sixteen and twenty.

Representatives of the *mahila samitis* were supposed to have monthly meetings, and a poll of the representatives of six such organizations indicated that all were following this practice. About one-third of the representatives did not regularly attend meetings, however, because of sickness, young children, or their husbands' objections. Approximately three-fourths of the representatives thought that these meetings were useful, although in the two oldest, or pilot, projects the figure of 88 per cent was higher. This figure seems to indicate that more representatives considered the meetings useful than attended and that the usefulness of the meetings was related to the age of the project. During the first year about one-fifth (19.2 per cent) of the *mahila samiti* representatives on the *vikas mandal* executive committees attended meetings regularly,[19] one reason for the low female attendance in a predominantly male group was the nature of the social conventions and the unsuitability of the meeting times. In fact, under these conditions, the fact that two-thirds of them reported attending some meetings was probably significant.

---

* Women representatives of the *mahila samitis* on the executive committees were even older than the men; 57.2 per cent of the men were over thirty-six compared with 63.4 per cent of the women.

Activities of the Mahila Samitis. The convenor of each *mahila samiti* called meetings to discuss and plan what could be done about the problems of the *vikas mandal* and the neighborhood. Some self-help activities were organized at the *vikas mandal* level, others at the *vikas parishad* level. Common projects carried out by the *mahila samitis* of the *vikas parishad* might involve all or only some *vikas mandals*. They included common craft classes; preschools for children between three and six; child-health competitions; best-kept home competitions; children's sports meets; dramatic shows; and celebrations of such religious and national holidays as Diwali and Independence Day.* Occasionally the women of a *vikas parishad* purchased sets of large utensils through their *vikas mandals* to be lent out for the typical large Indian marriage parties.

Other self-help projects for women included recreation for the children, social activities like picnics, and cultural activities like visits to historic places. In most areas, the first projects were in the areas of economics and health, and it was usually some time before interests broadened into other areas. Most self-help activities came in response to felt needs, but, in the cases of vaccinations, inoculations, and recreation, the workers often had to arouse awareness of the need by persistent and patient efforts.

Some self-help activities carried out by women were particularly striking. Not long after the Chinese invasion of India in late 1962, the various *mahila samitis* in one *vikas parishad*, being short of money and wishing to contribute their labor, decided to do something for the Indian *jawans*, or soldiers. The women knitted 150 pounds of wool into socks and sweaters and would have done more had wool not become difficult to procure. They also made five maunds, or 410 pounds, of Indian pickles.

The great single achievement of the women was the undertaking, in one *vikas mandal* area, of 1,000 families to operate a cooperative grocery store. To appreciate what this effort meant, one has to remember that Indian bazaar shops are operated by men. In this particular area, two cooperative grocery stores had been set up by *vikas mandals*. The *mahila samiti* decided that women would also organize and operate a store, probably one of the first of its kind in all India. Seventy women bought R.10 ($2) shares, and through friends they found thirty other women outside the area who would also contribute. With a 100-member group and a R.1,000 fund, they obtained additional help from the main bazaar. The store served as a source of great pride to the women of the area, and they were encouraged by the organizers, as this project might give them a new image of themselves.

A comparison of self-help activities and the problems in the areas as originally seen by women shows how much they changed their views as the projects developed. When first interviewed, 599 women thought almost exclusively about

---

* See Chapter 10 for a more complete discussion of self-help activities.

physical improvements and facilities, as well as about ways to increase their incomes. Few were concerned with health, education, recreation, and cultural activities. Surprisingly, 337, or 56 per cent, reported sanitation as a major problem. A considerable number reported no problems at all. When a later study was made of their self-help activities, social, cultural, and recreational interests were those mentioned most prominently, accounting for 44 per cent, or nearly one-half, of the total.

The extent to which women participated in the activities of *mahila samitis* varied according to many circumstances. Their limited mobility often made it difficult for them to participate in many activities, and many women had limited understanding of the objectives of a large-scale slum-improvement program. Their constant fight against poverty and hunger sometimes prevented them from doing more. If self-help contributions were required, they had to secure permission from their husbands, which was not always granted. In addition, the representatives of the *mahila samitis* often lacked the skill necessary to involve other people. There were also variations in social class. As might be expected, middle-class women were more highly motivated. Among regional groups, Punjabi women, both Sikh and non-Sikh, were most interested in self-improvement.

Although Indian women are conservative in matters of caste, particularly in relation to marriage and family relations, caste did not seem to interfere with the common activity programs for women. Perhaps the fact that subordinate status was shared by most women contributed to their solidarity. As caste and class are likely to be closely equated, it is likely that, in the choice of women representatives, class played a more important role than caste. There was no case, however, in which a Harijan (Untouchable) woman was a *samiti* representative except in one all-Harijan group. Women of different castes cooperated in buying sewing machines, sat together in nutrition and family-planning classes, and entered their homes in cleanliness contests and their children in child-health contests. One worker reported that, "There is no caste problem, except in matters of eating." In child-health competitions, women of various castes came to common meeting places and sat together for hours. The doctor who judged a contest did not, of course, know the caste of the child, and the women willingly accepted the fact that children of all castes were judged equally. A mixed caste group, however, would not visit the house of an Untouchable. In one zone, for example, where most of the women were Brahmins, the woman representative sought to exclude one woman from membership because she was an Untouchable. It was finally decided to include her because she could sing, but only with the provision that she come to other women's houses, thus precluding their going to hers.

Changes in Attitudes and Practices. Efforts were made in both the *vikas mandals* and the *mahila samitis* to increase the contacts among people of different castes, regions, and social classes in the areas. In a sample survey of the women of six *mahila samitis*, they were found to favor visiting the homes of people of other castes and communities—81 per cent of the women residents and 92 per cent of their elected representatives. Almost the same proportions, 78 per cent and 76 per cent, were in favor of allowing their children to play with children of other castes and areas. About 68 per cent of the women residents and 93 per cent of the representatives believed that there had been noticeable increases in communication among women; four residents and four representatives had not noticed change; and twenty-one residents and three representatives did not express an opinion either way. Two-thirds (61 per cent) of the residents, and two-thirds (66.7 per cent) of the representatives thought that quarreling among the women had decreased; 23.4 per cent and 27.8 per cent indicated no change; and 15.6 per cent and 5.5 per cent gave no opinion. The older the project the more likely the women were to answer that quarreling had declined; in fact, the percentage was almost twice as great in the older projects for both residents and representatives. This view was substantiated by the opinions of many women organizers, who found that fighting diminished as activities among women were organized into more constructive self-help activities. Differences of opinion among women could be vehemently expressed in an organized way in *mahila samiti* meetings rather than in fights before a street forum. The residents were evenly divided (40 per cent for each) between those who thought that there had been a change for the better in utilization of children's spare time and those who did not, with the rest having no opinion. On the other hand, thirty-three representatives (49 per cent of the total) believed that there had been a change for the better. On this point, there was no real relationship with the ages of the *vikas mandals*.

Despite being tradition-bound, illiterate, and constantly burdened with young children, slum women were more likely to work for social change than were the men, as such change seemed to reflect deep desires to demonstrate their abilities. Slum women had participated so little in an all-male society that they were more likely to be enthusiastic rather than skeptical about working for the solution of centuries-old slum problems. They had had few frustrating experiences in community service, political or otherwise, as the men might have had. Intellectually they had less resistance and could be more easily convinced. This desire for fuller participation and recognition was not, however, a desire to compete as equals with men, for their subordination to men continued as a matter of course.

If it is assumed that changes in practices are facilitated by changes in social organization, the new opportunities provided by the *mahila samitis* gave women a chance to gain status. Participation as members and even as officers of their own groups within the *vikas mandals* offered women this chance of recognition. The impact of this new role can be illustrated by the precedent-shattering attendance of two women representatives, veiled and in burkas (cloth outergarment covering face and body) at the regular meetings of *vikas mandal* executive committees consisting entirely of Muslims.

These changes were not easily accomplished because of the women's traditional image of themselves. The worker remarked that: "In the meeting ladies are very much reluctant to indulge in election business. It is due to their ignorance and feeling of inferiority and resistance to change. They feel afraid of taking any responsibility." The community organizers had to work hard to help bring about this change in self-image. In some cases they tried to present the possibilities of a new image to the women.

> The women told the community organizers that they would not be able to speak before the menfolk, as they had never done it before and it was against their custom. Some said that they did not mind attending meetings, that is, sitting with the men in the meetings, but that they would not be able to understand the proceedings or the discussions held in the meetings, so that there would not be much use in attending. The organizer told them that, in the beginning, it was creditable merely to sit with the men, as others would follow them and the men would become accustomed to women attending meetings. Once they started to attend the meetings, they could learn by observing, and eventually they would learn everything. If they were simply to sit at home, nothing would change.

Women representatives of the *mahila samitis* of the various *vikas mandals* were, on occasion, brought together for special meetings, either at points in the areas or at the offices of the Department, where, as representatives of their women's groups and of the men of the *vikas mandals* as well, they could compare their performances. In most instances, these occasions were the first "status" events in which women had ever participated and often the first visits so far from home without their husbands or other male relatives. The husbands in one all-Muslim *vikas mandal*, in fact, forbade their wives to attend a meeting. The women were allowed to go only after the organizers took the matter up with the executive committee of the *vikas mandal*, pointing out that theirs would be the only women's group unrepresented. The executive committee persuaded the husbands to agree that the two women could go in their burkas, provided that a taxi took them and brought them directly home. For the first time, Muslim women from this area went to a function without their men; the effect of this event on other Muslim women in the area can well be imagined.

A two-day training camp was held in 1961, attended primarily by the male officers of the various *vikas mandals*. Women representatives also attended these meetings but returned to their homes each night.[20] One session was devoted to the role of women in urban community development. This meeting was later followed by three special training sessions held by all *vikas parishads* for three women representatives of the *mahila samiti* from each *vikas mandal*. The programs lasted seven days and were attended by 110 women, eighty-three of whom received certificates and had their names listed in a publication on the course.[21] The participants later indicated that the chief advantages of the meetings were the opportunities to exchange views with women representing various other parts of the city.

Actually, all group activities, whether literacy classes, child care, family planning, nutrition, or discussion of community hygiene, contributed to a new self-image for the Indian slum woman who was actively participating in changing the community. In some instances, the women accomplished more than did the men. Sometimes individuals could gain even more status by winning prizes that were awarded annually in some areas for the best-kept houses. On occasion, they even represented the areas at important civic functions.

> There was a civic reception in honor of the Prime Minister of Denmark at the Red Fort in Delhi. Six ladies of the *mahila samitis* attended together and were glad because it was the first time they had received an invitation to such a function. They were very proud to have been given this invitation.

The horizons of the slum women were probably changed most through group participation in bus trips arranged by the *vikas mandals*, some of which were exclusively for women. Many women had not seen common historical sights around the city. In one *vikas parishad*, the women arranged a three-day, 340-mile round trip to the Taj Mahal, stopping at many places along the way. Although the trip was arduous, the worker wrote that the women continued to be "gay and interested even at the end of the trip." Other historical and important religious places were visited. In addition to the educational aspect of such trips, progress was also made in changing the women's attitudes about such things as other castes and religions. A visit to Parliament and a radio station, which was popular with nearly all *mahila samitis*, did much to broaden their approach to, and to bring about social change in, the everyday aspects of their lives.

Sometimes the introduction of new programs in connection with the project had unforeseen consequences. The Department was instrumental in securing one of the twenty television sets used in connection with the first regularly scheduled educational-television broadcasts in Delhi. It was given to a *vikas mandal* in a Muslim area that observed strict purdah. A special section was reserved for the women to observe the programs, which were seen by as many as a thousand closely huddled people. During the first televised program, it was discovered that the burkas covered the women's eyes so that they could not see the screen adequately. This problem was discussed at the next meeting of the executive committee, and it was decided that the women could throw back their head coverings for the first time in a public gathering.

Organization was a new idea to slum women, and the formation of *mahila samitis* and the program of activities brought them closer together. Many of the men eventually became reconciled to the participation of women inside or outside the project areas, and the women developed feelings of self-reliance. Women became more conscious of their children's health, and, as they themselves requested the health programs, they more readily accepted them. Attitudes of older women changed to some extent, particularly in allowing their daughters and daughters-in-law to leave their houses to participate in various self-help programs run by the *mahila samitis*. Perhaps the changed status of women and their new self-conception reached their culmination in one *vikas mandal*, when the women decided to run against the men in the general election for officers of the total group. At the last moment, it was decided by the organizers that all these efforts might tend to alienate the men and thus split the group into factions of men and women.

It is difficult to measure the degree of change that took place in the women's self-image; on the whole the judgment is impressionistic. One woman organizer, who had been with the project almost from the beginning, commented: "I remember the extreme apathy, the complete refusal to accept a lady community organizer in many projects; the skepticism with which the women of most project areas looked on us and called us 'mad.' Now, when I compare their attitudes with the efforts of many women in these and other areas I feel really amazed and proud even if we have not reached every woman in the slums."

RELATIONS WITH OTHER MUNICIPAL DEPARTMENTS

Coordinating urban community-development work with that of other departments of the Municipal Corporation presented persistent problems. Two issues were involved. First, some people believed, as had many in the early days of rural community-development work in India, that this new department was "duplicating" the services of other established government departments, health, education, sanitation, slums, social education, and so forth. This attitude developed from a misconception that community development is a concrete program rather than the introduction of a new philosophy of citizen participation into administrative programs and a self-generating process toward betterment on a self-help and mutual-aid basis. Although senior officers of the city government understood the nature of the project, many others in the line organizations were not properly "oriented" to the philosophy of community development and self-help.

Second, successful urban community-development efforts require the wholehearted cooperation of other municipal departments, as many area problems fall within their jurisdictions. Although it may be easy to mobilize community concern around existing problems, many of these problems have arisen because of inadequate municipal services. When these difficulties cannot be solved even with the help of the Department, the slum people become demoralized and begin to lose faith in the program and the possibilities of self-help. As an example, one *vikas mandal* attempted to improve the sanitation of its area by securing old tar barrels, painting and labeling them with zone numbers, and placing them as dust bins in each area. The municipal sweepers refused to empty them, as they said they were too heavy. The matter was discussed with the Sanitation Department, and, after some persuasion, it was temporarily solved by having the sweepers empty them. After other similar experiences, however, the *vikas mandal* lost interest in sanitation improvements. Still other cases involved delays in processing applications for additional water taps or similar facilities for which residents were willing to pay cooperatively. It might have been possible for other departments like public health and recreation to lend personnel that could have, with proper training, supplemented the meager manpower of the project. Although many departments came to recognize the benefits of people's participation, the process was gradual, and more vigorous administrative measures might have been helpful. The experience of the Delhi project has shown that a continuing task of any separate municipal agency in this field is to establish effective communication channels to other municipal departments.

SELF-HELP AND THE POLITICIAN

Experience has also shown that, in both developed and less developed countries, politicians are often important barriers to self-help by local citizens. Some instances of this occurred in the Delhi project. The slum dweller in an Indian city has difficulty in dealing with the government bureaucracy that might be able to supply him with facilities, handle his disputes with the landlord, or help him in other ways to deal with the frustrations of his everyday life. The city dweller must have help in coping with this system, which is why the politicians and, to some extent, the social-welfare agencies have entered the picture as intermediaries.[22] In a sense, they have become "patrons" of the slum dwellers. The local politician is then an "ambassador" who can manipulate the outside world and offer advice on how to deal with it.[23] As in Boston's West End, the politician is used by the people when they feel helpless because "government is, or is thought to be, personalized, capricious, and depriving."[24] Doing favors becomes the politician's most important function and the source of his most important contacts with his constituents.

The importance of differences between the objectives of citizen-participation programs and of the politicians was recognized from the beginning. Successful urban community-development work, however, is bound to become involved in the political process: The people and the political process must be linked.[25] Effective citizen participation requires the support of councilmen, aldermen, and important local political figures for improvements that the people may generate in slum areas. As one writer put it, "The basic weakness of slum programs since the earliest days is that slum people have not been storming city hall to get out of the slums."[26]

There was little evidence that councilmen used the *vikas mandals* for political purposes. Political considerations seemed neither seriously to help nor to hinder most organizational work of the *vikas mandals*. The political feelings of most urban slum people, when viewed at the area level, appeared to be "skin deep." Most of them had been discouraged for years by politicians with promises of future prosperity and complete solutions to their ever-growing problems, solutions that never seemed to materialize.* On the other hand, one weakness of citizen groups like the *vikas mandals* was their lack of sufficient power to influence "all-powerful government." Being small and nonpolitical in nature, they could not easily secure special benefits. Although the Department provided them with a channel to government, it was not a strong one.

Efforts were made to involve each councilman in a development project from its very beginning. Attempts were made to keep him informed of the work, he was asked to attend inaugural ceremonies for the *vikas mandals* and *vikas parishads*, and he was invited to other important gatherings. He was also made an ex-officio member of his *vikas parishad* or neighborhood council. In addition, the people of an area often publicly reported on their accomplishments to certain official committees of city councilmen. In spite of all these measures, a most persistent difficulty in the Delhi project was the inability to secure adequate support from city councilmen and other politicians. This failure can be charged partly to difficulties in communicating the idea of self-help and to a conflict in the roles of the politician and the *vikas mandal*. Some councilmen worked closely with the projects; nevertheless, opposition and misunderstanding on the part of the council and its committees were general for a long time.† Much more could have been done, however, at the outset of the project to explain the nature of community development work to all of the councilmen.

Many councilmen undoubtedly feared that urban community-development work would undermine their control over their constituencies. An organizer said: "One of the most difficult problems is that of giving credit for the work of the project. The councilmen are sometimes fearful of the work of the people. Sometimes the councilmen will not cooperate with the development councils because of the presence of other political parties on the executive committees." Consequently, one of the most delicate problems was that of giving credit to

---

* In the sample survey of 406 residents, one-third (33.3 per cent), however, thought that political groups in the area had adverse effects on the *vikas mandals*, the remainder believing that they had either neutral (36.7 per cent) or positive effects (23.3 per cent), with the answers of 6.7 per cent being not applicable because there were no political groups in their areas. See *Second Evaluation Study of the Vikas Mandals* (Delhi: Municipal Corporation of Delhi, May, 1965).

† One high-ranking member of the Planning Commission of India, in fact, believed that the failure to solve this problem adequately was one of the major difficulties encountered by the Delhi project.

the councilman for self-help work carried out in his area. If a *vikas mandal* executive committee happened to be of the councilman's party, it was possible to give him some credit, but often the committee was made up of members of various political parties. Then it was difficult to give the councilman credit for any accomplishments or even for him to work with the group. One councilman, in fact, stated that, although he would not interfere with the community-development work, he would not sit, if invited, on the same platform with the *vikas mandal* representatives of other parties. Some councilmen were concerned that new leadership would develop through the *vikas mandals*, which might threaten their political control of the areas.

The misunderstanding and opposition of the councilmen were reflected in the difficulties encountered in securing permanent status for the Department and in receiving necessary appropriations. Originally, the understanding with the Ford Foundation had been that the Municipal Corporation would assume more and more financial responsibility and that the Department would become a permanent agency of the municipality after a three-year period, if it were successful. Evaluation data and reports showing good progress were submitted periodically. In spite of these reports and because of political difficulties and indecision, the project and the Department continued for several years on a temporary basis. Beside political differences, other factors appear to have accounted for this indecision. They could not distinguish between the work of the Department and that of other departments, particularly the municipal social-education centers that offered individual training in literacy, citizenship, and crafts. Finally, they were suspicious of the organizational work being done by trained professional community organizers, who were receiving salaries considered high by their standards.

This political indecision seriously affected the project. Others objected to the experimental project on the grounds that it was supported by a "foreign foundation." The morale of the workers was lowered because job security is an important consideration in a country with great unemployment or under-employment among college-trained people. Some doubts were also raised in their minds about how their work was being received. This further lowered morale, and doubt came to be reflected in the minds of the slum citizens, many of whom learned of the continued precarious position of the Department. Other departments of the Municipal Corporation and even officials in higher places began to question the value of this work if it were not to be a permanent part of the city government. Evidence from the evaluation reports became secondary to rumor. One can only speculate as to whether or not there might have been even greater achievements if this pioneer Indian project had received the whole-hearted support of the politicians and the government.

Reports on urban-development projects in other parts of the world have suggested that effective relations between politicians and citizen self-help projects are generally difficult. Several self-help efforts in the United States have encountered similar difficulties: for example, Congressman Adam Clayton Powell's involvement in 1964 in Harlem Youth Opportunities Unlimited, later HARYOU-Act.* It is quite possible that greater acceptance could be gained among politicians for citizen self-help work if communication efforts could be improved.

1. Before work began, the program could be carefully explained to councilmen and the chairmen of all major committees. The councilmen could be briefed and given opportunities for questions in advance, so that they would not be so prone to develop negative positions based on misinformation.

2. In the selection of the first project areas, wards might be chosen in which councilmen were farsighted and understanding and would not feel themselves threatened by the program.

3. The councilmen should be kept constantly informed about organizational activities and problems presented by the projects; such information could be transmitted at the highest administrative levels in the project. If any suspicions about the project were detected in these frequent conversations, they could be allayed immediately.

4. The councilmen should be invited to all important gatherings. Such occasions make them feel important and also give the people the impression that they are interested in the work.

5. In preparing staff memoranda and announcements, reference to the councilmen should be included whenever possible. In explaining the nature of the work to a councilman, it should be pointed out that he cannot take care of everything and that self-help projects relieve him of some burdens. If the people's morale is improved, it should be an advantage to the councilman, rather than a disadvantage, providing that he is interested in their welfare aside from politics.

6. It is quite likely that nationwide programs in urban community development might change councilmen's attitudes.

Urban community projects, dealing of necessity as they do with heated political issues and organizing the interests of the average slum citizen, are indeed controversial. In fact, the controversies they arouse among politicians, welfare organizations, and government, are some indication of their success. The price of social change, particularly in an urban setting, is political controversy.

---

* See Kenneth B. Clark, *Dark Ghetto: Dilemmas of Social Power* (New York: Harper & Row, Publishers, 1965), pp. 155–68. A *New York Times* article on "The Troubles of Haryou" (October 13, 1965, p. 36–C) said that, "Some critics and neutral observers say they feel the boards [neighborhood] may not develop properly because the boards, by definition, will provide political power bases for the community that might offend, or even upset, politicians." Also see James Q. Wilson, *Negro Politics: The Search for Leadership* (New York: The Free Press, 1960); and William C. Loring, Jr., Frank L. Sweetser, and Charles F. Ernst, *Community Organization for Citizen Participation in Urban Renewal* (Boston: Massachusetts Department of Commerce, 1957).

§ *Conclusions*

In its over-all objectives of developing a program, organizing communities, enlisting self-help, identifying and training local leadership, and working out techniques of change, the Delhi project appears to have been reasonably successful. Administrative problems did arise, some *vikas mandals* were ineffective, and some workers did not perform up to expectations. Much more could have been achieved had it not been for several significant factors. Of major significance was the continued indecision about the future of the Department in the Municipal Corporation, which continued for more than five years until, in 1965, the work of the Department was finally made a permanent agency, the new Department of Community Services. Greater cooperation from other departments of the municipal government would also have increased favorable results as would stronger support from the central government in the early years of the project. A major problem in such urban community development is to devise ways of keeping up the original momentum of citizen self-help organizations.

Vikas mandals and *vikas parishads* were not magic lamps that could work miracles; they were human instruments much subjected to stresses and strains. The growth of community feeling is a slow process, and it can be fostered only as small groups like *vikas mandals* work jointly and continue to assume responsibility and initiative for improvements. At least several years, perhaps five or ten, are required to put a *vikas mandal* or a *vikas parishad* on firm footings, during which time some staff guidance and financial aids must be continued. The pace of change is slow in the face of centuries-old practices. As the Commissioner of Delhi, commenting in 1965 on the results of the second evaluation study, pointed out:

> To some, the findings of the study may appear somewhat depressing, since they indicate a lack of whole hearted cooperation and enthusiasm on the part of all participants. To my mind, however, there is nothing to be disappointed about, since giving a new form to an urban community, which has been drawn from backgrounds varying from one another and trying to achieve a homogeneity is not an easy matter or a matter of a few years. To expect a hundred per cent success would be expecting a miracle. Human nature and human society do not undergo a change very rapidly, particularly in the direction in which one wishes and tries to mould them.[27]

Over all, the results were encouraging when one recognizes that India is a difficult setting in which to work and not an easy place in which to bring about change of any kind. The slum, furthermore, presents serious problems for such an experiment anywhere, without added difficulties and hindrances like those faced in the Delhi project. With a more receptive bureaucratic setting and a different social and cultural situation, one might well expect even more encouraging results. If this much change was produced in the Indian slum, the possibilities for urban community development elsewhere, under more favorable conditions, seem encouraging. Perhaps the most practical evidence of the success of the Delhi and the later Ahmedabad projects was the adoption in India in 1965 of a national program of urban community development, patterned after the two projects. Such a decision to enlarge the scope of the work was reached after a careful study of the organization and achievements of these two pilot projects.[28]

PART FOUR

SOCIAL CHANGE AND THE SLUM

Chapter 12

THE PROCESS OF SOCIAL CHANGE IN SLUM AREAS

An understanding of the processes through which communities develop and take action is important in community development. Analysis of the steps, or patterns of process, involved in community change has been attempted by several writers, most of whom, however, have concentrated on change in smaller communities, rather than in large urban areas. As a result, several action models have been developed. For example, one model considers as processes in social change: (1) initiation of the idea, involvement of others, and legitimation of the idea; (2) preliminary study; (3) planning and establishment of goals; (4) establishment of a structure to coordinate the development process; (5) training and election of leaders; (6) the operational period, in which action is undertaken; and (7) continuation, with evaluation and follow-up. Within each phase, educational, legitimation, and evaluative processes are undertaken.[1] This model allows for some repetition of specific action processes like legitimation and education in the action phase.

An action model has been developed by Carl Taylor. It involves (1) systematic discussion of commonly recognized needs by members of the community; (2) systematic planning by residents for the first self-help undertaking selected by the community through sustained and systematic discussion; (3) almost complete mobilization and harnessing of the physical, economic, and social potentialities of community groups; and (4) the development of group aspirations.[2] Sower and his associates have suggested convergence of interest, establishment of an initiating set of relationships between several actors, legitimation and sponsorship, and establishment of an execution set of arrangements.[3] Lippitt and his associates have outlined six phases of planned change: (1) The client system discovers the need for help, sometimes with stimulation by the change agent; (2) the helping relationship is established and defined; (3) the change problem is identified and clarified; (4) alternative possibilities for change are examined and change goals or intentions established; (5) change is generalized and stabilized; and (6) the helping relationship ends, or a different type of continuing relationship is defined.[4]

Another analysis has divided the community-development process into three main stages: the introduction of a new concept, the possession of a belief, and the centering down of the process.[5] The total process involves: (1) definition of the problem (challenge and response); (2) tension and responsibility (new understanding); (3) imaginative openings (change considered); (4) development of confidence (change considered possible); (5) release and renewal (change made acceptable); (6) finding and facing the facts (technical knowledge acquired); (7) total involvement in active demonstration; (8) realization of practical accomplishments; (9) community-planning procedure initiated; (10) cyclical involvement of new people in community development; (11) establishment of associations and institutions designed to carry the process into future generations.

Beal and Capener have outlined fifteen more detailed steps: determining existing social systems, inception, prior social situation, delineation of relevant social systems, initiation, legitimation with key people and groups in the relevant power structure, diffusion sets or relationships, definition of the need in terms of more general relevant social systems, decision by relevant social systems to act, formalization and acceptance of goals by relevant social systems, decision on means to be used to carry out action, the plan of work for action, mobilizing and organizing resources for action, carrying out the action program, and total program evaluation.[6] Biddle has outlined the steps in the community-development process as exploratory, organizational, discussional, action, new projects, and continuation.[7] After analyzing a number of action models, Warren developed a five-part pattern of dynamic aspects of development and change in community-action systems: (1) initial systemic environment, (2) inception of the action system, (3) expansion of the action system, (4) operation of the expanded action system, and (5) transformation of the action system.[8]

One difficulty presented by such action models is the relative importance attached to task or activity accomplishments, that is, community action and strengthening community relations. Warren believes that the latter is the essence of community development, which he defines as the "deliberate and sustained attempt to strengthen the horizontal pattern of a community."[9] To him, community development is a process, and he does not regard it as a method for reaching certain objectives or performing certain activities. The problem is not how a particular task is accomplished but, rather, the dynamics of the social interrelationships involved. The latter factor Tumin has termed "the need for the development of concern for problem solving and a spirit of self-reliance in communities which have typically depended on others for the solution of their problems."[10] If one recognizes that the emphasis should be on strengthening the community, the successful accomplishment of tasks or activities, however, can help to develop community feeling.

§ *An Analysis of Social Process in Slum Areas*

In the Delhi project, the goal of the citizen groups was expressed in the preamble to their constitutions: "We, the residents of this *vikas mandal*, have solemnly resolved at our general meeting to work for improvement of our locality on the basis of self-help." Such a goal was not easily perceived by slum dwellers. Community change, or development, occurred through prolonged series of steps or processes, which gradually brought about conditions that differed significantly from those that had existed at the beginning. The following case history of a *vikas mandal* describes but does not explain this change:

In the beginning the area presented a look of filth and squalor, with narrow unpaved lanes and heaps of refuse lying about the choked drains. The sanitary conditions were poor. The residents lived in single-room tenements, most of which were in dilapidated condition. They worked in household shops manufacturing items like steel trunks. There was great apathy and suspicion.

The preliminary survey work was beset with difficulties because of this hostile attitude. The residents thought that their families were being counted in connection with food rationing or family-planning measures, and some thought the interviews were related to an increase in taxation or other political motives like checking the voter lists. Although many were suspicious, some were curious and listened to the worker about the purpose of the visits. They were assured again and again about the object of these visits. With these hostile groups, the workers established rapport, through perseverance and tact, winning their confidence. The local councilman, who later became an active supporter, was asked for his help.

After the door-to-door survey of all the residents by the organizers, the latter designated indigenous rather than traditional leaders who showed interest in making improvements in their area and in their homes. The next step was to organize meetings at the *vikas sabha* level, separate groups for men and women, to elect representatives to the executive committee of the *vikas mandal*. Then a general meeting of all residents, men and women, was called for the adoption of a constitution and the election of officers. The executive committee prepared various programs covering such aspects as health, sanitation, education, and recreation and ways to carry out such programs.

During the first six months of the project, the workers noticed changes in the behavior and thought patterns of the people. The people showed encouragement and interest in improvement of their lives through their own efforts. Today the area presents a neat appearance, with swept lanes, dust bins at each house, and all houses whitewashed. Various activities are being carried out for men, women, and children. During the first two years approximately seventy self-help projects were completed in physical improvements, health and sanitation, crafts, and education. The people had their lanes paved and electric lighting installed, put cement flooring around five new water taps to help the area remain drier and cleaner, and improved the area school. Signs hung across lanes and on walls saying that people should keep the area clean and "Dirt Breeds Disease." One of the major achievements was to prepare a volleyball ground through voluntary labor in an area which had long been used for storage of materials for people working in small craft shops in the area. This required a great deal of discussion and cooperation. They were also planning a dispensary and a cooperative society. They were willing to contribute their share to both. They were even dreaming that they could build houses on a cooperative basis in the area where they have lived for generations, provided they could secure encouragement and help from the government.

The people later invited the officers of the other *vikas mandals* to their area, and they made elaborate arrangements for the reception of their guests. Everyone participated actively, and they worked hard for two weeks prior to the event. All the houses were whitewashed, the lanes cleaned and sprinkled with water. A sum of R.250 was collected at the rate of 4 annas per head, on a voluntary basis, to meet expenses, and the area was then decorated with buntings and welcome arches. The area had a festive look, and the enthusiasm and cooperation witnessed on this occasion were said to be a totally new experience in the history of the area. According to a subsequent poetic composition that the residents wrote: "The drains are no longer choked, the lanes are not dirty, the people no longer remain isolated and do not have any fear complex. The community is full of group activities."

Not all projects, of course, went through such dramatic changes, but change did occur in all of them. Although certain organizational procedures were developed in the Delhi project, they did not provide a full understanding of the actual change processes, many of them informal. Consequently, a process analysis was made of fourteen *vikas mandals*, using as data the daily reports of the male and female organizers for each *vikas mandal* for the first year. Complete daily reports for similar periods were not available for the other *vikas mandals*. This process analysis constituted one of the first efforts at a quantitative approach to measuring community change in a project; nearly all previous studies had been based on single communities or projects and comparisons are therefore difficult.

The organizers were participant observers, and as such each kept daily reports of progress and observations in his area. The organizers recorded such material as their initial reactions to the communities and of the communities to them; problems connected with the identification of indigenous leaders; significant contacts and conversations with people both within and outside the area; trends in area opinions; problems and successes; and any other information they thought pertinent. The daily notes were to be completely frank, and the workers were urged to be objective because of the experimental nature of the project. The processed data came from the reports of twenty-eight community organizers in fourteen areas for a period of one year. All the projects had been organized through the intensive method. The reports varied in length from fewer than 100 single-spaced typed pages to more than 300, the average being about 150. A content analysis was made of each report according to an analytical model. Each important event or action that was part of the total development process within an organizer's area was recorded on special forms according to time intervals: weekly intervals during the first month, two-week periods for the second month, and monthly periods thereafter. The analyses of the *vikas mandals* were then compared, and when possible the project areas were ranked with Spearman rank correlation values computed by comparing the relative frequencies of important relationships for the various projects.

The flow of self-help activities was used as an index for ranking the projects according to the degree of successful achievement. Each time the organizer recorded that the people were in the process of acting directly on some problem or meeting their own desires through common effort an activity was coded with one check. The total volume of activities was considered the most effective measure, as there were community differences because some engaged in work with children or youth recreation more than did others, whereas others did more to encourage inoculations for diseases. The various projects were ranked separately according to the number of men's and women's activities. A significant correlation was found between the two.

After the initial study of several sample reports, an analytical model was prepared to measure the processes from the initiation of the project. It involved the following stages:

1. early reactions to the program;
2. stimulating the idea of self-help;
3. search for indigenous leadership;
4. developing new leadership;
5. establishing legitimation;
6. the organization and action phase;
7. development of a new self-image.

Three stages of action generally occurred in the projects: initiation of action, organization for action, and activity development. The first stage generally took one month, the second through the fourth month. By the end of the fourth month, eleven of the fourteen projects had completed the organization of their *vikas mandals*. The activity-development stage was generally concentrated in the last eight months, but all areas undertook some self-help activities prior to the formal inauguration of the *vikas mandals*. Some action processes were expected to be more critical than others. For example, if legitimation had not been achieved, fewer activities would be completed.

§ Initial Reactions to a Program of Change

The initial reaction of people to a program of change was one of apathy, overdependence upon outsiders, hostility, or suspicion. The people generally expressed fears or suspicions of the "real" purposes of the program. Doubts were commonly expressed about the organizers' true relationship with the city government: They really belonged to a political party and were soliciting votes, or they had come to pave the way for the demolition of the houses of the poor. It was hypothesized that these doubts and fears would have to be resolved before any effective action program could be undertaken. In eleven of the fourteen programs, these suspicions and doubts could not be resolved in less than a three-month period, and in three projects four or five months were needed. Many activities, however, were accomplished prior to the dispersal of these suspicions in contradiction of the hypothesis.

APATHY

Extensive apathy and confusion about the objectives of the project character-ized the initial experiences with slum dwellers. Many had been so disillusioned by unfulfilled promises of politicians, welfare groups, and government officials that they could not readily accept the organizers' reasons for coming into the area. Many political candidates had talked glibly about helping the people but had failed to fulfill their promises after election, and many social-welfare agencies had also failed to keep some of their promises. Finally, the people's feelings toward the municipal authorities' inability to meet the problems of the community had built up a lack of faith and even an atmosphere of hostility.

Some residents believed that the slum conditions under which they lived were acceptable or that improvements were no concern of theirs. Others believed that past experience or repeated failure to bring about improvement did not warrant any high hopes. Slum dwellers often expressed feelings of futility about helping themselves, an attitude easily understood if one realizes how long conditions had existed unchanged. People living under slum condi-tions for a long time could not readily recognize that something could be done by themselves or by working together with others. This sense of futility was particularly common among the older men and women. In one case the worker recorded, "As usual there were those who expressed the feeling by saying that nothing can be done in their areas and according to them the residents were so lethargic that they would like to live in the same dirty conditions."

In many cases, the residents critically evaluated their areas. They thought that the people of their area quarreled so frequently that they could not be expected to cooperate. This attitude correlated with the eventual total activity level (action accomplishment) with $r_s = .44$, a substantial correlation. The fewer the number of reports of this kind, the higher the action level.

OVERDEPENDENCE ON OUTSIDERS

People could not readily see that the idea of the project was to stimulate self-help and belief in their own capabilities. Reactions of dependence on outside systems occurred in nine of the fourteen *vikas mandals*. From their past experiences, the people believed that the organizers were closely connected with the municipal government and its politicians. Seeing two municipal employees present each day confirmed a belief that facilities were to be provided without much effort on the people's part. This belief was, in fact, confirmed when the organizers encouraged the people to apply for water-tap connections through the city, to obtain pest-control crews, or to have inoculation programs carried out. The workers did act as a link with city officials, but they attempted to discourage the initial reaction of dependence, as it was not in keeping with the image of a "self-help" program.

HOSTILITY

On some occasions in the early days of the projects, the attitude toward the workers went beyond suspicion to overt hostility toward the projects and to the workers. Hostility was directed against the "agent of authority," from whom the people generally expected much and always received much less. Some even said that, if the amount spent on the salaries of workers were made available to the *vikas mandals*, self-help could proceed without difficulty. Residents avoided the workers, refused to cooperate, and often insulted them as in these examples from two *vikas mandals*.

> The organizer found these ladies most uncooperative. They suspect her, which makes it difficult to obtain any information from them, and she has to give them assurances again and again. They are not pleasant to talk to, their remarks are ironical, and the worker feels that, being less privileged, these people are more insecure, which makes them suspicious.

> Then the community organizer, unfortunately, confronted an inhospitable and inhuman group of people. It was the second time that she had visited, on their assurances that they would let her know their views regarding the *vikas mandal*. But even in their second meeting they were uncooperative, amusingly asked irrelevant questions, and tried to provoke the organizer's anger.

SUSPICION

Many of the area residents looked upon the organizers' daily visits and their questioning not only as strange but also as threatening, and many rumors spread. Some believed that the visits were actually of a political nature; others were certain that the odd questions asked about such things as the sizes of families, the occupations of the residents, and the lengths of residence in the area were for the purpose of raising rents, moving the people to new housing colonies, increasing taxes, rationing food, or restricting the numbers of their children. Many old women complained even about the counting of the families.

They expressed doubt about the organizers' counting the number of families "ovenwise" (a family unit was defined as using a single *chulla*, or stove), as food rationing might soon be introduced or some trouble might come in connection with income taxes.

§ *Stimulating the Idea of Self-Help*

The idea of self-help was stimulated by changing the individual slum dweller's perception of the world around him through education in self-help and by demonstrating the possibilities of self-help in dramatic cases.

NEW PERCEPTION OF CAPABILITIES

It was essential to change the slum dweller's passive acceptance of the world around him to perception of the situation as amenable to change through his own efforts. In the initial interviews, the organizers asked questions intended to make people think about what *they* could do about certain problems in the areas, reversing the age-old process of dependence on government and others to solve their problems. The organizers began by asking, "What are some problems in the local area that you think the people here might be able to do something about?" This question usually seemed odd to slum dwellers who had been promised many things by politicians and social workers, and it elicited several types of response—tirades against the government or landlords for not solving their problems; mention of problems that could not be solved by the people themselves, such as the elimination of poverty, providing jobs, or large-scale construction of new houses; or simply apathetic looks. The organizers would then press the point, saying that such answers were not what was intended by the question, then repeating the query about what problems the respondents might think of that they could help solve. To this repetition, there was often continued silence, despite the countless observable problems of filth, insufficient facilities, and numerous children with nothing to do. At this point, the organizer might mention something specific in an attempt to convey the idea of a new and different approach.

The organizer followed up mention of problems offering self-help possibilities by inquiring in more detail about them, how long they had existed, whether or not anything had ever been done about them, and if the people sincerely wanted them changed. If a problem had existed for some time, the slum dweller often began to recognize that it was highly unlikely that the government, the politicians, or the social workers or landlords could be counted upon to do anything about it in the near future.

The slum dweller was then directly asked whether or not he himself would like to do something about the problems of his area, in an effort to stir him from his apathy. Regardless of the answer—and it was usually a polite "yes"—the question was intended to put the person, perhaps for the first time, in a position of visualizing his own role, and that of others like him, in the solution of the problems surrounding him. Finally, he was asked, "Would you be interested in attending a group meeting of persons in the area to discuss these various neighborhood problems?" He was also asked whether or not he had ever taken part in community activities. Usually the community organizers left behind them a trail of people thinking over the questions that had been asked and discussing the entire matter with family members and neighbors. During the interviews, the worker noted the degrees of response to these questions.

EDUCATION IN SELF-HELP

The workers were often asked to explain the purpose of the new program. Residents expressed disbelief in the possibility of such a program or in their own capabilities of carrying it out. Some workers attempted to overcome suspicions and lack of assurance by holding frequent discussions with the people. The number of such discussions was found to be correlated, at a low level, with decline in suspicion, but the relationship was not statistically significant.

While interviewing, the worker found the small blind alley to be quite dirty. Though the houses were kept clean, all kinds of rubbish were lying in the street, which was paved. The worker explained to them that there was no need to depend upon the municipal sweeper, as it is not a difficult task to clean it daily, in turn. The worker was surprised that each lady said that she had no objection if others were ready to do it because the lane was common, and if one cleaned and others did not it could not remain clean long. She suggested that, if each one had a certain day to clean, the lane could be kept in good condition. One of the children slipped and fell into filth, and the mother began to scold the child although it was not his fault. The worker remained silent and observed the mother. After a few minutes the worker said that it was not the fault of the child, as it was up to the adults to keep the lanes clean. Such incidents would not occur if the lanes were kept clean.

USE OF CRUCIAL SITUATIONS

Although it was sometimes difficult for the people to comprehend the possibilities of self-help, small incidents often provided opportunities to stimulate their thinking. In one case, the organizer found in unhinged latrine doors an opportunity to "sell" the possibility of self-help to a group of people.

On the worker's inquiry about the latrines, one of the people of the last lane led the organizer to the main *katra*. There all the doors of the six latrines (dry) for the men were unhinged from the wooden brackets. The chairman of the *mohalla* committee, who had come along with the organizer, began a harangue against the landlord and the municipal government. The worker patiently heard him, and when he had finished she asked the resident how long this condition had existed. When he said the doors had been that way for two or three months, the worker suggested that it would require only a few nails to repair the hinges. "You are right," was the reply. When the worker asked how much it would cost to buy the nails, the man replied that it would probably cost three or four annas (5 cents). The worker asked how many families used the latrines, and, when the resident said about 100 or more, she said, "Don't you think this much money can be contributed by the *katra* people to get each door repaired, or should we wait for the landlord or the city government to come and repair them?"

The chairman of the *mohalla* committee was listening to the discussion, and he at once became angry and pushed his hands into his pockets, saying: "I would pay three annas, four annas, or any amount from my pocket, but, sister, do you think we should start fixing the latrine doors? We would be working in filth and dirt." The worker then politely said that she was simply asking about the possibilities because it was inconvenient for the people and not the landlord and, in addition, the cost was meager. If they could find a professional blacksmith or the like, he could help to fix the doors. Furthermore, it was only an idea, and it could be dropped.

The other members of the group were already thinking about the matter, however, and remained silent. At least, the emphasis had been put on the over-all responsibility of the residents and not on the city government.

An impromptu discussion of space satellites was taken advantage of by one organizer to stimulate the group to thinking about more reading and the construction of a small room for a library and for discussion purposes.

A group of people was interested in listening to the community organizer tell about the Explorers and Sputniks traveling into outer space. The discussion was started when one of the people asked a question of the worker. They felt that they and others would like to read or hear about simple books on such topics if they could be made available to them. The worker suggested that the people join together to build a small room for such a cooperative library and discussion room.

§ *The Search for Indigenous Leadership*

The tasks of making the people conscious of the possibilities of self-help and assisting them in organizing and carrying out a wide range of developmental programs were formidable. No community organizer could do this work by himself. His chances of success, however, were greater if he worked through, and with, indigenous leaders. Such leaders were not the same as the formal or traditional leaders, who usually held their positions through appointment, inheritance, or social status or caste. Occasionally the two might coincide, and a formal leader might be extremely effective in mobilizing the efforts of the people. Leadership that must rely for its effectiveness on caste or religious authority, political party, or governmental position is generally not likely to be effective in social change. In fact, such formal leadership may stifle the average person's efforts to participate in changes in the local community. Indigenous leaders had the additional advantage of being identified with area groups, usually had similar backgrounds, and came from the same social classes. In a sense, they effectively "spoke the same language." To effect any marked change in the attitudes of members of an ex-criminal tribe in an urban community, for example, it was necessary to identify and use a natural leader among the group. It was also found that illiterate people often could more readily motivate other illiterate people than could literate leaders.

During the initial interviews, it was the community organizers' responsibility to identify possible potential leaders who could become a driving force for stimulating the idea of self-help and through whom the organizers could work to achieve their project objectives. In general, the majority of the officers would later come from this originally noted group. People with certain attributes were sought: those with previous experience in any type of self-help project; those whom others identified as leaders in times of crisis; those who offered services or made suggestions; those who showed unusual pride in their own homes; and those who were regarded as community leaders.*

PREVIOUS EXPERIENCE IN SELF-HELP ACTIVITIES

The initial interviews with slum dwellers provided opportunities to identify potential leaders for effecting social change. Each person was asked if he had had any previous experience with a mutual-aid program, cooperative welfare group, or voluntary organization. Occasionally an individual was found who had tried to promote a self-help water tap or some similar activity among the residents, even though unsuccessfully.

THOSE WHOM OTHERS DESIGNATED AS LEADERS IN TIMES OF CRISIS

In the initial interviews, the workers also asked the question, "To whom in this area would you turn in times of a crisis?" Leaders could be identified by finding out to whom the people themselves turned for help in such events as

---

* One study has made a comparison of several approaches to the problem of locating leaders in a single community: decision-making, voluntary activity, reputation, position, and organizational participation. See Linton C. Freeman, Thomas J. Fararo, Warner Bloomberg, Jr., and Morris H. Sunshine, "Locating Leaders in Local Communities: A Comparison of Some Alternative Approaches," *American Sociological Review*, 28 (October, 1963), 791–8.

floods, fires, epidemics, and serious family difficulties. Patterns of relationship could be discovered by analyzing these responses. One worker wrote about such a person: "He is a modest, unassuming person, who does not claim to be the leader of the *katra*. This role of his was revealed to the worker by the *katra* residents when they were being interviewed. All considered him to be a respected man and one who helped them solve disputes by mediation and arbitration."

Of the 115 people elected to the executive committees of twenty-one *vikas mandals*, 89.5 per cent of the men were considered "influential" in their *vikas sabha* or zone areas, and 59.5 per cent were "influential" in their *vikas mandal* areas.[11] Some influential people who were identified in this or in other manners, however, were not later elected as leaders of their groups. In fact, 10.5 per cent of the men elected to the executive committees of twenty-one *vikas mandals* were not influential in their zones, and 40.5 per cent were not influential in their *vikas mandal* areas. One explanation for this fact might be that a new, more formal organizational pattern provided the means by which people who were feared and respected because of tradition or other reasons and to whom the residents did turn for help were bypassed for new, more representative leaders.

OFFERING SERVICES OR MAKING SUGGESTIONS

Some people showed unusual interest in doing something about conditions and appeared anxious to make improvements. Several others offered their services in any manner that might be of help in the project.

> Then the community organizer met a lady who told her that she had asked the ladies to unite but that nobody bothered about it. Even though she had small children, she showed great enthusiasm and offered her free services to accompany the organizer in her work and to render help whenever needed.
> The lady asked the community organizer to explain the scheme once again. Then she started to think seriously about what could be done in the area. She assured the worker that she would introduce her to ladies who would like to take the lead. Meanwhile, she would herself talk to some of them.

Some people made reasonably good suggestions for development work, which showed that they had been thinking about the problems of the area.

> The male community organizer discussed the entire idea of developing the lane with a potential leader again. The latter wanted to discuss the plan with the other residents of the lane and was anxious to have the lane paved in front of the houses to avoid hardship to the residents during the monsoon. He said to the worker, "I have talked it over with many people, and half the residents have approved the idea and are ready to contribute labor and money."

UNUSUAL PRIDE IN THEIR HOMES

In every slum area, a few homes exhibited a certain pride of the occupants. The houses, and particularly the areas surrounding them, were clean and neat, often whitewashed on the inside or outside. The areas in front of the houses were free of litter, and, in some cases, attractive religious designs had been painted on the sides of the houses or on the doors. Such occupants were presumed to have pride in their surroundings and to be somewhat disturbed by the generally depressing conditions in the areas.

> The worker saw a house of pride today. The occupant of the house is a fitter who lives on R.80 a month and is so proud of his neat and clean house that he took the worker inside and explained the water-storage system, which he had devised himself. It consisted of a tank with a cover and tap fittings all cemented. The occupant had devised a small drain with a small outlet to stop the rats from coming in, and only the used water ran into the outside drain. He had a dust bin also. He said that because of cleanliness alone he and his family had been spared from last year's epidemic in the area. He discussed many things and seemed quite enthusiastic about a name plate, a dust bin with a wider opening, and some flower pots hanging on his door.

REGARDED AS LEADERS

Certain people were pointed out as "leaders" or people whose judgment was respected, even though they had no traditional or official leadership roles. Sometimes their leadership activities had been confined to their immediate areas, and they could be persuaded to help in much larger areas.

> He showed great interest in improving the present conditions of the area. He was particular about cleanliness. He told the community organizer that a meeting is conducted every Sunday morning at 7 A.M. in his *katra*. There are about twenty-five families. Each family gives 2 annas a month. Most of the residents of the *katra* take a keen interest in improving it. They have adopted certain regulations on how the water taps and latrines should be used, on cleaning the *katra*, and so forth. The meeting is attended by men only, but he suggested that, if the organizer were to call a meeting of women, they would help.

On the other hand, in developing an effective community organization, it was found important to avoid potential leaders who might antagonize other members of the group or who, rather than supporting new citizen organizations, might perpetuate former organizational structures and leadership under new names. Such people might be leaders of political groups with no real interest in the community, people too closely associated with specific groups, or caste leaders of formalized local *panchayats*. Sometimes people with bad reputations were able, however, if they took the initiative in doing things for the community, to make even greater impact than the others. In the process, they were often able to change the community's image of them.

In one case a woman was observed by the organizer to defend herself capably in a verbal argument with another woman before a large crowd of women. The organizer therefore approached her later for help in organizing a zonal *mahila samiti*. The woman took the initiative and helped the worker in many ways, arranged the use of her home, furnished a carpet and fan, and, with her children, helped to gather the women together. Only then did the worker learn that this widow had a reputation as a prostitute. The women came anyway and elected her their representative. She later took the initiative in forming a sewing group and in other activities. The men on the executive committee of the *vikas mandals* expressed strong disapproval of her. The worker noticed considerable favorable change in the attitude of the women, who also said she had changed a lot and even her children had changed. They were pleased that they had elected her. As the worker noted, "The men's executive committee had to keep quiet when they saw that everything went satisfactorily and that the lady proved to be an asset to the *vikas mandal*."

§ *Developing Indigenous Leadership*

A serious problem was the lack of previous leadership experience among potentially effective slum leaders. The organizer tried to win the confidence and respect of these individuals and to help them understand what they could help to accomplish. Through repeated visits, the organizer hoped to show his respect for their judgments and his need for help, and potential leaders were encouraged in any efforts they might make to improve the areas. The following case illustrates how such an indigenous leader was further developed.

Today the lady organizer visited a woman who had complained about dirty surroundings and that her child was always sick as a result of such dirt. The lady asked the worker what she had been doing and what she thought she could do. The worker told her about the efforts being made to pave the lane. Then she asked the lady what she thought could be done about the dirt that had been bothering her. The lady replied immediately, "Some improvement." The worker said to her that paving the lane would improve conditions but that keeping the houses clean was the responsibility of the women. The lady agreed. Then the worker asked her in what way she might be able to contribute to these efforts. She in turn asked the worker to suggest something. The worker suggested that a dust bin could be kept in front of each house and that everyone could make it a point to throw garbage in it only. The lady liked this idea, though she complained that the sweepers sent by the municipal corporation did not do their jobs properly. They spread the garbage in the lane instead of throwing it outside, and, as a result, the level of the lanes was rising, and the rain water flowed into the houses. The worker told her that, if the people would do their part, they could also ask the sweepers to do their part. The lady assured the organizer that she would make everyone have a dust bin.

After two days the organizer went to the lady's house. This time she could go in. The worker asked her about the dust-bin project, and she told the worker that her neighbors did not agree with her and said, "I have thrown the garbage in your house." The lady had retorted, "You dare not, and later when the lane is paved then we will see how you throw dust in the lane." Again, several days later, the lady organizer went to the dust bin project house and was informed that there was only one person who did not agree with the idea of dust bins; the rest had all put them out, and the lady was checking their use of the dust bins. The worker congratulated her on her achievement. Again the organizer went to the same house to make sure of the progress of the project. The organizer was assured that the project was going smoothly; except for some children, everyone was using the dust bins.

Later many of these people, identified and then encouraged to assume leadership, were elected to the executive committees. They had been motivated to assume leadership by a number of factors. Interviews with organizers from twenty-one *vikas mandals* revealed that prestige, status, and real desire to serve the people were the most important; political motives were of least importance. Of significance is the fact that nearly one-third were persuaded by others to assume leadership. The community organizers cited the following reasons, and the percentage reporting each reason, for the people's assumption of leadership roles:[12]

prestige and status	93.7
interest in helping people	87.5
persuaded by others	31.2
to work with friends	12.5
being a leader	12.5
personal gain	12.5
political motives	6.2
utilization of leisure time	6.2

§ Establishment of Legitimation

The important element of legitimation in action programs in rural and small town areas has been particularly stressed by Hoffer.[13] He describes it as the process of making a proposed action a legitimate one for the community by securing approval of individuals and groups who possess sufficient social power in the form of authority and influence. Legitimation has also been stressed by others, particularly Sower and his associates, who point out that it is essential to obtain access to groups, formal social structures, and influential individuals whose sponsorship or approval can legitimize action.[14]

In the Delhi project, the term "legitimation" was applied to the organizer's seeking for approval and even for assistance from influential people in carrying out the urban community-development project. Sometimes there were efforts to secure permission for the entire project; in others, for specific projects. In the formative stages of the Delhi project, there was a point at which each new organization was accepted as legitimate in its area. This acceptance often occurred before the formal organizational work was completed. Such recognition evolved in several ways: through important members of the power structure, through recognition or acceptance of what other projects had accomplished through self-help organization, and through successful self-help efforts.

IMPORTANT MEMBERS OF THE POWER STRUCTURE

Early in the project nearly all organizers, understanding the importance of acceptance, attempted to secure recognition, approval, or blessings of the self-help organizations to be formed from important people in the areas. The community organizers sought the support of municipal councilmen; political leaders; influential area individuals, particularly those with political, occupational, or other vested interests; *mohalla* committees and other important welfare groups in the areas; heads of existing youth and other groups; and even, in one case, a Hindu priest. These efforts are illustrated by this extract: "In the end, the worker went to L. K., who is an educated and important person in this area and is taking a keen interest. The worker had to spend a good deal of time, as four or five other people were sitting with him. L. K. explained the program and philosophy of self-help to these people and requested that they make the program a success." In this case, legitimation was given; in others it was delayed or refused.

The importance of such legitimation can be seen in instances in which residents demanded, as they occasionally did at the beginning, that the sanction of important people be obtained. In some areas, this desire for legitimation of the project was the result of previous unfortunate experiences with individuals or agencies claiming they had come to help the people. Either the residents felt that such efforts had been wasted, the charitable help had lasted only a short time, or money had been collected for limited self-help objectives by people who had then disappeared. In such areas many refused to cooperate actively, even in answering the initial survey questions, until the organizers' mission had been legitimated. The residents believed themselves incapable of deciding whether or not to cooperate with the project.

In all but two project areas, it was generally necessary for the women, or the female community organizers, to obtain the husbands' permission in order to participate in the projects. In granting permission, the husbands were greatly influenced by the projects' approval by important community figures. In one of the two areas where this permission was not necessary, many of the women were working as laborers and had some limited financial independence. In the other, the methods and results of a nearby successful project were already known to the residents.

In the first weeks of contact with ten of fourteen areas, a large proportion of the organizers sought out the most important people of the areas and asked to be shown around and introduced to other important people. Although this more cordial type of introduction helped to establish the organizers with the residents and to legitimate their work and their presence, in only five of the fourteen areas were both the men and woman organizers taken around and formally introduced by certain important people. Four of these five project areas eventually became the most successful in terms of self-help activity-rating levels. In nine of the areas, the municipal councilmen, the only politicians directly involved in area affairs, were approached directly by the organizers. In only four of these areas, however, was legitimation given by the municipal councilmen.

Legitimation was denied to the proposed organizations by some influential people in twelve of the fourteen project areas. In five of them, denials were equal to or exceeded legitimation. Such denials represented strong opposition to the program by important people in the areas, yet there seems to have been little connection between achievement of approval by important persons and the success of the projects. Successful projects were carried out without strong legitimation from them. In fact, in three of the top seven self-help projects, legitimation was more often denied than not. In at least half the projects, there were active opposition and obstruction from politicians and municipal councilmen.

There are several possible reasons for the differences that were found in the importance of legitimation for action programs in rural and small-town areas and in slum areas like those of Delhi. In the former, one might generally expect to find people who could be viewed as part of the power and influence structure, and their approval and legitimation of action programs might have pronounced positive consequences. On the other hand, in slum areas there is likely to be latent hostility to such power and authority figures as politicians, councilmen, landlords, and government officials who are presumed by the slum dwellers to have failed and even to have exploited them in the past. Politicians, for example, appear to many slum people to have functioned largely as a negative group. Consequently, slum dwellers often tended to disregard whether authority figures withheld or gave their approval; the fact that most did not therefore had little effect.

SELF-HELP EFFORTS

People often would not accept the project until they could see something tangible. In one area, for example, a member of the executive committee reported that it was difficult to collect the R.1 membership dues. "He said that the *vikas mandal* should do something as a sort of demonstration to the people of the area that it is actually an institution for the common welfare." Legitimation was accomplished in such cases by success in the first projects. Initial doubts, apathy, and suspicion were often overcome when people discovered that the organization they had established could really bring about results. It could then become accepted in the area, as in the following example:

> The wall news board, prohibitory boards, zoning, and dust-bin projects, which are visible and tangible, have helped the community to see the results of efforts they put in through these projects, and the *vikas mandal* is receiving more and more confidence from the community. The self-help milk distribution started today in the area. The number of children receiving milk is about 110. The president of the *vikas mandal* has consented to donate one tub for boiling water and mixing milk. The measuring utensils have been purchased out of the collection from the people of 2 annas (2 cents) per milk card. Also fuel and two pieces of cloth for mixing the milk have been purchased. The worker, who was in the area in the evening when the milk was being distributed, found that this project was regarded by the members of the executive committee as a major achievement. One of the members remarked: "Something concrete has been done by the *vikas mandal* at least. This will help us in winning the confidence of the people." In the meeting a resolution was passed to collect 8 annas from each family on the ground floor to provide a dust bin for their common use. The spadework had already been done by the male community organizer. Immediately the collections were taken and passed to a cashier elected that very moment. A tin drum to serve as a dust bin and a bamboo pole to clean the *katra* drain were purchased out of collected funds, and the minutes of the meeting and details of accounts were recorded in a notebook purchased from the bazaar. It was marked that every resident looked proud at the end of the meeting and felt he had gained something very valuable. Must it be said that today's effort had strengthened their confidence in self-help and cooperation, which had been lacking?

SEEING RESULTS OF OTHER PROJECTS

Sometimes legitimation was accomplished in a new project through visits to, or spreading knowledge about, another already existing and successful project. When it was decided that one highly successful project would be expanded into a neighborhood, a pamphlet was distributed to the neighborhood residents describing the achievements of the project. Visits to the project area were also arranged for them. In one area, the worker recorded, "They know about the work done in this area, and they want to start work as early as possible." In another *vikas mandal* visits were arranged for the women to "see the remarkable things for themselves." After the visit, the women said "there is no doubt that the condition of the area has changed as it was no joke to visit there in the rainy season." As a result, they no longer resisted the division of their areas into zones because this visit cleared up the doubts they had.

§ *The Organization and Action Phase*

Part of the action process occurred in the initial stages of *vikas sabha* formation, when the groups reviewed their problems and began to select projects that could be undertaken. Typically, such reviews occurred during the first few meetings of the *vikas sabhas*. This part of the total process oriented the people toward what could practically be accomplished. The early initiation of self-help activities appears to be positively related to the success of a project. The top three of the fourteen projects in performance had initiated or completed some activity or community-work projects by the third week. The bottom three had much later starts, well after six weeks.

Two types of organization activity occurred: first, that directed at forming a new social structure within the *vikas mandal* area; second, that directed principally at the solution of some specific problem. Organizational meetings at the *vikas sabha* and *vikas mandal* levels were primarily directed at building the *vikas mandal* structural unit through elections of representatives and officers. They also served to spread information, gather support from the people, identify problems, and initiate action groups. An action group, on the other hand, was considered in the process of formation when responsibility for a particular task was assigned to a resident or residents of the area. Action groups assigned to solve problems and to promote self-help activities did not necessarily result from these *vikas sabha* and *vikas mandal* meetings. Other action groups were formed when people informally came together and made decisions to solve particular problems.

When the total number of organizational meetings and the total self-help activity level were ranked, no significant relationship was found between them. Where informal action groups were formed, however, there was a strong relationship ($r_s = .84$) between them and the self-help activities score. The reason for the lack of significant relationship between the *vikas sabha* and *vikas mandal* organizational phase and outcome seems to be that, although organizers carried out the formal requirements for setting up *vikas mandals*, some were less interested in immediate concrete action programs. This observation was true of some people involved in the organizational programs also. In a number of cases, organizational meetings were held without being followed up immediately by the initiation of activities.

Under the intensive method of organization, the average length of time from the very beginning of a project to the first formal meeting of the *vikas mandal* was three months and three weeks, varying from two and a half to nearly eight months. No positive correlation was found between early initiation of the general meeting and the eventual level of activities. There was, however, a negative correlation of $r_s = -.21$ between rankings of the projects according to length of time required to initiate the *vikas mandals* and the levels of activity success. Little difference between length of time and level of activities was found when the more successful projects were compared with the less successful projects.

The expectations of people in a project area were, however, sometimes crushed when the *vikas mandal* was formed either too rapidly or over too long a period of time. If formed too quickly, the organization was quite likely to become a rather weak "paper" organization, simply because it had not been allowed to "jell." On the other hand, a protracted delay often meant that high expectations in the first few weeks were not capitalized upon at the most appropriate time to initiate activities.

Each *vikas mandal* experienced a number of hindrances to its organizational work. There was, however, very little correlation ($r_s = -.12$) between the numbers of hindrances experienced and the activity levels of the projects. The better project areas in activity performance had slightly smaller totals of recorded hindrances than did the poorer projects. The major incidence of obstructions occurred from the beginning of the second month of operation through the sixth month. In twelve of fourteen projects, more than two-thirds (67 per cent) of the recorded problems occurred in this five-month period. The last six-month period of operation was relatively free of hindrances.

No one problem—caste, politicians, or quarreling, for example—stood out as a single pervasive influence negatively related to project success. Certain situations did have varying effects, however, on the course of individual projects. Religious differences or problems were mentioned in one-half (seven of fourteen) areas. Nine areas mentioned conflicts between regional groups. Caste problems, for example, were mentioned in all but one project area, but, on the whole, the number of times they were recorded was limited.* Politicians interfered directly in several projects, in a different sense from refusing legitimation. Their interference, however, produced no significant differences in project performance. Such interference occurred in seven, or one-half, of the projects— in the three most successful and the four least successful. Much quarreling occurred in nearly all projects. Most of it was related to delays or related difficulties in the conduct of meetings. Slum people seemed to enjoy both watching and participating in such quarreling, and for this reason it probably had less serious effects than would otherwise have been the case. It was very serious when officers occasionally had heated arguments over personal difficulties or over rivalry for *vikas mandal* offices.

---

* Some substantiation for this finding is that only 3.3 per cent of the sample of 406 male heads of families thought that caste associations had a negative influence on the *vikas mandals* in their areas and only 6.7 per cent thought that religious groups had similar effects. Political groups, however, were thought to have negative effects among 33.3 per cent. See *Second Evaluation Study of the Vikas Mandals* (Delhi: Municipal Corporation of Delhi, May, 1965), p. 4.2.

§ *Development of a New Self-Image*

A change in identity or self-image is basic to successful community development, and a recognition of the individual's sense of who and what he is is vital to change in urban slum areas. Such change in the conception of the self among many people, its continuity with the past, and its commitment to the future are important in changing the way of life of a slum area. In most instances, such change represents a new sense of personal worth and organization of reality. In the beginning, most slum projects were characterized by apathy and lack of confidence in the people's own abilities because of their limited economic resources and their low social status. Confidence in themselves had to be developed in order for them to feel their own importance and recognize the possibilities for changing conditions with only modest help from outside sources.

Much difficulty was encountered in attempting to bring about this new perception of personal identity, as the slum dweller, reinforced by the slum culture, is inclined to be suspicious of, or to reject, change from without. Expectations and actions that differ from tradition in any way may be rejected. Slum dwellers are often even suspicious of those who cooperate with change agents from the outside world. Slum people may not try to avail themselves of opportunities to change their situations because they accept the view that their present identities are impossible to change. Sometimes they build up rationalizations to protect a world that seems secure and comfortable.

Through community development, changes are being attempted in the style of performance, roles, and norms that must be recognized by others and, in turn, perceived by themselves. Identity change under planned efforts includes the achievement of desire for change, revision of one's view of self through new experiences, commitment to change in self-identity, and recognition of new identities and roles.[15]

ACHIEVING A DESIRE FOR CHANGE

To achieve desire for change, it is often necessary to create among community members dissatisfaction with their present identities. Means must be found to stimulate this dissatisfaction with self so that a person greatly desires to change the self. In this respect, the creation of some discontent within slum areas can be not only useful but also essential. People must recognize this fact so that further prompting by outside agents will not be necessary.

In the Delhi project, an important step in the redefinition of self was to present the initial interview questions in such a way as to replace age-old dependence with ideas of a new independence from government and charity.

The men and women organizers' going from door to door helped to stimulate change in residents' perceptions of themselves and their situation. Even asking the question, "What problems do you think the people in this area could solve for themselves?" helped them to shake off some feelings of subordination. Even though few could make any suggestions, the question did stimulate discussion among the residents about this strange idea of their being capable of changing things themselves. Here were the beginnings of an awareness of the possibility of self-help and of a new view of themselves. The continued reiteration of belief in them by the community organizers and by others demonstrated W. I. Thomas's view that people come to act according to the expectations held of them.

REVISION OF ONE'S VIEW OF SELF THROUGH NEW EXPERIENCES

New experiences with different patterns of living may be effective in establishing new criteria for self-appraisal. One way to develop a new self-image is to achieve new experiences: It is in this way that self-identity is altered. Exposure to new experiences may lead to considerable alteration in the slum dwellers' views of themselves, provided, of course, that they really desire change. New experiences may give rise to new wants. In the Delhi project, efforts were made to expose people to activities of the new India by encouraging visits to the national radio station and various cultural centers and discussions of the Five-Year Plans for the development of the country. Exposure to new methods of child care and hopes for new roles for women were other examples of this approach.

Probably the best example of how new identity was encouraged in the projects was the printing of a small supply of letterhead stationery for the newly established citizen organizations. Each sheet displayed the name of the *vikas mandal* in Hindi, Urdu, and possibly English and, occasionally, the names of the officers. Supposedly, the stationery was to be used for communications with the municipal councilmen, the government, and other *vikas mandal* officials, but it was recognized from the beginning that such largely illiterate groups had little use for stationery. Although little use was made of it, it had great symbolic importance. It was one thing for people of low economic status to have stationery like that of government agencies and the wealthy: For largely illiterate people it was even more significant. The printed membership cards that members received and other small items built up similar feelings of importance. When a *vikas mandal* was formed, arrangements were made to photograph the officers and the ceremony; copies of these photographs, which were given to the group for display, were treasured not only because of their importance but also because they were probably the only, or at least among the few, pictures these people had of themselves.

Each *vikas mandal* had a small office, rented for $1 or 2 a month, which was deliberately kept only for the officers of the organization and not for the organizers. The name of the organization usually appeared on a large board above it, and some essential furniture was lent by the Department. This office and the equipment for activities that members had jointly purchased were proudly exhibited to any visitors as possessions that few other slum dwellers owned cooperatively and that they could never have purchased individually. Although most members of a *vikas mandal* were familiar at least with the boundaries of their area, it was customary to mark the limits of each area and each zone. These markings plus a community bulletin board set it apart from other areas.

A study of 351 male members and fifty-two female members of the executive committees of twenty-one *vikas mandals* showed that, in general, most (about two-thirds of the men and more than four-fifths of the women) had never before held positions of leadership.[16] One-fifth of the men elected (19.9 per cent) and nearly half the women (44.2 per cent) had no education whatever. Of the men, if those with fewer than three years of education are included, the figure was nearly one-third (31 per cent); with up to six years, two-thirds (63.2 per cent). If local leaders were to fulfill and to develop their roles as leaders, they needed opportunities to develop a feeling of importance. Beside the help of the community organizer, such opportunities were provided in part by various training meetings to which all the officers were invited and camp meetings. As the camp provided a special setting, it contributed a great deal to this feeling of importance. For example, a week-end camp, for the officers of the *vikas mandals*, was held in the summer of 1961.[17] Its primary purpose was to orient the leaders to the philosophy and approach of self-help work; to provide all *vikas mandal* officers with an opportunity to become better acquainted with one another, discuss matters of common interest, and exchange experiences; and to assist them in reviewing past work programs, fix priorities, and draw up future work plans.

Other methods were used to increase the residents' and officers' feelings of importance. On occasion, the officers reported to the area councilmen or to members of the standing committees, and they were also invited to participate in a city-wide civic meeting attended by a cabinet officer, the mayor, and other high dignitaries. Such meetings gave them, probably for the first time, except during elections perhaps, an opportunity to mingle with people of high prestige and served to break down the barriers that separated the slum population from activities of importance within the city. In a further effort to enhance the importance of slum dwellers, their officers were invited to the city-council chambers of Delhi to report on their activities to the Commissioner and Deputy Mayor of Delhi. One illiterate president said that he had never thought that he, a humble man, would ever sit in the hallowed chambers of the city government.

In the council chamber of the Municipal Corporation there were assembled the officers of the various *vikas mandals* and their community organizers. One officer introduced each of his fellows and then introduced the male community organizers last, an order that was suggested to him. The male community organizers introduced the women community organizers, who then introduced the women delegates present. The same *vikas mandal* officer reported to the Deputy Mayor and the Municipal Commissioner. Judging from the enthusiasm of the speakers and the attitude of the others present, this occasion was important for them, one of great pride. Each group listened attentively to the other groups. The women particularly displayed little of the shyness that one usually sees in slum women, and one sensed the feelings of pride and equality as well as of determination on their part. The meeting was even more impressive because hardly any of these people had ever been officials of any organization and probably had never been called upon even to give public addresses. The organizations they represented, the *vikas mandals*, had had no existence whatever several months earlier and were entirely artificial creations. Yet they talked about them as though they had always existed, and the fact that they were representing miscellaneous groups of people seemed entirely natural. After they had finished, the Deputy Mayor replied and gave an encouraging speech.*

The assignment of responsibility to slum dwellers is one way of changing not only their conceptions of themselves but also outsiders' conceptions of them. In general, Delhi slum dwellers responded to this approach. Two illustrations are significant. In one poor and highly illiterate *vikas mandal*, a valuable experimental television set was entrusted to the group, which took care of it for several years, operating it without loss or damage. In most *vikas mandals*, items like sewing machines and athletic equipment were entrusted to the people, who not only kept them safe but guarded them so well that they hardly lost even a needle. Perhaps it might be argued that slum people regard certain physical objects that they cannot afford with great respect and importance, provided that they have a personal interest in them.

COMMITMENT TO CHANGE IN SELF-IDENTITY

Individuals are often torn between old and new practices. Commitment to change in self-identity is a difficult step, as all such change requires some eradication of the former self. There is a need to understand what must be changed and how much it can be changed. The contents of new social roles must be known so that they can be properly played. Once new self-identities are acquired, people must continue to have experiences that fit them; otherwise, they will tend to step back into their old ways.

The idea of the *vikas mandal* implied confidence in the people's abilities to do things for themselves, making them more independent and in this sense

---

* This passage is taken from the notes of the author.

building prestige. On the other hand, charity under any name and from any source tends to perpetuate the image of the "poor unfortunate creature" of the slums. By its very nature, it develops dependence, which is the very antithesis of independent self-help. One example illustrates the development of this feeling. At the formation of one *vikas mandal*, an announcement was made that powdered milk was available for distribution to the group. A heated discussion then ensued as to the advisability of accepting the milk, as it was looked upon as "charity" and was thus diametrically opposed to the philosophy of the new organization. It was only after it was explained to them that the distribution would be made by the slum dwellers themselves that the free milk became acceptable in terms of their revised definitions of themselves. Another example shows the assumption of responsibility and the emergence of new self-conceptions.

> During the interviews the residents were made conscious of the unsanitary condition in their lane and the necessity for avoiding urinating in the drains. In the course of their discussions, they proposed putting up notice boards prohibiting urination, and this measure, too, became a subject of discussion. Various suggestions were made about the amounts to be contributed for these notice boards, but ultimately a nominal contribution of 1 *paise* (less than 1 cent) per family was decided upon. Some individuals and *katras* even offered to cover the entire cost of the notice boards, but the offers were not accepted, as they were contradictory to the "1 *paise* project," which could serve many purposes. First, all the residents would be associated or involved in the venture, and, second, the contribution was not much, and no one would grudge making it. If everyone contributed, everyone would be conscious of the purpose: "We should not urinate in the drains."

RECOGNITION OF NEW IDENTITIES AND ROLES

Recognition by others of new identities and roles is also crucial in social change. Urban community development can be regarded as a process of collective identity change in which people develop new conceptions of themselves when their former behavior patterns are no longer applicable. The praise of the outsider plays an important role in such change by helping to develop a new collective identity. On the other hand, humiliation from the outside may have an adverse effect. Recognition and acceptance by such key people in the community as government officials help to make new ideas and norms more acceptable. In the Delhi project, persistent efforts were made to give such prestige to slum dwellers. This approach might be regarded as "dangling a carrot," the carrot being recognition of identity change, but the very failure to do so often results in little change.

The importance of desire for status as a mechanism for changing social situations was seen in the first self-help project of the first *vikas mandal*. The executive committee decided to number all the houses as a joint project. Although the primary reason given by the committee was the facilitation of mail distribution, this goal seemed somewhat irrelevant as few residents received mail. The suggestion was a shock to those in charge of the Delhi project, as other problems were far more pressing and such a project had not even been mentioned in the training programs. Other project areas also often adopted this scheme among their first activities, often with the addition or substitution of name plates, with names painted on wood for 5 or 10 cents each. Yet the importance of these numbers and name plates became quite clear. It is customary in Indian cities for wealthy people, government officials, and others of high status to have house numbers, as well as their names on their houses. Consequently, when these numbers appeared on the shacks of largely illiterate slum dwellers, it seemed evident that they symbolized some wish for identity and importance in a largely impersonal urban setting and paved the way for closer unity within the areas. Later the use of numbers and name plates became a regular program activity and was encouraged by the organizers. In one very poor area of shacks, a small dwelling had not one but three name plates outside the door, one for each married couple in the joint family.

Some prestige was also achieved through the joint whitewashing of an area. This activity was popular and served to set the area apart in striking fashion from the surrounding neighborhood. To those living there, it meant that they came from a clean whitewashed area, whereas nearby neighbors did not. Whitewashing is commonly associated with the religious festival of Diwali: Doing it at other times may therefore have had added significance.

Finally, people come to feel a sense of new identity, an identity that is a product of what the group has done. In efforts to live up to this new self-image, further change is possible. Eventually people may come to regard themselves as no longer in need of the help of the change agent, as capable of doing things for themselves, and as having ability to take on bigger projects. Knowing that one woman organizer was to be transferred to another type of work, a few women sat around her and inquired, "What will the new organizer do?" "The same work I was doing" was the reply. "But you have done nothing," came the answer back. "It is the people who paved their lane, it is again they who paid for the water tap, and what did you do?"

The process of identity change explains the lengthy procedures necessary to modify group practices and habits that are collectively represented in the improved self-images of slum people. It is not something that can be accomplished on an individual basis, nor is it a change that can be successfully accomplished in a few months or even possibly in a few years. With some people it may never be accomplished. The process of identity change accounts for the difficulties of coping with slum sanitation problems in India, or with delinquency, drug addiction, and illegitimacy in slum areas in the Western world. It often takes a long time for people to see such behavior as a reflection on their new image of themselves.

The following factual description illustrates the changes that took place during the initial four months of one project.

Until a few years ago, the residents of this very poor area were largely indifferent to their surroundings. They were then organized into a *vikas mandal*, with an elected executive committee to plan and carry out improvements. The people began to sink roots into their area and to grapple with the realities of urban life. During the first six months, a process of social change was initiated. In July, there was an interview with each family to determine needs. Money was collected for four additional water taps. An adult literacy club, child-care classes, and a children's club were organized. In August, there was an election of a fourteen-member executive committee, all men. The children's club sponsored the area's first celebration of Independence Day—with decorations, flag-raising, songs, and tea. The residents began collecting funds for paving bricks and drainage tiles. A committee was organized to supervise community trash cans provided without cost by the government. In September, the executive committee approved the constitution and elected officers. A television club was organized to raise funds to maintain a community television set promised by the government. A women's sewing class began, with a machine lent by the government. A public-health nurse started twice-weekly visits. The children's club visited the railway station and made a carom board. In October, brick paving and concrete drains were completed in one large lane. Residents began collecting funds for a new tiled latrine. Two water taps were installed. The *vikas mandal* chalked up the sixtieth dues-paying family. The executive committee decided to appoint women to subcommittees. The children's club visited All-India Radio, bought cricket equipment with funds saved from dues, and challenged outside teams.

By November, there were 100 dues-paying families. Another lane was paved. All homes were whitewashed by the owners, with the government providing whitewash. The first literacy class was completed, but the sewing class was extended from three to six months because members were still confused by terms. A weaving class was organized, with the government advancing a loan for a loom. The children's club voted to help parents every Sunday, took a bicycle tour of Delhi with another club, and undertook daily distribution of powdered milk from UNICEF to infants, the sick, pregnant women, and nursing mothers. The executive committee passed its first crisis—one resident refused to dismantle a hut encroaching on a lane but changed his mind under public pressure and asked for a permit to rebuild.

The area was originally one of the dirtiest in Old Delhi, and the area surrounding the project was exceptionally filthy. After the first few months, the area was far cleaner and more orderly than before. The residents no longer threw so many things out of their houses into their neighbors' yards. The drains were much cleaner, and there was little evidence of children easing in the drains. Rather than being apathetic they seemed to have considerable optimism about the future of their area.

An analysis was made of changes in the self-image during this period, using the daily reports of the organizers, statements of the residents, and the opinions of the organizers. Although these sources recorded nothing explicitly about self-image, they revealed a definite shift from initial apathy and dependence on the organizer to an attitude of self-importance. The process seemed to follow these steps:

1. apathy of people toward self-help;
2. blaming some group landlords, politicians, and city government officials for conditions;
3. role of politics in project cleavages along lines of caste and region, with leaders' conflicts interfering with organization;
4. distrust of organizer and his reason for being there;
5. cleavages among age groups about self-help ideas, with young men being more enthusiastic;
6. acceptance of the community organizer and legitimation of project;
7. assumption of responsibility for initial activities largely by the community organizer;
8. change in superstitions and failure to utilize vaccination;
9. persistent follow-up by leaders in spurring the people on to new visions of possibilities;
10. establishing patterns of communication and cooperation among residents;
11. development of a new self-image of importance and recognition that things can be changed through self-help;
12. common activity programs leading to community feeling;
13. common activity programs leading to other activities;
14. shift from dependence on community organizer to community initiation of activities;
15. expansion to more complex projects as confidence increases;
16. belief that what is being accomplished arises from the people's own efforts and not from the work of the community organizer.

Chapter 13

THE SLUM AND APPLIED SOCIOLOGY

Although slums may vary from one type to another, certain general patterns of slum life are world-wide. The slum is generally, but not always, characterized by inadequate housing, deficient facilities, and congestion, but it is far more than these physical attributes. Sociologically, it is a way of life, a subculture with a set of norms and values, which is reflected in poor sanitation and health practices, deviant behavior, and characteristic attributes of apathy and social isolation. Rather than being "disorganized," the slum often simply has developed its own organization, a type of organization usually regarded as unconventional by the middle class. Slum dwellers are isolated generally from the power structure and regarded as inferior; they, in turn, reflect their own suspicions toward the outside world.

Society reacts negatively to slum dwellers; the nonslum dweller often associates the physical conditions of the slum with a belief in the "natural inferiority" of its inhabitants. This reaction has important consequences in the social isolation and alienation of slum dwellers and their exclusion from power and participation in urban society. Slum residents lack effective means of communicating with the outside world because of lack of communication experience, their own powerlessness to make their voices heard, and their own apathy. Because of their powerlessness, they also feel unable to alter their life situations. This powerlessness is accompanied by long-standing patterns of behavior and beliefs that are based on current realities about this weakness.

Throughout the centuries many groups have lived in the slums and have moved out of them; others have stayed on. In most cities the slums have continued for centuries, in many instances either growing larger or expanding into new areas. In this sense slums can be said to be self-perpetuating, either being replenished from within or being infused with new populations through migration from outside the city. In the past, in the United States at least, it has generally taken about three generations for a substantial proportion of families to move from the tenements of the city slums to middle-class areas. In developing countries, this movement out of the slums has hardly occurred at all, or if it has occurred it has taken many generations. Such a "natural" method of moving people out of the slums has generally worked, but it has been inefficient, slow, sometimes barbaric, and wasteful of manpower and human talents. The problem is how to produce in one generation what might require three generations in more affluent societies and how to bring about change in one or two generations in developing countries, which might otherwise require as many as five or more generations if it could be accomplished at all. Furthermore, most city slums contain not a few hundred or even a few thousand but hundreds of thousands and, in countries like India, even millions of people. Unless some solution can be found to produce widespread change by dealing with these great masses of slum people, little real progress can be made.

The problem is more than that of moving people out of the slums; rather it is one of change or even eradication of the slums themselves. It seems evident that slums cannot be rapidly changed simply by providing more professional help and guidance, greater economic and educational opportunities to overcome poverty, and more and better-coordinated services. Some slum dwellers, however, may be changed. The past history, as well as the present status, of slum programs has suggested that such efforts alone have not been highly successful. Many slum dwellers have limited aspirations and do not have enough desire for material wealth, education, and better lives to strive for them. In developed countries in particular, urban people tend to think more of themselves, often being afraid to be involved in enterprises beyond their own immediate satisfaction, which has even been reflected in a trend against active intervention when acts of violence are being committed against other urban citizens. Slum people may disdain to engage in activities yielding what appear to them to be the highest rewards.*

Some have believed that social change in the slum will follow from mere exposure and contacts with new ideas and economic opportunities. This explanation is too simple, as mere contact with more scientific ways of living or new sets of values does not necessarily lead to their adoption. A community may become even more apathetic about these new ways or styles of living, and this principle holds even for nations as a whole. In some countries, great social change did not occur, despite centuries of contact with Western ways, as in Indonesia.[1] In rural community-development programs, for example, the problems are greater than merely supplying adequate fertilizers, seed grains,

---

* One writer commented on these difficulties in relation to community development in Indian villages: "There are others, and they probably form the majority, who, in spite of the efforts of the extension services and the inducements offered by them, seem inert and indifferent. They pass up repeated opportunities to increase production and income; even when opportunity knocks at their very door." Kusum Nair, *Blossoms in the Dust: The Human Element in Indian Development* (London: Gerald Duckworth & Co., Ltd, 1961), p. 195.

and new agricultural techniques: The peasant farmer has to want to change his practices.*

Widespread and effective change in the slums requires assumption of responsibility for, and contributions by, the people affected. They must have a stake in the results and an appreciation of the need for change. "When change in custom is the immediate objective, the client community's cooperation is obviously essential."[2] As they contribute to change by doing things for themselves, a total situation develops in which slum dwellers are likely to be more receptive to change as a whole. As Haggstrom has pointed out, the poor have then found themselves in a problematic situation and have themselves been moved to do something about it.[3] In early nineteenth-century England, for example, many working-class people began to educate themselves individually or in groups, as part of the rising labor movement.[4] Illiterate people would gather each week in pubs to listen and discuss serious books and periodicals that were read aloud.

Today the average American Negro slum dweller, for example, makes few efforts, except through protest movements, to do things for himself. He has little local community organization, and he insists that the "white world" deal with his problems as products of racial discrimination and denial of economic opportunity. Yet the solutions to the innumerable problems that he faces must come also through his own efforts if they are to be effective. The image of the Negro slum dweller must be modified not only through changes in opportunities but also through self-initiated changes in the norms and values of the Negro slum areas relating to delinquency and crime, violence, illegitimacy, drug addiction, lack of family responsibility, and apathy toward educational opportunities. This change may, in turn, affect others' images of the "urban Negroes" and may facilitate overcoming discrimination and limitations on economic opportunity.

> But the worst of it is that important tasks, necessary ones on the agenda of American Negroes, are shirked and ignored. These are tasks that conceivably no one but Negroes can do. It is probable that no investment of public and private agencies on delinquency and crime-prevention programs will equal the return from an investment by Negro-led and Negro-financed agencies. It is probable that no offensive on the public school system to improve the educational results among Negroes will equal what may be gained from an equivalent investment by Negro-led and Negro-financed groups, and an increase in the numbers of Negro teachers and principals. It is possible that no effort to change the patterns of the Negro lower-class family will be effective at a time when the white family is in disorder,

---

* Bert F. Hoselitz, "Problems of Adapting and Communicating Modern Techniques to Less Developed Areas," *Economic Development and Cultural Change*, 2 (January, 1954), 249–69. For example, the Japanese method of paddy culture was introduced into India more than ten years ago, yet it has not been generally accepted, and India's rice yield per acre remains the lowest in the world.

when strong families of whatever kind, native and ethnic, show signs of disintegration; but if anything can be done, it is likely that Negro agencies will be far more effective than public agencies and those of white Protestants.[5]

Changes in slums can be accelerated through the use of the large potential source of manpower and resources provided by the slum dwellers' own efforts. People who live in slum areas can do a great many things for themselves. There are large-scale possibilities for physical improvements, health and sanitation, education, and recreational and cultural activities (see Chapter 10). It is a curious contradiction that middle-class people, whose problems are not so serious and who often have the funds to arrange for help, engage in far more self-help activities, either individually or cooperatively, than do the poor who have greater problems and less ability to pay. People in urban slum areas in the United States could, for example, make minor repairs and improve the maintenance of their housing, whether owned by private or public landlords, perhaps with community-owned tools; improve the sanitation of their neighborhoods;* help protect public property like schools and parks from vandalism; assist in the control of drug addiction, delinquency, and illegitimacy; establish credit unions and cooperative stores and promote the cooperative ownership of recreational equipment and library materials;† and cooperate with teachers and serve as assistants to help with school problems and increase motivation for learning. The protection of women from assault has been assumed recently in New York City slum areas by citizen groups, which furnish evening escorts home and maintain citizen patrols.[6] Self-help efforts in job training have also been conducted by some local communities.

§ A Conceptual Framework for Changing the Slum

Few people would question the necessity for directly involving the mass of people in order to cope successfully with the mounting urban problems of both developed and developing countries. The issue is how and whether or not it can be done on a sufficiently large scale to effect appreciable changes in urban communities. Is it possible to create effective identification with a neighborhood or community in the face of general urban apathy? Can groups of citizens who will actually raise morale and neighborhood standards be organized? How can

---

* In one large United States city, the head of the municipal rodent-eradication bureau recently said that, if the tenement slum dwellers really wanted to get rid of rats, they could do it in a few months. The garbage left about by the slum dwellers and their failure to plug entry ways for the rats and to help eradicate them are what make rat control impossible for city administrations.

† For example, a group of families or a local community could jointly own an encyclopedia for the children, which is generally too expensive for a single slum family. This approach might increase the children's desire for education and improve their performances in school.

we achieve urban communities committed to procedures and goals involving genuine democratic participation?

The initiation of effective change in slum areas requires the recognition of several principles. As Lippitt and his associates have pointed out, the new profession of community-development work seeks to use knowledge of the behavioral sciences in efforts to bring about community change and to stimulate self-help.[7] An agent of change must have a scientifically formulated theory of human behavior, a clear idea of what is to be changed, an accurate knowledge of the specific situation, an understanding of his own values and motives, and a knowledge of how to record his experiences, in order to contribute to a body of knowledge about social change.[8] After a study of a large number of village community-development projects, Goodenough summarized one set of principles based on the human factors affecting developmental programs: (1) Development proposals and procedures should be mutually consistent; (2) the agents of change must have thorough knowledge of the main values and principal features of the client community's culture; (3) development must take the whole community into account; (4) the goals must be stated in terms that have positive value to the community's members; (5) the community must be an active partner in the process; (6) agents of change should start with what the community has in the way of material, organizational, and leadership resources; (7) development procedures must make sense to the community's members at each step; (8) the agents of change must earn the personal respect of the community's members; (9) the agents of change should try to avoid making themselves indispensable in the development situation; and (10) good communication and coordination among workers and their respective agencies are essential.[9]

Although these broad principles may be useful, they are perhaps not sufficiently detailed to suggest the elements involved in change. A more specific set of principles or concepts for developing community feeling and self-help in a slum area is proposed here: (1) a group approach to slum problems; (2) recognition of community differences; (3) creation of a new type of social organization; (4) group perception of the need for change; (5) the pursuit of self-imposed change; (6) the use of voluntary groups for change; (7) change in identity or self-image; (8) the utilization of indigenous workers and leadership; (9) representative community leadership; (10) the giving of responsibility and credit to ordinary people; (11) the use of conflict and the need for power in social change; (12) the utilization of competition among groups; (13) the utilization of chain reactions in social change; (14) the utilization of outside assistance in attaining objectives; and (15) decentralization of some governmental functions.[10] This frame of reference does not imply that this approach alone will solve slum problems, with their complex mixtures of physical, economic, educational, and political factors. Any effective solution requires changes within a balanced framework in which all ingredients are recognized.

The problems that have developed in slum areas everywhere have generally originated in group practices condoned and continued by the groups. Groups must therefore be used in the solution of these problems. A group, rather than an individual, approach must be used, and slum people, as a group, must desire change. A development program will be effective only as a community sees the need for change and as it collectively evolves its own capacity for achieving it. New economic- and cultural-improvement programs can be presented to people without being fully utilized. Change can be effectively accomplished only with the cooperation of the citizens as a group and through their perception of the need for change and their desire to cooperate with outside agencies in bringing about social change. Slum neighborhoods often have different conduct norms, and the efforts of law-enforcement officers, school teachers, and social workers may be either supported, ignored, or ridiculed by the people. Certainly there is no way for a few policemen or outsiders to eradicate community-approved behavior like stealing, other forms of juvenile delinquency, begging, fighting, gambling, prostitution, and the illegal use of drugs.* Nor can municipal authorities alone deal in slum areas with poor sanitation, health problems, the misuse of public housing, and inadequate recreational facilities. School programs and the motivation for learning cannot succeed without the support of the neighborhood people. As Conant pointed out, "One needs only to visit a [slum] school to be convinced that the nature of the community determines what goes on in the school."[11]

RECOGNITION OF COMMUNITY DIFFERENCES

Slum communities exhibit considerable variations in racial, ethnic, regional, tribal, occupational, caste, and religious backgrounds; age composition; and length of residence in the areas. They often have certain distinct norms, value systems, or ways of life, and it is therefore quite likely that slum communities will respond in different ways to urban community development and will require modifications in organizational procedures and techniques to produce social change. For example, one of the reasons for some difficulties in rural community-development programs in India has been, as Kusum Nair has

---

* Furthermore, much of the "slum-making process," insofar as it generates deviant behavior, arises from deficiencies in two aspects of social control. Slums are deficient in social controls originating in conventional institutions that define the limits of permissible behavior for persons living there, particularly adolescents, and controls by means of which the community is enabled to resist encroachments by such deviants as adult criminals, drug peddlers, prostitutes, and corrupt politicians who espouse values to which certain members of the local community may be strongly antagonistic. See Harold Finestone, "Narcotics and Criminality," *Law and Contemporary Problems*, 22 (Winter, 1957), 69-85.

pointed out, that the tailor-made government program has not sufficiently recognized the differences among the 550,000 villages.[12]

Any attempts to change prevailing practices must be preceded by recognition and familiarity with community beliefs. Each slum area has to be studied carefully from the point of view of physical characteristics; population composition, with emphasis on its main divisions; family and age distribution; prevailing attitudes and opinions of different groups; and the "power structure" of the local community.[13] Attitudes of men and women toward health, sanitation, and recreation must be ascertained.

A successful urban community-development program can hardly rely upon a set pattern of general procedures alone. Organizational work to develop self-help involving a well-settled ethnic community may present a different situation than that involving a highly diversified new housing development. Similarly, Negro slum areas in large United States cities generally lack the basic cultural unity of ethnic communities. This variation has made the problem of effective community work in these areas much more difficult.

CREATION OF A NEW TYPE OF SOCIAL ORGANIZATION

Slum residents participate in organized groups to minimal degrees, particularly in comparison with the middle class. They take little part in the affairs of the larger community.[14] Various studies have revealed, in fact, that between 60 and 80 per cent of the lower class in the United States belongs to no formal organizations. This lack of social participation is not limited to civic affairs. One study of about 500 lower-class people who had lived in Bombay for an average of 21.5 years showed that the majority was completely apathetic toward participating in any group or social activity; about three-fourths did not participate in any such activity.[15]

Several characteristics of the lower- and working-class slum dweller explain this relative lack of participation in community and neighborhood affairs.[16] In the first place, there is a common feeling of futility and defeatism, a set of self-defeating attitudes that acts as a barrier to the slum dweller's participation. Second, differences in racial and ethnic background often create antagonism that prevents cooperation. Third, most organizations have been staffed or promoted by middle-class people, and the average lower- and working-class slum dweller has not been able to discern benefits to himself in the organizations.

The creation of a new type of organization of their own is likely to increase participation in community affairs among slum dwellers and to provide a mechanism for effective change among a group of heterogeneous people. It also may furnish a way of minimizing resistance to change among the traditional leadership of an area by developing new indigenous leadership. Such a new organization can be provided by forming a unit based on the ties where the people live such as a block, a neighborhood, a *kaifong*, a *vikas mandal*, or a *mohalla*. In many cases such a unit is the only one around which slum dwellers can be organized and mobilized for change.* After evaluating the role of block organizations in the Chicago Hyde Park-Kenwood Community Conference, one study concluded that "citizen participation is essential to a workable program of [urban renewal] conservation."[17]

The problem, however, is how to develop sufficient neighborhood cohesion, sufficient sense of belonging in the area, as well as indigenous leadership capable of identifying neighborhood problems and acting upon them. It is essential but not easy to build indigenous group activities into neighborhood organizations that can identify and support area needs, can put pressures on private and public authorities, and can assume initiative for improving opportunities within the neighborhood.

A new organization helps to focus on issues common to the community. When new issues like cooperative paving of a lane, construction of a new latrine, mass cleanliness and vaccination campaigns, and efforts to control delinquency come under discussion, it is possible to obtain a degree of unity among people with diverse ethnic, caste, regional, religious, tribal, and occupational backgrounds.[18] Self-help activities like posting of common bulletin boards, community whitewashing projects, and local community sports programs for children also help to develop community spirit.

GROUP PERCEPTION OF THE NEED FOR CHANGE

Slum people will not necessarily change through being told what to do or being furnished the means for change. People appear to be willing to participate in actions directed at adjusting or changing conditions in their neighborhoods if they perceive the need for change and are adequately aroused.[19] The desire for change seems to precede any successful program of self-help. In urban community development, permanent change is likely to come as a community sees the need for it and develops the capacity for making it. People may resist change if it appears to threaten their traditions, if they cannot understand it, or if it comes as a result of pressures from outside. "It is a mistake to think that

---

* The East Harlem Project, for example, which began in 1957 in a heavily Puerto Rican slum of New York City, has emphasized self-help and the development of block organizations. Patricia Cayo Sexton, *Spanish Harlem* (New York: Harper & Row, Publishers, 1965). Also see David Borden, "East Harlem Block Community Development Program, First Edition, East Harlem Project," Mimeographed. In 1965, a city-wide Puerto Rican Council for Economic and Social Development was set up as a clearinghouse for a variety of Puerto Rican self-help programs in New York City neighborhoods. See "A Proposal for a Self-Help Puerto Rican Community Development Project in the City of New York," Puerto Rican Forum, Inc., New York, Mimeographed.

everyone in the slums is hopelessly beaten, defeated, at war with society, or incompetent and that therefore they can not do things for themselves."[20]

PURSUIT OF SELF-IMPOSED CHANGE

Of great importance is the ordinary citizen's direct role in changing his immediate physical and social surroundings and his day-to-day living. In such direct roles, slum people themselves help to improve and maintain public facilities like housing, schools, and parks. They learn to accept proper health and sanitation practices and the importance of education in their world. They assume direct roles in dealing with delinquency, drug addiction, prostitution, illegitimacy, and intergroup conflict in their areas. Self-imposed changes have more meaning and therefore more permanence than those imposed from without, no matter how well intended the latter may be. Although an outsider can often produce quick changes or do much for a community, the important and persistent questions are "How long will they last?" and "Will the community return to the old practices?" Self-directed changes, however modest, become lasting bases for the community's confidence in its own abilities to meet and solve its own problems. Outside resources may not be completely accepted, because they are not "ours." With a self-help approach it is possible to persuade people to take new views of old traditions. In the Liyari urban community-development project in Karachi,[21] for example, the men were originally opposed to education for girls and women because it would remove them from the homes and the control of men. Their attitude greatly changed, however, as they themselves assumed responsibility for community development, and they came to favor education, even for girls and women.

USE OF VOLUNTARY GROUPS FOR CHANGE

Slum areas often have a number of voluntary groups, some of them traditional. They may be based on tribal, village, caste, and ethnic ties, as well as on some types of formal organization; *mohalla* committees, sports groups, lodges, and clubs, for example. Sometimes such groups carry on a few organized self-help activities for the communities. In general, however, they are poorly organized and functionally weak. In addition, their organization and functions often have continued with no re-examination in the light of changing social conditions. These groups can often be redirected, and new goals can do much to change slum conditions. In Delhi, for example, some *mohalla* committees, which had long histories, were revitalized, and their objectives were changed toward more useful functions. The identification and utilization of similar groups in slum areas of other cultures may furnish further mechanisms for social change. In slum areas in the United States, for example, there are churches, fraternal organizations, ethnic-group organizations, social clubs, and neighborhood taverns with largely regular clienteles, which already command the loyalties of many people.[22] Groups like the store-front churches, which are not usually reached in traditional community-organization efforts, are encouraged, for example, by Mobilization for Youth on New York's Lower East Side to plan cultural, social, and social-action programs emphasizing the interests and "styles" of lower-income groups.

CHANGE IN IDENTITY OR SELF-IMAGE

Apathy and lack of confidence in self-help characterize most beginning slum-improvement projects, but newly created self-images provide motivating forces for slum people to change their practices. Change in identity or self-image and recognition of different expectations are essential in any successful slum-action program. Planned identity change includes awakening the desire for change, new experiences to change self-image, commitment to change in self-identity, and recognition by others of new identities and roles.[23] Haggstrom has suggested that successful social or community action by a poorer person enhances his conception of his own worth and helps to overcome his feelings of powerlessness.

> In our society inner worth as expressed in action, striving, the struggle is held eventually to result in attainment of aspirations. If one is not successful, one is viewed as worthwhile so long, and only so long, as one struggles. The poor tend to be regarded as failures and not struggling, and hence as worthless. This perception of worthlessness is incorporated in the conception which others have of the poor and also, to some extent, in the conceptions which the poor have of themselves. One way in which the poor can remedy the psychological consequences of their powerlessness and of the image of the poor as worthless is for them to undertake social action that redefines them as potentially worthwhile and individually more powerful. To be effective, such social action should have the following characteristics:
>
> 1. The poor see themselves as the source of the action;
> 2. the action affects in major ways the preconceptions, values, or interests of institutions and persons defining the poor;
> 3. the action demands much in effort and skill or in other ways becomes salient to major areas of the personalities of the poor;
> 4. the action ends in success;
> 5. the successful self-originated important action increases the force and number of symbolic or nonsymbolic communications of the potential worth or individual power of individuals who are poor.[24]

The desire for status has been a useful tool in changing the self-image, for as one student of urban affairs has declared: "The awakening of self-respect is the most powerful agent for renewing our cities socially, and for that matter physically. Partly this must be earned; partly it must be freely given."[25] In the Delhi project, efforts were made to develop feelings of importance, prestige, and respectability, among slum dwellers. A new self-conception was developed in several ways: numbering and whitewashing houses, acquiring offices and supplies, printing letterhead stationery, and visiting historical and cultural centers. Similarly, wider participation in the larger society, through reporting the community's activities to important people, camping trips for officers, discussions of the Five-Year Plans, and other techniques, helped to lend respectability. Women assumed greater responsibility for change within the new type of organization based on territorial ties, and their active participation helped to demonstrate their social equality as well as to change their images of themselves. Similarly, change in the Liyari self-help project in Karachi slums has been greatly helped by the fact that some residents are now able to mingle with members of the more respectable classes of the city, partly through meetings of their citizen leaders with others but also partly through pride in the achievements of their groups. For example, the Girl Guide troop of Liyari, supported by the citizen-development council, won first place in the All-Pakistan competition for cleanliness; the Liyari Boy Scout troop won second in a drama contest.

The importance of changes in identity has been particularly stressed in the Black Muslim movement in the United States.[26] Working largely in some of the most difficult lower-class Negro slums, this movement tries to develop a new image of the Negro. In their small mosques in neighborhood areas great stress is placed on their proud African heritage and the rejection of the appendages carried over from slavery. The new convert experiences a "rebirth" in self-image, in which he changes his name (the names of most Negroes are those of their slave owners), his religion (Christianity was imposed by slavery), his idea of his African homeland, his moral and cultural values, and his very purpose in life. Among Black Muslims pride in Africa means that new patterns of behavior must be practiced by the lower-class slum Negro if behavior and the new self-image are to be reconciled. A strict private and public morality is emphasized for the "new Negro"; crime, delinquency, drug addiction, and illegitimacy no longer fit this new self-image. Family roles are also redefined; a patriarchal system is substituted for a matriarchal. Family responsibility is expected of the men, who are also expected to live soberly and with dignity, be honest, work hard, and devote themselves to their families' welfare. Women are to be treated with dignity and respect, given protection and security. In turn, women should dress and behave circumspectly, they should learn modesty and thrift, and the women's auxiliary often even learns how to set "a middle-class table" worthy of the "new Negro."

Although derived from a sect based on religious conflict, this general approach is highly suggestive for slum work elsewhere. Interest among American slum Negroes in Africa and its achievements has been developed as a method of change by others than Black Muslims, as for example, in the Harlem Youth Opportunities project (HARYOU-Act). Efforts are directed at increasing pride in Africa, such ancient cultures as the highly developed Ashanti culture, the Benin bronzes, and the new independent African nations. This emphasis helps to overcome the stigma of former slavery and the void in ancestral pride that had existed.*

USE OF INDIGENOUS LEADERS AND NONPROFESSIONAL WORKERS

Change in slum areas is unlikely to occur by itself: Certain people must act as agents to initiate the process of change. It has long been customary to use educated people, generally professionally trained, in the slums. They have generally been social workers, community organizers, or urban-extension agents. Certainly, the role of some outsiders is to act as indispensable catalysts of change. "New forms and patterns of action have often come about only when an outside element has been added to the political chemistry."[27] A new trend is emerging, however, toward relying on such professional people but working through indigenous leaders. The latter are viewed not merely as extensions of the professional workers but as players of distinct roles in their own right.[28] This view has great implications for developed countries, but in the less developed countries, where professional persons are few in number, the consequences of such an approach, if it is valid, are even greater.† In Sweden, citizen youth boards, rather than the courts, deal with juvenile delinquents, and juvenile and adult offenders are placed on probation to volunteer probation officers. Various union groups in the United States have shop stewards who perform many of the functions of social workers or professional counselors.

The possibilities for using volunteer and paid indigenous leaders to deal with the problems of the slums are extensive. In the Delhi project, as in others, such people were used as volunteer community organizers and effective leaders

---

* In Detroit, Negro faces and allusions have been incorporated into first-grade primers as an act of respect, particularly for the large number of Negro children attending schools in the slum areas.
† Actually, the use of ordinary citizens in dealing with various problems is not a new approach. Great numbers of civilians were brought into defense work during World War II as volunteer firemen, policemen, first-aid nurses, airplane spotters, and rationing officials. Citizen groups have assumed responsibility for dealing with common problems with which members are personally concerned. These groups include Alcoholics Anonymous, Narcotics Anonymous and Synanon, Recovery Incorporated, and clubs of older people. Such groups have been formed by the members to aid in the rehabilitation of the alcoholic, the drug addict, and former mental patients and to help overcome the loneliness of old age. The best-known example is the membership of Alcoholics Anonymous, which claims 300,000 members in 6,000 chapters. These self-help groups deal with the difficult problems of alcoholism without professional assistance. See Marshall B. Clinard, *Sociology of Deviant Behavior* (rev. ed.; New York: Holt, Rinehart & Winston, Inc., 1963), Chapter 22, "The Group Approach to Social Reintegration."

in capacities ranging from community planning to the distribution of milk. In a New York City project, slum women have been used as education aides in the schools, making home visits and carrying out other duties. Homemakers with little education have been hired to help welfare recipients at home. In the bus depot in Chicago, women from the poor areas of the southern Appalachian mountains work at Traveler's Aid to assist new arrivals from those areas. High-school students from slum areas have been employed as tutors for others. Those slum dwellers who have vocational skills could also be employed to teach others.

Indigenous or nonprofessional people have an advantage in stimulating social change, as they are more closely linked to the people and their problems.[29] Many slum residents are "significant others," with considerable power and influence.[30] Themselves part of the problem-producing environment, they may be more able to establish effective communication patterns in the area. Many have more inside knowledge of "traditional efforts" to deal with the slum and can even change the professional workers' thinking about their problems, as the indigenous workers may perceive problems differently from the professional. This leadership also provides large-scale supplements to manpower, resulting in wider coverage of slum areas, and helps to reduce unemployment among that very group whose limited education and training may keep it unemployed or underemployed. Even when such people are employed on a part- or full-time paid basis, the approach is likely to be less costly and more effective.

The indigenous worker may present a new image to slum dwellers, a model that the professional worker can seldom be, as most have had no previous slum experience. Participation of the indigenous leaders in wider community activities gives greater power to slum groups, and, as a result, apathy and perception of inferiority may decrease and the desire for change may increase. Indigenous leadership also develops skill in dealing with the police and other public agencies. Such skill helps residents gain confidence in dealing with community problems and may even lead eventually to attacks on more specialized and technical problems. It may be that, out of such indigenous leadership in community development, may come a new and more dedicated group of political leaders, who are badly needed in large urban areas, particularly those in developing countries like India.

Finally, this type of work produces jobs for slum dwellers in a field in which limited professional staff is available, which is the case in most developed countries and particularly in developing countries. Many middle-class professionals and other people are becoming reluctant to work directly with slum people. "The current trend in most of the human service areas, such as social work and psychiatry, is for an increasing ratio of time to be spent on consultation, supervision, teaching, and a decreasing proportion of time in direct service."[31]

The task of the professional in social work, adult education, or extension is to identify and train effective indigenous leaders. The identification of effective local leadership that is also representative is not easy. It is often easy enough to find volunteers, but they may not be representative. The more representative are likely to be poorly educated and may even themselves exhibit many of the problem attitudes of the area. Training indigenous leaders requires extensive reorientation in professional thinking. It calls for the selection of what is important in the indigenous leader's world. Training also must emphasize nonpartisan roles, the confidential nature of the activities, and changes in attitudes toward outside authority.[32]

Although the development of widespread indigenous and nonprofessional, rather than professional, leadership is essential in dealing with the slum, several problems arise, including how to keep the indigenous leader "indigenous" and the nonprofessional "nonprofessional." Such leaders can easily adopt the attitudes and mannerisms of the professional and middle classes, as they become pleased with their new roles, status, and influence. In such cases, they may reject the very people whom they are to lead. The use of nonprofessional slum dwellers in providing homemaker services to slum families in the United States, for example, has presented such problems. People who have lived in slums and have managed to move up have themselves often developed middle-class attitudes toward the poor. As Pearl and Riessman have put it, "We were, in effect, asking our indigenous staff to walk through those very doors which they had managed to slide by most of their lives."[33]

There is also the constant danger of political and partisan influences on the indigenous worker. Motivations for personal power may become important, and power struggles may develop among leaders. The initial enthusiasm of such lay leaders must be maintained, for they are likely to overreact to reverses. These problems can be met, in part, through training programs and the informal guidance of professional workers, provided they can overcome suspicion of their professionalism and their higher social class. In this connection, more professional and nonprofessional people with lower-class backgrounds and experience in slums might be recruited. Providing they do not reject their backgrounds, they can use knowledge that may improve work with indigenous leaders.

REPRESENTATIVE COMMUNITY LEADERSHIP

The mobilization of slum people for effective action requires that they participate in leadership at both the neighborhood and city-wide levels, something which they now rarely do anywhere. "Citizen participation has relevance to improving the slum conditions," as one writer has suggested, "because one of the attributes of slum people is that they are out and they feel out. . . . The poor and the slum residents know that things are run by somebody else. They have no stake in the larger community, they do not make its decisions and most do not expect to get anywhere in it."[34] In the cities of most countries, the boards of city and neighborhood welfare groups, including health, welfare, and hospital boards, consist primarily of what are called "public-spirited" citizens. Close inspection reveals that they often do not represent the larger population and that most come from the middle and upper socioeconomic groups. Exceptions can be found, of course, but the ordinary people of the slum remain in the minority, whereas they often constitute a large proportion of the urban population with which such boards are mainly concerned.*

People of the middle class may become involved with the problems of the slums, either because they are concerned with the welfare of slum residents and want to help them or because their own neighborhoods are being encroached upon by slums and they wish to prevent blight. When middle-class residents work together in community-organization efforts to improve their own neighborhoods, the chances for success are fairly high, because the middle class, unlike the lower classes, is more experienced in analyzing problems and taking the necessary steps to solve them. Its members are better able to deal with city officials, are better equipped to work cooperatively in neighborhood organizations, and have more financial backing for whatever action may be necessary to reach their objectives. It is nevertheless often true that, however well middle-class people may be able to cooperate, attempts to foster mutual action between the middle and lower or working classes are sometimes ineffective. In some attempts at joint action, the members of the middle class are likely to take over or be given leadership that tends to create hostility among the less educated, lower-income members.[35] Such was the case in the Hyde Park-Kenwood Community Conference in Chicago, which was intended to represent all the neighborhood residents but which nevertheless mainly advanced the interests of the middle-class leaders of the project.[36]

Even more common perhaps is the preponderance of the better educated and of area businessmen among the leaders of slum communities. Citizen participation often means participation of the upwardly mobile person who will leave the slum anyway or of businessmen, clergymen, teachers, and government employees who live in or near the area and officers and staff members of various welfare and cultural organizations. Some people may believe that such participation is good, as leaders of this type have backgrounds, accomplishments, and experience that can provide more "intelligent leadership" for the

---

* An important study of a large city found that the average individual had no voice in policy determination. The most important policy group, the community council, "does not represent all members of the community . . . Generally speaking, the ordinary citizen is not represented upon these boards." The residential location, primarily in suburban areas, of those in power tends, furthermore, to isolate them from the mass of the people and the problems of the community. Floyd Hunter, *Community Power Structure: A Study of Decision Makers* (Chapel Hill: University of North Carolina Press, 1953), p. 251.

city and the various slum areas. All too often, however, decisions and planning are made for the poor on the assumption that they are not competent. "Successful people" are supposed to make decisions, and typical slum residents are by definition not successful.

It should be quite apparent, however, that "successful" neighborhood leadership may not have the backing of the majority of the average neighborhood residents; there may be "leaders" without followers. The type of "neighborhood organization" that involves round-table discussions by the leading citizens of a neighborhood may provide interesting pastimes for the middle-class elements of the community, but its effectiveness as an instrument of slum improvement through urban community development is open to serious question. As Hunter has put it, phoniness in citizen participation is not wanted: "Reform or improvement efforts will not get far if the people who are 'improved' are not themselves engaged in the improvement process."[37] Leadership from the lower-status groups may often be slow and cumbersome, but in the long run it may produce greater results. Slum dwellers tend to be reluctant to cooperate with those who do not also live in the slums and who will gain most of the credit for any positive changes. The problem is largely one of effective communication and motivation, and, in a sense, the people "speak the same language."

The basic purpose of urban community development is the preparation of ordinary people for assuming democratic responsibilities. Potential indigenous leadership must be identified and developed. It is a mistake to rely upon formal, traditional leaders and the better educated, for leadership from higher-status groups may inhibit the growth of leadership from below. The election of indigenous leaders is more effective than the use of well-meaning volunteers, for in this way the energies and enthusiasms of the average slum dwellers, many of whom have never before held positions of leadership, can be released.

A program for creating new citizen leadership, for example, was initiated in 1965 by Community Progress, Inc., a large-scale experimental project begun in 1962 in New Haven to deal with the problems of the poorer areas of the city. A representative from each of the seven neighborhood project areas was elected to the board of directors, and a twenty-one-member residents' advisory committee of three representatives from each neighborhood was also elected. The purpose of this new approach was to expand and formalize the participation of inner-city residents in the policy making, planning, improvement, and evaluation of New Haven's community action programs in problem areas. The residents of each neighborhood developed their own election mechanisms and conducted elections; in four neighborhoods the elections were by public balloting at designated polling places.

Encouraging participation in community affairs has the beneficial effect of raising the perceived status of a slum dweller and thus paves the way for solving many slum problems. It demonstrates to the low-income community that the larger community is interested in its point of view, provides "success models" in upward mobility for slum residents, and introduces new perspectives and new realism into the solution of community problems.*

GIVING RESPONSIBILITY AND CREDIT TO ORDINARY PEOPLE

Too often responsibility and credit for accomplishments in the slums go primarily to private or governmental agencies or to political parties, whose leaders may bask in the glory of accomplishments while blaming the people for lethargy and failures. In many, welfare centers or workers may be the means of "identifying" the slum group. Other well-meaning business and professional organizations may boast of their efforts to better the slums, whereas what is actually reflected is the work of thousands of ordinary slum citizens. Although the purpose of urban community development is the improvement of slum areas and the city as a whole, the local social-welfare or government agency, rather than the people, often becomes the point of emphasis.

Local leadership must be given credit as well as responsibility, particularly when it is truly representative. Such credit develops confidence and pride. There can be little compromise on the principle of giving credit to the people of the slums. Either they receive practically all the credit, which is in itself a motivating factor, or they lose their continuing enthusiasm and may become disillusioned by work with private or governmental agencies and their workers even when it benefits the area. People who are doing something for themselves can be a potent force, whether in improving health and sanitation or in curbing juvenile delinquency.

THE USE OF CONFLICT AND THE NEED FOR POWER IN SOCIAL CHANGE

Social conflict may have a positive function, as Simmel and more recently Coser have pointed out.[38] Conflict may help to establish or re-establish group unity and cohesion, serving as a binding element among parties that have previously had little relationship with one another. Conflict also helps to revitalize existing norms or contributes to the emergence of new norms, and it helps to establish and maintain a balance of power among contending parties. Conflict can "serve as a means for ascertaining the relative strength of antagonistic interests within the structure, and in this way constitute a mechanism for the maintenance or continual readjustment of the balance of power.

---

* Hunter also points out, however, that a slum resident who suddenly becomes a member of community-wide voluntary organizations and activities will perhaps gain status among the middle class of his city, but he may be regarded by his fellow slum dwellers as a "traitor" and may lose all his influence in his neighborhood. See David R. Hunter, *The Slums: Challenge and Response* (New York: The Free Press, 1964), p. 196.

Since the outbreak of the conflict indicates a rejection of a previous accommodation between parties, once the respective power of the contenders has been ascertained through conflict, a new equilibrium can be established and the relationship can proceed on this new basis. Consequently, a social structure in which there is room for conflict disposes of an important means for avoiding or redressing conditions of disequilibrium by modifying the terms of power relations."[39]

The use of conflict tactics may be called for in urban community-development projects when the problems of a slum are viewed as "political." The slum dweller's dilemma has been his own lack of power. Being lower in economic status, moving outside the sources of social and political power, and usually being apathetic or subject to political manipulation, he has often become a pawn in the urban world. It has been suggested that slum dwellers need to achieve some unity among themselves, as well as some degree of militancy, which will eventuate in their recognition as part of the power structure and in their proper demands for services and opportunities being met.

The problem of the poor involves not simply an economic nexus but a power nexus as well.[40] Slum dwellers generally react with apathy to their own powerlessness. They are constantly reminded of this powerlessness by public and private welfare agencies, by the police, by absentee landlords, and by urban-renewal programs. When slum dwellers do engage in successful social action, they gain a certain degree of power, even though their incomes are not materially changed. Consequently, their attitudes may change. Through demonstration of their power in successful social change, additional situational changes may come about, which are defined as desirable by the slum dwellers themselves rather than by powerful outsiders.

> Work done with the residents of slum communities should aim at two targets: giving the poor a sense that they can, through their own initiative (and political action), affect the world around them, and giving the poor a sense that they can, through solidarity with others, organize to alter successfully their environment. Individual initiative, group initiative, and political action: These are also major weapons. The beginning of salvation for the poor will be the realization that they can, through their own initiative and effort—and not by depending on hand-me-downs from higher authorities—control their own destinies.[41]

The people of the slum are poor, poorly educated, and ineffective in their communications with the outside world. In some areas, no unity may exist, and ethnic, regional, tribal, caste, or religious groups may actually be hostile toward one another. Under these circumstances, slum people are often ignored or exploited by more powerful and organized groups; the "haves" are committed to the maintenance of the *status quo* within the slums, and the "have nots" struggle to change it. A conflict-group approach to slum problems assumes that, in order for the "have nots" to bring about improvement and change that are ignored or opposed by such powerful institutions as city government, large industrial plants, and the more wealthy who may have to pay for them, it is necessary to accumulate *power* to escape the control of such institutions. According to this position, as Alinsky has pointed out, there are only two sources of power: money and people.[42] As slum people have little money, their only way to achieve power is through organizing the people. The creation of a power structure in the slum that would be capable of bringing about improvements requires arousing the slum dweller from his typical apathy and hopelessness. This effort demands extensive and careful organization techniques, and the slum dweller must be offered something of interest once he has been brought into a neighborhood organization. In this respect, the use of conflict offers a second advantage, for the excitement and activity it generates tend to maintain the enthusiasm and support of the slum dweller. If conflict and controversy are allowed to wane, the interest of the people in the neighborhood will also fade. These citizens' organizations constitute new power groups, and any new power group automatically becomes an intrusion and even a threat to the existing power structure of a city. It may become a conflict group when for various reasons it attempts to make changes in housing, rental practices, or public services.

Conflict provided some motivating force in the Delhi project. In nearly all the projects, the "government," in the form of the Municipal Corporation, had been regarded as responsible for many slum difficulties, whether in sanitation, in health, or in insufficient water facilities. The people's doing things for themselves and putting pressure on the "inefficient" municipality to aid them in their efforts were important forces for change. Difficulties with private landlords (and, in some cases, the municipality was the landlord) also furnished an important rallying point for developing *vikas mandals* and performing functions that the "miserable" landlords had long neglected.*

Conflict tactics have been used in several urban community-development projects carried out in the United States.† They have been widely used in civil-rights demonstrations. The use of conflict tactics has been indirectly employed in several projects like Mobilization for Youth in New York City, in campaigns against landlords to improve their slum properties, in rent strikes,

---

* Conflict has been found to play a role in bringing about more successful social integration in slum areas in Latin America. After studying slums in Cali, Lima, and San Juan, Rogler concluded that only adversity and hostility will produce effective neighborhood organization by recreating quasi-rural patterns as an aggressive response to the progressive limitation of options. Lloyd H. Rogler, "Slum Neighborhoods in Latin America," unpublished paper quoted in Richard M. Morse, "Recent Research on Latin American Urbanization: A Selective Survey with Commentary," *Latin American Research Review*, 1 (Fall, 1965), 35–74.

† Conflict tactics are used by the Black Muslims to weld the group together; they include emphasis on strict racial separation, the evil of the white man, the failure of traditional churches, and definition of middle- and upper-class Negroes as selfish "Uncle Toms."

and in campaigns to register slum voters. These tactics have served to solidify communities and to give them some sense of power. Over the past thirty years the Industrial Areas Foundation, whose founder and director is Saul Alinsky, has assisted in the formation of forty-four citizens' organizations involving more than two million people throughout the country, including four in Chicago and several in Mexican-American communities. It uses conflict as the main mechanism for change.[43] Alinsky's conflict model of social action appears to produce results, for even a critic has stated that :

> Alinsky's model deserves careful attention for a number of factors it demonstrates: (1) Social action and community organization can be accomplished in low-income communities (The poor, apparently, are not as apathetic as they are said to be when given appropriate alternatives to be unapathetic about.); (2) Social action can be quite inexpensive and does not require a huge outlay of government funds; (3) Representatives of all religions and classes can be united in community action groups; (4) Social action organizations can withstand witch hunt tactics; and (5) It is relatively easy to find indigenous leadership in poor communities.[44]

An example of work done by the Industrial Areas Foundation is The Woodlawn Organization (TWO) in a Negro area immediately south of The University of Chicago, which has one of the highest population densities in the city.[45] Conflict tactics came into play in 1961, when the university announced plans for an urban-renewal project in which North Woodlawn would be annexed for campus expansion. The entire Woodlawn community was aroused, and a planning committee was formed to bargain with the city and the university. This group, which hired planning consultants, drew up a plan emphasizing rehabilitation of existing buildings rather than mass clearance. Favorite tactics of The Woodlawn Organization have included picketing and other mass demonstrations. Stores suspected of giving false weights have been boycotted and picketed, rent strikes have been organized against landlords who have failed to comply with housing codes, and, when strikes have failed, groups of Woodlawn citizens have gone to the homes of absentee landlords to picket with signs like "Your Neighbor is a Slumlord." One well-publicized display of strength and effort to build community spirit came soon after the formation of The Woodlawn Organization, when forty-three buses were chartered to take residents to the city hall to register to vote. Other activities of the organization have been directed at school integration, help for families in financial distress, youth-recreation programs, and the establishment of "community living rooms," special rooms reserved in apartment houses for social and educational functions of nearby residents.

Hunter has questioned the use of conflict, however, as a means to achieve change in slum areas. He questions how the energy generated by the deliberate use of conflict and the exacerbation of raw issues can be translated into institutional change.[46] Militancy must be accompanied by the subtle involvement of bureaucracy in efforts to bring about change. It is difficult to distinguish the line between the good and bad effects of conflict in social change. In some situations, it may be a prerequisite to overcoming apathy and roadblocks imposed from outside, and, in others, it may become an end in itself within the slum neighborhood.

The use of conflict by slum dwellers is likely to result in strong negative reactions from the middle class, which may take the view that lower-class people should not use tactics like strikes and protest marches. If the middle class uses conflict tactics, the question is different; because of its social position, it may have the right to do so. Furthermore, politicians and others are likely to grow uneasy as the slum dwellers gain independence and power through the use of conflict.

COMPETITION AMONG LOCAL GROUPS

Within a broad program of urban community development, competition for status among communities can increase the unity, pride, and involvement of slum dwellers and can also facilitate change. For example, in the Delhi project regular inter-*vikas mandal* athletic competitions were used to stimulate self-help and local pride; contests were also held to choose the healthiest or best-cared-for child, and visits between projects were arranged. At such meetings, officers of the various projects learned what other groups working together under similar conditions had been able to achieve and what objectives they had found impossible to achieve or perhaps had not even considered. These and other procedures helped to create community identity among the diverse groups. Officers became conscious of the fact that they represented "areas" and that any personal shortcomings might reflect upon the status of the areas. At one meeting of citizen-council presidents, an illiterate president was observed avidly "reading" a newspaper so that he would not embarrass his group in the presence of literate leaders. In another, an illiterate person who was chairing a meeting of officers of other *vikas mandals* was seen to "follow" carefully an agenda of the meeting by pointing, as though he could read, to items on the list that had been prepared by the community organizers.

CHAIN REACTIONS IN SOCIAL CHANGE

Well-entrenched slum practices, difficult to change under any conditions, may be approached in circuitous fashion. Success in the accomplishment of easier and more readily accepted objectives enables groups to tackle those of increasing difficulty. In this way, a chain reaction may be set in motion. This principle can be illustrated from the Delhi project, where a beginning was made with such traditional practices as the singing of religious songs and followed, step by step, through child-care competitions, child-care classes, and then family planning. The principle can also be illustrated by the relation of sewing classes to literacy training. One of the more popular self-help schemes was the craft classes, at which women learned to use sewing machines and to make clothes. This training offered them opportunities to clothe their families better and also possibly to earn supplemental income. As many of the women were illiterate, they could not easily take measurements or even place material properly for cutting. They could neither read the tape measure or ruler nor add the inches or feet, and they said, "Teach us this counting." This recognition of their own inadequacy often made them interested in self-help literacy programs. A Venezuelan urban community-development project also illustrates this principle.[47] It started with volleyball teams, which led to building a recreation area; later the teams were divided into bucket brigades to clean up the slum.

OUTSIDE ASSISTANCE IN ATTAINING OBJECTIVES

Slum people need help in recognizing their own needs and in organizing themselves to achieve their objectives. Although sometimes they may not be satisfied with many of the conditions under which they live and have often settled into patterns of acceptance, they have not had many opportunities to talk over their problems or their needs as a group. Outside intervention seems necessary almost by definition, for the continued existence of slum problems apparently demonstrates that slum dwellers, without some outside help or stimulation, are unable or have not wanted to change what are commonly thought of as problems. Assuming that they desire to change those features, they have not done so for several reasons. First, they lack experience in dealing with the middle-class world, they lack self-confidence, and they have not developed the ability to work effectively within an organization. A slum community seldom has a pattern for making decisions, and there may thus be no way of deciding that outside help is necessary. This lack stems from the slum dweller's inability to plan for the future, his apathy toward present conditions, his distrust of those who are not of his own group, and his limited educational and vocational aspirations. Projects that attempt to produce community change are thus likely to encounter unwillingness to admit weakness, fear of failure or awkwardness in initiating new practices or patterns, fatalistic expectations of failure reinforced by previous unsuccessful attempts to change, and fear of losing current satisfactions.[48]

This desire to preserve existing satisfactions has great significance in the slum when outside help is offered, for, as has been pointed out, the slum provides many outlets that slum dwellers cannot risk losing, even if it can be shown what benefits can be attained through community development. Other factors interfere with outside efforts to bring about community change. They include shortages of time, energy, and money; competition of other projects for these resources; lack of information about how to execute projects; and an environment that is simply intractable.[49]

Some important sources of outside intervention or help in slum improvement have been private citizen associations, welfare organizations, churches, and such various governmental units as extension services, adult education, separate departments to assist urban community development, public health services, and the schools. If such outside intervention is to be at all successful, the slum residents must accept it. Lower- and working-class people are highly suspicious of "outsiders," and the middle class, city-government employees, the police, and the settlement-house workers are often viewed by the lower and working classes with suspicion and often hostility. Opportunities, temptations, and pressures of the larger society are evaluated in terms of their effects upon the way of life built around the family circle or peer group, and any offer of outside help that threatens this pattern is likely to be rejected.

The outside-intervention approach can be illustrated by the government cooperative or agricultural-extension program that has existed for years in rural areas of the United States. One objective of the urban-extension technique is to encourage people to understand their needs as the education process takes hold and then to have them participate in satisfying these needs. A more recent application of this technique has been in experimental urban-extension work in slum and "gray" areas, an approach used extensively in Pittsburgh, where a large private organization is attempting to encourage acceptance of such a program. Programs have included homemaker service on a block basis; discussion guides for certain groups; radio programs in which experts answer questions from listeners; clinics on lawn care, tree planting, and yard work; and "how-to-do-it" classes in simple remodeling and painting of houses.[50]

The problems of slums and the apathy of urban populations are so great and so complex that outside intervention can hardly be left to hit-or-miss efforts by private welfare agencies and other private action groups. Even in those cities that have the most extensive neighborhood and settlement-house activities, only a fraction of the slum inhabitants is involved, and the operation of scattered projects supported by unintegrated organization has resulted neither in extensive coverage nor in coordinated attacks. Even an effective privately organized health-and-welfare council cannot adequately meet this problem. Private organizations interested in citizen involvement in renewal, delinquency, and similar projects only scratch the surface of the whole city, and they directly involve relatively small proportions of the people. For this reason, the city-wide effects of most settlement houses, neighborhood centers, and neighborhood councils have been very limited, for example, in the United States. Although one part of a city, with a high delinquency rate and deteriorated physical conditions, may be organized into a citizen council, nothing may be done in an adjoining area. "Islands of community work" remain largely islands of ineffectiveness.

The involvement of citizens in the development of neighborhood councils and the overcoming of public apathy toward urban problems are as much the responsibility of local government as are adequate water supplies and good school systems. Such efforts need not be confined to slum areas but can also be directed at creating new and improving existing community organizations of citizens in middle-class areas. An agency, a municipal department of urban community development or community services, might well be created to take responsibility for working toward the following objectives: (1) development of civic consciousness and responsibility among urban people; (2) development of the idea of self-help and assumption of responsibility by neighborhood people for solving their own problems; (3) the social integration of communities on a neighborhood basis through participation in self-help mutual-aid programs; (4) preparation of the ground for decentralizing some municipal services among the communities; and (5) planning citizen-involvement programs and their coordination with other private and public agencies.

The assumption of such responsibilities as a proper function of municipal government would give citizen participation both recognition and status. Such a department would be responsible for organizing and coordinating the work of citizen groups and would also help to represent them in the administration of governmental functions, a task now chiefly performed by elected officials like councilmen who, in large urban centers, may represent far more people than they can possibly deal with effectively. It could make plans on a city-wide basis, concentrating on certain areas where there might be particular needs for citizen groups. Furthermore, it could coordinate the activities of private organizations and health-and-welfare councils, along with the work of other municipal agencies. The establishment of a similar urban agency at the state or national level could further reinforce these efforts.

Some might fear the intrusion of politics into such work. Opportunities for political considerations have been present in many areas of municipal government, and, where such considerations are no longer major elements, it is partly because the problems have become too serious for political interference. Many slum problems like delinquency, violence, health, and sanitation have reached that point. Much would depend on the urban situation and the type of leadership and freedom given such a municipal department.

As a great deal of citizen work to improve urban conditions is being done by churches, business organizations, labor unions, and such other voluntary associations as tribal, ethnic, and village groups in the cities, this work could be coordinated and improved through some type of training program. Liaison officers from the staff of a municipal department could also help to improve the organization and work of these groups, as is done, for example, by Hong Kong *kaifongs* or volunteer-citizen neighborhood councils. In fact, a citizen approach to urban problems through governmental organization has been established in the last few years in several less developed areas, chiefly India, Pakistan, the Philippines, Colombia, Venezuela, and Hong Kong.[51] The philosophy and techniques of urban and rural community-development programs may become one of the chief exportable contributions of less developed countries to their more highly developed brethren. Certainly the sanitation and health problems of Dacca and Delhi are no greater than the juvenile-delinquency problems of New York, Chicago, and London.

A separate governmental agency charged with encouraging citizen participation may be regarded by some as a duplication of effort, as this function might well be handled by the old-line governmental agencies responsible for health, sanitation, and education. Urban community development is actually, however, a method for introducing a new dimension, through which urban people are given more responsibility and citizen cooperation in administrative programs is sought. Part of the continuing task of a separate municipal agency would be the education of other municipal departments in this important new approach to urban life. Private agencies would find this task difficult.*

DECENTRALIZATION OF SOME GOVERNMENTAL FUNCTIONS

The modern metropolis is so huge and sprawling that efficient management has become all but impossible, and the basic need for direct contact between the people and administrators of city services has frequently receded into the background. The very government designed to serve the people has become unwieldy. Political units like wards are too large and the problems too complicated for one councilman or alderman to handle.

An important goal of urban community development is the effective decentralization of some governmental authority and services through neighborhood citizen boards. A controlled decentralization of civic authority in an urban setting might result in greater support for government and might overcome some of the apathy and hostility of many urban citizens toward government. Greater neighborhood governmental responsibility might well improve the work of the police by changing slum people's attitudes toward them, develop greater interest in education and school programs, result in closer cooperation on sanitation problems, and afford protection to various public facilities like schools, parks, public water taps, and street lighting. One might, for example,

---

* Private welfare organizations in community work serve, and should continue to serve, an important function. Many have served as pioneers in this field. In any long-term effort to deal with the problems of the large city, the combined approaches of groups of citizens, private welfare agencies, and the municipal government would be required.

foresee the possibility of decentralized lay panels, in place of juvenile-court judges, to deal with delinquents, as is done in England and Sweden. Or slum school districts could have their own school boards, coordinated, of course, with the city school board. Programs operating through the schools to change slum ways need the support and backing of the adults in the community.

Such decentralization would depend upon the city's being divided into a series of smaller political units and the coordination of organized citizen groups in each of these units, which could consist of blocks, neighborhoods, and districts, according to population. In a number of countries, such units consist of urban wards with their own elective councils, like those in Tokyo,[52] Yugoslavia, Moscow, and Dar-es-Salaam, whose purpose is to improve the administration of government as a whole. In Pakistan, each city is divided into small units or basic democracies, whose committees help to coordinate the services of government with those of people.[53]

§ *Conclusions*

In conclusion, it should be reiterated that certain aspects of the slum problem in the developed or the less developed countries reach far beyond small areas and the possibilities of self-help. Certain functions of government in urban areas cannot be decentralized, and certain problems cannot be corrected at the local level. In both affluent and poor countries, there is a need for more equitable distribution of wealth and elimination of poverty, as well as for greatly improved housing conditions; in less affluent societies, there are acute problems of increased industrialization, overcoming widespread unemployment, and increasing health facilities. Despite these reservations, there is still much that can be done by slum people, and, for that matter, all urban people, to help themselves.

NOTES

CHAPTER 1

1   Eric Partridge, *Origins: A Short Etymological Dictionary of Modern English* (London: Routledge & Kegan Paul, Ltd, 1958).

2   Allan A. Twichell, "Measuring the Quality of Housing in Planning for Urban Redevelopment," in Coleman Woodbury, ed., *Urban Redevelopment: Problems and Practices* (Chicago: University of Chicago Press, 1953), pp. 25–30.

3   Urban Renewal Administration, Housing and Home Finance Agency, *Urban Renewal Manual* (Washington, D.C.: U.S. Government Printing Office, 1959), Section 10.1, "Selection and Treatment of Project Areas."

4   *United States Census of Housing: 1960*, Vol. 1, Part 1, United States Summary (Washington, D.C.: Department of Commerce, Bureau of the Census, 1961), p. lxiii.

5   *Ibid.*

6   David R. Hunter, *The Slums: Challenge and Response* (New York: The Free Press, 1964), p. 32.

7   William G. Grigsby, "Housing and Slum Clearance: Elusive Goals," *The Annals*, 352 (March, 1964), 107–18.

8   Quoted in Ruth Shonle Cavan, *Criminology* (2nd ed.; New York: Thomas Y. Crowell Company, 1955), p. 87.

9   Terrence Morris, *The Criminal Area: A Study in Social Ecology* (London: Routledge & Kegan Paul, Ltd, 1957).

10   Miles L. Colean, *Renewing Our Cities* (New York: The Twentieth Century Fund, 1953), p. 41.

11   Herbert J. Gans, *The Urban Villagers: Group and Class in the Life of Italian-Americans* (New York: The Free Press, 1962), p. 310.

12   See Jane Jacobs, *The Death and Life of Great American Cities* (Vintage ed.; New York: Alfred A. Knopf, Inc., 1961).

13   Michael Harrington, *The Other America: Poverty in the United States* (New York: The Macmillan Company, 1962), p. 70.

14   William F. Whyte, *Street Corner Society* (Chicago: University of Chicago Press, 1943), p. 283.

15   Charles Abrams, *Man's Struggle for Shelter in an Urbanizing World* (Cambridge, Mass.: The M.I.T. Press, 1964), p. 6.

16   E. Franklin Frazier, *The Negro in the United States* (rev. ed.; New York: The Macmillan Company, 1957), p. 636.

17   See Jacobs, *op. cit.*, pp. 55–73.

18   Chester W. Hartman, "Social Values and Housing Orientations," *Journal of Social Issues*, XIX (April, 1963), 113–31.

19   Maurice R. Davie, *Negroes in American Society* (New York: McGraw-Hill Book Company, 1949), p. 220.

20   The Indian Conference of Social Work, *Report of the Seminar on Slum Clearance* (Bombay: Mouj Printing Bureau, 1957), p. 81.

21   Abrams, *op. cit.*, p. 5.

22   United Nations, *Report on the World Social Situation* (New York: United Nations Publication, 1957).

23   David Hunter, *op. cit.*, p. 77.

24   Kenneth B. Clark, *Dark Ghetto: Dilemmas of Social Power* (New York: Harper & Row, Publishers, 1965), p. 31.

25   David Hunter, *op. cit.*, p. 71.

26   For a survey of the studies, see Ernest R. Mowrer, *Disorganization, Personal and Social* (Philadelphia: J. B. Lippincott Co., 1942).

27   *Final Report to Honorable Frank P. Zeidler, Mayor, City of Milwaukee* (Milwaukee: Study Committee on Social

Problems in the Inner Core of the City, 1960).

28 R. B. Navin, W. B. Peattie, and F. R. Stewart, *An Analysis of a Slum Area in Cleveland* (Cleveland: Metropolitan Housing Authority, 1934).

29 Calvin F. Schmid, "Urban Crime Areas: Part II," *American Sociological Review*, 25 (October, 1960), 655–78.

30 Henry Allen Bullock, "Urban Homicide in Theory and Fact," *Journal of Criminal Law, Criminology, and Police Science*, 45 (January-February, 1955), 565–75; and Marvin E. Wolfgang, *Patterns in Criminal Homicide* (Philadelphia: University of Pennsylvania Press, 1958).

31 See Clifford R. Shaw, *Delinquency Areas* (Chicago: University of Chicago Press, 1929); Shaw, Henry D. McKay, and James F. McDonald, *Brothers in Crime* (Chicago: University of Chicago Press, 1938), especially Chapter V, "The Community Background"; Shaw, *The Natural History of a Delinquent Career* (Chicago: University of Chicago Press, 1931), especially Chapter II, "A Delinquency Area"; Shaw, *The Jack Roller* (Chicago: University of Chicago Press, 1930); and Frederic M. Thrasher, *The Gang* (Chicago: University of Chicago Press 1927), especially Chapter I, "Gangland."

32 Shaw and McKay, *Juvenile Delinquency and Urban Areas* (Chicago: University of Chicago Press, 1942).

33 *Indices of Social Problems* (New York: New York City Youth Board, 1960).

34 Isidor Chein, Donald L. Gerard, Robert S. Lee, and Eva Rosenfeld, *The Road to H: Narcotics, Delinquency and Social Policy* (New York: Basic Books, Inc., 1964), p. 73.

35 Morris, *op. cit.* For discussions of delinquent neighborhoods in cities of Scotland, see John Mack, "Full-Time Miscreants, Delinquent Neighborhoods and Criminal Networks," *The British Journal of Sociology*, XV (March, 1964), 38–53.

36 See United Nations, *op. cit.*; and Marshall B. Clinard, "The Organization of Urban Community Development Services in the Prevention of Crime and Juvenile Delinquency, with Particular Reference to Less Developed Countries," *International Review of Criminal Policy*, 19 (1962), 3–16.

37 Shankar S. Srivastava, *Juvenile Vagrancy: A Socio-Ecological Study of Juvenile Vagrants in the Cities of Kanpur and Lucknow* (New York: Asia Publishing House, 1963).

38 See, for example, Whyte, *op. cit.*

39 Solomon Kobrin, "The Conflict of Values in Delinquency Areas," *American Sociological Review*, 16 (October, 1951), 653–61.

40 Robert E. L. Faris and H. Warren Dunham, *Mental Disorders in Urban Areas* (Chicago: University of Chicago Press, 1939); and Dunham, "Current Status of Ecological Research in Mental Disorders," *Social Forces*, 25 (March, 1947), 321–7. Also see H. Warren Dunham, *Community and Schizophrenia: An Epidemiological Analysis* (Detroit: Wayne State University Press, 1965).

41 August B. Hollingshead and Frederick C. Redlich, *Social Class and Mental Illness* (New York: John Wiley & Sons, Inc., 1958).

42 Leo Srole, *et al.*, *Mental Health and the Metropolis: The Midtown Manhattan Study* (New York: McGraw-Hill Book Company, 1962), p. 213; and Thomas S. Langner and Stanley T. Michael, *Life Stress and Mental Health* (New York: The Free Press, 1963). Also see Frank Riessman, Jerome Cohen, and Arthur Pearl, *Mental Health of the Poor* (New York: The Free Press, 1964).

43 Quoted in Arthur Hillman, *Neighborhood Centers Today: Action Programs for a Rapidly Changing World* (New York: National Federation of Settlements and Neighborhood Centers, 1960), pp. 20–1.

44 See particularly Oscar Lewis, *The Children of Sanchez: Autobiography of a Mexican Family* (New York: Random House, Inc., 1961), especially the introduction; and Lewis, "The Culture of Poverty," *Trans-Action*, 1 (November, 1963), 17, 19. Also see Lewis, *Five Families: Mexican Case Studies in the Culture of Poverty* (Vintage ed.; New York: Alfred A. Knopf, Inc., 1959).

45 See Lewis, *The Children of Sanchez*, pp. xxv–xxvii; Walter B. Miller, "Lower Class Culture as a Generating Milieu of Gang Delinquency," *The Journal of Social Issues*, XIV (March, 1958), 5–19; Jerome Cohen, "Social Work and the Culture of Poverty," *Social Work*, 9 (January, 1964), 3–11; Elizabeth Herzog, "Some Assumptions about the Poor," *Social Service Review*, XXXVII (December, 1963), 389–402; Joseph A. Kahl, *The American Class Structure* (New York: Holt, Rinehart & Winston, Inc., 1957), pp. 211–12; St. Clair Drake and Horace Cayton, *Black Metropolis* (New York: Harcourt, Brace & World, Inc., 1945); Whyte, *op. cit.*; and Gans, *op. cit.*

46 Herzog, *op. cit.*

47 Sydney M. Miller, "The American Lower Class: A Typological Approach," *Social Research*, 31 (Spring, 1964), 1–22. Also see S. M. Miller, Riessman, and Arthur A. Seagull, "Poverty and Self-Indulgence: A Critique of the Non-deferred Gratification Pattern," in Louis A. Ferman, Joyce L. Kornbluh, and Alan Haber, eds., *Poverty in America* (Ann Arbor: University of Michigan Press, 1965), pp. 285–302.

48 S. M. Miller, "The American Lower Class."

49 Gans, *op. cit.*, p. 246.

50 *Ibid.*, p. 244.

51 See Gans, *op. cit.*, p. 170.

52 Srole, *et al.*, *op. cit.*

53 Hollingshead and Redlich, *op. cit.*

54 David Hunter, *op. cit.*, p. 18.

55 *Ibid.*

56 Hollingshead, *Elmtown's Youth* (New York: John Wiley & Sons, Inc., 1949), p. 111.

57 Walter Firey, *Land Use in Central Boston* (Cambridge, Mass.: Harvard University Press, 1947), p. 179.

58 Whyte, *op. cit.*, p. xv.

59 John R. Seeley, "The Slum: Its Nature, Use, and Users," *Journal of the American Institute of Planners*, XXV (February, 1959), 7–14.

60 Gans, *op. cit.* Also see Edward J. Ryan, "Personal Identity in an Urban Slum," in Leonard J. Duhl, ed., *The Urban Condition: People and Policy in the Metropolis* (New York: Basic Books, Inc., 1963), pp. 135–50.

61 W. B. Miller, *op. cit.*; and Martin Loeb, "Implications of Status Differentiation for Personal and Social Implications," *Harvard Educational Review*, XXIII (Summer, 1953), 168–74.

62 See, for example, Faris, *Social Disorganization* (New York: The Ronald Press Company, 1948), p. 203; and Svend Riemer, *The Modern City* (Englewood Cliffs, N.J.: Prentice-Hall, Inc., 1952), p. 148.

63 See, for example, Whyte, *op. cit.*; Gans, *op. cit.*; and Thrasher, *op. cit.*

64 W. B. Miller, "Implications of Lower Class Culture," *Social Service Review*, 33 (September, 1959), 219–36.

65 Whyte, "Social Organization in the Slums," *American Sociological Review*, 8 (February, 1943), 34–9.

66 W. B. Miller, "Lower Class Culture," p. 19.

67 Richard A. Cloward and Lloyd E. Ohlin, *Delinquency and Opportunity* (New York: The Free Press, 1960), pp. 203–10.

68 Harvey W. Zorbaugh, *The Gold Coast and the Slum* (Chicago: University of Chicago Press, 1929), p. 82.

69 Shaw, *The Natural History of a Delinquent Career*, p. 15.

70 Charles E. Silberman, *Crisis in Black and White* (New York: Random House, Inc., 1964), p. 321.

71 Lawrence Frank Pisani, *The Italian in America* (New York: Exposition Press, 1957), pp. 62–4.

72 Moses Rischin, *The Promised City* (Cambridge, Mass.: Harvard University Press, 1962).

73 Seeley, *op. cit.*

74 Marc Fried and Peggy Gleicher, "Some Sources of Residential Satisfaction in an Urban Slum," *Journal of the American Institute of Planners*, 27 (November, 1961), 305–15.

75 Whyte, *Street Corner Society*, p. xvi.

76 Firey, *op. cit.*, p. 179.

77 Fried and Gleicher, *op. cit.*, pp. 305–15.

78 Riemer, "The Slum and Its People," in C. E. Elias, Jr., James Gillies, and Riemer, *Metropolis: Values in Conflict* (Belmont, California: Wadsworth Publishing Co., Inc., 1964), p. 251.

79 Riemer, *The Modern City*, p. 147.

80 Donald J. Bogue, *Skid Row in American Cities* (Chicago: Community and Family Study Center, University of Chicago, 1963), Chapter 2, "Who Lives on Skid Row and Why—Views of Resource Persons," pp. 46–77.

81 Donald A. Cook, "Cultural Innovation and Disaster in the American City," in Duhl, *op. cit.*, pp. 87–93.

82 Seeley, *op. cit.*, pp. 7–14.

83 Robert K. Merton, *Social Theory and Social Structure* (rev. ed.; New York: The Free Press, 1957), p. 180; and Lewis A. Coser, "Some Functions of Deviant Behavior and Normative Flexibility," *American Journal of Sociology*, 68 (September, 1962), 178–81.

84 Ernest W. Burgess, "The Growth of the City," in Robert E. Park and Burgess, *The City* (Chicago: University of Chicago Press, 1925), and Louis Wirth, ed., *Contemporary Social Problems* (Chicago: University of Chicago Press, 1939), p. 32.

85 Zorbaugh, *op. cit.*, pp. 127–9.

86 Homer Hoyt, *The Structure and Growth of Residential Neighborhoods in American Cities* (Washington, D.C.: Federal Housing Administration, 1939), pp. 75–7; and Hoyt, "The Structure of American Cities in the Post-War Era," *American Journal of Sociology*, 48 (January, 1943), 475–81.

87 Gideon Sjoberg, *The Preindustrial City: Past and Present* (New York: The Free Press, 1960), Chapter IV. Also see Noel P. Gist, "The Ecology of Bangalore, India; An East–West Comparison," *Social Forces*, 35 (May, 1957), 356–65.

88 Sjoberg, *op. cit.*, p. 98.

89 Leo F. Schnore, "On the Spatial Structure of Cities in the Two Americas," in Philip M. Hauser and Schnore, eds., *The Study of Urbanization* (New York: John Wiley & Sons, Inc., 1965), p. 366.

90 Abrams, *The Future of Housing* (New York: Harper & Row, Publishers, 1946), p. 21. For another argument that slums are caused by the shortage of houses, see Robert Lasch, *Breaking the Building Blockade* (Chicago: University of Chicago Press, 1946).

91 Colean, *op. cit.*, p. 41.

92 J. M. Mackintosh, *Housing and Family Life* (London: Cassell & Company, Ltd, 1952), p. 16.

93 *Ibid.*, p. 113.

94 Claude Gruen, "Urban Renewal's Role in the Genesis of Tomorrow's Slums," *Land Economics*, 39 (August, 1963), 285–91.

CHAPTER 2

1 Marvin Lowenthal, *The Jews of Germany* (New York: Longmans, Green, and Company, 1936), p. 93. Also see Louis Wirth, *The Ghetto* (Chicago: University of Chicago Press, 1928), p. 23.

2 "Ghetto," *The Columbia Encyclopedia* (3rd ed.; New York: Columbia University Press, 1963), p. 823; and Cecil Roth, *A Short History of the Jewish People* (London: East & West Library, 1948), p. 297.

3 Israel Abrahams, *Jewish Life in the Middle Ages* (Philadelphia: The Jewish Publication Society of America, 1894), p. 67.

4 Wirth, *op. cit.*, pp. 47–8.

5 Lowenthal, *op. cit.*, p. 211.

6 David Philipson, *Old European Jewries* (Philadelphia: The Jewish Publication Society of America, 1894), p. 56, quoted in Wirth, *op. cit.*, p. 44.

7 M. Dorothy George, *London Life in the Eighteenth Century* (London: Routledge & Kegan Paul, Ltd, 1925), p. 70.

8 *Ibid.*, p. 69.

9 Lewis Mumford, *The City in History* (New York: Harcourt, Brace & World, Inc., 1961), pp. 462–3.

10 Edwin Chadwick, *The Sanitary Condition of the Labouring Population of Gt. Britain 1842* (Edinburgh: T. & A. Constable Ltd, reprinted, 1965), pp. 111–12.

11 Pauline Gregg, *A Social and Economic History of Britain, 1760–1955* (London: George C. Harrap & Co., Ltd, 1950), p. 480.

12 Thomas Burke, *The Streets of London Through the Centuries* (London: B. T. Batsford, Ltd, 1940), p. 101.

13 Mumford, *op. cit.*, pp. 466–7.

14 George R. Sims, *How the Poor Live* (London: Chatto & Windus, Ltd, 1889); and Robert Blatchford, *Dismal England* (London: Walter Scott, Ltd, 1899).

15 B. Seebohm Rowntree, *Poverty: A Study of Town Life* (London: Macmillan & Co., Ltd, 1902).

16 Burke, *op. cit.*, p. 155.

17 John F. C. Harrison, *Learning and Living 1790–1960: A Study in the History of the English Adult Education Movement* (Toronto: University of Toronto Press, 1961) pp. 12–30.

18 W. J. Reader, *Life in Victorian England* (London: B. T. Batsford, Ltd, 1964), p. 86.

19 Friedrich Engels, *The Condition of the Working Class in England in 1884* (London: George Allen & Unwin, Ltd, 1892), p. 128.

20 For a description of the conditions of workers in assorted street trades in nineteenth-century London, see Henry Meyhew, *London Labour and the London Poor: The Condition and Earnings of Those That Will Work, Cannot Work, and Will Not Work* (London: Charles Griffin and Company, Ltd, 1851).

21 Chadwick, *op. cit.*, p. 411.

22 Harrison, *op. cit.*, p. 17.

23 Rowntree, *op. cit.*, p. 59.

24 Sims, *op. cit.*, p. 21.

25 Rowntree, *op. cit.*, p. 5.

26   Charles Booth, *Life and Labour of the People in London*, I (London: Macmillan & Co., Ltd, 1892), pp. 37–8.

27   *Ibid.*, p. 150.

28   Sims, *op. cit.*, p. 86.

29   Booth, *op. cit.*, p. 160.

30   *Ibid.*, p. 131.

31   Quoted in James Ford, *Slums and Housing: History, Conditions, Policy* (Cambridge, Mass.: Harvard University Press, 1936), p. 62.

32   Mumford, *op. cit.*, p. 433.

33   Robert Ernst, *Immigrant Life in New York City, 1825–1863* (New York: Columbia University Press, 1949), p. 49.

34   Maldwyn Allen Jones, *American Immigration* (Chicago: University of Chicago Press, 1960), p. 225. Also see Robert DeForest and Lawrence Veiller, *The Tenement House Problem*, II (New York: The Macmillan Company, 1903), p. 73.

35   Ernest Flagg, "The New York Tenement House Evil and Its Cure," in Robert A. Woods, *et al.*, *The Poor in Great Cities* (New York: Charles Scribner's Sons, 1895), pp. 370–92.

36   Ford, *op. cit.*, p. 869.

37   Jacob A. Riis, *How the Other Half Lives: Studies Among the Tenements of New York* (New York: Charles Scribner's Sons, 1920), pp. 55–6.

38   DeForest and Veiller, *op. cit.*, I, p. 293.

39   Quoted in *ibid.*, p. 299.

40   Moses Rischin, *The Promised City* (Cambridge, Mass.: Harvard University Press, 1962), p. 80. In Chapter 13, we present a long discussion of Mobilization for Youth, which was started in 1962 as a large-scale county development project to deal with the Lower East Side.

41   *Ibid.*, p. 144.

42   Cecil Woodham-Smith, *The Great Hunger: Ireland 1845–9* (London: Hamish Hamilton, 1962), p. 248.

43   Robert Hunter, *Tenement Conditions in Chicago* (Chicago: City Homes Association, 1901).

44   *Ibid.*, Chapter VI, "Outside Sanitary Conditions," pp. 111–43.

45   *Ibid.*, Chapter VII, "Social Pathology, Diseases and Death," pp. 144–60.

46   *Ibid.*, p. 36.

47   Edith Abbott, *The Tenements of Chicago, 1908–1935* (Chicago: University of Chicago Press, 1936), p. 80.

48   Jane Addams, *Forty Years at Hull House* (New York: The Macmillan Company, 1935).

49   Addams, *The Spirit of Youth and the City Streets* (New York: The Macmillan Company, 1910), p. 111.

50   Paul Underwood Kellogg, ed., *The Pittsburgh District, Civic Frontage* (New York: Survey Associates, Inc., 1914), p. 90.

51   Charles Frederick Weller, *Neglected Neighbors in the National Capital* (New York: Holt, Rinehart & Winston, Inc., 1909).

52   Margaret Leech, *Reveille in Washington* (New York: Harper & Row, Publishers, 1941), pp. 9, 10.

53   Charles Loring Brace, *The Dangerous Classes of New York and Twenty Years' Work Among Them* (New York: Wynkoop & Hallenbeck, 1880), p. 152.

54   DeForest and Veiller, *op. cit.*, p. 6. Also see Robert Hunter, *op. cit.*

55   Gordon Atkins, *Health, Housing and Poverty in New York City, 1865–1898* (Ann Arbor: University of Michigan Press, 1947), p. 30.

56   Reported in DeForest and Veiller, *op. cit.*, I, p. 79.

57   Robert Hunter, *op. cit.*, p. 104.

58   *Ibid.*, p. 108.

59   *Ibid.*, p. 21.

60   William Elsing, "Life in New York Tenement Houses," *Scribner's Magazine*, May, 1892, pp. 699–717.

61 Riis, *op. cit.*, p. 246.

62 Robert Hunter, *op. cit.*, p. 147.

63 William I. Hull, "The Children of the Other Half," *The Arena*, 17 (April, 1897), 1046.

64 Ernest C. Moore, "The Social Value of the Saloon," *American Journal of Sociology*, 3 (July, 1897), 1–12. Also see Raymond Calkins, *Substitutes for the Saloon: An Investigation Made for the Committee of Fifty* (Boston: Houghton Mifflin Company, 1901).

65 Moore, *op. cit.*, pp. 4–5. Charles Booth reports the same function of the saloon among the lower classes in his *Life and Labour of the People in London*.

66 Langdon W. Post, *The Challenge of Housing* (New York: Holt, Rinehart & Winston, Inc., 1938), p. 101.

67 Quoted in Edith Elmer Wood, *The Housing of the Unskilled Wage Earner* (New York: The Macmillan Company, 1919), p. 29.

68 Robert H. Bremner, *From the Depths: The Discovery of Poverty in the United States* (New York: New York University Press, 1956), pp. 6–7.

69 Jay Rumney, "The Social Costs of the Slums," *The Journal of Social Issues*, VII (1951), 69–85. Also see Roy Lubove, *The Progressives and the Slums: Tenement House Reform in New York City 1890–1917* (Ithaca: Cornell University Press, 1962).

70 See Booth, *op. cit.*; Sims, *op. cit.*; and Rowntree, *op. cit.*

71 Bremner, *op. cit.*, p. 69.

72 *Ibid.*, Chapter 6.

73 *Ibid.*, p. 89.

74 *Child of the Dark: The Diary of Carolina Maria De Jesus*, translated by David St. Clair (New York: E. P. Dutton & Co., Inc., 1962).

CHAPTER 3

1 Charles J. Stokes, "A Theory of Slums," *Land Economics*, 38 (August, 1962), 187–97.

2 *Ibid.*, p. 189.

3 *Ibid.*

4 *Ibid.*, p. 192.

5 *Ibid.*, p. 197.

6 Harvey W. Zorbaugh, *The Gold Coast and the Slum* (Chicago: University of Chicago Press, 1929), pp. 128–9.

7 Herbert J. Gans, *The Urban Villagers: Group and Class in the Life of Italian-Americans* (New York: The Free Press, 1962), p. 28.

8 *Ibid.*

9 John R. Seeley, *Redevelopment: Some Human Gains and Losses* (Indianapolis: Community Surveys, Inc., 1956); and Seeley, "The Slum: Its Nature, Use, and Users," *Journal of the American Institute of Planners*, XXV (February, 1959), 7–14.

10 *Ibid.*, p. 12.

11 Seeley, *Redevelopment*, pp. 50–1.

12 *Ibid.*, p. 56.

13 *Ibid.*, p. 57.

14 *Ibid.*

15 Charles Abrams, *Man's Struggle for Shelter in an Urbanizing World* (Cambridge, Mass.: The M.I.T. Press, 1964), p. 4.

16 Abrams, *The Future of Housing* (New York: Harper & Row, Publishers, 1946), pp. 22–8.

17 *Report on The World Social Situation* (New York: United Nations Bureau of Social Affairs, in cooperation with the International Labour Office, the

Food and Agriculture Organization, the United Nations Educational, Scientific and Cultural Organization, and the World Health Organization, 1957), p. 132.

18 Abrams, *Man's Struggle for Shelter*, pp. 21–2.

19 *Ibid.*, p. 13.

20 Richard W. Poston, *Democracy Speaks Many Tongues: Community Development Around the World* (New York: Harper & Row, Publishers, 1962), p. 28.

21 See Floyd Dotson and Lilian Ota Dotson, "Ecological Trends in the City of Guadalajara, Mexico," *Social Forces*, 32 (May, 1954), 367–74.

22 Philip M. Hauser, ed., *Urbanization in Latin America* (New York: Columbia University Press, by arrangement with UNESCO, 1961), p. 56.

23 Poston, *op. cit.*, p. 30.

24 *Report on the World Social Situation*, p. 186.

25 José Matos Mar, "Migration and Urbanization," in Hauser, *op. cit.*, pp. 170–7.

26 Ozzie G. Simmons, "The Clinical Team in a Chilean Health Centre," in Benjamin D. Paul, ed., *Health, Culture and Community* (New York: Russell Sage Foundation, 1955), p. 328.

27 Jacquelyn Gross, "As the Slum Goes, So Goes the Alliance," *The New York Times Magazine*, June 23, 1963, p. 12.

28 Quoted in *Report on the World Social Situation*, p. 185.

29 Gross, *op. cit.*, p. 12.

30 *Child of the Dark: The Diary of Carolina Maria De Jesus*, translated by David St. Clair (New York: E. P. Dutton and Co., Inc., 1962).

31 Robert C. Schmitt, "Implications of Density in Hong Kong," *Journal of the American Institute of Planners*, XXIX (August, 1963), 210–7.

32 *Ibid.*, p. 216.

33 Michael Banton, *West African City: A Study of Tribal Life in Freetown* (London: Oxford University Press, 1957), p. 83.

34 Peter C. W. Gutkind, "Congestion and Overcrowding: An African Problem," *Human Organization*, 19 (Fall, 1960), 130.

35 "Some Considerations on the Prevention of Juvenile Delinquency in African Countries Experiencing Rapid Social Change," *International Review of Criminal Policy*, 16 (October, 1960), 43.

36 UNESCO, *Social Implications of Industrialization and Urbanization in Africa South of the Sahara* (Lausanne: United Nations Educational, Scientific and Cultural Organization, 1956), p. 49.

37 Harm J. de Blij, *Dar Es Salaam: A Study in Urban Geography* (Evanston: Northwestern University Press, 1963), p. 33.

38 Peter Marris, *Family and Social Change in an African City: A Study of Rehousing in Lagos* (London: Routledge & Kegan Paul, Ltd, 1961), p. 82.

39 *Ibid.*

40 *Ibid.*, p. 83.

41 See, for example, R. E. Phillips, "The Bantu in the City: A Study of Cultural Adjustment on the Witwatersrand"; E. Hellman, "Rooiyard: A Sociological Survey of an Urban Native Slum Yard"; M. Hunter, "An Urban Community, East London"; and I. Schapera, "Migrant Labour and Tribal Life in Bechuanaland," in UNESCO, *op. cit.*, pp. 174–208.

42 J. C. De Ridder, *The Personality of the Urban African in South Africa: A Thematic Apperception Test Study* (London: Routledge & Kegan Paul, Ltd, 1961), p. 32.

43 *Ibid.*, p. 38.

44 Robert C. Weaver, *The Negro*

Ghetto (New York: Harcourt, Brace & World, Inc., 1948), p. 27.

45 Oscar Handlin, *The Newcomers: Negroes and Puerto Ricans in a Changing Metropolis* (Cambridge, Mass.: Harvard University Press, 1959), p. 48.

46 St. Clair Drake and Horace R. Cayton, *Black Metropolis* (New York: Harcourt, Brace & World, Inc., 1945), p. 576.

47 Weaver, *op. cit.*, p. 83.

48 Woody Klein, *Let in the Sun* (New York: The Macmillan Company, 1964), a "life history" of a tenement building in East Harlem.

49 James Ford, *Slums and Housing* (Cambridge, Mass.: Harvard University Press, 1936), p. 322.

50 E. Franklin Frazier, *The Negro in the United States* (New York: The Macmillan Company, 1957).

51 *Ibid.*, p. 304.

52 Drake and Cayton, *op. cit.*, p. 583.

53 Kenneth B. Clark, *Dark Ghetto: Dilemmas of Social Power* (New York: Harper & Row, Publishers, 1965), pp. 47–9.

54 *The Negro Family: The Case for National Action* (Washington, D.C.: Office of Policy Planning and Research, United States Department of Labor, March, 1965), Introduction. Also see "New Crisis: The Negro Family," *Newsweek*, August 9, 1965, pp. 24–8.

55 Harlem Youth Opportunities Unlimited, Inc., *Youth in the Ghetto* (Mimeographed, 1964), p. 109.

56 *Ibid.*, p. 127.

57 *Ibid.*, p. 183.

58 Drake and Cayton, *op. cit.*, p. 590. Also see Clark, *op. cit.*, pp. 71–4.

59 Clark, *op. cit.*, p. 31.

60 *Ibid.*, p. 87.

61 See James B. Conant, *Slums and Suburbs* (New York: McGraw-Hill Book Co., Inc., 1964).

62 Harlem Youth Opportunities, *op. cit.*, p. 197. For a discussion of present-day conditions and problems of Harlem schools, see Clark, *op. cit.*, Chapter 6, "Ghetto Schools: Separate and Unequal."

63 Clark, *op. cit.*, p. 125.

64 Harlem Youth Opportunities, *op. cit.*, p. 178.

65 Clark, *op. cit.*, p. 133.

66 Harlem Youth Opportunities, *op. cit.*, p. 157.

67 Clark, *op. cit.*, pp. 86–7.

68 *Ibid.*, p. 90.

69 United States Department of Justice, Federal Bureau of Investigation, *Crime in the United States: Uniform Crime Reports, 1960* (Washington, D.C.: United States Government Printing Office, 1961), pp. 95, 101.

70 R. C. Bensing and Oliver Schroeder, Jr., *Homicide in an Urban Community* (Springfield: Charles C Thomas, Publisher, 1960), p. 41.

71 Marvin E. Wolfgang, *Patterns in Criminal Homicide* (Philadelphia: University of Pennsylvania Press, 1958), pp. 31–3.

72 Handlin, *op. cit.*, pp. 105–17. For a discussion of the powerlessness of Negro communities, see Clark, *op. cit.*, particularly pp. 154–98. Also see Floyd Hunter, *Community Power Structure: A Study of Decision Makers* (Chapel Hill: University of North Carolina Press, 1954); and Ernest A. T. Barth and Baha Abu-Laban, "Power Structure and the Negro Sub-Community," *American Sociological Review*, 24 (February, 1959), 69–76.

73 See Nathan Glazer and Patrick Moynihan, *Beyond the Melting Pot* (New York: Columbia University Press, 1958), p. 92. Also see Elena Padilla, *Up from Puerto Rico* (New York: Columbia University Press, 1958); and Handlin, *op. cit.*

74 Patricia Cayo Sexton, *Spanish*

Harlem: Anatomy of Poverty (New York: Harper & Row, Publishers, 1965).

75 See, for example, Lawrence R. Chenault, *The Puerto Rican Migrant in New York City* (New York: Columbia University Press, 1938); Beatrice B. Berle, *80 Puerto Rican Families in New York City* (New York: Columbia University Press, 1958); Christopher Rand, *The Puerto Ricans* (New York: Oxford University Press, Inc., 1958); and John H. Burma, *Spanish-Speaking Groups in the United States* (Durham, N.C.: Duke University Press, 1954).

76 Glazer and Davis McEntire, *Studies in Housing and Minority Groups* (Berkeley: University of California Press, 1960), p. 172.

77 Lewis Yablonsky, *The Violent Gang* (New York: The Macmillan Company, 1962), pp. 171–94. This term has also been used by Richard A. Cloward and Lloyd E. Ohlin, in *Delinquency and Opportunity: A Theory of Delinquent Gangs* (New York: The Free Press, 1960), p. 173.

78 Maurice R. Stein, *The Eclipse of Community* (Princeton: Princeton University Press, 1960), p. 131. He suggests a theory of slums based on historical analysis rather than one derived from problems connected with ethnic acculturation.

79 Oscar Lewis, *The Children of Sanchez: Autobiography of a Mexican Family* (Vintage ed.; New York: Alfred A. Knopf, Inc., 1963), p. xvi.

80 *Ibid.*, p. xv.

81 Michael Harrington, *The Other America* (Baltimore: Penguin Books, Inc., 1962), p. 153.

82 *Ibid.*, p. 154.

83 Chester W. Hartman discusses "territorial" and "selective" use of space for the working class and middle class respectively in "Social Values and Housing Orientations," *Journal of Social Issues*, XIX (April, 1963), 113–31.

84 William F. Whyte, *Street Corner Society* (Chicago: University of Chicago Press, 1962); Gans, *op. cit.*; and Walter Firey, *Land Use in Central Boston* (Cambridge, Mass.: Harvard University Press, 1947), Chapter V, "The Influence of Localized Social Solidarity Upon Land Use: The North End."

85 Zorbaugh, *op. cit.*

86 Whyte, "Social Organization in the Slums," *American Sociological Review*, 8 (February, 1943), p. 36.

87 *Ibid.*, p. 39.

88 Firey, *op. cit.*, p. 183.

89 Harrington, *op. cit.*, p. 157.

90 Gans, *op. cit.*, p. 236.

91 Edward J. Ryan, "Personal Identity in an Urban Slum," in Leonard J. Duhl, ed., *The Urban Condition* (New York: Basic Books, Inc., 1963), p. 147.

92 Gans, *op. cit.*, pp. 265–6.

93 *Ibid.*, p. 267.

94 Hartman, *op. cit.*

95 *Ibid.*

CHAPTER 4

1 See the still limited but growing literature on the cities of India, as surveyed in, for example, Bert F. Hoselitz, "A Survey of the Literature on Urbanization in India," in Roy Turner, ed., *India's Urban Future* (Berkeley: University of California Press, 1962). Also see S. N. Sen, *The City of Calcutta: A Socio-Economic Survey, 1954–55 to 57–58* (Calcutta: Bookland Private, Limited,

1960); A. Bopegamage, *Delhi: A Study in Urban Sociology* (Bombay: University of Bombay Press, 1957); R. L. Singh, *Banaras: A Study in Urban Geography* (Banaras: Nand Kishore & Bros., 1955); K. N. Venkatarayappa, *Bangalore: A Socio-Ecological Study* (Bombay: University of Bombay Press, 1957); H. C. Malkani, *A Socio-Economic Survey of Baroda City* (Baroda: Sadhana Press, 1958); D. R. Gadgil, *Poona, A Socio-Economic Survey*, 2 vols. (Poona: Gokhale Institute of Politics and Economics, 1945, 1952); N. V. Sovani, D. P. Apte, and R. G. Pendse, *Poona: A Re-Survey; The Changing Pattern of Employment and Earnings* (Poona: Gokhale Institute of Politics and Economics, 1956); and S. Kesava Iyengar, *A Socio-Economic Survey of Hyderabad-Secunderabad City Area* (Hyderabad: Government Press, 1957).

2 See comments by Kingsley Davis in *The Population of India and Pakistan* (Princeton: Princeton University Press, 1951), pp. 148–9; by Nels Anderson in *The Urban Community: A World Perspective* (New York: Holt, Rinehart & Winston, Inc., 1959); and by Anderson in *Our Industrial Urban Civilization* (New York: Asia Publishing House, 1964).

3 Robert I. Crane, "Urbanism in India," *American Journal of Sociology*, LX (March, 1955), 463–70. Hoselitz has written in a like vein about the primate or great cities of other Asian countries in "Urbanization and Economic Growth in Asia," *Economic Development and Cultural Change*, VI (October, 1957), 43.

4 Stuart Piggott, *Prehistoric India to 1,000 B.C.* (Harmondsworth, Middlesex: Penguin Books, 1950); and Piggott, *Some Ancient Cities of India* (Bombay: Oxford University Press, 1945). Also see Gideon Sjoberg, *The Pre-Industrial City: Past and Present* (New York: The Free Press, 1960).

5 See Turner, *op. cit.*; also see Crane, *op. cit.*; G. S. Ghurye, "Cities of India," *Sociological Bulletin*, II (March, 1953), 47–71; Vishwambhar Nath, "Urbanization in India, with Special Reference to the Growth of Cities," in United Nations, *Proceedings of the World Population Conference, 1954*, II (New York, 1955), 843–54; and C. B. Mamoria, "Rural and Urban Composition of the Indian Population," *Modern Review*, XCIX (February and March, 1956), 118–24, 195–202.

6 Davis, "Urbanization in India: Past and Future," in Turner, *op. cit.*, p. 8.

7 Ghurye, *op. cit.*, p. 48.

8 Davis, *The Population of India and Pakistan*.

9 Davis, "Urbanization in India," p. 11.

10 *Ibid.*, p. 25.

11 *Ibid.*, pp. 22–6.

12 *Ibid.*, p. 26.

13 See, for example, Pitambar Pant, "Urbanization and the Long-Range Strategy of Economic Development," in Turner, *op. cit.*, pp. 182–92; Sachin Chaudhuri, "Centralization and the Alternate Forms of Decentralization: A Key Issue," in Turner, *op. cit.*, pp. 213–39; and William Bredo, "Industrial Decentralization in India," in Turner, *op. cit.*, pp. 240–61.

14 Chaudhuri, *op. cit.*, p. 224.

15 Ministry of Works, Housing and Supply, *The Problem of Housing in India* (Delhi: National Printing Works, 1957), p. 16.

16 Nirmal K. Bose, "Calcutta: A Premature Metropolis," in *Cities* (New York: Alfred A. Knopf, Inc., 1965), p. 60.

17 Bharat Sevak Samaj, *Slums of Old Delhi: Report of the Socio-Economic Survey of the Slum Dwellers of Old Delhi City* (New Delhi: Atma Ram & Sons, 1958), p. 7.

18   Ministry of Works, Housing and Supply, *op. cit.*, p. 12.

19   Beatrice Pitney Lamb, *India: A World in Transition* (New York: Frederick A. Praeger, Inc., 1963), p. 264.

20   Bose, *op. cit.*, pp. 60–1.

21   Quoted in Mamoria, *Social Problems and Social Disorganization in India* (Allahabad: Kitab Mahal, 1960), pp. 155–6.

22   Hoselitz, "The Cities of India and their Problems," *Annals of the Association of American Geographers*, 49 (June, 1959), 223.

23   Mamoria, *Social Problems*, p. 158.

24   S. V. Desai, "Public Health in Slum Areas," in *Report of the Seminar on Slum Clearance* (Bombay: Indian Conference of Social Work, 1957), p. 86.

25   Gerald F. Winfield, *China: The Land and the People* (New York: William Sloane Associates, Inc., 1948), p. 258.

26   Lewis Mumford, *The City in History* (New York: Harcourt, Brace & World, Inc., 1961), p. 290.

27   Mahatma Gandhi, *India of My Dreams* (Ahmedabad: Navajivan Publishing House, 1947), p. 134.

28   Ministry of Works, Housing and Supply, *op. cit.*, p. 15.

29   Bharat Sevak Samaj, *op. cit.*, p. 30.

30   Charles Abrams, *Man's Struggle for Shelter in an Urbanizing World* (Cambridge, Mass.: The M.I.T. Press, 1964), p. 9.

31   Bharat Sevak Samaj, *op. cit.*, p. 172.

32   *Ibid.*, p. 166.

33   Bose, *op. cit.*, p. 63.

34   *Indian Express*, July 13, 1961.

35   Bharat Sevak Samaj, *op. cit.*, p. 28.

36   B. H. Mehta, "Community Organization in Urban Areas," in Government of India, *Social Welfare in India*, (New Delhi: The Planning Commission, 1960), pp. 79–80.

37   P. N. Prabhu, "Bombay: A Study of the Social Effects of Urbanization," in *The Social Implications of Industrialization and Urbanization: Five Studies of Urban Populations of Recent Rural Origin in Cities of Southern Asia*, Calcutta: United Nations Educational, Scientific and Cultural Organization Research Centre on the Social Implications of Industrialization in Southern Asia, 1956 (New Delhi: Oxford Printing Works, 1956), p. 83.

38   See Sen, *op. cit.*, pp. 241–2; and Bopegamage, *op. cit.*, pp. 157, 161.

39   See Shankar Sahai Srivastava, *Juvenile Vagrancy: A Socio-Ecological Study of Juvenile Vagrants in the Cities of Kanpur and Lucknow* (New York: Asia Publishing House, 1963); Perin C. Kerawalla, *A Study in Indian Crime* (Bombay: Popular Book Depot, 1959); Delhi School of Social Work, *The Beggar Problem in Metropolitan Delhi* (Delhi: Kingsway Press, 1959); and Indian Conference of Social Work, *Beggar Problem in Greater Bombay* (Bombay: Mouj Printing Bureau, 1959).

CHAPTER 5

1   Charles Abrams, *Man's Struggle for Shelter in an Urbanizing World* (Cambridge, Mass.: The M.I.T. Press, 1964), especially Chapters 5 and 11.

2   *Report of the Advisory Committee on Slum Clearance*, Government of India, New Delhi, July 18, 1959, p. 5.

3   Asoka Mehta, "The Future of Indian Cities: National Issues and Goals," in Roy Turner, ed., *India's Urban Future*

(Berkeley: University of California Press, 1961), p. 418.

4   Richard L. Meier, "Relations of Technology to the Design of Very Large Cities," in Turner, *op. cit.*, pp. 299–307.

5   Ministry of Works, Housing and Supply, *The Problem of Housing in India* (New Delhi: National Printing Works, 1957), p. 7.

6   Richard L. Park, "The Urban Challenge to Local and State Government: West Bengal, with Special Attention to Calcutta," in Turner, *op. cit.*, p. 388.

7   For a discussion of India's limited economic resources, see John P. Lewis, *Quiet Crisis in India* (Anchor Books ed.; Garden City, N.Y.: Doubleday Company Inc., 1964).

8   *Report of the Advisory Committee on Slum Clearance*, p. 21.

9   Ministry of Works, Housing and Supply, *The Problem of Housing*, p. 10.

10   Government of India, *Third Five-Year Plan* (New Delhi: Planning Commission, 1961), p. 687.

11   H. S. Dhillon, "Group Dynamics in a Bustee—A Study of Groups and Leadership," *Report of the Seminar on Urban Community Development* (Hyderabad: Yura Press, 1959), p. 128.

12   Kurt W. Back, *Slums, Projects, and People: Social Psychological Problems of Relocation in Puerto Rico* (Durham: Duke University Press, 1962), pp. 106–7.

13   Abrams, *op. cit.*, p. 54.

14   Nirmal K. Bose, "Calcutta: A Premature Metropolis," in *Cities* (New York: Alfred A. Knopf, Inc., 1965), p. 64.

15   Abrams, *op. cit.*, p. 252.

16   William and Paul Paddock, *Hungry Nations* (Boston: Little, Brown and Company, 1964), p. 119.

17   *Ibid.*, p. 120.

18   Martin Anderson, *The Federal Bulldozer: A Critical Analysis of Urban Renewal, 1949–1962* (Cambridge, Mass.: The M.I.T. Press, 1964), pp. 219–33.

19   A. H. Schaaf, "Public Policies in Urban Renewal: An Economic Analysis of Justifications and Effects," *Land Economics*, XL (February, 1964), 67–87.

20   Herbert J. Gans, *The Urban Villagers: Group and Class in the Life of Italian-Americans* (New York: The Free Press, 1962), Chapter 14 "An Evaluation of the Redevelopment Plan and Process," pp. 305–35.

21   *Ibid.*, p. 308.

22   *Ibid.*, p. 328.

23   Jane Jacobs, *The Death and Life of Great American Cities* (New York: Random House, Inc., 1961), p. 4.

24   For a discussion of how urban renewal merely shifts the slums from one place to another, see Claude Gruen, "Urban Renewal's Role in the Genesis of Tomorrow's Slums," *Land Economics*, 39 (August, 1963), 285–91.

25   Jacobs, *op. cit.*, pp. 270–1. Also see Abrams, "City Planning and Housing Policy in Relation to Crime and Delinquency," *International Review of Criminal Policy*, 16 (October, 1960), 23–8.

26   Harrison E. Salisbury, *The Shook-Up Generation* (Crest ed.; Greenwich, Conn.: Fawcett World Library, 1958), p. 62. Also see Catherine Bauer, "The Dreary Deadlock of Public Housing," *Architectural Forum* (May, 1957).

27   See Michael Harrington, *The Other America: Poverty in the United States* (Baltimore: Penguin Books, Inc., 1962), p. 160.

28   Nathan Glazer and Daniel Patrick Moynihan, *Beyond the Melting Pot: The Negroes, Puerto Ricans, Jews, Italians, and Irish of New York City* (Cambridge, Mass.: The M.I.T. Press, 1963), pp. 62–3.

29   See Robert K. Brown, *Public Housing in Action: The Record of Pitts-*

burgh (Pittsburgh: The University of Pittsburgh Press, 1959), Chapters 8, "The Paradox of Public Housing," and 9, "The Rent Subsidy Program." For a discussion of racial segregation and the problems it presents in public housing, see Davis McEntire, *Residence and Race* (Berkeley: University of California Press, 1960), Chapter XVIII, "Low-Rent Public Housing."

30 William W. Biddle and Loureide J. Biddle, *The Community Development Process: The Rediscovery of Local Initiative* (New York: Holt, Rinehart & Winston, 1965), p. 186.

31 Urban Renewal Service Technical Guide No. 3, *Selecting Areas for Conservation*, 1960.

32 See, for example, David Hunter, *The Slums: Challenge and Response* (New York: The Free Press, 1964), p. 222.

33 Judah Gribetz, "New York City's Receivership Law," *Journal of Housing*, 21 (July, 1964), 297–300.

34 Anderson, *The Federal Bulldozer*, p. 5. For an evaluation of both sides of slum clearance and urban renewal, see Abrams, *The City Is the Frontier* (New York: Harper & Row, Publishers, 1965).

35 *Ibid.*, particularly pages 219–23, for a list of "beliefs" compared with "facts" about federal urban renewal. Anderson suggests that much of this effort can be more effectively carried out by private enterprise.

36 See, for example, Robert A. Woods and Albert J. Kennedy, *The Settlement Horizon: A National Estimate* (New York: The Russell Sage Foundation, 1922). Also see David E. Owen, *English Philanthropy, 1660–1960* (Cambridge, Mass.: The Belknap Press of Harvard University Press, 1964).

37 See Arthur Hillman, *Neighborhood Centers Today: Action Programs for a Rapidly Changing World* (New York:

National Federation of Settlements and Neighborhood Centers, 1960). Also see Hillman, *Community Organization and Planning* (New York: The Macmillan Company, 1950).

38 Gans, *op. cit.*, p. 146.

39 Gans, *op. cit.*, Chapter 7, "The Caretakers: Missionaries from the Outside World."

40 Arthur Evans Wood, *Hamtramck: A Sociological Study of a Polish-American Community* (New Haven: College & University Press, 1955), p. 191.

41 Gans, *op. cit.*, p. 152.

42 See, for example, Marshall B. Clinard, "Contributions of Sociology to Understanding Deviant Behavior," *The British Journal of Criminology*, XVII (October, 1962), 110–29.

43 David Hunter, "Slums and Social Work or Wishes and the Double Negative," in Bernard Rosenberg, Israel Gerver, and F. William Howton, *Mass Society in Crisis: Social Problems and Social Pathology* (New York: The Macmillan Company, 1964), pp. 594–603.

44 William F. Whyte, *Street Corner Society* (Chicago: University of Chicago Press, 1943).

45 *Ibid.*, p. 99.

46 Gans, *op. cit.*, pp. 149–50.

47 *Ibid.*, p. 152. A descriptive account, in novel form, of the life of a New York City social-welfare worker has demonstrated the virtual impossibility of solving the social problems of the slum through traditional casework methods. See Julius Horowitz, *The Inhabitants* (Cleveland: World Publishing Company, 1960).

48 David Hunter, "Slums and Social Work," p. 596.

49 See Wayne E. Thompson, "Developing a City's Human Resources," *Public Management*, XLV (April, 1963), 74–8.

50 "Statement of Goals," Oakland Interagency Project (Mimeographed, January, 1964).

51 For a discussion, see David Hunter, *The Slum*, pp. 143–70.

52 Robert K. Merton, *Social Theory and Social Structure* (rev. ed.; New York: The Free Press, 1957); and Merton, "Anomie, Anomia, and Social Interaction: Contexts of Deviant Behavior," in Clinard, ed., *Anomie and Deviant Behavior: A Discussion and Critique* (New York: The Free Press, 1964), pp. 213–42.

53 See particularly Clinard, "The Theoretical Implications of Anomie and Deviant Behavior," in Clinard, *Anomie and Deviant Behavior*, pp. 38–46. In the same source, see Edwin M. Lemert, "Social Structure, Social Control, and Deviation," pp. 57–98; James F. Short, Jr., "Gang Delinquency and Anomie," pp. 98–128; and Alfred R. Lindesmith and John Gagnon, "Anomie and Drug Addiction," pp. 158–89.

54 Charles Winick, "Physician Narcotic Addicts," *Social Problems*, 9 (Fall, 1961), 174–86.

55 Edwin H. Sutherland, *White Collar Crime* (New York: Holt, Rinehart & Winston, Inc., 1949; reissued 1960); and Clinard, *The Black Market* (New York: Holt, Rinehart & Winston, Inc., 1952).

56 Richard A. Cloward, "Illegitimate Means, Anomie, and Deviant Behavior," *American Sociological Review*, 24 (April, 1959), 164–76.

57 Cloward and Lloyd E. Ohlin, *Delinquency and Opportunity* (New York: The Free Press, 1960), pp. 151–2 and 159–60.

58 *Ibid.*, p. 86.

59 Clinard, "Theoretical Implications," p. 30. Also see David J. Bordua, "Delinquent Subcultures: Sociological Interpretations of Gang Delinquency," *The Annals*, 338 (November, 1961), 135; and Bordua, "Some Comments on Theories of Group Delinquency," *Sociological Inquiry*, 32 (Spring, 1962), 252–5.

60 Warren C. Haggstrom, "The Power of the Poor," in Frank Riessman, Jerome Cohen, and Arthur Pearl, eds., *Mental Health of the Poor* (New York: The Free Press, 1964), pp. 205–26.

61 Daniel Seligman, "The Enduring Slums," *Fortune*, December, 1957, pp. 144–9.

62 See Mobilization for Youth, Inc., *A Proposal for the Prevention and Control of Delinquency by Expanding Opportunities* (Mimeographed, December 9, 1961); Harlem Youth Opportunities Unlimited, Inc., *Youth in the Ghetto: A Study of the Consequences of Powerlessness and a Blueprint for Change* (Mimeographed, 1964); *New Haven Youth Development Program* (New Haven: Community Progress, Inc., 1963); and *Neighborhood Program Reports* (New Haven: Community Progress, Inc., May 1, 1964).

63 Also see Daniel Glaser, "New Trends in Research on the Treatment of Offenders and the Prevention of Crime in the United States of America," *International Review of Criminal Policy*, 23 (1965), 8–9.

CHAPTER 6

1 For estimates, see Charles Abrams, *Man's Struggle for Shelter in an Urbanizing World* (Cambridge, Mass.: The M.I.T. Press, 1964), p. 3.

2 See Nels Anderson, *The Urban Community: A World Perspective* (New York: Holt, Rinehart & Winston, Inc., 1959); and Marshall B. Clinard, *Sociology*

of Deviant Behavior (rev. ed.; New York: Holt, Rinehart & Winston, Inc., 1963), Chapter 3.

3 See, for example, the following publications of the United Nations Educational, Scientific and Cultural Organization (UNESCO): Philip M. Hauser, ed., *Urbanization in Latin America* (New York: Columbia University Press, 1961); Hauser, ed., *Urbanization in Asia and the Far East* (New York: UNESCO, 1957); *The Social Implications of Industrialization and Urbanization: Five Studies of Urban Populations of Recent Rural Origin in Cities of Southern Asia* (Calcutta: UNESCO, 1956); and *Social Implications of Industrialization and Urbanization in Africa South of the Sahara* (Switzerland: UNESCO, 1956). In addition, see Hortense Powdermaker, *Copper Town: Changing Africa* (New York: Harper & Row, Publishers, 1962).

4 "Some Considerations on the Prevention of Juvenile Delinquency in African Countries Experiencing Rapid Social Change," *International Review of Criminal Policy*, 16 (October, 1960), 43.

5 Morris Janowitz, *The Community Press in an Urban Setting* (New York: The Free Press, 1952), p. 19. Also see Gregory P. Stone, "City Shoppers and Urban Identification: Observations on the Social Psychology of City Life," *American Journal of Sociology*, 60 (July, 1954), 36–45; Stone, "Flint City-Fringe Survey," Social Science Research Project, The University of Michigan, Ann Arbor, Michigan, 1955, cited in Harold L. Wilensky and Charles N. Lebeaux, *Industrial Society and Social Welfare* (New York: Russell Sage Foundation, 1958); and Joel Smith, William H. Form, and Stone, "Local Intimacy in a Middle-Sized City," *American Journal of Sociology*, 60 (November, 1954), 276–84.

6 See, for example, *Report of the*

European Seminar on Community Development and Social Welfare in Urban Areas, Bristol, England, September 12–22, 1959, Geneva, United Nations, p. 23.

7 Scott Greer, *The Emerging City: Myth and Reality* (New York: The Free Press, 1964).

8 Paul N. Ylvisaker, *Community Action: A Response to Some Unfinished Business* (New York: The Ford Foundation, n.d.), p. 4.

9 *Community Development and Related Services* (New York: United Nations Department of Economic and Social Affairs, 1960), p. 1.

10 Richard W. Poston, *Democracy Speaks Many Tongues: Community Development Around the World* (New York: Harper & Row, Publishers, 1962), pp. 180–1.

11 Ernest F. Witte, "Community Development in Selected Countries," *Community Development Review*, 7 (June, 1962), 2.

12 See Carl C. Taylor, Douglas Ensminger, Helen W. Johnson, and Jean Joyce, *India's Roots of Democracy: A Sociological Analysis of Rural India's Experience in Planned Development Since Independence* (Bombay: Orient Longmans, 1965); B. Mukerji, *Community Development in India* (Calcutta: Orient Longmans, 1961); S. C. Dube, *India's Changing Villages: Human Factors in Community Development* (Ithaca: Cornell University Press, 1958); Rajeshwar Dayal, *Community Development Programme in India* (Allahabad: Kitab Mahal, 1960); S. K. Dey, *Community Development* (Allahabad: Kitab Mahal, 1960); Dey, *Panchayat-i-Raj: A Synthesis* (London: Asia Publishing House, 1961); Government of India, *A Guide to Community Development* (Delhi: Ministry of Community Development, 1957); and Albert Mayer, *Pilot Project, India: The*

Story of Rural Development at Etawah, Uttar Pradesh (Berkeley: University of California Press, 1959).

13 Taylor, et al., p. 170.

14 Ibid., p. 213. Detailed description of the program, as well as a critical analysis of its actual operation can be found in this work.

15 For a discussion of community-development programs in other countries, see particularly Poston, op. cit. Also see T. R. Batten, Communities and Their Development (London: Oxford University Press, 1957); Phillips Ruopp, ed., Approaches to Community Development (The Hague: W. Van Hoeve Ltd., 1953); Ward H. Goodenough, Cooperation in Change (New York: Russell Sage Foundation, 1963); United Nations Bureau of Social Affairs, Social Progress through Community Development (New York: 1955); Ramon P. Binamira, The Philippine Community Development Program (Manila: Office of Presidential Assistant on Community Development, 1957); Colonial Office, Community Development: A Handbook (London: Her Majesty's Stationery Office, 1958); Peter Du Sautoy, Community Development in Ghana (London: Oxford University Press, 1958); I. C. Jackson, Advance in Africa—A Study of Community Development in Eastern Nigeria (London: Oxford University Press, 1956); Jack D. Mezirow, Dynamics of Community Development (New York: Scarecrow Press, Inc., 1963). In addition, see various issues of The International Review of Community Development, Community Development Review, Community Development Bulletin, and Rural Sociology.

16 Taylor, A Critical Analysis of India's Community Development Program (Delhi: Community Projects Administration, Government of India, 1956), p. 51. Also see Kusum Nair, Blossoms in the Dust: The Human Element in Indian Development (London: Gerald Duckworth & Co., Ltd., 1961).

17 The literature is quite extensive. See particularly Clarence King, Working with People in Small Communities (New York: Harper & Row, Publishers, 1958); Burton W. Kreitlow, E. W. Aiton, and Andrew P. Torrence, Leadership for Action in Rural Communities (Danville, Ill.: The Interstate Printers & Publishers, Inc., 1960); Charles Loomis and J. Allan Beegle, Rural Sociology: The Strategy of Change (Englewood Cliffs, N.J.: Prentice-Hall, Inc., 1957); Everett M. Rogers, Social Change in Rural Society (New York: Appleton-Century, 1960); Wayland J. Hayes, The Small Community Looks Ahead (New York: Harcourt, Brace & World, Inc., 1947); Marvin B. Sussman, ed., Community Structure and Analysis (New York: Thomas Y. Crowell Company, 1959); Severyn T. Bruyn, Communities in Action: Pattern and Process (New Haven: College & University Press, 1963); Christopher Sower, John Holland, Kenneth Tiedke, Walter Freeman, Community Involvement (New York: The Free Press, 1957); and Edward O. Moe, "Utah Community Development Program," Community Development Review, 8 (June, 1963), 61–71.

18 Such an effort in the remote areas of Italy by UNLA (Unione Nazionale per la Lotta contro l'Analfabetismo), or the Association for the Fight Against Illiteracy, has been described by Friedmann. See Fredrick G. Friedmann, The Hoe and the Book: An Italian Experiment in Community Development (Ithaca: Cornell University Press, 1960).

19 See, for example, Melford E. Spiro, Kibbutz: Venture in Utopia (New York: Schocken Books, Inc., 1963).

20 Colonial Office, Community Development, pp. 19–20.

21 *Community Development and National Development* (New York: United Nations Department of Economic and Social Affairs, 1963), p. 73. Also see the report by the Secretary-General of the United Nations, *Community Development in Urban Areas* (New York: The United Nations Department of Economic and Social Affairs, 1961).

22 Murray G. Ross, *Community Organization: Theory and Principles* (New York: Harper & Row, Publishers, 1955), p. 5.

23 H. L. Witmer and E. Tufts, *The Effectiveness of Delinquency Prevention Programs*, Publication No. 350, Children's Bureau, United States Department of Health, Education and Welfare (Washington, D.C.: United States Government Printing Office, 1954), p. 15. Also see Southside Community Committee, *Bright Shadows in Bronzetown* (Chicago: South Side Community, 1949), pp. 104–5.

24 Saul D. Alinsky, *Reveille for Radicals* (Chicago: University of Chicago Press, 1946); and Jane Jacobs, *The Death and Life of Great American Cities* (Vintage ed.; New York: Random House, Inc., 1961), pp. 297–9.

25 Sidney Dillick, *Community Organization for Neighborhood Development —Past and Present* (New York: William Morrow & Co., Inc., 1953).

26 See particularly Ross, *op. cit.* Also see Arthur Dunham, *Community Welfare Organization: Principles and Practice* (New York: Thomas Y. Crowell Company, 1958).

27 Julia Abrahamson, *A Neighborhood Finds Itself* (New York: Harper & Row, Publishers, 1959); and Peter H. Rossi and Robert A. Dentler, *The Politics of Urban Renewal: The Chicago Findings* (New York: The Free Press, 1961).

28 *The New York Times*, February 15, 1965, p. 21.

29 Robert S. Strother, "Self-Help on Slums," *National Civic Review*, LIV (January, 1965), 12–5.

30 See, for example, *The New York Times*, May 28, 1964, p. 30, and December 16, 1964, p. 45.

31 *Adams-Morgan: Democratic Action to Save a Neighborhood* (District of Columbia: Office of Urban Renewal, 1964), p. i.

32 See Warren C. Haggstrom, "The Power of the Poor," in Frank Riessman, Jerome Cohen, and Arthur Pearl, eds., *Mental Health of the Poor* (New York: The Free Press, 1964) p. 220.

33 See Chapter 7.

34 Salima Omer, "Urban Community Development: The Experience of Pakistan," *International Social Service Review*, 6 (March, 1960), 26.

35 See pp. 197–8.

36 Secretary-General of the United Nations, *Community Development in Urban Areas*.

37 *Urban and Rural Community Development*, Proceedings of the XIth International Conference of Social Work (Rio de Janeiro: Brazilian Committee of the International Conference of Social Work, 1962).

38 See Chapter 8, pp. 160–5.

39 Secretary-General of the United Nations, *Community Development in Urban Areas*, p. 1.

40 Batten, *op. cit.*, p. 6.

41 Asoka Mehta, "The Future of Indian Cities: National Issues and Goals," in Roy Turner, ed., *India's Urban Future* (Berkeley: University of California Press, 1962), p. 419.

42 See, for example, Irwin T. Sanders, *The Community: An Introduction to a Social System* (New York: The Ronald Press Company, 1958).

43 Roland L. Warren, *The Community in America* (Chicago: Rand McNally & Co., 1963), pp. 325–9.

44 Batten, *op. cit.*, p. 5.

45 Taylor, "Community Development Programs and Methods," *Community Development Review*, 3 (December, 1956), 34–42.

46 See James V. Cunningham, *The Resurgent Neighborhood* (Notre Dame, Ind.: Fides Publishers, Inc., 1965), pp. 116–42.

47 Economic Commission for Asia and the Far East, *Report of the Asian Seminar on Urban Community Development* (Mimeographed; Singapore, 1962), p. 21.

48 For a discussion of these efforts, see *General Report on Self-Help and Mutual Aid Housing*, World Planning and Housing Congress, San Juan, 1960; and Abrams, *op. cit.*, pp. 168–74.

49 Abrams, *op. cit.*

50 See, particularly, Abrahamson, *op. cit.*; Strother, *op. cit.*; and reports of ACTION-Housing Extension Projects in Pittsburgh.

51 Per G. Stensland, "Urban Community Development," *Community Development Review*, 8 (March, 1958), 32–9.

52 Sjoerd Groenman, "Community Development in Urban Areas," *International Review of Community Development*, 7 (1961), 61–9. Also see B. Chatterjee, "Some Issues in Urban Community Development," *International Review of Community Development*, 9 (1962), 113–24.

53 Sanders, *op. cit.*, pp. 406–7; and Sanders, "Theories of Community Development," *Rural Sociology*, 23 (March, 1958), 1–12.

54 Sanders, *The Community*, p. 407.

55 Louis M. Miniclier, "Values and Principles of Community Development," *International Review of Community Development*, 5 (1960), 57–8.

56 *Community Development—A Handbook*, Conference on Community Development, Buckinghamshire, 1957.

57 Warren, *op. cit.*, p. 326.

58 Adapted from *Report of the European Seminar*, p. 25.

59 William W. Biddle and Loureide J. Biddle, *The Community Development Process: The Rediscovery of Local Initiative* (New York: Holt, Rinehart & Winston, Inc., 1965), p. 224.

60 Thomas D. Sherrard, "Community Development and Community Organization—Common Elements and Major Differences," in *Urban and Rural Community Development*, pp. 9–18. Also see Sherrard, "Community Organization and Community Development: Similarities and Differences," *Community Development Review*, 7 (June, 1962), 11–20.

61 Sherrard, "Community Development and Community Organization," p. 9.

62 Warren, *op. cit.*, p. 324.

CHAPTER 7

1 A. Bopegamage, *Delhi: A Study in Urban Sociology* (Bombay: University of Bombay, 1957), p. 33.

2 Kingsley Davis, "Urbanization in India: The Past and Future," in Roy Turner, ed., *India's Urban Future* (Berkeley: University of California Press, 1962), p. 25.

3 *The Statesman*, Delhi, June 30, 1959.

4 See, for example, M. N. Srinivas, ed., *India's Villages* (rev. ed.; Bombay: Asia Publishing House, 1960); McKim Marriott, ed., *Village India: Studies in the Little Community* (Bombay: Asia Publishing House, 1961); and G. Morris Carstairs, *The Twice-Born* (London: Hogarth Press, Ltd, 1961).

5 K. M. Kapadia, "Caste in Transition," *Sociological Bulletin*, XI (March–September, 1962), 73–89. In Calcutta there appears to be considerable concentration of population by caste and region. See Nirmal K. Bose, "Calcutta: A Premature Metropolis," in *Cities* (New York: Alfred A. Knopf, Inc., 1965), pp. 59–75.

6 Kapadia, *op. cit.*, p. 74.

7 Taya Zinkin, *Caste Today* (London: Oxford University Press, 1962), p. 49.

8 Bert F. Hoselitz, "The Role of Urbanization in Economic Development: Some International Comparisons," in Turner, *op. cit.*, p. 173.

9 P. N. Prabhu, "A Study of the Social Effects of Urbanization," in *The Social Implications of Industrialization and Urbanization* (Calcutta: United Nations Educational, Scientific and Cultural Organization Centre on the Social Implications of Industrialization in Southern Asia, 1956), p. 94.

10 Gertrude Marvin Woodruff, "An Adidravida Settlement in Bangalore, India: A Case Study of Urbanization," Unpublished Doctoral Dissertation, Radcliffe College, 1959.

11 Arthur Niehoff, *Factory Workers in India*, Milwaukee Public Museum Publications in Anthropology, Number 5 (Milwaukee: Radtke Bros. & Kortsch Co., 1959), p. 102.

12 *Ibid.*, p. 103.

13 *Ibid.*

14 *Ibid.*, pp. 103–4.

15 Hoselitz, "The Urban–Rural Contrast as a Factor in Socio-Cultural Change," *The Economic Weekly*, 12 (January, 1960), 145–52.

16 Davis, *The Populations of India and Pakistan* (Princeton: Princeton University Press, 1951), pp. 170–6.

17 P. R. Nayak, "The Challenge of Urban Growth to Indian Local Government," in Turner, *op. cit.*, pp. 366–7.

18 See Marshall B. Clinard and B. Chatterjee, "Urban Community Development in India: The Delhi Pilot Project," in Turner, *op. cit.*, pp. 71–94. Also see Clinard, "The Delhi Pilot Project in Urban Community Development," *International Review of Community Development*, 7 (1961), 161–71; Chatterjee, "India Applies Rural Techniques of Self-Help to Rapidly Growing City Neighborhoods," *Journal of Housing*, 18 (May, 1961), 193–7; and Chatterjee, "Urban Community Development, Delhi Project: A Review," *Indian Journal of Social Work*, October, 1962.

19 L. F. Rushbrook Williams, *The State of Pakistan* (London: Faber & Faber, Ltd, 1962), Chapter 11.

20 See various reports of the Presidential Assistant on Community Development. Also see Jose V. Abueva, *Focus on the Barrio* (Manila: Institute of Public Administration, University of the Philippines, 1959).

21 United Nations Report of the Secretary-General, "Popular Collaboration with Municipalities," *Community Development in Urban Areas*, 1961.

22 Caroline F. Ware, "Community Development in Urban Areas, Initial Experience in Bogotá, Colombia," *Community Development Review*, 7 (June, 1962), 43–57.

23 Carola Ravell, "Community Development in Venezuela," *Community Development Review*, 8 (June, 1963), 79–89.

CHAPTER 8

1 Herbert A. Thelen, *Dynamics of Groups at Work* (Phoenix ed.; Chicago: University of Chicago Press, 1954), pp. 13–30; and Julia Abrahamson, *A Neighborhood Finds Itself* (New York: Harper & Row, Publishers, 1959). Also see Peter H. Rossi and Robert A. Dentler, *The Politics of Urban Renewal: The Chicago Findings* (New York: The Free Press, 1961).

2 Abrahamson, *op cit.*, p. 77.

3 For a description of detailed organizational procedures, see B. Chatterjee and Marshall B. Clinard, *Organizing Citizens' Development Councils* (Delhi: Municipal Corporation of Delhi, 1961).

4 See Chatterjee, "Some Issues in Urban Community Development," *International Review of Community Development*, 9 (1962), 113–24.

5 For excellent summary and discussion of these issues, see Gilbert Herbert, "The Neighborhood Unit Principle and Organic Theory," *The Sociological Review*, 11 (July, 1963), 165–213.

6 *Ibid.*, pp. 166–79.

7 Beatrice Pitney Lamb, *India: A World in Transition* (New York: Frederick A. Praeger, Inc., 1963), p. 158.

CHAPTER 9

1 The Secretary-General of the United Nations, *Community Development in Urban Areas* (New York: United Nations, 1961), p. 9.

2 José Matos Mar, "The 'Barriados' of Lima: An Example of Integration into Urban Life," in Philip M. Hauser, ed., *Urbanization in Latin America* (New York: International Documents Service of Columbia University Press, 1961), pp. 170–90.

3 Ann Ruth Willner, "Social Change in Javanese Town-Village Life," *Economic Development and Cultural Change*, 6 (April, 1958), 234.

4 The Secretary-General of the United Nations, *op. cit*, p. 9. Also see Kenneth Little, "The Role of Voluntary Associations in West African Urbanization," *American Anthropologist*, 59 (August, 1959), 579–96.

5 Ioné Acquah, *Accra Survey, 1953–1956* (London: University of London Press, 1958).

6 Michael Banton, *West African City: A Study of Tribal Life in Freetown* (London: Oxford University Press, 1957), p. xv. Also see Banton, "Social Alignment and Identity in a West African City," in Hilda Kuper, ed., *Urbanization and Migration in West Africa* (Berkeley: University of California Press, 1965), pp. 131–47.

7 Oscar Lewis, "The Culture of the *Vecindad* in Mexico City," UN/UNESCO Seminar on Urbanization Problems in Latin America, 1958 (Information Document No. 1), p. 7. Also see Lewis, *The Children of Sanchez: Autobiography of a Mexican Family* (Vintage ed.; New York: Alfred A. Knopf, Inc., 1963).

8 R. P. Dore, *City Life in Japan* (Berkeley: University of California Press, 1958). See particularly Chapter 17, "The Ward," pp. 269–90.

9 *Ibid.*, p. 287.

10 Nicholas Babchuk and C. Wayne Gordon, *The Voluntary Association in the Slum* (Lincoln, Neb.: University of

Nebraska Studies, No. 27, October, 1962).

11 Department of Urban Community Development, Delhi Municipal Corporation, *A Study of Mohalla Committees: Community Associations* (Delhi: Municipal Corporation of Delhi, 1962).

CHAPTER 10

1 See R. M. Varma, "The Problem of Communication in Urban Community Development," *Social Work Forum*, III (July, 1965), 1–3.

2 *A Study of Women's Attitudes and Practices and Working of the Mahila Samitis* (Delhi: The Department of Urban Community Development, Municipal Corporation of Delhi, August, 1963).

3 See p. 162.

CHAPTER 11

1 Otto Klineberg, "The Problem of Evaluation," *International Social Science Bulletin*, 7 (1955), 347.

2 Herbert H. Hyman, Charles R. Wright, and Terence K. Hopkins, *Applications of Methods of Evaluation: Four Studies of the Encampment for Citizenship* (Berkeley: University of California Press, 1962), pp. 3–4. Also see Howard E. Freeman and Clarence C. Sherwood, "Research in Large-Scale Intervention Programs," *Journal of Social Issues*, 21 (January, 1965), 11–28; and Michael P. Brooks, "The Community Action Program as a Setting for Applied Research," *Journal of Social Issues*, 21 (January, 1965), 29–40.

3 For a more complete discussion, see Marshall B. Clinard, "Evaluation and Research in Urban Community Development," *International Review of Community Development*, 12 (1963), 187–98.

4 For a more complete discussion of these steps, as they apply to community development in general, see Samuel P. Hayes, Jr., *Measuring the Results of Development Projects* (New York: United Nations Educational, Scientific and Cultural Organization, 1959). Also see Hyman, *et al., op. cit.*

5 D. Ghost, "Programme Evaluation and Research," *Report of the Asian Seminar on Planning and Administration of National Community Development Programmes* (New York: The United Nations, 1962), p. 149.

6 For a detailed evaluation of an American urban community-development project, see Rossi and Dentler's study of the Hyde Park–Kenwood Community Conference. Peter H. Rossi and Robert A. Dentler, *The Politics of Urban Renewal: The Chicago Findings* (New York: The Free Press, 1961), pp. 102–55.

7 *Evaluation Study of the Formation and Working of the Vikas Mandals* (Delhi: Department of Urban Community Development, Municipal Corporation of Delhi, June, 1961). This study was carried out by Mr. V. Gopalan, then Deputy Director, Department of Urban Community Development, and now Deputy Director, Social Welfare Program Evaluation Organization, Planning Commission, Government of India.

8 *Second Evaluation Study of the Vikas Mandals* (Delhi: Municipal Corporation of Delhi, May, 1965). This study was conducted by the research and evaluation unit under the direction of Rajeshwar Prasad, Senior Research Assistant. The author assisted in planning it.

9 *Evaluation Study*, p. 12.

10 *Ibid.*, p. 35.

11 *Ibid.*, p. 37.

12 *Second Evaluation Study*, pp. 5.1–5.6.

13 *Ibid.*

14 *A Study of Women's Attitudes and Practices and Working of the Mahila Samitis* (Delhi: The Department of Urban Community Development, Municipal Corporation of Delhi, August, 1963).

15 *Second Evaluation Study*, pp. 5.15–5.17.

16 *Evaluation Study*, pp. 24–5.

17 *Second Evaluation Study*, p. 6.5.

18 *Evaluation Study*, p. 9.

19 *Evaluation Study*, p. 11.

20 *Training Community Leaders: First Week-End Camp for Office-Bearers of Vikas Mandals* (Delhi: Department of Urban Community Development, Municipal Corporation of Delhi, 1961, Mimeographed).

21 *Training Women Workers of Vikas Mandals* (Delhi: Department of Urban Community Development, Municipal Corporation of Delhi, 1961, Mimeographed).

22 Daniel Melnick, "Politics in a Delhi Ward," Senior Thesis for a B.A. degree in political science, University of Wisconsin, 1963. Melnick spent a year in Delhi and speaks fluent Hindi.

23 Herbert J. Gans, *The Urban Villagers: Group and Class in the Life of Italian-Americans* (New York: The Free Press, 1962), pp. 170–80. Gans has suggested that the local politician's other functions are representation and providing reliable information on the motivations and decisions of the outside world. Also see J. T. Salter, *Boss Rule: Portraits in City Politics* (New York: McGraw-Hill Book Company, 1935).

24 Gans, *op cit.*, p. 170.

25 See David R. Hunter, *The Slums: Challenge and Response* (New York: The Free Press, 1964), pp. 189–92; and Nicholas von Hoffman, "Reorganization of the Casbah," *Social Progress*, 3 (April, 1962), 33.

26 Carl Feiss, quoted in David B. Carlsen, "Urban Renewal: Running Hard, and Sitting Still," *Architectural Forum*, 116 (April, 1962), 183.

27 Foreword to *Second Evaluation Study*.

28 See Ahmedabad Municipal Corporation, *Urban Community Development: Ahmedabad Project, 1962–65* (Ahmedabad: Janta Printing Company, 1965); and Urban Community Development Department, Ahmedabad Municipal Corporation, "Evaluation Study of Formation and Working of the *Vikas Mandals*," Mimeographed, 1965.

CHAPTER 12

1 Frank H. Sehnert, *A Functional Framework for the Action Process in Community Development* (Carbondale: Department of Community Development, Southern Illinois University, 1961, Mimeographed), pp. 87–92.

2 Carl C. Taylor, Douglas Ensminger, Helen W. Johnson, and Jean Joyce, *India's Roots of Democracy: A Sociological Analysis of Rural India's Experience in Planned Development Since Independence* (Bombay: Orient Longmans, 1965), pp.

601–3; and Taylor, "Community Development Programs and Methods," *Community Development Review*, 3 (December, 1956), 37–9. This framework is also repeated by Lowry Nelson, Charles E. Ramsey, and Coolie Verner, *Community Structure and Change* (New York: The MacMillan Company, 1960), pp. 419–22.

3   Christopher Sower, John Holland, Kenneth Tiedke, and Walter Freeman, *Community Involvement* (New York: The Free Press, 1957), pp. 308–14.

4   Ronald Lippitt, Jeanne Watson, and Bruce Westley, *The Dynamics of Planned Change: A Comparative Study of Principles and Techniques* (New York: Harcourt, Brace and World, Inc., 1958), pp. 123–42.

5   Severyn T. Bruyn, *Communities in Action: Pattern and Process* (New Haven: College and University Press, 1963), pp. 133–46.

6   George Beal and Harold R. Capener, "A Social Action Model," presented at the Rural Sociological Society Meeting, Pullman, Washington, August, 1958.

7   William W. Biddle with Loureide J. Biddle, *The Community Development Process: The Rediscovery of Local Initiative* (New York: Holt, Rinehart & Winston, Inc., 1965), pp. 90–102.

8   Roland L. Warren, *The Community in America* (Chicago: Rand McNally & Co., 1963), pp. 315–20. The action process has been analyzed by others, including Murray G. Ross, *Community Organization: Theory and Principles* (New York: Harper & Row, Publishers, 1955), Chapters 6 and 7; H. Curtis Mial, "Community Development—A Democratic Social Process," *Adult Leadership*, 6 (April, 1958), 277; Dorothy and Curtis Mial, *Our Community* (New York: New York University Press, 1960), ix–xiii;

T. R. Batten, *Communities and Their Development: An Introductory Study with Special Reference to the Tropics* (London: Oxford University Press, 1957), pp. 224–7; Harold F. Kaufman, "Toward an Interactional Conception of Community," *Social Forces*, 38 (October, 1959), 13; and Robert W. Janes and Harry L. Miller, "Factors in Community Action Programs," *Social Problems*, 6 (Summer, 1958), 57.

9   Warren, *op. cit.*, p. 324.

10   Melvin M. Tumin, "Some Social Requirements for Effective Community Development," *Community Development Review*, 11 (December, 1958), 4.

11   *Evaluation Study of the Formation and Working of the Vikas Mandals* (Delhi: Department of Urban Community Development, Municipal Corporation of Delhi, June, 1961), p. 9.

12   *Evaluation Study of the Vikas Mandals* (New Delhi: Department of Urban Community Development, Municipal Corporation of Delhi, March, 1962), p. 9.

13   Charles R. Hoffer, "Social Action in Community Development," *Rural Sociology*, 23 (March, 1958), 43.

14   Sowers, *et al.*, *op. cit.*, Chapter 4.

15   The theoretical scheme of identity change presented here has been partially derived from Ward H. Goodenough, *Cooperation in Change: An Anthropological Approach to Community Development* (New York: Russell Sage Foundation, 1963), Chapter 9.

16   *Evaluation Study of the Vikas Mandals* (1962), p. 9.

17   *Training Community Leaders*, A Report of the First Week-end Camp for Office-Bearers of *Vikas Mandals* (Delhi: Summer, 1961, Department of Urban Community Development, Municipal Corporation of Delhi).

CHAPTER 13

1   Everett E. Hagen, *On the Theory of Social Change: How Economic Growth Begins* (Homewood, Ill.: Dorsey Press, 1962), p. 25.

2   Ward H. Goodenough, *Cooperation in Change: An Anthropological Approach to Community Development* (New York: Russell Sage Foundation, 1963), p. 18.

3   Warren C. Haggstrom, "Poverty and Adult Vocations," Mimeographed, Syracuse University, January, 1965, p. 4.

4   Edward P. Thompson, *The Making of the English Working Class* (London: Victor Gollancz, Ltd, 1963), pp. 711–3.

5   Nathan Glazer and Daniel Patrick Moynihan, *Beyond the Melting Pot: The Negroes, Puerto Ricans, Jews, Italians, and Irish of New York City* (Cambridge, Mass.: The M.I.T. Press, 1963), p. 84.

6   *The New York Times*, May 28, 1964, p. 30; and December 16, 1964, p. 45.

7   Ronald Lippitt, Jeanne Watson, and Bruce Westley, *The Dynamics of Planned Change: A Comparative Study of Principles and Techniques* (New York: Harcourt, Brace & World, Inc., 1958).

8   Goodenough, *op. cit.*

9   *Ibid.*, pp. 22–3.

10   Also see Marshall B. Clinard, "The Sociologist and Social Change in Underdeveloped Countries," *Social Problems*, 10 (Winter, 1963), 207–19; and Clinard, "Perspectives on Urban Community Development and Community Organization," *Social Welfare Forum* (New York: Columbia University Press, 1962), pp. 65–85.

11   James B. Conant, *Slums and Suburbs* (New York: The New American Library of World Literature, Inc., 1961), pp. 25–6.

12   Kusum Nair, *Blossoms in the Dust: The Human Element in Indian Development* (London: Gerald Duckworth & Co., Ltd, 1961), pp. 190–4.

13   See pp. 169–70. Also see William C. Loring, Jr., Frank L. Sweetser, and Charles F. Ernst, *Community Organization for Citizen Participation in Urban Renewal* (Boston: Massachusetts Department of Commerce, 1947), p. 179.

14   Nicholas Babchuk and C. Wayne Gordon, *The Voluntary Association in the Slum* (Lincoln: University of Nebraska Studies, New Series No. 27, 1962), p. 116. Also see Joseph A. Kahl, *The American Class Structure* (New York: Holt, Rinehart & Winston, Inc., 1957).

15   P. N. Prabhu, "A Study on the Social Effects of Urbanization," in *The Social Implications of Industrialization and Urbanization: Five Studies of Urban Populations of Recent Rural Origin in Cities of Southern Asia* (Calcutta: United Nations Educational, Scientific and Cultural Organization, 1956), p. 104.

16   David R. Hunter, *The Slums: Challenge and Response* (New York: The Free Press, 1964), pp. 177–8.

17   Peter H. Rossi and Robert A. Dentler, *The Politics of Urban Renewal: The Chicago Findings* (New York: The Free Press, 1961), p. 283. Also see Herbert A. Thelen and Bettie B. Sarchet, *Neighbors in Action: A Manual for Community Leaders* (Chicago: University of Chicago Human Dynamics Laboratory, 1954); and Julia Abrahamson, *A Neighborhood Finds Itself* (New York: Harper & Row, Publishers, 1959).

18   Coleman's studies of community conflict and organization around such issues as fluoridation and urban renewal in the United States have suggested the same thing. James S. Coleman, *Com-*

munity *Conflict* (New York: The Free Press, 1957).

19 Lippitt, *et al., op. cit.*, p. 131.

20 David Hunter, *op. cit.*, p. 175.

21 See pp. 124–5.

22 See particularly Babchuk and Gordon, *op. cit.*, pp. 90–1; and Clinard, "The Public Drinking House and Society," in David J. Pittman and Charles Snyder, eds., *Society, Culture and Drinking Patterns* (New York: John Wiley & Sons, Inc., 1962), pp. 270–92. Also see Mass-Observation, *The Pub and the People* (London: Victor Gollancz, Ltd, 1943).

23 See pp. 301–8. Also see Goodenough, *op. cit.*, Chapter 9.

24 Haggstrom, "The Power of the Poor," in Louis A. Ferman, Joyce L. Kornbluh, and Alan Habers, eds., *Poverty in America: A Book of Readings* (Ann Arbor: The University of Michigan Press, 1965), p. 332.

25 Paul N. Ylvisaker, *Community Action: A Response to Some Unfinished Business* (New York: The Ford Foundation, 1963), p. 4.

26 See Charles Eric Lincoln, *The Black Muslims in America* (Boston: Beacon Press, 1961); E. U. Essien-Udom, *Black Nationalism: A Search for an Identity in America* (Chicago: University of Chicago Press, 1962); and Walter B. Simon, "Schwarzer Nationalismus in Den U.S.A.," *Kölner Zeitschrift für Soziologie und Sozialpsychologie*, Summer, 1963. Essien-Udom is a lecturer at the University of Ibadan, Nigeria. In pointing out the efforts of the Black Muslims to change self-images, there is no endorsement of the antiwhite philosophy and tactics of this group.

27 Nicholas Von Hoffman, "Reorganization of the Casbah," *Social Progress*, 3 (April, 1962), 33.

28 Frank Riessman, "The Revolution in Social Work," *Trans-Action*, 2

(November–December, 1964), 15. Also see Arthur Pearl and Riessman, *New Careers for the Poor: The Nonprofessional in Human Service* (New York: The Free Press, 1965).

29 *The Indigenous Nonprofessional: A Strategy of Change in Community Action and Community Mental Health Programs*, Report Number 3, National Institute of Labor Education Mental Health Program, New York City.

30 David Hunter, "Slums and Social Work or Wishes and the Double Negative," in Bernard Rosenberg, Israel Gerver, and F. William Howton, *Mass Society in Crisis: Social Problems and Social Pathology* (New York: The Macmillan Company, 1964), p. 601.

31 Pearl and Riessman, *op. cit.*, p. vii.

32 Riessman, *op. cit.*, p. 13.

33 Pearl and Riessman, *op. cit.*, p. 135.

34 David Hunter, *The Slums*, p. 173. Also see Clinard, "Perspectives on Urban Community Development," pp. 65–85.

35 David Hunter, *The Slums*, p. 193.

36 See Rossi and Dentler, *op. cit.*

37 David Hunter, *The Slums*, p. 174.

38 Georg Simmel, *Conflict*, trans. by Kurt H. Wolff (New York: The Free Press, 1955); and Lewis Coser, *The Functions of Social Conflict* (New York: The Free Press, 1964).

39 Coser, *op. cit.*, pp. 154–5.

40 Haggstrom, "The Power of the Poor."

41 Patricia Cayo Sexton, *Spanish Harlem* (New York: Harper & Row, Publishers, 1965), p. 194.

42 Saul Alinsky, *Reveille for Radicals* (Chicago: University of Chicago Press, 1946). Alinsky's techniques and philosophy are explained in this book and in his *Citizen Participation and Community Organization in Planning and Urban Renewal* (Chicago: Industrial Areas Foundation, 1962). Also see Charles E.

Silberman, *Crisis in Black and White* (New York: Random House, Inc., 1964), pp. 321–8; "The Professional Radical: Conversations with Saul Alinsky," *Harpers*, June, 1965, pp. 37–47; and "A Professional Radical Moves in on Rochester: Conversations with Saul Alinsky, Part II," *Harpers*, July, 1965, pp. 52–9.

43   Alinsky, *Citizen Participation*.

44   Riessman, "Self-Help Among the Poor: New Styles of Social Action," *Trans-Action*, 2 (September–October, 1965), 35.

45   For a discussion of The Woodlawn Organization, see Silberman, *op. cit.*, Chapter 10, "The Revolt Against 'Welfare Colonialism,' " especially pp. 318–55.

46   David Hunter, *The Slums*, p. 180. Also see Riessman, "Self-Help Among the Poor."

47   See various reports of ACCION (Americans for Community Cooperation in Other Nations), New York, New York.

48   Lippitt, *et al.*, *op. cit.*, pp. 180–1.

49   *Ibid.*, pp. 86–8.

50   See *A Report on the Pilot Program for Neighborhood Urban Extension, Homewood Brushton, 1960–1963*, ACTION-Housing, Inc., Pittsburgh, Pennsylvania. For a discussion of the urban-extension approach in Pittsburgh, see James V. Cunningham, *The Resurgent Neighborhood* (Notre Dame, Ind.: Fides Publishers, Inc., 1965), particularly Chapter 9.

51   See pp. 160–5.

52   R. P. Dore, *City Life in Japan: A Study of a Tokyo Ward* (Berkeley: University of California Press, 1958).

53   L. F. Rushbrook Williams, *The State of Pakistan* (London: Faber & Faber, Ltd), 1962.

Appendixes

MUNICIPAL CORPORATION OF DELHI
DEPARTMENT OF URBAN COMMUNITY DEVELOPMENT

CONSTITUTION OF A VIKAS MANDAL

Preamble

We the residents of the————————have solemnly resolved in our general meeting on————(day) dated————to work for improvement on the basis of self-help. In pursuance thereof we have decided to organize ourselves as set forth below.

I. NAME

A. The name of the organization shall be————————Vikas Mandal.
B. The office of the organization shall be in the————————.

II. AIMS AND OBJECTIVES

The aims and objectives of the Vikas Mandal shall be as follows:

A. to foster the spirit of self-help and cooperation among the dwellers of the area;

B. to devise ways and means to solve local problems and to meet local needs;

C. to raise funds for the various activities of the Vikas Mandal;

D. to pool and share ideas for the promotion of the general welfare of the neighborhood and the city;

E. to promote and foster civic consciousness and a spirit of public service to ensure full and proper use of public property and services available in the community.

III. NATURE

The Vikas Mandal shall be a nonpartisan, nonsectarian, and nonprofit-making organization.

IV. AREA

The Vikas Mandal shall function for the people living in the area popularly known as————————and bounded by————————on the North, ————————on the South,————————on the East, and————————on the West.

V. MEMBERSHIP

A. The membership of the Vikas Mandal shall be of two types:

1. contributing, *i.e.*, voting members;
2. noncontributing, *i.e.*, nonvoting members.

B. All members living in the Vikas Mandal area and of the age of eighteen years or older shall be members of the Vikas Mandal.

C. The membership fee of the contributing members shall be R.1 per member per annum payable in two six-monthly installments of 50 *naya paisa* each.

D. The membership will be open only to those who reside in the area.

VI. THE EXECUTIVE COMMITTEE

The Executive Committee of the Vikas Mandal shall consist of

A. the officers:

1. President	1
2. Vice-President	1
3. Secretary	1
4. Treasurer	1
TOTAL	4

B. One member from each *vikas sabha* of the area shall be elected by members residing in the *vikas sabha* zones.

C. Community organizers of the Municipal Corporation of Delhi shall be ex officio members.

VII. VIKAS SABHAS

There shall be a *vikas sabha* in each zone, which shall

A. elect one member to the Vikas Mandal Executive Committee;

B. supervise and execute in its zone the decisions of the Executive Committee.

VIII. ELECTIONS

The officers named in VI. A. shall be elected in a general meeting of the Vikas Mandal by ballot according to rules and by law framed by the Executive Committee of the Vikas Mandal.

IX. TERMS OF OFFICE

The officers of the Vikas Mandal shall hold office for terms of one year each and until the respective successors have been elected at the next general meeting and have assumed office.

X. MEETINGS

A. General

1. The annual general meeting of the Vikas Mandal shall be held at such place, day, and time as may be determined by the Executive Committee.

2. It shall, however, be obligatory on the Executive Committee to call at least one ordinary general meeting between two annual general meetings. Notice of such meetings shall be given ten days in advance.

3. The meeting shall be presided over by the President, in his absence by the Vice-President, and in the absence of both by one elected for such purpose by the Executive Committee.

4. One-third of the membership or twenty contributing members, whichever is less, shall constitute a quorum for the transaction of business.

5. Special meetings may be called by the President or the Executive Committee or upon the request of one-third of the membership or fifty members of the general body, whichever is less. All members must receive at least seven days' notice of the special meeting.

B. Executive Committee

1. The Executive Committee shall meet at least once a month.

2. The quorum for the transaction of business shall be one-third of the total membership of the Executive Committee.

3. The meeting shall be presided over by the President of the Vikas Mandal, in his absence by the Vice-President, and in the absence of both by one elected at the meeting by the Executive Committee.

XI. FUNCTIONS AND POWERS

A. General Body

1. In its half-yearly meetings it shall put to a vote approval of the report presented by the Secretary of the Vikas Mandal.

2. In its annual general meeting it shall

a. put to a vote approval of the report of the Executive Committee for the preceding year;
b. lay down a broad program of work for the ensuing year;
c. elect the officers of the Vikas Mandal;
d. put to a vote approval of the annual budget of the Vikas Mandal and adopt the audited statement of accounts for the previous year;
e. appoint auditors for the ensuing year.

B. Executive Committee

The Executive Committee shall

1. appoint subcommittees and *ad hoc* committees for specific purposes;

2. appoint a finance committee for the purpose of helping the officers in raising and administering funds;

3. take decisions on holding Executive Committee meetings and fix their dates, times, and places;

4. take decisions on holding meetings of the general body and fix their dates, times, and places;

5. take any steps that it may consider necessary for the furtherance of the aims and objectives of the project;

6. fill vacancies among the officers caused for any reason (vacancies among *vikas sabha* representatives shall, however, be filled by elections in the zones concerned);

7. approve the Secretary's annual report before it is submitted to the general body at its annual session;

8. approve the audited statement of accounts for submission to the general body;

9. outline a program for the following year in terms of local needs and finances.

XII. NOTICES OF MEETINGS OF THE GENERAL BODY

A. The dates, times, and places of the meetings shall be fixed by the Executive Committee.

B. Ten days' notice shall be necessary for ordinary meetings, and three days' notice shall be given for special or emergency meetings.

C. Except for amendments to the constitution, all decisions in the general body shall be taken by a simple majority of votes.

XIII. FUNDS

All funds of the council shall be deposited in a scheduled bank approved by the Executive Committee and shall be controlled jointly at one time by any two among the President, Treasurer, and Secretary.

XIV. PROCEDURE FOR AMENDING THE CONSTITUTION

Every proposal regarding an amendment to the constitution shall be initiated in an Executive Committee meeting especially called for the purpose, and two-thirds of the members present and voting must approve the amendment before it is sent to the general body for final approval. In the general body, the amendment must be approved by two-thirds of the members present and voting before it goes into effect.

XV. GENERAL

A. The Executive Committee shall have the power to frame bylaws for carrying out its own work and the work of the Vikas Mandal not inconsistent with the constitution and to alter, rescind, or modify the bylaws by a simple majority of votes.

B. In the event of dissolution of the Vikas Mandal, the ownership of all property of the Vikas Mandal derived from membership fees or donations shall inevitably vest in the Department of Urban Community Development, to be used for similar work elsewhere in Delhi.

XVI. RULES OF BUSINESS FOR THE EXECUTIVE COMMITTEE

A. The President shall preside over the meetings of the Executive Committee. In his absence the Vice-President shall preside. If neither of them is present, then the Executive Committee shall elect any of its members to act as chairman for the meeting.

B. Three days' notice shall be necessary for ordinary meetings and twenty-four hours' notice for emergency meetings.

C. The Secretary, with the approval of the President, shall fix the dates, times, places, and agendas of the meetings.

XVII. DUTIES OF THE PRESIDENT

A. To note whether or not a quorum is present and, if so, to call the meeting to order and declare a quorum present;

B. to preside over all meetings of the general body and the Executive Committee;

C. in the case of a tie vote on any issue, to exercise his own vote;

D. to adjourn a meeting of the general body under unavoidable circumstances;

E. to control the Vikas Mandal's accounts in the bank jointly with the Treasurer or Secretary;

F. to approve expenditures up to R.10 pending sanction from the Executive Committee.

XVIII. DUTIES OF THE SECRETARY

A. To serve as the chief executive officer of the general body and the Executive Committee;

B. to issue all notices of meetings and to carry on the routine work of the Vikas Mandal;

C. to prepare the agendas of the meetings and to have them approved by the President and, for general meetings, to have them approved by the Executive Committee;

D. to keep and maintain the records of the general body, its membership, the Executive Committee, and the subcommittees;

E. to keep on hand a cash account of R.15;

F. to prepare reports of the work of the Executive Committee and to present an annual report of the activities of the Vikas Mandal to the general body at its annual meeting;

G. to call meetings of the general body in accordance with the rules adopted for such procedures;

H. to record the proceedings of the meetings;

I. to control the Vikas Mandal's accounts in the bank jointly with the President or Treasurer.

XIX. DUTIES OF THE TREASURER

A. To receive, disburse, and maintain proper accounts of all funds of the Vikas Mandal;

B. to control jointly with the President or the Secretary of the Vikas Mandal the accounts in the bank;

C. to prepare the budget of the Vikas Mandal and to present it to the Executive Committee for its information and approval;

D. to keep proper accounts of income and expenditures of the Vikas Mandal, to have them duly audited, and to submit them when called upon by the Executive Committee.

XX. DUTIES OF THE AUDITOR

To submit his report and remarks to the Secretary for submission to the Executive Committee and the general body at the end of the financial year.

THE STATISTICS ON VARIATIONS IN PERFORMANCE

The statistics on variations in performance were computed from totals for each *vikas mandal*. Thirty-one *vikas mandals* were studied, but, as three had breakdowns of population ages radically different from the others, they were omitted from the calculations. The total number of degrees of freedom for all calculations was twenty-eight (see Table B1). Looked at in one way, the sample of *vikas mandals* used to analyze the variations was the universe, as it constituted almost all those that had been organized up to March, 1963. Viewed in another way, it was possibly not a random sample of slum areas in Delhi.

Table B2 summarizes the information on the major variables. All the variables were defined only for positive values. For symmetric distributions the mean and median* are equal. For unimodal distributions skewed to the right (left) the mean is greater (less) than the median. From Table B2 one can infer that the distributions of participation were symmetric, whereas those of projects were skewed slightly to the right. The distributions of homogeneity, as proportions of family origins from the various regions, were also skewed slightly to the right. Sizes of *vikas mandals* were skewed to the right, whereas ages of *vikas mandals* were skewed to the left. All the other variables seemed reasonably symmetric.

In order to make maximum use of the data, especially as the number of degrees of freedom was so small, four indexes were constructed: homogeneity, literacy, occupations, and age structure of the population in the *vikas mandal* (see Table B3). These indexes were used in the regression analysis.

The homogeneity index H was defined by

$$H = \sum_{i=1}^{K} Wi\,Pi, \qquad K = 1, 2, 3, 4$$

where Pi is the largest proportion of the population to a single state of origin. The states considered were Delhi, Uttar Pradesh, Rajasthan, and Punjab

---

* The median is that value of the variable such that half the distribution has values less than the median and half greater. The mean is, of course, the ordinary arithmetical mean.

(including West Pakistan). The W_i are the weights defined by

$$W_1 = 1, \quad W_2 = \frac{4-1}{4} = \frac{3}{4}, \quad W_3 = \frac{4-2}{4} = \frac{1}{2}, \quad W_4 = \frac{4-3}{4} = \frac{1}{4}$$

Such an index reflects two tendencies. First, the larger the number of groups in which an area is split, the less homogeneous it is. Second, the more even the distribution among the groups, the less homogeneous is each group and vice versa. For any size of K, the upper limit of H is 1.00, and the lower limit for K equal to four is 0.20.

The remaining three indexes were similarly constructed. The literacy index was defined by

$$L = \sum_{i=1}^{3} i \, Pi$$

where $i = 1$ for illiterate, $i = 2$ for literate, $i = 3$ for matriculation (eleven years) and above. The proportion having the ith literacy level is Pi. For the occupation index

$$O = \sum_{i=1}^{4} i \, Pi$$

where $i = 1$ for service and other trades, $i = 2$ for unskilled and semiskilled occupations, $i = 3$ for trade and business, $i = 4$ for professional occupations. The last index was that for the age structure of the population defined by

$$A = \sum_{i=1}^{3} i \, Pi$$

where $i = 1$ for ages zero to seventeen, $i = 2$ for ages eighteen to thirty-five, $i = 3$ for ages above thirty-six. Table B3 lists the means and standard deviations of these indexes over the twenty-eight *vikas mandals*.

Table B4 shows the simple correlations between projects and participation per 1,000 population and per type of activity after allowing for the effect of length of operation of the *vikas mandal*. The second series shows the correlation without allowing for length of operation. The differences were not very striking but did indicate that length of operation accounts for some of the variation in size of the projects. The effects of length of operation on participation and projects are more thoroughly discussed in the regression analysis.

In Table B5 simple linear least-squares regression analysis was applied to the data; each line in the table represents the finally accepted regression estimate. If time had permitted, more extensive tests to verify the assumptions made in order to calculate the regression estimates would have been done. If one assumes that the regression coefficients are the same for each *vikas mandal* and that the conditional distribution of the dependent variable given the regressors is randomly distributed, then the estimates in Table B5 are unbiased. Furthermore, if one assumes the normal distribution with constant variance for the conditional distribution of the dependent variables, the estimates are also efficient, and the usual hypothesis tests are valid. The assumptions underlying regression analysis are, from this point of view, less restrictive than those for estimating the parameters of unconditional distributions.

The value of the constant term's coefficient summarizes the net effect of the omitted variables, which effect is assumed to be constant except for random disturbances. This assumption was one of the more important ones to be tested by further analysis. The R^2 quoted is the ordinary multiple-correlation coefficient between the dependent variable and the independent variables. It can be interpreted as a measure of the proportion of the total variation of the dependent variable, which is explained by the independent variables. R^2 is a corresponding measure in which allowance has been made for the number of regressors used and the number of degrees of freedom.* An R^2 value calculated on only a few independent variables with a large number of degrees of freedom is better than the same value calculated on a large number of independent variables and a small number of degrees of freedom. The F value quoted in the table is the statistic for testing the joint statistical significance of all the included independent variables. In all the regressions the quoted independent variables were jointly significant statistically.

It should be pointed out that although a variable may have a *statistically* significant coefficient, yet its effect on the explanation of the variation in the dependent variable may be very small indeed. One should not include variables with statistically significant coefficients if their contributions to the explanation are very small. By these means one gets the simplest equation that explains the variation in the dependent variable. In the regressions quoted no variable was retained that added less than 1 per cent to the multiple-correlation coefficient.

The independent variables considered, some of which were rejected, were the age of the *vikas mandal* in months, the size of the *vikas mandal* in numbers of families, and the four indices of homogeneity, age structure, literacy, and occupation. In no case was the multiple-correlation coefficient higher than 59 per cent, that is, the independent variables "explained" a maximum of 59 per cent of the total variations in the dependent variables. Which variables do have effects and which do not, however, were determined.

One should note that the "dependent" variables are examined, both on a per-1,000-population basis and on a per-month-of-operation basis. The only difference arising from the addition was a change in the "scale" of the coefficients, that is, all the conclusions one may infer from the data with respect to participations and projects still hold for participations and projects per month of operation. With respect to the age of the *vikas mandal* this result was a little surprising. One can conclude, however, that participations per head per month of operation increase slightly with the age of the *vikas mandal*.

---

* H. Theil, *Economic Forecasts and Policy* (Amsterdam: North-Holland, 1961), pp. 211–2.

Table B1

The Thirty-One Vikas Mandals Studied up to March, 1963

NAME OF THE VIKAS MANDAL	DATE OF FORMATION	NUMBER OF FAMILIES	TOTAL POPULATION	AVERAGE SIZE OF THE FAMILIES
Pilot Projects				
Bagichi Ramchand	September 9, 1959	273	1,014	3.7
Chowk Shah Mubarak	October 2, 1959	265	1,428	5.4
Magazine Road Colony	October 4, 1959	429	1,695	3.9
Serai Khalil	August 27, 1959	396	2,322	5.8
Shora Kothi	November 8, 1959	238	1,200	5.0
Tihar Colony	September 13, 1959	275	2,360	4.9
	Totals	1,876	9,019	Average 4.8
Sadar Idgah Neighborhood				
Bagichi Raghunath	May 29, 1960	169	754	4.5
Basti Raghunath	May 22, 1960	403	1,982	4.9
Gali Chulhewali	April 3, 1960	354	1,759	4.9
Gali Lallu Misra	May 15, 1960	277	1,348	4.8
Katra Multani	May 15, 1960	216	1,986	4.5
Krishna Nagar	May 21, 1960	422	2,047	4.8
Patli Gali	May 15, 1960	265	1,259	4.7
Peepalwali Gali	May 15, 1960	239	1,210	5.1
T. T. Shah	May 29, 1960	243	1,180	4.9
Uttari Dwar	May 14, 1960	331	1,440	4.3
	Totals	2,919	13,965	Average 4.8

Table B1 (cont.)

Shora Kothi Neighborhood				
Dhruv	April 17, 1960	173	861	4.9
Gali Ganesh	May 22, 1960	286	1,411	4.9
Punjabi Mohalla	May 1, 1960	195	969	4.9
Shorawali Gali	June 12, 1960	217	1,202	5.5
Shora Kothi Main Gate	May 8, 1960	114	504	4.4
	Totals	985	4,947	Average 5.0
Paharganj Neighborhood				
Gali Chandiwali	May 7, 1961	128	672	5.2
Gali Sangtrashan	January 15, 1961	142	723	5.1
Jan	May 29, 1961	358	1,998	5.6
Ghee Mandi	May 21, 1961	195	1,003	5.2
Krishna	January 11, 1961	291	1,405	4.8
Mantola	April 9, 1961	98	571	5.8
Naveen	June 28, 1961	262	1,406	5.4
Panch Gali	December 4, 1960	203	716	3.5
Poorvi Mantola	August 5, 1961	246	1,361	5.5
Prem	May 20, 1961	277	1,567	5.6
	Totals	2,200	11,424	Average 5.0
	Grand Totals	7,980	39,355	4.9

Table B2

Medians, Means, and Standard Deviations of Basic Variables Used in the Analyses of Twenty-Eight Vikas Mandals up to March, 1963

Variable	Median	Mean*	Standard Deviation of Mean
Total participations per 1,000 population†	6,270	6,630	2,870
Physical participations per 1,000 population	1,970	1,910	1,210
Sanitation-health participations per 1,000 population	2,040	2,120	1,190
Education participations per 1,000 population	70	140	220
Recreation participations per 1,000 population	1,020	1,090	750
Total projects per 1,000 population	37.55	41.58	19.27
Physical projects per 1,000 population	4.48	6.53	6.16
Sanitation-health projects per 1,000 population	8.57	9.62	5.36
Education projects per 1,000 population	2.43	2.52	1.76
Recreation projects per 1,000 population	12.26	16.21	10.84
Economic projects per 1,000 population	4.23	4.47	2.81
Age of the *vikas mandals* (in months)	34.00	31.54	6.68
Size of the *vikas mandals* (in families)	244.50	250.39	86.10
Percentage of families from Delhi	18.05	23.00	22.34
Percentage of families from Uttar Pradesh	20.79	20.44	16.37
Percentage of families from Rajasthan	2.55	5.97	6.89
Percentage of families from Punjab	12.17	15.01	12.50
Percentage of families from West Pakistan	58.00	66.64	57.66
Percentage of population under seventeen	48.68	48.34	2.33
Percentage of population from eighteen to thirty-five	31.32	31.77	2.43
Percentage of population over thirty-six	20.87	19.89	2.93
Percentage of population illiterate	49.20	48.52	17.58
Percentage of population literate	50.80	51.83	17.20
Percentage of population matriculates (eleven years)	7.96	9.61	7.79
Percentage of families professional	3.94	5.44	4.75
Percentage of families trade and business	33.33	29.79	11.43
Percentage of families skilled and unskilled	32.87	30.51	20.13
Percentage of families service and other	33.36	34.26	10.68

* Certain groups of percentages do not have means that add up to 100 because of the double counting involved in some categories.

† Projects and participations are not equated by month of *vikas mandal* operation.

Table B3
Mean and Standard Deviations of the Indexes Used in the Regression Analysis of Twenty-Eight Vikas Mandals up to March, 1963*

Index	Mean	Standard Deviation
Homogeneity	85.29	8.62
Literacy	181.00	38.48
Occupation	206.40	17.30
Age	171.50	4.62

* Values shown are in percentages. The lower limit on the indexes of literacy, occupation, and age is 100.00.

Table B4
Correlations Between Participations and Projects for Breakdowns of Both, Defined by Equivalent Definitions (All Variables per 1,000 Population), Equated and Not Equated For Age of the Vikas Mandal*

NOT EQUATED FOR AGE OF PROJECTS†		EQUATED FOR AGE OF PROJECTS§	
Definition	Correlation	Definition	Correlation
Total	0.40	Total	0.53
Physical	0.38	Physical	0.32
Sanitation-health	0.59	Sanitation-health	0.66
Education	0.63	Education	0.69
Recreation	0.26	Recreation	0.44
Economic	0.53	Economic	0.44

* The standard errors of the estimates of the correlation coefficients were not calculated. It was decided that the precision of the estimates could not be relied upon because of the possible nonrandomness of the sample. These estimates are only indicative values.
† Not equated for age per month of operation of the *vikas mandals.*
§ Equated for age per month of operation of the *vikas mandal,* as well as per 1,000 population.

Table B5

Least-Squares Regressions of Projects and Participations on Age of Vikas Mandal, Literacy, Occupation, Homogeneity, Age Composition, and Size for Twenty-Eight Vikas Mandals to March, 1963*

Dependent Variables	CONSTANT†	AGE OF VIKAS MANDAL	LITERACY	OCCUPATION	HOMOGENEITY	AGE STRUCTURE	SIZE OF VIKAS MANDAL	R^2 AND R^{-2}§	F^{**}
Projects per 1,000 population (total)	78.06 (8.81)						−0.146 (0.033)	42.4 (40.1)	118.39 (1,26)
Projects per 1,000 population per month of operation (total)	2.781 (0.301)						−0.0056 (0.0014)	48.0 (46.0)	
Projects per 1,000 population (physical)	−17.58 (11.02)	0.605 (0.174)	0.068 (0.032)				−0.029 (0.012)	45.8 (39.0)	17.93 (3,24)
Projects per 1,000 population per month of operation (physical)	−0.246 (0.343)	0.0116 (0.0054)	0.0017 (0.0009)				−0.0009 (0.0004)	37.9 (30.1)	
Projects per 1,000 population (sanitation-health)	19.11 (2.56)						−0.038 (0.010)	37.1 (34.7)	76.72 (1,26)
Projects per 1,000 population per month of operation (sanitation-health)	0.681 (0.084)						−0.0014 (0.0003)	44.5 (42.3)	
Projects per 1,000 population (education)	4.442 (0.981)						−0.008 (0.004)	14.1 (10.8)	34.44 (1,26)

Projects per 1,000 population per month of operation (education)	0.155 (0.031)						19.3 (16.2)	
Projects per 1,000 population (recreation)	-23.32 (6.40)	-1.038 (0.342)	-0.169 (0.064)		0.689 (0.405)	-0.0003 (0.0001)	44.0 (34.2)	22.65 (4,23)
Projects per 1,000 population per month of operation (recreation)	0.075 (2.18)	-0.055 (0.012)	-0.0055 (0.0022)		0.022 (0.014)	-0.062 (0.022)	59.3 (52.2)	
Projects per 1,000 population (economic)	-32.23 (16.83)	0.191 (0.070)			0.179 (0.099)		32.4 (27.0)	36.39 (2,25)
Projects per 1,000 population per month of operation (economic)	-0.734 (0.491)	0.0014 (0.0020)			0.0048 (0.0029)	-0.0020 (0.0007)	12.6 (5.6)	
Participations per 1,000 population (total)	-11.26 (4.88)	0.279 (0.087)	0.050 (0.015)				35.2 (30.1)	75.67 (2,25)
Participations per 1,000 population per month of operation (total)	-0.112 (0.166)	0.002 (0.003)	0.001 (0.001)				30.6 (25.1)	
Participations per person per 1,000 population (physical)	-11.42 (4.21)	0.154 (0.044)	0.015 (0.006)	0.0280 (0.015)			35.8 (27.7)	27.63 (3,24)
Participations per person per 1,000 population per month of operation (physical)	-0.234 (0.154)	0.0023 (0.0016)	0.0004 (0.0002)	0.0007 (0.0005)			19.8 (9.8)	

Table B5 (cont.)

	CONSTANT†	AGE OF VIKAS MANDAL	LITERACY	OCCU-PATION	HOMO-GENEITY	AGE STRUCTURE	SIZE OF VIKAS MANDAL	R² AND R⁻²§	F**
Participations per person per 1,000 population (sanitation-health)	31.86 (9.21)	0.015 (0.007)			-0.069 (0.026)	-0.131 (0.046)	-0.0050 (0.0030)	33.3 (24.9)	32.53 (3,24)
Participations per person per month of operation (sanitation-health)	0.935 0.282	0.0003 (0.0002)			-0.001 (0.0008)	-0.004 (0.001)	-0.0002 (0.0001)	33.0 (24.7)	
Participations per person per 1,000 population (education)	-1.071 0.387	0.015 (0.007)	0.004 (0.001)					32.4 (27.0)	9.38 (2,25)
Participations per person per month of operation (education)	-0.026 (0.013)	0.0003 (0.0002)	0.0001 (——)					28.3 (22.5)	
Participations per person per 1,000 population (economic)	-1.623 (0.377)	0.030 (0.007)	0.005 (0.001)					48.0 (43.8)	15.84 (2,25)
Participations per person per month of operation (economic)	-0.043 (0.011)	0.0008 (0.0002)	0.0001 (——)					46.0 (41.7)	

* Each column shows the coefficients in each regression. Figures in parentheses give the standard errors. Only those variables whose coefficients were significant and that added at least 1 per cent to the multiple-correlation coefficient were included. The superscript symbol (⁻) indicates standard deviation less than 0.0001.

† The value of the coefficient of the constant term summarizes the net effect of those variables omitted from the regression.

§ R^2 and $\bar{R}^2$ are both expressed as percentages. $\bar{R}^2$ is the multiple-correlation coefficient corrected for degrees of freedom, which is listed below the corresponding value of R^2, the ordinary multiple-correlation coefficient.

** The corresponding degrees of freedom are listed below each computed F value.

INDEXES

NAME INDEX

The numbers following each name are the page numbers where authors are quoted or their works cited as valuable references.

SUBJECT INDEX

Date Due

Through the *vikas mandal*, women help to purchase a cooperative sewing machine, contributing pennies monthly in hopes of supplementing family incomes through handiwork. The city furnishes the instructor. Because of their illiteracy, the women have difficulty reading patterns and taking measurements, and many later enroll in self-help literacy classes.

Continued on overleaf

Photographs 4 and 5 courtesy Marshall B. Clinard; all others courtesy the Department of Urban Community Development, Delhi Municipal Corporation.